Twenty Things to Do
with a Computer
Forward 50

Future Visions of Education Inspired by Seymour Papert and
Cynthia Solomon's Seminal Work

Edited by Gary Stager, PhD

Constructing Modern Knowledge Press

Copies of this book may be purchased at volume discount through the publisher at cmkpress.com.

Publisher:
Constructing Modern Knowledge Press
Torrance, California, USA
cmkpress.com

EDU034000   EDUCATION / Educational Policy & Reform
EDU016000   EDUCATION / History
EDU039000   EDUCATION / Computers & Technology

ISBN: 978-1-955604-00-0 (paperback)
ISBN: 978-1-955604-01-7 (hardcover)

Layout: Sylvia Libow Martinez
Cover design: Yvonne Martinez

Contents

Foreword   i
    Cynthia Solomon
Introduction   1
    Gary Stager

Section 1 — Our Vision

Twenty (Poetic) Things to Do with a Computer   11
    Angi Chau
Progress   13
    Gary Stager
Spiraling   19
    Artemis Papert & Cynthia Solomon
Adventures on the Road to Mathland   25
    Dan Lynn Watt
Twenty Things is the Foundation for Constructionism   39
    Fred Martin
Life in Logoland   43
    Marian B. Rosen
The First Thing I Did with a Computer   49
    Bryan P. Sanders
Twenty Things and Onwards   51
    Stephen Heppell
Purple Constructionism   55
    Nettrice Gaskins
My Rules   57
    Jennifer Orr
Radical Ideas: Joy and Empowerment   61
    Ken Kahn

An Eternal Source of Inspiration or What the Bulgarian Turtle Told Achilles This Time   63

    Evgenia (Jenny) Sendova

I Learn How to Code and Lengthen My Reach #makingliberation   93

    Susan Klimczak

The Best Day Ever   101

    Cathy Hunt

Section 2 — Intellectual Timidity

The Computer Programs the Child   105

    Audrey Watters

Where Have All the Metaphors Gone?   107

    Gary S. Stager

Hitchhiking to Logo's Mathland   117

    Molly Lynn Watt

When You Wake Seymour Papert in the Middle of the Night   127

    Gary Stager

2020 Things to Do with a Computer   129

    Dale Dougherty

Intellectual Timidity   135

    Eleonora Badilla-Saxe

Seeking the Magic: One Teacher's Evolution Story   139

    Carol Sperry

Bad Design is Violence: Powerful Ideas and Powerful Politics in Constructionist Education   145

    Paulo Blikstein

Thou Shalt Not Write Curriculum   151

    Peter Rawitsch

The Wider Walls   153

    Bill Kerr

Let's Kill the Pencil   157

    Gary Stager

Whatever Happened to the Revolution?   159

    Geraldine Kozberg

Section 3 — Personal Computing

A Dreamer Given Sight 165
David Loader

Personal Computing 171
Gary Stager

Kid Power 181
Dennis O. Harper

Education Technology @ Fifty Something: My Personal Perspective 187
Karen J. Billings

To Be or Not to Be ... (a Programmer) 191
John Stetson

Change Is Certain, Progress Is Not 195
Ron Canuel

Twenty Things and Moving Forward: An Embodied-based Scenario for Kindergarten Children 199
José Armando Valente

Math Classes Are Failing the AI Age Workforce 207
Conrad Wolfram

The End of Knowing – and a New Way to Learn 209
Sugata Mitra

The Evolution of Logo Connections to the Physical World, From 1971 to Today 221
David D. Thornburg

Learning Together 227
David Cavallo

Section 4 — Recursion Line

Thoughts on XX 237
Tom Lough

Reflections on Papert and Solomon from the History and Civics Classroom 241
Heather Allen Pang

A Language for Making Physical Things 245
Leo McElroy

Things to Do with a Computer in an English/Language Arts Classroom (Besides Word Processing) 253
Kate Tabor

Twenty Things to Make with Biology   257
   Yasmin B. Kafai & Justice T. Walker

For Real: Some Modern Things to Do with a Computer   267
   Martin Levins

Twenty Ways to Facilitate Twenty Things to Do with a Computer   273
   Carmelo Presicce, Giulio Bonanome, & Angela Sofia Lombardo

A Place for Experimentation: The Library   281
   Carolyn Foote

Computer Modeling, Data Collection, and Programming in Middle School Science   283
   Donna Collins

Theo's Rockets   295
   Gary Stager

Ten Things to Do with the Internet   299
   Tom Lauwers

Three European Robotics Projects Inspired by Twenty Things   303
   Michele Moro & Dimitri Alimisis

A Robot Petting Zoo   305
   John Umekubo

Collaboration Rules! Twenty Insights About Online Collaborative Learning   311
   Yvonne Marie Andres

Make a Turtle!   317
   Miles Berry

#11: Make a Music Box and Program a Tune   323
   Walter Bender & Devin Ulibarri

The Future is Computational   333
   Gary Stager

Isn't it Time for Us to Grow Up?   345
   Seymour Papert

Toolbox   346
Contributor Biographies   347
Twenty Things to Do With a Computer (1971)   359
   Seymour Papert & Cynthia Solomon

Also from Constructing Modern Knowledge Press   401

Foreword

Cynthia Solomon

Twenty Things to Do with a Computer represents a collaborative effort to create a computer *place*, an environment in which children expand their knowledge by exploring and inventing real and imagined objects aided by a programming language designed for them. This essay describes things Seymour and I did teaching children in 1968–69 and in 1970–71 and things we hoped to do in the future. Beside programming we introduced physical activities such as juggling, balancing on a bongo board, and stilt walking. We looked for more activities that we could talk about procedurally. Actually, Seymour and I focused on how we talk about things, developing a meta-language, debugging strategies, and projects that were expansive in nature.

Underlying our activities was the idea of creating a *mathland*, a place and a culture where participants could explore and invent objects through a programming language designed for them. But, of course, to do those things required the help and inventiveness of many people.

Amongst our collaborators in this endeavor were Marvin Minsky (a founder of the field of Artificial Intelligence) and a slew of MIT AI Lab hackers—students and staff. This collaboration started in the 1960s and continued into the 21st century and was joined by a coterie of interesting teachers, researchers, and learners from all over the world.

Seymour was the one to declare that children needed their own programming language–not one designed for adults. Logo, the first language designed for children, was Seymour's brainchild (Solomon et al., 2020). The idea formed when he consulted at Bolt, Beranek and Newman (BBN) for Danny Bobrow (head of the AI Group) and Wally Feurzeig (head of the Educational Technology group). From its inception in 1966 to current times Logo has gone through many improvements and adjustments. Several papers in this collection reflect that fact.

Logo and the idea of a computer environment and culture for children came about at a time when dramatic change in education seemed possible. The United States had lost the race with the Soviet Union to be the first to launch a satellite. This competition led to a large amount of funding to improve K-12 education and especially math and science. Change was proposed in what was taught as well as how things were taught. Change was also happening for how people of color and women were educated. In some ways it was a heady time full of outspoken and courageous protests about the way things had been.

As our first year-long Logo class drew to a close, Seymour saw success and yet a need for something more. It wasn't enough for learners to play with words and numbers and sentences. A more concrete object was needed. And so, the turtle was born—a creature on wheels that could be commanded to move and turn. By 1970 there were floor turtles and a display turtle, both had pens with which to leave a trace of their paths.

Although Seymour encouraged people to think about other microworlds, the turtle world with turtle geometry has remained the fullest, richest, and most copied microworld. For example, after fifty years of playing with turtles I am deeply absorbed with a turtle that makes designs for computerized embroidery machines. I use TurtleStitch, a program built into the Snap! programming language. TurtleStitch has one turtle which follows the conventions of Snap! with a few additional features specifically for embroidery.

My current work with an embroidery machine has reminded me why I haven't rushed to use fab lab equipment. In its early years I was disappointed in the lack of focus on software and user interface issues. Improvements have been slight and yet folks plug away. Remixing is key to progress, and good user interfaces encourage remixing, especially by newcomers who might have fabulous ideas. 3D printing reminds me of the early 60s when folks were putting data on decks of cards, submitting the decks to be run on mainframe computers, and then waiting a day or a week to get the results. How frustrating it was when the bug might be trivial, but the fix would take so long. And so it is today with 3D printing.

Today not only do I have my own computer but I have my own reliable computerized embroidery machine. I program in TurtleStitch on my computer. I then download my design in an embroidery machine file format to a flash drive. Next, I insert the drive into the embroidery machine and choose my fabrics, threads, and needles. Most of the jobs I run take no more than three minutes, but some take over thirty minutes. The machine is quite robust. I do encounter problems with fabrics, threads, or needles, but the issues are manageable, and feedback is quick. So, I can share the device and designs with others quite easily. Easy access makes a difference for any learner or doer.

What keeps me intrigued and stretches my skills with design and programming in TurtleStitch? My answer is the immediacy of the design process including bugs in the computer programs and bugs with the machine due to the interaction of fabric, needle, thread as well as design.

With TurtleStitch you can experience bugs turning into features as you allow yourself to be playful in what you are doing. Experiment! Bugs are often welcome. When they are not, TurtleStitch offers an easy and visual way to play with numbers, to change values. And there is a diverse and growing community of users whose projects are available for remixing (as in Scratch and Snap!).

I might as well come clean and say I have a slight aversion to using my hands with various construction kits from LEGO to paper circuits. Either my finger muscles are weak or my hands shake. I did love Tinkertoys and identified when Marvin (2019a) talked about them. I also liked soldering. I do enjoy talking to devices, getting LEDs to light up in funny patterns, opening and closing pathways etc. In other words, I like to chatter with devices.

I bring up likes and dislikes to point out that Seymour's and my search for twenty things and more was guided by our respect and love for children and the way they learn and what they want to learn. Our presentations as teachers can certainly influence how children treat their likes and dislikes. As teachers we know that what we teach and how we teach greatly influences children's love for learning. But we often get caught up in what was done in the past. Marvin Minsky illustrates this point when he offered an answer to the question *Why do some children find math hard to learn?* and suggested that "this is often caused by starting with the practice and drill of a bunch of skills called Arithmetic — and instead of promoting inventiveness, we focus on preventing mistakes" (2019b).

Seymour also reminded us that "The role of the teacher is to create conditions for invention rather than provide ready-made knowledge." In other words don't just tell learners a set of facts and then test them on their retention. One of his dreams was that this Logo environment would give rise to a mathland where learners could fall in love with what they were doing as they reflected on their actions.

In keeping with Papert's saying "you can't think about thinking without thinking about thinking about something" we concentrated on thinking about how children learn and how machines can be taught to learn.

After turtles were introduced, we continued to think about the most important parts of creating a culture of learning. This is an excerpt from my paper, *Teaching Young Children to Program in a Logo Turtle Computer Culture* (1978).

The Computer Culture

"Logo" is the name of a programming language, but it is also used as the name of an environment, a culture, a way of thinking about computers and about learning and about putting the two together. The environment is made of ideas, of things, and of people.

The things include not only the computer, but computer controlled devices like turtles. There are mechanical turtles which move along the floor and are often equipped with touch or light sensors, and there are also graphics turtles, which live on TV-like screens where they draw in phosphor white or in multi-color. The computer system which gives life to all of this understands the Logo language. The computer and the programming language play a vital role in creating an exciting atmosphere where programs, people, turtles and other computer controlled devices Interact with one another and learn from one another.

In the environment people become researchers, and actions and ideas take on animate qualities. Ideas from computer science like naming, procedurization, and debugging become intermixed with anthropomorphic thinking to become lively tools in problem-solving situations.

Different turtle types naturally develop distinct attributes, but there are also common elements. For example, the turtle's state is its position and its heading. Its state can be changed by either telling it to go FORWARD (or BACK) a number of steps or telling it to turn RIGHT (or LEFT) some number of degrees. It can also leave a trace (PENDOWN) of its path or not (PENUP). While the culture is closely tied to turtles, it is certainly more universal. The turtles were invented as vehicles to convey this culture to beginners. They make certain images more vivid and certain ideas more concrete. But the goal is to convey these ideas and images, to make them real, comfortable, personal for a beginner of any age.

A Functional Description

Functionally, the Logo environment is made up of the following:

1. a computer

2. a programming language and an operating system

3. a collection of computer peripherals, usually including graphics and turtles

4. a collection of projects

5. a meta-language - a consistent way of talking about the language, the projects, etc.

6. a relationship between teacher and learner

7. a collection of "bridge activities" like juggling, puzzles, etc.

All of these components are interdependent and the special virtues of the environment follow from their coherence with one another. Taken individually, they have no great merit or utility. *For example, one would expect very limited educational benefits to come from teaching programming, even Logo programming, in an "abstract" environment or from using turtles as toys without a vision derived from the computer culture.*

The design of the Logo environment as a whole is strongly influenced by certain general ideas of which three are particularly relevant to work with young children: procedurizatlon, anthropomorphization, and debugging. The following three sections discuss these in turn.

A procedural view of the world

A procedural view of the world touches upon all aspects of our culture. Taken in its simplest sense, a procedure is a description of how to do something, and when applied to the world, leads to a perception of complicated processes in terms of subprocesses. That is, complicated processes are reduced to an interconnected cluster of simpler processes, each of which can be clearly described. In the Logo world, whether a child is learning to walk on stilts or to juggle three balls or to make the turtle walk in a square, the main intellectual activity is to look for a set of procedures which, when knit together, will do the job. The intellectual environment we are describing is designed to exploit this commonality in order to channel prior real-world procedural knowledge into the service of mastering the computer and also to channel whatever is so learned back into improvements of knowledge about the non-computer world.

As a support to procedural thinking emphasis is placed on giving words meanings, naming processes, and making descriptions for how to do things. These ideas are embodied in Logo, the programming language. (A real attempt was made to minimize the formalisms of language so as not to detract from naming, procedurizing, subprocedurizing, recursion. Further work is needed here and became dramatically apparent in work with young children.)

An anthropomorphic view of the computer

Anthropomorphizing, "ascribing human characteristics to non-human things," has been a natural way to understand aspects of the world. It can also be seen as a powerful problem solving tool. Its pervasiveness is supported by the fact that we talk about a "Logo turtle environment" or a "computer culture" or "Logo worlds," etc., and are understood. Turtles themselves are concrete realizations of this thinking. On a more abstract level, programs as well as turtles are looked at anthropomorphically. This gives rise to powerful teaching strategies such as the use of metaphors like "playing computer," "being the turtle," "being the procedure," "naming the actors and describing their roles," "teaching the computer new words," and "teaching the turtle how to do something."

A further extension of these teaching strategies is embodied in the idea of encouraging young students to think of themselves as *studying* turtle behavior or computer behavior in order to learn about themselves—both how they are the same and how they are different. Thinking in terms of using what we know in order to teach the computer requires us to know some of its essential attributes as well as our own, and at the same time feeds into and is supported by a procedural view of the world.

Debugging

The important message that comes from ideas about debugging is that we learn from our mistakes; that the intricate process of making things work or learning new skills has to do with hypothesizing, testing, revising, etc. Debugging in the Logo world becomes the most important and integrating activity. It is supported by procedural thinking as well as an anthropomorphic view of the world. Giving things names so you can talk about those things aids in debugging. Debugging something can vary from making a broken thing work to find the way a thing works though different from the plan is better. Bugs thus can easily become features. We just have to adjust our view or modify and improve our plan and let ourselves be open to change. Applying some of the debugging strategies gleaned in programming to our thinking bugs in other situations gives us an opportunity to talk about them.

When debugging is embedded in a computer world where procedural and anthropomorphic thinking come into play the process becomes one of the most engaging activities in the environment. Children collect, classify and enjoy bugs. Sometimes bugs are serendipitously adopted as features worth perpetuating, sometimes procedures must be constructed to deal with the phenomena caused by their appearance, and sometimes the bugs and their side effect need to be removed. But in this pursuit, children become creative researchers studying behavior, making up theories, trying out ideas, etc.

A Philosophy of Learning

To the extent that the children are really able to see themselves as "creative researchers," they are learning something much more important than using computers.

We believe that the computer when used as proposed here is the ideal carrier for this self-image of learner-as-researcher.

This approach applies to teachers as well as students. When I teach Logo, I honestly see myself and the child as engaged in a genuine joint research activity—we are jointly trying to understand what is happening in the unique situation created by this turtle project. The exact situation really has never occurred before. It poses problems I have never seen before. I do not know in advance what the answers are. One of the most exciting discoveries made by the children is just that: "You mean you really don't know how to do it," exclaimed one child in amazement and in reaction to a hundred remembered situations in which teachers put on the stance of "let's do it together" while really knowing the answer in advance. For some children the prospect of an honest relationship with the teacher is something new and inspiring. This environment is especially good for developing such relationships because it is so "discovery rich." One of my goals is to convey to other teachers the possibility of this "teacher-and- student-as-research collaborators" kind of relationship. The extent that we can achieve this, we see one way in which the effect of the computer presence goes beyond "using computers." Its real impact is on the total culture of which teacher and child are part.

―――――――――◆―――――――――

Forward Fifty More

Looking back at the fifty years since *Twenty Things* was written creates both nostalgia and wonder. How idealistic and optimistic we were that we could change the world. How wonderful that so many people came along for the journey. How impactful that many children had experiences that changed their lives. We could be pessimistic and claim that nothing has changed, and our work has been forgotten, but I choose to keep learning, keep teaching, and keep moving forward, one turtle step at a time.

References

Minsky, M. (2019a). The Infinite Construction Kit. In C. Solomon & X. Xiao (Eds.), *Inventive Minds: Marvin Minsky on Education* (pp. 3-18). MIT Press.

Minsky, M. (2019b). What Makes Mathematics So Hard to Learn? In C. Solomon & X. Xiao (Eds.), *Inventive Minds: Marvin Minsky on Education* (pp. 41-57). MIT Press.

Solomon, C., Harvey, B., Kahn, K., Lieberman, H., Miller, M., Minsky, M., Papert, A., Silverman, B., & Shepard, T. (2020). History of Logo. *Proceedings of the ACM on Programming Languages, 4*(HOPL). doi.org/10.1145/3386329

Solomon, C. J. (1978). Teaching young children to program in a LOGO turtle computer culture. *ACM Sigcue Outlook, 12*(3), 20-29.

Introduction

Gary Stager

Remember 1971?

- *Marcus Welby, M.D.* was TV's #1 show
- "Joy to the World" by Three Dog Night topped the charts
- *Fiddler on the Roof* was the most popular film
- A gallon of gas cost $0.36
- China was admitted to the United Nations
- Richard Nixon was *Time's* Man of the Year
- Intel released the first commercially available microprocessor

1971 is also when Cynthia Solomon and Seymour Papert published *Twenty Things to Do with a Computer*, a revolutionary document that would set the course of education for the next fifty years and beyond. This book is a celebration of the vision set forth by Papert and Solomon a half-century ago. Four dozen experts from around the world invite us to consider the original provocations, reflect on their implementation, and chart a course for the future through personal recollections, learning stories, and imaginative scenarios.

Followed literally, *Twenty Things to Do with a Computer* remains more ambitious than most current school tech plans and, if pursued, would introduce students to powerful ideas rooted in modernity. However, *Twenty Things* was never intended as either a utopian vision or a prescription for educational practice. It was intended as an "object-to-think-with"—about being receptive to the learning adventures afforded by emerging technology. *Twenty Things* is not about using computers to teach children things we've always wanted them to know, perhaps with greater efficiency or comprehension. Rather it is an invitation to learn and do in ways previously unimaginable.

Twenty Things may not be widely known, but its impact is all around us. In 1971, Solomon and Papert predicted 1:1 personal computing, the maker movement, children programming computers, robotic construction kits, computer science for all, and integrating computing across the school curriculum. All of this, years, or perhaps decades, before such notions became commonplace. The paper is remarkable for its omniscience, yet Papert and Solomon were not soothsayers. *Twenty Things* was in many ways a report chronicling what they had already achieved with children and computers a year before the Watergate break-in.

> *But our purpose here is not to complain of what other people have not done, but to tell of some exciting things you can do with the computer you have row or with the one you will be incited to get by the pages that follow. More than half the suggestions we are about to make have been implemented and tested in our elementary school teaching program. This does not imply that they are not of equal or greater value at other levels of education; on the contrary, we are convinced that they give a glimpse of the proper way to introduce everyone of whatever age and whatever level of academic performance, to programing, to more general knowledge of computation and indeed (we say courageously steeling ourselves for the onslaught) to mathematics, to physics and to all formal subjects including linguistics and music. — Solomon & Papert, Twenty Things*

In fewer than thirty pages, *Twenty Things to Do with a Computer* introduces readers to a world in which children may use computers they own to create, solve problems, control their world, and bring powerful ideas to life across subject areas. More importantly, *Twenty Things* situates the ideals of progressive educators from John Dewey to Malaguzzi, Holt, Kozol, Meier, Kohn, Sizer, Hawkins, Katz, and Weber in a modern context. It demonstrated how computing could be creative, humane, whimsical, childlike, and a way to learn "everything else," even ideas at the frontiers of mathematics and science. For a time, the work of Papert, Solomon, and their colleagues made educational technology the epicenter of progressive thought. This would be an extraordinary feat today, but that it was accomplished in 1971 renders the work miraculous.

It's a cheap parlor trick to talk about how education is about to be disrupted and schools will become extinct. *Twenty Things* is not a YouTube talk taking a courageous stand for creativity, absent any substantive alternatives. You will not find more passionate critics of schooling than Seymour Papert and Cynthia Solomon. However, nearly all their research was conducted in schools, most often in disadvantaged communities or developing countries. Seymour and Cynthia were never happier than when working in real schools, a rare trait among academics. I witnessed that joy working alongside them. We do not give up on schools because that is where the kids are. It should be possible to criticize the school system without abandoning its inhabitants. This book does not concede that schools are obsolete, but the ideas within are certainly applicable to informal learning environments as well.

Papert and Solomon's work was predicated upon the notion that teachers are competent and love children. They embraced the humanity and creativity of progressive education and built a bridge to a computational age in which STEM subjects could be experienced naturally in the spirit of the arts. The authors of *Twenty Things,* and those celebrating its anniversary in this book, give voice to underrepresented stakeholders and powerful ideas in education.

Each time I use one of the technologies or techniques inspired by Solomon and Papert I remember what the legendary jazz musician Jimmy Heath taught me, "What was good, is good." Their programming language, Logo, is timeless. If you do not believe me, try Logo with children. Kids today feel as creatively expressive and intellectually alive as I did when I first met the turtle nearly forty years ago.

Papert and Solomon

Seymour Papert is widely considered the father of educational technology. Cynthia Solomon's contributions thoroughly qualify her for long-overdue recognition as the mother of educational technology.

Cynthia Solomon

In the early 1960s, Cynthia Solomon graduated from Radcliffe with a history degree. She was extremely interested in computer programming, but that was not something women *did* back then. A friend of Solomon's helped her land a job as a secretary to MIT professor and artificial intelligence pioneer, Dr. Marvin Minsky. While working at MIT, Solomon taught herself to program in LISP. By 1967, she, along with Seymour Papert, Wally Feurzeig, and others, invented the first programming language for children—Logo. That led to Cynthia to working with Seymour Papert, who by that time was a professor in the MIT Applied Mathematics Department and continued working with him in the MIT Artificial Intelligence Lab and its Logo Group.

Not only did Solomon help create the first programming language for children, but she developed many of the pedagogical approaches and activities we currently use to teach students to use computers. More than fifty years later, Logo is still in use by millions of children around the world in the form of Scratch, Snap!, Lynx, Turtle Art, and other dialects.

Cynthia was a cofounder of Logo Computer Systems, an educational software company still in existence, and directed the development of Apple Logo, the first commercial version of Logo. She also wrote the Apple Logo manual. Later, she was Director of Atari Cambridge Research, where the focus was on building a "play station of the future". The lab produced many experimental prototypes of technologies now central to human-computer interaction.

Along with Margaret Minsky and Brian Harvey, Solomon published *Logo Works: Challenging Programs in Logo* (1986), which demonstrated the sorts of sophisticated computer science projects in which kids could engage.

Throughout her career, Solomon has been committed to introducing creative computer education to students and educators. Her doctoral thesis was the basis for the seminal book, *Computer Environments for Children: A Reflection on Theories of Learning and Education* (1986). She worked with the One Laptop Per Child Foundation to develop learning activities for computing in the developing world. Most recently, she edited the important book, *Inventive Minds: Marvin Minsky on Education* (2019).

I met Cynthia Solomon in 1985 at the height of Logo's popularity. I had just parked my car at MIT, an institution way above my paygrade, to attend the Logo '85 conference. Within what seemed like seconds, I encountered a woman who said, "Hey kid, come to dinner with us." My hostess was Cynthia Solomon. She has been my mentor, colleague, and friend ever since. It has been a great joy to travel the world with Cynthia, co-lead teacher workshops, and share her as an indispensable teammate and Senior Fellow of Constructing Modern Knowledge.

Seymour Papert

Seymour Papert (1928-2016) was a mathematician and one of the early pioneers of artificial intelligence. In addition, he is internationally recognized as the seminal thinker regarding computers and modern pedagogy for children. Born and educated in South Africa, Papert was an active participant in the anti-apartheid movement of the early 1950s. His dissident status caused Papert to flee his country without a passport. Seymour had earned two PhDs in mathematics prior to being recruited by Jean Piaget to collaborate at the University of Geneva. Papert helped Piaget consider using mathematics in the service of understanding how children can learn and think.

In the early 1960s, Papert came to MIT, where, with Marvin Minsky, he founded the Artificial Intelligence Lab and co-authored the seminal book *Perceptrons* (1969). In addition to publishing countless papers and articles, Seymour Papert was the author of *Mindstorms: Children Computers and Powerful Ideas* (1980), arguably the most influential book in the field. That was followed by *The Children's Machine: Rethinking School in the Age of the Computer* (1993) and *The Connected Family: Bridging the Digital Generation Gap (1996)*.

Papert was a cofounder of the MIT Media Lab, longtime director for the Media Lab's Epistemology and Learning Group, later the Future of Learning Group, and the first LEGO Papert Professor of Learning Research at MIT. He was a driving force behind Maine's law providing every 7th & 8th grader with a laptop and the One Laptop Per Child Foundation. His inventions not only include the Logo programming language, but also the first robotics construction kit for children, created in collaboration with LEGO.

Seymour Papert is the originator of the learning theory *constructionism* and served as inspiration for the movement known as one-to-one computing.

In 2006, Dr. Papert was struck by a motorcycle while crossing a Hanoi street. This accident left him with a debilitating brain injury for his remaining years.

Although I first read *Mindstorms* in 1982 and saw Papert speak at Logo '85, I do not recall meeting him for about another year and then we interacted regularly at conferences. I was part of his entourage to Australia in 1990 for the World Conference on Computers in Education and was invited to MIT soon after to report on the work I had been doing with laptops in K–12 schools. Seymour generously keynoted two New Jersey Educational Computing Conferences I organized and contributed to the *Logo Exchange* journal I edited.

I advised Papert and Maine officials preparing for their statewide laptop rollout. We were both keynote speakers at a 2004 conference in Sydney, organized to kickoff Apple's introduction of laptops in education and I was invited to join Seymour as a member of his Future of Learning Group at MIT and One Laptop Per Child Learning Team. That work took me to Brazil, Mexico, and Costa Rica.

From 1999–2002, we worked closely together in creating a high-tech, project-based, constructionist, alternative learning environment inside Maine's troubled prison for teens. I was the principal investigator in what became Papert's last institutional research project, "The Constructionist Learning Laboratory." This collaboration solidified my commitment to constructionism and formed the basis for my doctoral dissertation (2006).

The enormity of Papert's wit, wisdom, and accomplishments are barely explored in this text. Over time, many books will be written about his contributions. I miss him every day.

The Audacity of Seymour Papert

Mathematician, social justice warrior, scientist, artificial intelligence pioneer, author, inventor, computer scientist, pilot, chef, teacher… Seymour Papert was quite a complex figure. People interested in his work often focus on a tiny piece of Seymour, like his one of his favorite parables, "The Blind Men and the Elephant."

Seymour Papert's singular genius may be described as follows:
1. Developed a theory about learning, constructionism
2. Created tools for implementing constructionism
3. Described through vivid examples and learning stories what it would look like in practice
4. Always predicted how school would reject that innovation

The last point is enormously important. Critics of Papert often show contempt for his idealism. They cynically dismiss him as a fanciful utopian. This just isn't the case. Nearly every piece of writing about education, teaching, or learning from 1968–2006, talks about what could be, accompanied by examples, and an acknowledgment of how the body of school is likely to reject this new organism. That cold reality never tempered Papert's belief that progress was possible.

Why This Book?

I often remark that if one seeks to improve education, the first step is finding a cure for amnesia. This book is an effort to preserve a historical document and share it with future of generations seeking a more creative, personal, empowering, and meaningful educational experience for young people. Each of us stands on the shoulders of giants. Few have laid such a broad and strong foundation for sustaining progressive education than Seymour Papert and Cynthia Solomon. The contributors to this volume have spent fifty years extending that legacy.

Nearly fifteen years ago it became clear to me that certain changes having to do with computers were going to seep into the culture and become part of everyone's life. These changes would occur because of economic and historical and intellectual forces vastly more powerful than those of any school board, or even the National Science Foundation. The computer is a product of history, a cultural force, and we cannot change that fact. What we can do, however, is try to deviate this force a little. Thus, I arrived at the idea of integrating a programming language with the concrete world of visual events, making graphics available through "turtles," making programming and all the mathematics and conceptual events programming entails—making that concrete instead of abstract.

The importance of the computer is that a whole range of abstract entities which could not physically be manipulated before can be now. They can become concrete. One can play with them, push them around. The computer is a universal machine, and if we are clever enough, if enough of us get involved in the process, perhaps one day we can use it to fill all the gaps. That is the general goal. (Papert, 1984)

One lesson I learned from Seymour is that every time the system accepts your intervention, metaphorically saying, "I got it," we should do something more radical. If you are trying to pull a wagon attached to a rope, the rope needs to be taut or no forward progress is possible. We must keep the rope taut.

Who is This Book For?

Both Seymour Papert and Cynthia Solomon were exceptional at presenting complex concepts and powerful ideas in a way that resonated with experts and the general public. This book seeks to continue that tradition by welcoming a wide audience. Sadly, Papert was often despised by the education establishment for daring to believe that teachers could be better. My fervent wish is that readers will represent a broad cross-section of teachers, administrators, preservice educators, technology designers, and parents. Each of this book's authors were invited based on their multiple perspectives, roles, and contributions to education. I hope will find something to make you think and consider how things need not be as they seem. Although satisfying the standards set by *Twenty Things* remains elusive in many schools, the essays in this book chart a course for the foreseeable future.

How is This Book Organized?

This book combines history, theory, politics, technology, epistemology, pedagogy, mathematics, sociology, computer science, art, and developmental psychology to create a lens through which we may make the world a better place for children. Such an eclectic mix of topics and voices is impossible to categorize in a definitive fashion. Therefore, the book is organized loosely around four themes found in the Solomon and Papert paper:

- Learning with computers
- Educational conservatism and resistance
- Personal computing
- Future possibilities

Essays were arranged based on a variety of criteria, some profound and others mundane. Books are linear yet each contribution to this anthology is worthy of your attention. You should also read the original *Twenty Things* paper at the end of the book.

Meet My Friends

Nothing brings me more joy than sharing my friends, heroes, sheroes, mentors, and colleagues with fellow educators. That is one of the primary motivations behind my Constructing Modern Knowledge institute and the creation of this book. Contributors to this book include scholars and tech pioneers who worked with Papert and Solomon in the 1970s, phenomenal classroom teachers, inventors, researchers, school administrators, university professors, and educational technology leaders. Revisiting a half century's worth of their work, as well as the new essays written just for this book has inspired me beyond words. Through the words of these authors, you will surely come to love and respect them as I do.

But Wait, There's More!

Should this book inspire you to revisit the literature, learn more, or try computing projects, a host of additional resources may be found online at the following sites.

- **Cmkpress.com/20things** – The official web site for this book. Come here for further reading recommendations and learning resources.
- **Dailypapert.com** – The online archive of Seymour Papert's writing, audio, and video
- **Logothings.github.io/logothings** - Cynthia Solomon's History of Logo web site
- **Inventtolearn.com** – A collection of resources supporting learning by making

Bibliographic Note

Since dozens of essays in this volume cite *Twenty Things to Do with a Computer*, we made the editorial decision not to include the bibliographic citation repeatedly. Here is the citation.

Papert, S., & Solomon, C. (1971). Twenty Things to Do with a Computer. *MIT Artificial Intelligence Memo Number 248.*

Acknowledgments

While I could easily write a book just raving about the contributors, please indulge my desire to single out a few for special mention. Of course, everyone who generously contributed to this text shapes my thinking.

By their example, Dan and Molly Lynn Watt taught me everything I know about teaching teachers. First as a participant in their legendary Logo Institute and then as a faculty member of the same event, I gained confidence in the efficacy of constructionism. Now both retired, Dan was an engineer who became one of the principal investigators of Logo 1970s research and Molly was a social activist heavily steeped in progressive education movements. Dan was the first "star" I met while attending my first education conference in 1983. There were no two more popular figures in the world of educational computing in the 1980s than the Watts. Dan authored one of the most successful educational computing books in history and together, their written output taught even great teachers to teach better. Their authentic generosity of spirit and faith in the inherent goodness of humanity created opportunities for so many of us to become more sensitive educators and understand complex concepts like recursion, even if it was via contra dancing. The education system would be so much healthier if fearless, ukulele-toting, homespun geniuses like Dan and Molly were more popular than the slick merchants of word salad theatrics who are lionized today.

Tom Lough is a true southern gentleman, science educator, and one of the few veterans and certainly only Olympian to have been a leader in the Logo community. Tom founded *Logo Exchange*, the long-running journal for Logo-using educators that did so much sustain a community of educators engaged in the Sisyphean task of teaching computer programming to children in the 1980s and '90s, a time when computer access was hardly ubiquitous. I first met Tom at the Logo '85 conference and enjoyed the great honor of following in his footsteps as the last editor of *Logo Exchange*. Tom delights in the efforts of others and like Dan and Molly, trusted me to contribute in ways I didn't know I could.

In 1986, I traveled solo across the country for the first time to attend the West Coast Logo Conference. At the opening reception I observed David Thornburg and Brian Silverman engaged in a fierce conversation about Ada Lovelace. I remember thinking to myself, "I want to be able to do *that* someday." It was not long before both David and Brian became great friends and colleagues. David contributed to this book and although Brian did not so in words, his legacy is enormous. If you have used a dialect of Logo or robotics construction kit over the past four decades, there is a good chance that Brian Silverman helped create it. Without him, I would not have any software to use with children. It has been a great joy to share David, Brian, Dan, and Molly with educators at Constructing Modern Knowledge and other professional learning events I have organized over the years.

Soon after meeting David Loader at the 1990 World Conference on Computers in Education in Sydney, I was invited to spend months at a time helping to bring Solomon and Papert's ideas to life in the Southern Hemisphere's largest girls school. I was given carte blanche to do anything I thought would improve the institution. Decades later, I asked David what he was thinking in trusting me so unequivocally. He seemed genuinely confused by the question, but after further pressing replied something along the lines of, "Well, anyone who showed your level of initiative was given that level of authority." Upon reflection, I realized that was true and that is what made him arguably the most significant school principal of the past fifty years.

The time I had the privilege to spend with Seymour and Cynthia in person and via their written artifacts shapes every hour of my life and will do so forever. I am grateful for their friendship, mentoring, and collegiality. The laughs and conversations have been priceless. It is humbling to think about how a wannabe jazz musician and serial Algebra failure could spend his professional life sharing their profound genius with educators across the planet.

I owe my career and the learning adventures enjoyed over three million air miles to Brian, David, Molly, Dan, Tom, Seymour, and Cynthia. Without their faith in me, there would be no career.

Words cannot express my depth of gratitude to Sylvia Martinez who lovingly and tirelessly assembled, edited, and designed the book you are now reading.

My parents, Brian and Arlene, supported any nutty direction I decided to take my life while Sylvia, Leon, Vivian, and Yvonne gave me my own family. I am madly in love with my grandchildren Theo and Irene. They alone make the world a better place.

References

Minsky, M., & Papert, S. A. (1969). *Perceptrons: An Introduction to Computational Geometry*. MIT Press.

Papert, S. (1980). *Mindstorms: Children, Computers, and Powerful Ideas*. Basic Books.

Papert, S. (1984). Computer as Mudpie. In D. Peterson (Ed.), *Intelligent Schoolhouse: Readings on Computers and Learning*. Reston Publishing Company.

Papert, S. (1993). *The Children's Machine: Rethinking School in the Age of the Computer*. Basic Books.

Papert, S. (1996). *The Connected Family: Bridging the Digital Generation Gap*. Longstreet.

Solomon, C. (1986). *Computer Environments for Children: A Reflection on Theories of Learning and Education*. MIT Press.

Solomon, C., Minsky, M., & Harvey, B. (Eds.). (1986). *LogoWorks*. McGraw-Hill Book Company.

Solomon, C., & Xiao, X. (Eds.). (2019). *Inventive Minds: Marvin Minsky on Education*. MIT Press.

Stager, G. S. (2006). *An Investigation of Constructionism in the Maine Youth Center* [Ph.D., The University of Melbourne]. Melbourne, Australia.

Section 1 — Our Vision

In our image of a school computation laboratory, an important role is played by numerous "controller ports" which allow any student to plug any device into the computer. The ports are protected by fuses and suitable Interfaces so that little harm will be done if anyone carelessly puts the main voltage into a computer output port. The laboratory will have a supply of motors, solenoids, relays, sense devices of various kinds, etc., etc. Using them the students will be able to invent and build an endless variety of cybernetic systems.

Our purpose here is not to complain of what other people have not done, but to tell of some exciting things you can do with the computer you have now or with the one you will be incited to get by the pages that follow. More than half the suggestions we are about to make have been implemented and tested in our elementary school teaching program. This does not imply that they are not of equal or greater value at other levels of education; on the contrary, we are convinced that they give a glimpse of the proper way to introduce everyone of whatever age and whatever level of academic performance, to programing, to more general knowledge of computation and indeed (we say courageously steeling ourselves for the onslaught) to mathematics, to physics and to all formal subjects including linguistics and music.

—*Twenty Things to Do with a Computer* (1971)

Twenty (Poetic) Things to Do with a Computer

Angi Chau

In Solomon and Papert's original paper, one of the most striking things to me was the open-ended nature of their prompts. Beginning with "Build a Turtle" and going all the way to "Puppets" (and of course, the tongue-in-cheek "Recursion Line"), the brevity and vagueness of each prompt opens up whole worlds of exploration.

Taking the prompts as inspiration, I challenged myself to create similarly world-opening, exploration-rich prompts, grounded in my own practice of teaching computer science using creative and artistic projects. Harking back to the brevity of Solomon and Papert's original prompts, I used the haiku form to keep the prompts short, sweet, and poetic in nature.

Although these prompts were originally conceived in the context of creative coding, one can also imagine responding to some of these prompts using other "computerly" ways of creating—from physical computing to stop-motion animation to 3D modeling.

1. You want to be who?
    What are your likes, dreams, and hopes?
    Create your avatar.

2. Five, four, three, two, one!
    Countdown timer that ends with…
    what? A surprise please!

3. Who was Sol Lewitt?
    His "Wall Drawings" were simple,
    but complex. Code one.

4. Math of emojis?
    How to build calculator
    for your emotions?

5. Start with a photo
    Of a trip you took somewhere.
    Make it rain, or snow.

6. A favorite poem?
    Made even better if it
    is animated.

7. Go out for a walk.
    Patterns everywhere. Look there!
    How can you make that?

8. Fishes in the sea...
    So many kinds! Imagine
    them interacting.

9. Joy of rotations -
    mandalas, kaleidoscopes.
    What will you rotate?

10. A mindful moment
    is good for our well-being.
    What does yours look like?

11. Have you looked so close
    at something, it's just colors?
    Evoke that detail.

12. Tick-tock, tick-tock, tick...
    Make a clock, but not for hours.
    Track time that matters.

13. Let's surprise a friend
    who is feeling low, with jokes
    and confetti, and more!

14. Invisible ink
    made something out of nothing.
    Think we can code that?

15. Chatbots can be nice,
    or funny, or confused, or...?
    Make one who is wise.

16. Find a sound poem.
    Your sound poetry...listen,
    and what would I hear?

17. Beauty of chaos
    in clouds, smoke, fire, waves. Mimic
    that somehow, some way.

18. Snowflakes, pineapples,
    Lightning, and mountain ranges.
    All fractals. Make one.

19. Life changes, evolves.
    Can a machine evolve too?
    What would that mean then?

20. Nineteen poems you've made.
    For this last, twentieth prompt,
    pick any. And do more.

Progress

Gary Stager

At the end of a particularly stressful and exhausting week early in our project creating a multiage, constructionist, technology-rich, project-based, alternative school inside a troubled prison for teens, Seymour Papert asked me, "Any plans for tonight?" I responded, "What do you have in mind, Seymour?" to which he replied, "I thought we could go out for a nice dinner and continue that conversation about changing the world."

Such determined optimism is what attracted me to educational computing and to "the Logo community." Many of the educators (my people) and researchers attracted to Logo during its 1980s heyday embraced a desire to make the world a better place for kids. It should come as no surprise that so many of the Logo developers and leading advocates were veterans of the civil rights, women's rights, and anti-war movements. Logo offered a tool for turning their social justice activism into modern classroom practice.

> *I have been in other movements... I didn't see it as more special than what was happening in the "whole language" and other things that I had been part of before. What was happening in Logo seemed every bit as important and significant to me... So, we saw Logo as one more of a very powerful handful of important endeavors happening in our lifetime and we threw our energy into it... The ideas weren't radical to me, I was already in those ideas. (Molly Watt, quoted in Agalianos, 1997)*

The new opportunities to democratize computational ideas by making mathematical accessible to children was a bonus. Papert often argued that the use of computers in the spirit of *Twenty Things* created ways for doing mathematics with a similar personal, creative, and emotional investment as one might find in a great art or social studies lesson (Papert, 1991). Many of the educators who embraced Logo viewed it more broadly as a vehicle for empowerment. Papert saw computers and Logo not only as a continuation of the progressive vision of Dewey, but also as a next step in addressing how humans really learn.

Dewey remains a hero to those who believe in a twentieth-century vision of a child as a person with the right to intellectual self-determination, and there can be little doubt that a child treated with respect and encouragement rather than threatened with rejection and punishment will fare better under any system of education. But while Dewey's influence has surely removed some of the crudest impediments to the healthy development of the child, it has been so diluted that it barely addresses the next serious question: In trying to teach children what adults want them to know, does School utilize the way human beings most naturally learn in non-school settings? (Papert, 1993)

Computers, generally, and their use as proposed by Solomon and Papert more specifically, expand the breadth, depth, and range of possible projects. Computing as a creative, intellectually rich activity adds colors to the crayon box and supercharges project-based learning. The hope is that students will not only learn what the education system values but will prepare kids to solve problems their teachers have never imagined and explore previously inaccessible intellectual domains.

Logo's first decade (1967-77) coincided with the second golden age of progressive education. By the late 1970s – early 1980s, school integration, affirmative action, federally funded CETA job training programs, and feminism improved the quality of life for many people. By the time Papert published *Mindstorms* (1980) and microcomputers entered classrooms, the Black/White achievement gap in US schools had narrowed to its smallest differential in history (Darling-Hammond, 1997). The Logo community's period of maximum influence benefited from social policies and political forces not only aligned with the personal values of its teachers but were good for the children they taught.

> *I came into the project [Logo] with ideas of teaching that I still hold very strongly, that are associated with what might be loosely called "progressive education" in this country. Logo fitted within that stream of thought. To me Logo was not inventing something new in its approach to education... student-centered learning, groups of people learning together. When I came to this environment I already had a belief in these ideas. (Paul Goldenberg, quoted in Agalianos, 1997)*

Twenty Things, Mindstorms, and *Logo Exchange* were invitations to those of us seeking to supercharge progressive education with computing. Logo conferences around the world offered communion to those seeking to share a new way of teaching and learning. Countless Logo books were published to satisfy a growing community of evangelists and teachers in search of new ideas.

Each new microcomputer release was followed by a new dialect of Logo software. By adding word processing to the Logo environment, LogoWriter (1986) made programming accessible to teachers across the curriculum. Logo was no longer the exclusive plaything of math instruction, in fact, much of the most interesting mathematical thinking could now be found in the service of storytelling, language arts, and social studies. LogoWriter's introduction of the site license made it possible for entire schools, districts, and states to offer programming software for children in classrooms and at home. As a result, project work was no longer constrained by the school bell and could commence anytime anywhere.

Logo's ascendant popularity mirrored the increasing availability and affordability of personal computers. Schools who viewed computers as a symbol of modernity needed something to do with the hardware and Logo programming was one of the few available options. Conventional wisdom suggests that in an app-centric world, options for using computing devices abound. That makes differentiating the Logo's grandiose goals—agency, intellectual empowerment, social justice, creativity, classrooms as incubators of democracy, making accessible to children ideas at the frontier of mathematics and science—from the passive consumption favored by today's cheerleaders for edtech even more critical. There is a profound difference between the vision described in *Twenty Things* and the ways in which a parent might pacify a toddler with an iPad at a pancake house.

While excitement over the new widespread access to microcomputers and a relative scarcity of other "educational" software packages might explain part of Logo's popularity in the 1980s, the success and lasting impact of the ideas of Solomon, Papert, and their colleagues should not be viewed merely through the lens of market forces or technological progress. Their powerful ideas, as embodied by Logo-like software environments, physical computing, and robotics kits endure and are even viewed as aspirational fifty years later. John Berlow, editor of Mindstorms, recalled:

> *I think mainly what happened was that because of Seymour's kind of breadth of interest and perspective a lot of teachers... took it up as a new kind of way into progressive educational reform...The influence of progressive education was still alive. Logo was seen as a way to give some kind of backbone to progressive education. (Agalianos, 1997)*

Why Logo (and the ideas found in *Twenty Things*) peaked in popularity during the 1980s is a complex phenomenon worth exploring. It is too simplistic to conclude that interest in Logo resulted from the initial availability of microcomputers or that it was marginalized once other software reached the marketplace and teachers had more options for using computers in the classroom. In its heyday, Logo represented something very special—a set of powerful ideas that not only defined educational computing, but also formed the basis for a global community of practice demonstrating the creative and intellectual potential of children. For lots of children and educators such as myself, Logo made us feel smart, capable, and creative—perhaps for the first time.

> *But despite the many manifestations of a widespread desire for something different, the education establishment, including most of its research community, remains largely committed to the educational philosophy of the late nineteenth and early twentieth centuries, and so far, none of those who challenge these hallowed traditions has been able to loosen the hold of the educational establishment on how children are taught. (Papert, 1993)*

While it is likely that schools changed Logo more than Logo changed schools, one should not be quick to dismiss the impact Logo and *Twenty Things* continue to have on children and their teachers. Survey the contributors to this book and you will hear moving tales of how Logo programming enriched relationships with their students, their intellectual power, and themselves. The popularity, visibility, and influence of Papert and Solomon's ideas ebb and flow over time as a reflection of social, political, and policy mores.

While the initial impetus for Logo was to create a Mathland where children could be mathematicians rather than be taught math, the motivation of its early funders was more prosaic. During the post-Sputnik space race era of the late 1960s, Logo was viewed as an instrument of national security. This is ironic given the counter-culture impulses of Logo's developers. Paradoxically, it was national security concerns of the Reagan-era that stifled the educational climate in which Logo flourished during most of the 1980s. Besting one's rivals was no longer viewed as requiring acts of creativity and innovation, but as brute force, compliance, and standardization.

When I studied to become a licensed primary school teacher (PK – 8), we were required to learn to teach reading, writing, literature, math, science, social studies, music, art, and physical education. We were taught the cognitive value of manipulatives and how to create our own. We learned how to use cardboard boxes, hammers, nails, and scraps of cloth to bring literature and storytelling to life and were *required* to learn to play the piano at least a little bit. Teachers made connections between subjects and children with a variety of interests, skills, needs, and expertise. Authentic and playful tasks were celebrated, and our teacher preparation included explicit instruction in what to write in your plan book if you chose to play Scrabble in class for three months.

There was an expectation that we would know what and who we taught. Rich interdisciplinary projects were how learning was made memorable, meaningful, and memorable. Science corners, pets, living plants, puppets, a piano, cardboard castles, costumes, microscopes, were the reason for classrooms. Our attire was to be "smart casual." Teacher preparation was equal parts art and science.

That all ended in the mid-80s with the publication of *A Nation at Risk* (Gardner et al., 1983), the Reagan administration's antagonism towards government as promoter of the common good, and the accompanying efforts to privatize public treasure, like schools. By the late 1980s, legislatures across the globe were removing the art of teaching from teacher credentialing programs and leaving behind little more than animal control and curriculum delivery. This standardization was codified in the United States by George W. Bush's *No Child Left Behind* and Barack Obama's equally vulgar *Race to the Top* legislation. Now, in the name of "science," schools became instruments for delivering standardized curriculum in competition, not just with global adversaries, but in a perpetual war between children, teachers, and communities. Twenty years later, there is little talk of "science" because one cannot continue to blame teachers and kids for a failing system when the "data" would reveal that the system has been engaged in *your* failing experiment for a generation.

I would describe the dominant education practice of 2000-2021, perhaps even dating as far back as the mid 1980s, as being guided by a downward policy spiral in which:

1. Agency, discretion, choice, and control are removed from teachers
2. Teaching becomes more automatized and less thoughtful
3. "Results" suffer
4. So, more agency, discretion, choice, and control is removed from teachers.

It is the recursive nature of this public shaming ritual that jeopardizes the types of learning experiences found in *Twenty Things*. The result is that not only are the wondrous accoutrements of progressive education absent from many schools, including Logo, but few working educators even know about them.

Hints of Progressivism

I student taught with a veteran educator on the cusp of retirement, named Arlene Schoenberger. A casual observer would find little evidence of progressive education in her classroom. She followed the curriculum, the desks were in rows, and her bulletin boards had not been redecorated in epochs. A more nuanced eye would notice Mrs. Schoenberger's calm confident authority, free of the frantic terror many of today's teachers display. Sure, her confidence may have resulted from experience, but that didn't explain why she embraced Logo and robotics in her classroom. In fact, she was so enthusiastic that she enrolled her retired engineer husband in my LEGO TC Logo workshops so he could assist her students on classroom robotics projects during the school day.

The best advice dispensed by my mentor was, "They're never all here. When you can grab five kids, do math. Just keep track of who has done what." Mrs. Schoenberger never fell prey to the fantasy that she was the center of educational universe or that learning was the result of having been taught. She had not internalized the delusional notion that every student hangs on the word of every teacher every second of a lesson with perfect retention. Her sense of satisfaction was not tied to someone else's standard of student achievement. Although she had little interest in learning Logo herself, she saw value in it for her students, perhaps most of all because they seemed to enjoy it. Engaged students were a source of pride. Mrs. Schoenberger valued powerful learning experiences for her students even when they did not revolve around her.

I've given some thought to explaining how an older traditional teacher could create such a fertile environment for Logo-like learning. So, here's my hypothesis. Although Mrs. Schoenberg would not likely identify as a progressive educator, her career was **progressive adjacent**. She taught at a time when educationally progressive ideas were in the air. Her career spanned the 60s, 70s, and 80s when whole language, the project approach, classroom centers, open education, Elementary Science Study, and Cuisenaire rods were part of the dialogue. In fact, Schoenberger taught in a school based on the "Open Classroom" for a few years during the 1970s. Although she (or her school) strayed from these practices over time, she must have learned from them. The best evidence for this diagnosis is that Mrs. Schoenberger felt no need to dominate the classroom either as a dictator, lecturer, soloist, conductor, or choreographer. She was a realist who understood the unpredictability of classrooms, respected her students, welcomed collaboration, and delighted in the company of all kids, including the nutty ones no matter how serious she appeared.

Building Bridges to the Future of Progressive Education

> *But despite the many manifestations of a widespread desire for something different, the education establishment, including most of its research community, remains largely committed to the educational philosophy of the late nineteenth and early twentieth centuries, and so far none of those who challenge these hallowed traditions has been able to loosen the hold of the educational establishment on how children are taught. (Papert, 1993)*

On countless occasions, I have introduced Papert and Solomon's ideas to teachers who consider themselves learner-centered or whose experiences as a learner, teacher, or parent were progressive adjacent. In each case, their reaction is "OK, I get it." If you return to their classroom a few weeks later, you are likely to find nice examples of computationally rich project work in the spirit of *Twenty Things* on display. This kind of teaching is not impossible, or even difficult, but requires an explicit attention to making it happen.

Is there hope for teachers whose preparation has been mechanistic or vocational in nature? What about for today's young teachers who experienced impoverished classroom experiences as No Child Left Behind-era students? I am optimistic that there is, but only if we nurture those who Seymour Papert called "the Yearners."

> *Large numbers of teachers manage to create within the walls of their own classrooms oases of learning profoundly at odds with the education philosophy publicly espoused by their administrators; some public school districts, perhaps those where Yearners have moved into administration, have made space for Yearners within School by allowing for the establishment of alternative programs within the School system, allowing such programs to deviate from district policies on method and curriculum. (Papert, 1993)*

Piaget (1973) teaches us that knowledge is a consequence of experience. If we desire for teachers to create new, more progressive learning environments for children, their preservice and ongoing in-service education needs to provide firsthand experience learning in ways similar to the ones they desire for their students. Such productive contexts for learning use the computational and constructive materials and technologies of their time (or at least the ones detailed in 1971). Papert urged teachers participating in workshops to take off their teacher hats and put on their learner hats. This philosophy forms the basis for our Invent to Learn workshops and Constructing Modern Knowledge institutes. Much is possible when we produce learning contexts in which Yearners become progressive adjacent.

One thing I observed is that Seymour Papert knew all the major figures in progress education. If he didn't know then personally, he was quite familiar with their work. By the 1990s, Papert was explicitly connecting his work to progressive education while simultaneously describing how it extended that tradition.

> *There is a family resemblance (and I will accept the word **progressive** to name it) between the vision of learning I am presenting here and certain philosophical principles expressed in the diverse forms of innovations that go under such names as **progressive** or **open** or **child-centered** or **constructivist** or **radical** education. I certainly share with this broad movement the criticism of School as casting the child in the role of passive recipient of knowledge. (Papert, 1993)*

Great constructionist software and flexible accessible hardware are critical, but insufficient, to bring about what Papert called "megachange" or even to complete Papert and Solomon's *Twenty Things*. Situating pedagogical and technological achievements in that specific milieu may enable us to understand how to maintain the spirit of *Twenty Things* for future generations. Most

17

importantly, the future of progressive education is at stake.

Teachers, whether Yearners or not, cannot choose pedagogical paths they have not experienced themselves. It is imperative that preservice teacher education and ongoing professional development stands on the shoulders of giants like Cynthia Solomon and Seymour Papert, but also shares the lessons of the legions of progressive educators who proceed us.

Educators who "meet the turtle," love her and are inspired to introduce her to their students. This has been demonstrated repeatedly in classrooms from Melbourne to Milan to Montgomery. It is not unusual for teachers to remember "the turtle" from their own schooling and wonder where she went.

Every time a 4th grader leaps up in class and exclaims, "I know what I did wrong. It's not greater than, it's less than!" or a teacher professes to enjoying math for the first time or bursts with pride while demonstrating their interactive robotic invention, we are reminded of the gifts Papert and Solomon gave us.

Therefore, educational progress requires that we keep their ideas alive, nourish the Yearners, and inspire educators merely dissatisfied with the system. Access to great constructionist materials and models of learner-centered practices need to be accompanied by a theoretical basis for justifying pedagogical behavior. Since education occurs in real time, we need to build the plane while flying it. A greater sense of urgency is required to honor the children we are blessed to serve.

Logo and the broader ideas introduced by Papert and Solomon represent the modern embodiment of progressive education.

> *Logo makes a dramatic difference in the lives of children when Logo-the-language is embedded in Logo-the-environment. Logo at its best has motivated teachers to rethink their relationship with curriculum and with children, and has encouraged children to reflect on their own relationship with learning. (Solomon et al., 2020)*

Logo is an invitation for progressive educators to explore new technology-enriched learning opportunities, just as it is a means for introducing constructionism and social justice to a wider universe of educators. Logo can introduce, amplify, and sustain the pedagogical ideals of progressive education, just as progressive traditions create the fertile soil necessary to harvest the greatest yield from *Twenty Things*. The fruits of such optimism are well within reach. As Carol Sperry reported overhearing two kindergartners discussing what happens in the computer lab, "It's fun. It's hard. It's Logo."

References

Agalianos, A. S. (1997). *A Cultural Studies Analysis of Logo in Education* [Doctor of Philosophy, Institute of Education, University of London]. discovery.ucl.ac.uk/id/eprint/10018887/7/Agalianos%2C%20 Angelos%20S.pdf

Darling-Hammond, L. (1997). *The Right to Learn: A Blueprint for Creating Schools that Work* (1st ed.). Jossey-Bass.

Gardner, D., Larsen, Y., Baker, W., Campbell, A., & Crosby, E. (1983). *A Nation at Risk: The Imperative for Educational Reform*.

Papert, S. (1980). *Mindstorms: Children, Computers, and Powerful Ideas*. Basic Books.

Papert, S. (1991). Situating Constructionism. In I. Harel & S. Papert (Eds.), *Constructionism* (pp. 1-11). Ablex. papert.org/articles/SituatingConstructionism.html

Papert, S. (1993). *The Children's Machine: Rethinking School in the Age of the Computer*. Basic Books.

Piaget, J. (1973). *To Understand is to Invent: The Future of Education* (G. A. Roberts, Trans.). Grossman Publishers.

Solomon, C., Harvey, B., Kahn, K., Lieberman, H., Miller, M. L., Minsky, M., Papert, A., & Silverman, B. (2020). History of Logo. *Proceedings of the ACM on Programming Languages*, 4(HOPL), 1-66.

Spiraling

Artemis Papert & Cynthia Solomon

For us, spirals are inspiring objects to think with. They can be stitched, they can be drawn. In this essay we are sharing our love of spirals with you.

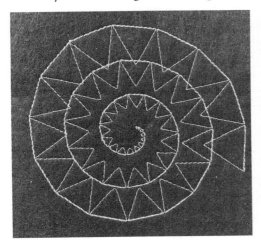 

Cynthia on Polygons and Spirals

Lately I've been thinking about spirals; in particular how to get Logo turtles to make spirals. Seymour Papert first invented these turtles in 1969 at Bolt, Beranek and Newman (BBN) and at the MIT AI Lab. The need for them was in reaction to Seymour and me teaching a year-long Logo-math class to twelve-year olds. Papert felt the children did well but could have done even better if they had a concrete object to interact with. In the sixties Papert himself was steeped in work on robotics at MIT with Marvin Minsky, his close collaborator. Papert didn't think of the turtle as a robot nor as an automaton just a thing to control. But turtles had pens and could leave a trace of their paths. A whole new world of computerized drawing, graphics, and animation opened up to children in 1970 when both floor and display turtles were set up in an elementary school where Seymour and I taught ten-year-olds in a year-long computer class.

Analysis of turtle behavior falls into the category of differential geometry and has come to be known as turtle geometry. This led to an interesting theorem, the Total Turtle Trip Theorem: the turtle will return to its starting state if it moves a fixed amount and turns a fixed amount. The exception occurs if it turns 0 or 360 degrees where upon it will walk in a straight line and never get back to its starting state. The turtle's state is described by its position and heading. A display turtle's position is where it is on a grid which is marked by the intersection of horizontal (x) and vertical (y) lines. The center position has x as 0 and y as 0.

I have to admit I love making the turtle draw polygons whether they be regular polygons or star polygons. The turtle I have in mind takes two forms. It lives on a graphics screen and it lives on the floor as a wheeled mechanical creature. A turtle understands and obeys a cluster of commands. Logo was the first computer language that had commands I could give to the turtle.

The basic turtle commands in Logo are: move forward or back a number of steps, and turn left or right a number of degrees. Two of today's block languages, Scratch and Snap! and their offshoots have three commands: move, turnleft, and turnright. TurtleArt, on the other hand, is devoted to turtle behavior and follows the original Logo commands of forward, back, left, and right.

The reasons I love making the turtle draw polygons have to do with a kind of aesthetics. With the same procedure, the turtle draws a plethora of polygons. All I have to do is change the forward step or the right or left turn. I have been playing around with turtles and polygons for a very long time. Nonetheless, I often stumble upon something new and beautiful.

I can make polygons in different sizes and colors. I can make designs out of polygons and then capture the screen results on paper or have the turtle draw on paper. I can now, thanks to TurtleStitch, transfer the designs to a computerized embroidery machine and stitch on felt, cardstock, or other fabrics.

Here is *poly* in TurtleStitch,

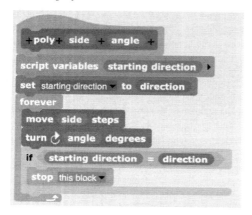

and the results from running the procedure.

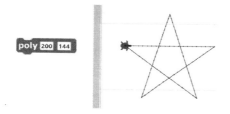

Using the 5-pointed star *poly* I tried different turnings. The resulting design was captivating.

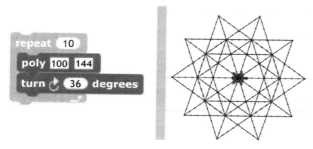

I had similarly surprising experiences when I turned to spirals. I wanted to play on the 5-pointed star theme and so I ran *polyspi* with an angle of 144 (a 5-pointed star). I then ran it three times and stopped because I liked the result.

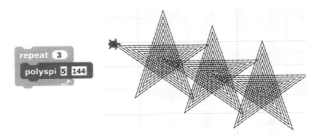

Here is the TurtleStitch code I used. Of course, I made a new stop rule and altered the code somewhat from the poly or polyspi code in the *Twenty Things* paper. I embroidered the poly and polyspi drawings.

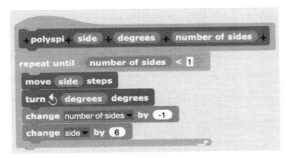

My closing remarks are about a call I made to Artemis Papert. I asked her, "How many multiples of 360 degrees does the turtle turn to make different star polygons?" She replied, "I don't know, that's a question for Brian Silverman, he must know." Brian didn't have an immediate answer. But we started exploring together. After a while Margaret Minsky and Oliver Steele joined us in the exploration. Each of us tackled the problem in a slightly different way. We knew from the Total Turtle Trip Theorem that no matter how many vertices the polygon had, the turtle would eventually draw a closed figure and return to its starting state. The turtle goes round and round. But how many times? This is called its winding number. We computed it using a variety of methods. Our discussion led to more questions like how many polygons have the same number of vertices or what polygons cannot be made by the poly procedure?

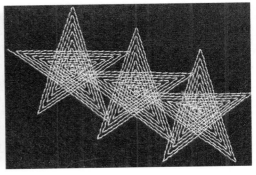

Artemis, the Artist

I first started programming in the 1970s, with Logo at the MIT AI Lab. I was about ten years old. I found being at MIT and programming exciting. I have to admit that I do not remember what my programs were but I do remember that I felt there was something missing. I was excited about programming but I was not really excited about my Logo projects. I am an artist at heart and somehow art didn't seem to be what people did with Logo. Or maybe it was not what the people of that particular Logo culture did.

As an adult, I reconnected with Turtle Geometry. Paula Bontá and Brian Silverman had created TurtleArt, a microworld for making art through code. It was what I wished I had as a child. The turtle had learned about color. This was exciting. What was also exciting was that Brian and I were exchanging artistic ideas and bouncing images off each other. One of us would make an image and the other one would alter it in some way. Sometimes it was minor, sometimes major.

At the beginning I was at times struggling with the geometry or with some algorithm. Brian was my programming and math expert and was there to help me when I felt stuck. Over time the programming part became kind of invisible and I could just focus on the art—color, lines, shapes, and composition. I was excited, I was hooked, I was spending hours creating image after image.

TurtleArt allows a novel kind of dialog between artist and image. Explorations in TurtleArt take the form of a repeated set of explorations. An image can be drawn, redrawn, reconsidered, and redrawn with tiny variations.

Cynthia likes spirals. I like them too.

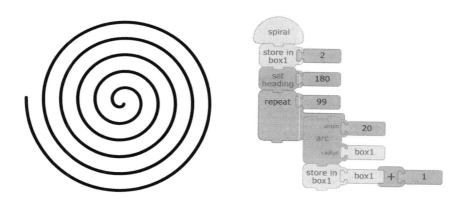

It's nice but not very imaginative. What I really had in mind was a coiled snake.

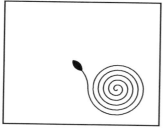

Better.

Better still.

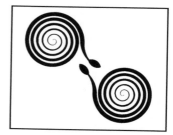

Better to have a companion.

Each snake is made out of a body – i.e. a spiral

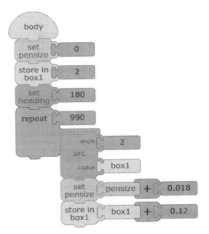

a neck – a piece of a spiral

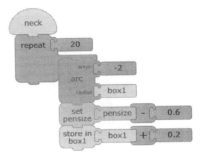

and a head.

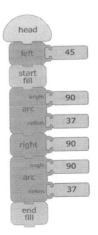

So where's the big idea? The big idea is that at times very small changes can make a huge difference. Before reaching the final image, there were a lot of iterations. Some nice, some not so nice. The artistic exploration is what fascinates me.

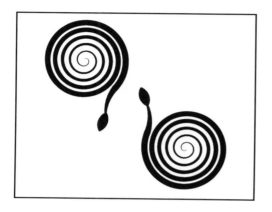
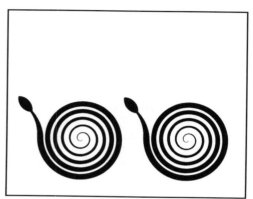
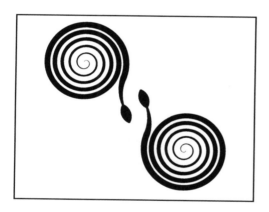
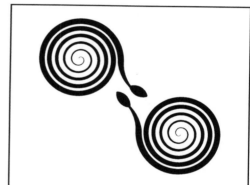
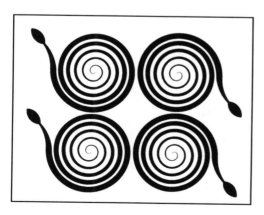

Adventures on the Road to Mathland

Dan Lynn Watt

It is snowing brightly and heavily outside my window in Cambridge as I begin this adventure, remembering one of the most fertile and exciting periods of my professional and personal life. For almost twenty years, starting in 1976 I was deeply enmeshed, first in the MIT Logo Group, and later in a broad national and international community of Logo educators.

My journey began more than ten years earlier while I was a graduate student in engineering at Cornell. I studied abstract topics with bizarre names like Theory of Elasticity, Magneto-Aerodynamics, Partial Differential Equations, and Tensor Analysis. Long before I completed my dissertation, I knew that I did not want to be an engineer. I was a civil rights activist at Cornell, and I wanted to contribute to society in a much more progressive, egalitarian way than engineering.

I was fortunate to learn about a project called Elementary Science Study (ESS) in Newton Massachusetts. ESS was hiring scientists and educators to collaborate on creating hands-on science kits for elementary school, and I was thrilled to be offered a position. At ESS we worked to find engaging materials and challenges for children, lead them to create their own questions, and their own experiments, about an important science domain. We wanted children to *be scientists* and discover the excitement of exploring the physical and living worlds.

Before ESS and other hands-on science curricula developed during the sixties, elementary school science teaching consisted mostly of textbooks of science facts and, if students were lucky, cute demonstrations by teachers. We were determined to bring dramatic changes to elementary school classrooms in the name of science education. Students in our classes were going to be active, moving around, talking, questioning, sharing, making messes, and of course, learning to clean up after themselves. We were consciously out to upset the educational applecart.

The first unit I worked on was *Whistles and Strings* (Watt & Romney, 1971b). For one activity we gave kids plastic tubes to blow across and make a sound (like blowing across a soda bottle). They could cut the tubes to different lengths to investigate how the length of the tube affected the sounds. What if they blew across the tube harder or softer? What if they covered the end of a tube or left it open? It was not easy to predict what would happen, leading to more questions. That made this a good unit. While I tried these activities in a classroom to see if kids enjoyed and engaged with the experience, an observer carefully took note of the kids' questions, the experiments they did with the tubes, problems they ran into, and so forth. (I don't need to tell you that this classroom was noisier than usual in an elementary school!) Afterwards I wrote up the activities, kids' questions and challenges in a trial teaching guide, and asked several Boston area teachers to try it out and give feedback on which activities worked well, which fizzled, which caused problems, and so forth. Only after trying in several classrooms and revising the teachers' guide based on the feedback we received, did we publish a teacher's guide for the final version of the unit.

This was the process for all the ESS units. We provided engaging kits of materials—enough for every child in a class—and interesting challenges for kids. In our teacher's guides we emphasized ways teachers could help children generate questions and think of experiments related to their questions. We put in examples of children's questions so teachers would have an idea of what to expect. Along with *Whistles and Strings*, we published a companion teacher's guide, *Musical Instrument Recipe Book* (Watt & Romney, 1971a), a collection of instructions for children and teachers to build instruments from readily available materials.

While working at ESS I met my future wife Molly at a teacher workshop. We discovered that we both owned Appalachian dulcimers, and both loved folk music, progressive education, the civil rights movement, and each other. Later, as you may already know, we became professional as well as life partners.

I had been hired at ESS as a scientist. By the time I left after three years I had become an educator. I took a job as a classroom teacher in Brookline, Massachusetts to see if the progressive education theory and practice I had learned at ESS, could be used in other areas of the curriculum. ESS was Brookline's official science curriculum, and our curriculum coordinators were advocating inquiry learning in all subject areas. The Brookline schools were supportive of open education. We wanted children to have different activities and projects to choose from. We built as much content knowledge as we could into investigations that interested and engaged children.

As a teacher I was challenging myself as well as my students. It was sometimes exciting, sometimes frustrating, to be an open education teacher. After seven years of teaching fifth grade, I was burnt out and applied for a sabbatical. By another stroke of good luck I managed to get myself invited to spend the 1976-77 school year as a visiting research associate with the MIT Logo Group. I was on my way to *Mathland*.

Before I met Seymour Papert or anyone else at MIT, I read two research memos that introduced me to Logo. I was excited by Cynthia Solomon's and Seymour Papert's *Twenty Things to Do with a Computer*, and Seymour's *Teaching Children to Be Mathematicians vs. Teaching Them About Mathematics*, both published in 1971. The title of Seymour's paper immediately drew me in. What he advocated was exactly what I had been doing at ESS for science learning, and what I had tried to do as an inquiry teacher in Brookline. Give kids exciting materials to explore, and let them choose their own questions and projects they wanted to do next. Reading these papers, I knew I wanted to be part of this new educational movement as much as I wanted to be part of ESS ten years earlier.

The projects described in *Twenty Things* were immediately engaging to children and could easily launch them into investigations of their own. Every activity involved students controlling a computer, making it do things of great interest: programming a robot, drawing designs on a screen, exploring unexpected properties of geometric shapes, creating a simple animation, controlling the actions of a mechanical erector set, and much, much more.

What got my attention more than the intriguing activities was the Logo computer language which used normal English words to *tell the computer* what the child wanted it to do. By keeping a record of those instructions and seeing the effects they caused, students could understand and explain what they had done, and *debug* their programs, that is, experimentally change their programs to resolve problems when the instructions did not do what they expected. And as Seymour further explained in *Teaching Children to Be Mathematicians*, this process gave children access to their own thinking. As a teacher, I realized that it would also allow me access to the students' thinking—something I had struggled with as a classroom teacher.

Seymour's paper demonstrated that by inventing programs to control the Logo turtle, students could learn powerful mathematical and computer science concepts that were not taught in conventional math classes. Seymour called the Logo language and the geometry of the shapes drawn by the turtle, "a mathematics made for learning." Because of the level of student engagement, Seymour argued, the learning would be deeper and longer lasting than mathematics learned in school. He showed how students could "identify with the turtle" by using their own bodies as tools to think with. They could *play turtle*, that is, imagine themselves in the turtle's place and think, for example, "Should I go forward here? How far?" "Which way should I turn? How far?" I had always loved geometry but found it difficult to teach using paper and pencil. I was hooked!

A few years later, in *Mindstorms: Children Computers and Powerful Ideas* (1980), Seymour described in luminous prose and with many examples, how someone could fall in love with mathematics by learning Logo. He coined the term "Mathland," a learning environment designed to engage children in conversations with a math-speaking entity, specifically the Logo language and turtle geometry. He used the metaphor of learning a foreign language. I paraphrase his argument:

> Even though many English-speaking people, children and adults, have difficulty learning French in a classroom, it is absurd to say, "French is difficult to learn." Children who grow up in France, surrounded by French speakers learn the language at a very young age. Similarly, it is absurd to say, "math is difficult to learn." Think how natural it would be to learn mathematics in Mathland, engaging with a math-speaking computer, and surrounded by others speaking mathematics with the computer and each other.

There are many more brilliant psychological insights and metaphors in *Mindstorms*. I reread much of it while preparing this chapter.

The classroom experiments carried out by Cynthia and Seymour in 1968 and 1969, and described in the two 1971 research reports, convinced them that children could learn powerful mathematics by programming the Logo turtle. But those experiments were carried out using teletype consoles connected by phone lines to a mainframe computer at MIT. The time lag between entering a command and the resulting action was frustrating. The computer displays were crude cathode ray tubes. The teachers were MIT computer scientists. Further classroom experiments would have been impractical and expensive at the time.

By 1976, when I joined the MIT Logo Group, Seymour was certain that personal microcomputers were on the horizon. He and his colleagues at MIT wanted a proof-of-concept experiment showing the viability of Mathland in an elementary school, with average children and a public school teacher. I had ten years of elementary school classroom teaching and curriculum development behind me. I would be a perfect candidate for implementing Mathland in a public school.

During my sabbatical at MIT I fell in love with the Logo language and the mathematics of turtle geometry. The way Logo used English words to tell the turtle how to move inspired me to invent meaningful names for the procedures and designs I made. As I constructed patterns and shapes with the turtle, I loved the way a small change in a program command or a variable could produce unexpected effects. And I loved the way, so very often, what I intended turned out differently than I expected. Put another way, I discovered the joy of bugs and debugging.

If I was ecstatic during my first year in Mathland, it was also due to the heady atmosphere and the community I found in the MIT Logo group, with Seymour, other MIT faculty, Hal Abelson, Andy diSessa and Jean Bamberger, and the group's amazing office manager Greg Gargarian, who carried the daily business of the group on his back. There was a feeling of camaraderie, of being involved in a common learning endeavor. The group included undergraduate computer science majors, visiting psychologists, musicians, physicists, international visiting educators, and some brilliant programmers. Everyone was pleased to show each other what we were working on and to talk endlessly about education and computers. If I got stuck in learning Logo, programing people who knew more than I did were always around to help me get unstuck. After I read *Mindstorms* I realized that the MIT Logo Group in the seventies was the embodiment of a *samba school*.

One task for my sabbatical was to find a way to return to Brookline with the means to bring a group of children along with me to Mathland. This would be the proof-of-concept experiment that Seymour and the group had been working towards. Seymour, with my assistance, wrote a proposal that convinced the National Science Foundation (NSF) to fund a small one-year study, of children learning Logo in a school setting. And so, the Brookline Logo Project was born.

During the 1977–78 school year we set up a classroom of four computers in the basement of Lincoln School—where I taught before my sabbatical. The computers were huge heavy, stand-alone behemoths with special high-resolution displays costing about $15,000 each. (We were anticipating the near future when much smaller and cheaper microcomputers using TV monitors would be readily available.)

Over the course of the year I taught and documented the learning of sixteen sixth grade students, four groups of four, for about four hours per week, for an average of about thirty hours. The students selected for the project represented a range of backgrounds and prior school success.

Each student had their own computer. Students could share ideas and collaborate if they wished. My teaching strategy was to introduce basic turtle commands and simple procedures, and let the students take it from there. I would suggest project ideas from time to time and encourage students to share ideas with each other. I introduced new features of Logo and more complex programming techniques, as students needed them to accomplish their goals. Between classes I spent hours reviewing printouts of the student work. This was a very rich experience of *action research*. The *research* was to document the students' problem solving and mathematical thinking. The *action* was the suggestions I made to students if they were stuck, or to extend their projects, and introduce new programming techniques, all based on the ways they were already thinking.

Sylvia Weir, a visiting senior researcher at MIT, and I wrote two massive reports documenting the learning of our sixteen students, *Final Report of the Brookline Logo Project, Volume II and Volume III*. (The reports are still available in an archive at MIT—check them out!) *Volume II* documented specific content our students learned of programming, problem solving, and mathematics over the course of about thirty hours of Logo immersion. *Volume III* describes the learning approaches of each individual student, showing how they created their own projects, progressed by different paths, and learned in their own ways. We showed that students at all levels of mathematical and academic abilities were able to succeed, and equally important, feel successful in the Logo classroom. They did not all learn the same content—some learned more mathematics and programming than others. In essence they learned what they needed to know to carry out the projects they invented. The quantity and quality of the student's work, and the mathematics they learned informed my work for more than fifteen years.

Consider these two projects completed successfully by two students with different levels of programming skill and mathematical ability.

Donald's Head	Deborah's Rabbit
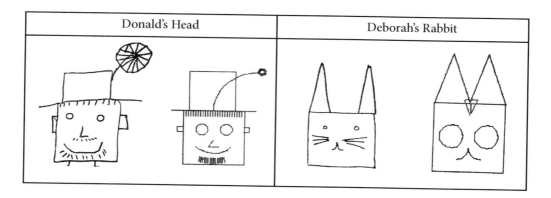	

Donald was academically successful in the regular school curriculum. He planned his project in advance, sketching all the small details he wanted. Then he worked *top-down* by writing a super-procedure listing each feature of the head as a separate sub-procedure. He invented complicated sub-procedures to draw the hair and the beard. But Donald was not good at visualizing the position and heading of the turtle. For instance, he decided to use an arc procedure to draw the mouth—and spent an entire class period using trial and error to place and orient the turtle to make the mouth come out where he wanted it.

Deborah's teachers considered her a "slow learner." But she had one mathematical ability that Donald did not. She had good visual intuition, could see where the turtle was heading and comfortably predict where it would move next. Deborah worked *bottom-up*. She sketched the rabbit she wanted the turtle to draw, and then constructed her design one piece at a time. Early in the semester she discovered that she could draw many designs using only 30-degree turns. And she used only 30 degrees for almost all her work. When she drew the square for the turtle's head, she knew that three 30-degree turns made one 90-degree turn, but continued using 30 degrees exclusively. She would slowly and methodically turn the turtle 30 degrees, see where it was heading, then decide whether to turn once again, or to move forward. Once she had these strategies in place, she could work through the steps of her project at her own pace. When I suggested a few times that she combine three 30-degree turns to make one 90-degree turn, she shook her head—"I know what I'm doing!" When I complemented her on her mathematical problem solving, she retorted, "This ain't math! I hate math!"

By 1980 when *Mindstorms* was published, some schools had begun to acquire microcomputers without yet knowing how they were going to be used. Seymour promoted Logo as a learning environment with "no threshold, no ceiling." Someone could start constructing simple geometric shapes within a few minutes after experimenting with just a few turtle commands. *Mindstorms* led readers to believe that learners could progress to more complicated projects of their own choosing with very little direct teaching. "No ceiling" meant that Logo could be used to write complex programs. For example, it had list processing commands for manipulating and sorting data and could be used to teach a course in computer science.

Rather than learn in a conventional classroom atmosphere, Seymour proposed that learning occur in a *community* of Logo users, with people with all different levels of knowledge and interests requesting help and giving help as needed. He invoked the example of Brazil's samba schools, and used them as a metaphor for a kind of learning environment that he suggested would be superior to a conventional classroom.

I'd like to point out that Seymour's *samba school* had much in common with the richly-provisioned open classroom environments that Molly established successfully in her primary grade classrooms year after year. (See her essay "Hitchhiking to Logo's Mathland.")

Thousands of readers found the Seymour's vision exciting. They were eager to try out Logo in classrooms. Many educators were convinced after reading *Mindstorms* that once a student was introduced to the basics of Logo, they could progress on their own, "without direct teaching." Actually Seymour described a very sophisticated kind of facilitative teaching, conducted informally in a *samba school* environment.

Mindstorms was released in 1980. At about the same time programmers at MIT implemented a version of Logo on Apple II microcomputers. They licensed it to different software companies. The Apple company chose to give a copy of Apple Logo with every computer sold to a school. This was an exciting time. People all across the country became computer enthusiasts and bought microcomputers for their homes. Some of these folks were also school teachers. This helped create an advocacy group for computers in the schools.

Schools were starting to have computers and Logo software. But there were major challenges before it could be used successfully.

- Instructional materials did not come with the software. The technical manual for Logo was useless for ordinary humans.
- Teachers were unfamiliar with turtle geometry, the gateway to Mathland.
- Schools were used to programs for specific ages. But what grade(s) did Logo belong in?
- Should the computer be placed in a regular classroom, or should they be grouped in labs?
- Teachers did not yet know the Logo language.
- A community of Logo learners did not yet exist.

My time at MIT was up, and the Reagan administration had cut off funding for the NSF education programs. Then in 1981, I got lucky again. The editor-in-chief of Byte Books in Peterborough, New Hampshire wanted to publish a line of Logo books for educators. He invited me to join his company as an editor and a writer. He had already contracted with Hal Abelson, a professor at MIT to write a readable, comprehensive Logo manual describing all of Logo's features with examples of how to use them. I was hired to edit Hal's book, *Logo for the Apple II*, and would be paid part-time to write my own Logo book for teachers and students.

Thus *Learning With Logo* was incubated. A book is a static object. Could a book help create a dynamic, exploratory learning experience? I did not want to write a textbook with lessons, followed by problem sets with answers in the back.

I wanted kids who could read at a fifth or sixth grade level to be able to learn Logo at home. I wanted teachers to be able to learn Logo, and have activities they could immediately use to learn along with their students. The book would start with the very simplest turtle commands (no threshold), and gradually take learners to some complex projects using variables, conditional expressions, and recursion, and to make interactive games, animations, quizzes, and so forth.

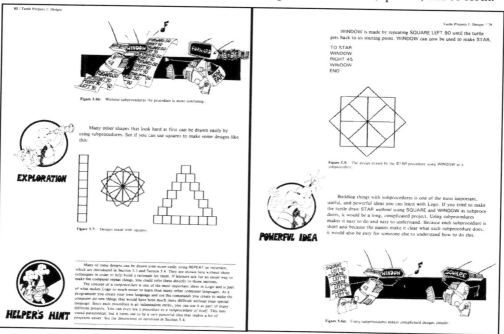

I wanted to balance opportunities for individual initiative and creativity yet ensure that Logo's powerful ideas were featured in the text just when students might need them. It is tempting to want to keep exploring, trying new projects, without stopping to reflect on a powerful idea embedded in a particular project—an idea that will make one's future work easier to understand, and easier to program.

I introduced a few ideas in each chapter along with many suggestions for explorations. I had the advantage of having access to projects built by the sixteen children in the Brookline Logo Project. Therefore many of the challenges in the book were children's ideas, not mine. And I used plenty of turtle designs as visual challenges, without words explaining how to do them. Many other ideas in book came from colleagues at the MIT Logo Group. Some ideas had been floating around the group for years and I never really knew who originated them in the first place.

Some Logo educators wanted students to *discover by trial and error* the angle (90 degrees) needed to make then turtle draw a square. By contrast, I showed students very early on that they could draw a square using 90-degree rotations. They could create so many more interesting geometric designs using angles that are factors of 360, such as 30, 45, 60, 90, and 120. I didn't ask kids to memorize these, but to think of them as tools for thinking in the turtle's world. Later I challenged them to explore the effects of using other angles.

Children often want to create designs with circles, but Logo does not have a circle command. I provided *tool procedures*[1] throughout the book including tools that drew circles and quarter-circle arcs using the radius to determine a circle's size. I learned in the Brookline Project that designs using circles were so motivating to children that creativity flowed naturally. I found that *after* students used circles in their designs they were more interested in learning how they are made. So in a later chapter on repeating patterns, I introduced the challenge of making the turtle draw a circle—so students could find out that a Logo circle is technically a regular polygon with very small sides and very small angles.

I was fortunate to find a brilliant young cartoonist, Paul Trap, who specialized in drawing fanciful robots. I used his cartoons to illustrate the metaphor that a Logo procedure is like a robot. It can only do exactly what someone tells it to do. This metaphor also let me illustrate how procedures pass inputs to other procedures, one of the most difficult programming concepts for beginners.

Trap also drew icons for *Powerful Ideas*, *Pitfalls* (common bugs and how to avoid them), *Explorations* and *Helper's Hints*. The last were in smaller print for teachers. (Children could read them too, of course.)

You may be surprised to know that computers were so new to most people in 1983 that in the first chapter I had to explain how to turn the computer on and how to insert a floppy disk to start up Logo!

In 1983 when *Learning With Logo* was published, schools had many different brands of microcomputers, so McGraw-Hill, the parent company of Byte Books, put out four different editions for different computers.[2] Spanish and Italian translations were published by McGraw-Hill's international division. An unauthorized Chinese translation was published by the People's Education Press in Beijing. When Molly and I were invited to teach Logo to leading Chinese educators in 1986, we learned that 100,000 copies of the translation, had been printed in a pocket-sized format on thin paper, and distributed to Chinese schools costing about what a cup of coffee cost in America at the time! We were thrilled—and I never mentioned the Chinese edition to McGraw-Hill.

Timing is everything! *Learning With Logo* was the first Logo book published for teachers and children and was very popular. Since there was little else to do with classroom computers Logo was being introduced in thousands of classrooms. The various editions and translations (including Chinese) sold over 200,000 copies.

Learning With Logo, and other Logo books that came along a year or two later helped thousands of teachers get started. However, teaching Logo so that children learned the powerful programming and mathematics ideas was the exception rather than the norm. Many schools decided that rather than have one computer in the back of each classroom, it would be better to establish a computer lab, with a dedicated specialist—a better trained and enthusiastic teacher. Students would come to the lab once or twice a week. Usually, the emphasis was on learning to program, rather than on the mathematics and mathematical habits of mind students might be learning. If students had some experience of Mathland, it was more or less a byproduct of programming with the turtle.

Looking back I realize that some of this was my responsibility. *Computer literacy* was a major buzzword in the 1980s, and I was a strong advocate for children learning to program using Logo.

By this time, Molly Lynn Watt had joined me on the road to Mathland. (See "Hitchhiking to Logo's Mathland.") Together we embraced the challenge of doing our part to support a national and international community of educators to use Logo effectively. We made a joint decision to work and travel together on this road. It proved to be a wonderful adventure for us. I don't think we would have been able to sustain the work if we hadn't been doing it together.

While I was working for Byte Books, Molly taught the first ever graduate-level Logo course for teachers, for Lesley University. Then Lesley hired her to teach weekend courses for teachers in Colorado. She flew out with her Apple computer and a small monitor in her luggage! Molly also taught 3-credit Logo courses for Continuing Education students at Keene State, near our home in New Hampshire.

Molly and I began speaking, teaching, and traveling together. There were Logo conferences, and educational computing conferences with Logo threads. We spoke at conferences and led workshops for teachers across the US and in several Canadian provinces. We led Logo workshops for teachers in China, Italy, Bermuda, and Australia.

Here's a little anecdote from our travels. Once we were invited to give a workshop in Australia. We took a vacation in Australia's Northern Territory and booked a small one-day outback tour in Kakadu National Park. Just ourselves, an Australian couple, and a guide in a four-wheel-drive vehicle. I happened to be wearing a Logo t-shirt. The woman sitting across from us stared for a while, then finally said, "I teach Logo in grade five back home." "What curriculum do you use?" Molly asked. "Well," she said, "we use a wonderful big book, with a drawing of a man with a beard on the cover." "That man is me!" I blurted out. "I had a beard back then. The cover design was created by one of my students."

In 1984 we were each invited to teach a month-long graduate course for teachers at Simon Fraser University in a suburb of Vancouver British Columbia. "Hitchhiking to Logo's Mathland," describes Molly's experience teaching beginning Logo programmers. My course was for teachers with some prior Logo experience and was about using Logo to create specialized *microworlds*.

This was based on an idea from *Mindstorms*. In Chapter 5, "Microworlds, Incubators for Knowledge," Seymour used the term to describe a consciously constructed, deliberately limited environment in which students could learn powerful ideas by exploration. He explained how he designed the turtle geometry microworld as an entry to Mathland. He next described in detail a microworld for learning Newtonian physics by creating a turtle with commands for speed and acceleration, and another microworld for simulating feedback in animal behavior. In this microworld the turtle is endowed with sensors that could detect light or sound. Students could explore simple feedback mechanisms, for example, by programming the turtle to turn toward or away from the light and increase or decrease the amount of the turn depending on how near it was to the light.

My challenge to teachers at Simon Fraser was to use a Logo program to create a limited microworld with a set of powerful ideas in some particular domain. The microworld had to include interesting phenomena that students would want to explore, as well as powerful ideas. The microworld could take the form of a game, but it could not be a lesson with right and wrong answers. I gave the teachers starting points, like the physics and animal behavior simulations described above. And I gave some examples from *Learning With Logo,* for instance, a game for young students to explore angles and distances in the turtle world. Students turn the turtle to aim at a randomly placed target and decide how far to move to hit the target. In this way they learn about angles and distances on the screen.

These projects challenged teachers to learn more sophisticated programming techniques, and more importantly, to identify powerful ideas kids could learn by exploring. Fortunately we had teachers in the class with different levels of programming experience and content knowledge, teachers who taught different ages, so we all learned from each other. We tried out each other's projects and critiqued each other on the basic criteria of a microworld. Why are those ideas powerful for particular students? Are the challenges interesting enough, are they fun, so that children will want to explore them?

Even with *Learning With Logo,* and other books that were becoming available, we knew it was a major challenge to teach Logo effectively, the way we wanted it to be taught—as a project-based experience engaging a community of learners rather than being totally teacher directed. What would it take for a teacher inspired by *Mindstorms* to create a Logo Mathland with her students?

We identified a few major barriers blocking the road to Mathland. One of these barriers was that many teachers had very little experience with Logo programming beyond using Forward and Back, Right and Left and teaching the computer to draw simple shapes. They needed time to learn Logo at an adult level—to know more than their students so they could help students progress beyond the simplest level of programming. They needed to know the powerful programming ideas embedded in Logo and the powerful ideas in the world of turtle geometry.

A mantra in teacher professional development is *teachers teach as they were taught.* To be specific, in order to establish a Logo *samba school* environment in their classrooms, it could be wonderful if they could learn Logo in a samba school themselves.

So we established an intensive, residential Logo Institute for teachers, starting in the summer of 1984, immediately after we came back from Vancouver. The first three Logo Institutes were held at Keene State College, offering graduate credit through the friendly auspices of Keene's Continuing Education Department. Our friend Tony Stavely, a psychology professor at Keene, co-led those three institutes with us. He knew a lot about Logo programming using list processing to manipulate data. This fulfilled a need for participants who wanted to explore more advanced Logo programming.

Molly is a brilliant teacher and creator of learning environments for all ages. She invented the underlying structure that supported open-ended learning at the Logo Institutes. Some of the content of the Institute was informed by my deeper knowledge of programming and mathematics.[3] Molly and I sought the same goals, but thought about things differently, which made us a powerful team.

The Institutes were designed as *samba schools* for teachers—an immersion for two or three weeks to develop their programming skills, participate in collaborative project-based learning, and develop a national and international cohort of Logo buddies. After Keene we were invited to lead the Institute at Union College in Schenectady, New York, and then to co-lead it with Ricky Carter for two summers at Lesley University in Cambridge Massachusetts. Molly's essay in this book, "Hitchhiking to Logo's Mathland," tells some of the ways we structured the learning experience for teachers. My course at the Institute, which I taught every year, was based on the microworlds course I developed at Simon Fraser. And every year I had more examples of teacher-made microworlds to demonstrate.

Gary Stager was twenty-three when he showed up at the third Logo institute at Keene State in 1986. Although much younger than most of the participants, all experienced classroom teachers, Gary became everybody's favorite go-to guy for ideas and help with programming projects. The rumor was that he stayed up all night in the dorms, helping people with their projects. From that point on, we never had a Logo Institute without Gary!

Molly and I were proud to be invited by Gary to come out of retirement in our late seventies to serve as "elder" faculty members at the Constructing Modern Knowledge Summer Institute several years ago. It was a privilege to be part of the maker movement, which is carrying on the creative energy and much of the ethos of the Logo community of the 1980s. To me CMK is another *samba school*, offering way more than twenty things to do with a computer.

Our next project, *Teaching With Logo: Building Blocks for Learning,* was published by Addison-Wesley in 1986. The introduction featured a list Molly had developed of twenty powerful ideas embedded in Logo. We painted a picture of a fifth-grade classroom in order to give teachers a vicarious experience of a Logo *samba school.* Throughout the book we followed the learning of five students—representative of many students we had known. The students worked in different ways, had different learning styles, mathematical abilities, interests, and project ideas. We started, as all good Logo work does, with a few basic commands and watched to see where the students' ideas would take them.

Subsequent chapters showed us working with the students to support each one's creative ideas and gradually elaborate them into complex interactive projects. We described everything we did as teachers to support students' learning: established an expectation of mutual help and collaboration among students; illustrated how students kept journals of their work; showed examples of our notes on each student's progress; revealed how we intervened occasionally to give suggestions—not all of which were accepted by the students.

Each chapter in the book highlighted one or two new powerful ideas about programming and Mathland. We hoped that teachers would use these approaches in their own classrooms.

In recent years we've met several people who were inspired and guided by the teaching approaches described in *Teaching With Logo*—even though they are no longer using the version of Logo we used, probably not using Logo at all. We were surprised by one friend, a computer science professor, who has himself written textbooks using Logo to teach computer science. He came up to us at a conference recently and said that *Teaching With Logo* was his favorite Logo book!

In the late 1980s Molly and I were invited back to Education Development Center (EDC), where we both had worked and where we met in the 1960s. We were encouraged to write a proposal to the NSF to pursue an idea for a Logo research project we had been thinking about for a while.

Most Logo evaluation studies at the time were conducted by outsiders, in classrooms with teachers just starting to learn Logo themselves. They typically compared students' scores on math tests for example, before and after some number of hours of Logo instruction. They often concluded that Logo students showed no statistically significant gains. One obvious difficulty was that the tests of standard school math did not include the mathematics of turtle geometry. Another was, they did not collect data on what students were actually learning in class as they worked on their Logo projects. We wanted to take a different approach. We wanted to collaborate with experienced Logo teachers to document what their students were learning.

For several years Molly had been teaching action research to teachers in New Hampshire as part of Antioch New England's master's degree program for experienced teachers. *Action research* is based on the idea that meaningful classroom change can occur when teachers study their own teaching practices and the learning of their students, and then change their practice based on what they have observed. Molly had also supervised teachers' action research dissertations.

The Logo Action Research Collaborative (LARC) was a four-year project supported by the NSF over two funding cycles. LARC was based on two synergistic ideas. The first was to document what students were learning in Logo classrooms using observations and examples collected and analyzed collaboratively with teachers. The second was training teachers to become action researchers, that is, to use the examples and observations of students to make incremental improvements to their teaching.

Action research is perfectly suited for Logo teachers as it parallels the cycle of creating Logo projects. Try something, study what happens to fix a problem or make an improvement, then try again, etc. The LARC project paralleled the action research I had done in the Brookline Logo Project ten years earlier. My role then as teacher/researcher had been to document examples of student work and student learning, *and* to use my observations to support students learning more effectively.

By 1988 when the first LARC project started, there were dozens of educators in and around Boston who had been teaching Logo for three or more years. Most of them had taken graduate Logo courses at Lesley University. We invited nine Boston area teachers to join a research team to collect examples of student work. We met regularly to analyze the examples together to articulate the knowledge of Logo programming and mathematics their students were learning. We looked at the student's actual programs, and the designs the programs produced. We used a process that Molly developed to look at one example at a time. We went around the group three times asking ourselves: What knowledge is the student using? We looked only at what we could see in the data. What knowledge is the student *not* using that could be helpful to them? And finally, what is *one* step that each of us would suggest to the teacher? It was totally up to the teacher to decide whether or not to use one of the ideas. By spending the time it took, looking deeply at the work of one student collected by one teacher, all the teachers gained knowledge about how some of their students might be thinking and were free to use any of the teaching suggestions in their classes.

To disseminate the data gathered by the teachers, Molly and I published a small book of examples of student projects collected by teachers, to illustrate what students actually were learning in mathematics and Logo programming. *Logo Learning: Strategies for Assessing Content and Process* (1992) was published by the International Society for Technology in Education (ISTE). The examples were accompanied by a comprehensive checklist of important Logo learning goals. This was intended as a practical tool for teachers to assess their students or to create rubrics students could use to document their own progress.

The second LARC cycle was designed to build on and disseminate the action research methods of the first project. We used a train-the-trainers model to include several school districts across the country. One teacher from each district attended a summer training to learn methods of facilitating an action research collaborative. Then each facilitated a LARC project in their own community, training their participants in action research.

To disseminate some of the research done by teachers, we hosted a one-day mini-conference of Logo teacher researchers at the 1991 National Educational Computing Conference in Phoenix.

Molly and I edited a monograph of several teacher research papers, *New Paradigms in Classroom Research on Logo Learning* (D. Watt & M. Watt, 1993), also published by ISTE.

The LARC project ended in 1992, almost thirty years ago! Molly and I had one more adventure in Mathland a year later. We were invited, along with many of our Logo colleagues, to a small international conference held at Methodist Ladies College, a private girls' school for grades K–12 in Melbourne Australia. Every student in grades 5–12 had their own laptop, and Logo was used in every grade. That was the last time Molly and I shared our experiences using Logo with teachers.

By then Molly and I had gone on to other exciting professional adventures. Molly established an Action Research Center at EDC. One of its projects was training science education leaders in several states as part of the NSF's State Systemic Initiative program to improve science education nationally. I joined a project at EDC called Math and More, funded by IBM's Education Division, to develop powerful computer-based microworlds for elementary school mathematics. (These were exciting exploratory learning environments, but did not include Logo.)

Now it's about thirty years later. So much has changed. Logo itself changed dramatically during the eighties and nineties. First LogoWriter added word processing to Logo, and the emphasis shifted from turtle geometry projects to making storybooks and simple games. The turtle was still there, and it could carry different shapes making cool animations possible by changing shapes. In his speeches I noticed Seymour stopped talking as much about Mathland.

Then MicroWorlds, the most elaborate version of Logo, added multiple turtles called sprites, so more interesting animations were possible. Kids could import their own photos and put their photo on a sprite. They could record and playback speech to make an animated joke book or a talking storybook. They could download sounds and background images from the internet. With MicroWorlds students could produce very creative and attractive projects with less programming. With MicroWorlds, students could do many more than twenty things. But Mathland in the form of the turtle geometry wasn't explored very much.

I am happy to say that Mathland still exists in different forms. Some schools still teach Logo the old-fashioned way. Brian Silverman and Paula Bontá developed TurtleArt, a wonderful tool that uses an expanded form of turtle geometry to produce elegant works of art. Artemis Papert and Brian are actively promoting it and disseminating some fascinating artwork created with it. Sylvia Martinez and Gary Stager's book, *Invent to Learn: Making, Tinkering, and Engineering in the Classroom* (2019) has a chapter about many educational programming languages including versions of Logo, which are available in and out of schools today, and most of which I know nothing about.

Mathland may exist in places where it is not quite as visible as it was in the old days. I am sure that readers of this book are familiar with Scratch, the newest and most exciting descendant of Logo, created at the MIT Media Lab under the leadership of Mitch Resnick. Scratch uses blocks for commands. Programs are assembled by snapping blocks together like LEGO bricks. More than creating a new programming paradigm, the Scratch Group has forged a massive international community of children and adults that I think of as *Scratchland*. Kids all over the world are sharing projects and remixing and extending them. I find it exciting to see so many young people of so many different ethnicities and languages, so deeply and enthusiastically working in Scratchland.

Mitch's book *Lifelong Kindergarten: Cultivating Creativity Through Projects, Passion, Peers and Play* (sometimes called *the four Ps*), is one of my favorite contemporary education books. *Mindstorms* was inspiring because it showed a path towards what might be possible in learning with computers. *Lifelong Kindergarten* is inspiring because shows how learning is happening with computers and computer networks today. I am moved by Mitch's eloquence, and the stories he relates about students using Scratch, sharing projects and helping each other in a safe, creative online environment.

Yet I was surprised to find no emphasis on mathematical thinking or Mathland, anywhere in *Lifelong Kindergarten*. And I am convinced that a lot of Mathland is deeply embedded in Scratchland. No one can engage in this kind of project work without being a mathematician some of the time (as well as a designer, engineer, artist, and so forth). I wonder if kids know when they are thinking mathematically. And I wonder, in Scratchland, how are kids encouraged to consolidate and articulate what they are learning as they move from project to project?

I also believe that Mathland is deeply embedded in today's educational Maker Movement. Kids and teachers making things that use computers to produce actions with real world objects, must be thinking mathematically much of the time. After all, computers are still math-speaking devices.

I'll end with a shout out to the Constructing Modern Knowledge Summer Institute (CMK). The annual teacher workshop for making things with technology that Gary Stager and Sylvia Martinez have led for many years now is a wonderful *samba school*. To me it is like a Logo Institute, combined with Molly's richly-provisioned open classroom, raised to the nth power. All of this, and much more is explained in Sylvia and Gary's book, *Invent to Learn: Making, Tinkering, and Engineering in the Classroom* (2019), which pays homage to Cynthia and Seymour's writings of fifty years ago, and articulates so many wonderful things to do with computers today.

There is so much to do in a huge open space at CMK, so many things and people to do it with. It is a wonderful kindergarten for teachers. They come to play, have an unexpected, often powerful learning experience, and at the end have something to take with them when they leave. Or if not the actual thing they made, a video of the thing in action they can take home and show their friends, colleagues and students.

If students in the makerspaces that these teachers teach in have half the fun and half learning their teachers experience at CMK, the world will be a better place for it.

References

Abelson, H. (1982). *Logo for the Apple II*. McGraw-Hill, Inc.

Martinez, S. L., & Stager, G. (2019). *Invent to Learn: Making, Tinkering, and Engineering in the Classroom* (2 ed.). Constructing Modern Knowledge Press.

Papert, S. (1972). Teaching Children to Be Mathematicians versus Teaching about Mathematics. *International Journal of Mathematical Education in Science and Technology, 3*(3), 249-262.

Papert, S. (1980). *Mindstorms: Children, Computers, and Powerful Ideas*. Basic Books.

Papert, S., Watt, D., diSessa, A., Weir, S. (1979a). Final Report of the Brookline Logo Project, Part II, Project Summary and Data Analysis. In *MIT A.I. Memo 545 and Logo Memo 53*. Cambridge, Massachusetts: Massachusetts Institute of Technology.

Papert, S., Watt, D., diSessa, A., Weir, S. (1979b). Final Report of the Brookline Logo Project, Part III, Detailed Profiles of Each Student's Work. In *MIT A.I. Memo 546 and Logo Memo 54*. Cambridge, Massachusetts: Massachusetts Institute of Technology.

Resnick, M. (2017). *Lifelong Kindergarten: Cultivating Creativity Through Projects, Passion, Peers, and Play*. MIT Press.

Watt, D. (1983). *Learning With Logo*. McGraw-Hill Book Co.

Watt, D., & Romney, E. (1971a). *Musical Instrument Recipe Book Teacher's Guide. Elementary Science Study*. Webster Division, McGraw-Hill Book Co.

Watt, D., & Romney, E. (1971b). *Whistles and Strings Teacher's Guide. Elementary Science Study*. Webster Division, McGraw-Hill Book Co.

Watt, D., & Watt, M. (1992). *Logo Learning: Strategies for Assessing Content and Process*. International Society for Technology in Education.

Watt, D., & Watt, M. (1993). *New Paradigms in Classroom Research on Logo Learning.* International Society for Technology in Education.

Notes

1 A ***tool procedure*** is a procedure written in Logo, that students could use as if they were built-in commands. Tool procedures were provided on a disk that came with the book. The last chapter in *Learning With Logo* explained how all the tool procedures worked.

2 *Learning With Logo* (1983), *Learning With Apple Logo* (1984), *Learning with IBM Logo* (1985) and *Learning With Commodore Logo* (1985). MCGraw Hill Book Co. *Learning with TI Logo* was planned but never published—Texas Instruments microcomputers did not catch on in many schools.

3 Other faculty members who contributed to the Institute content were Tony Stavely, Peter Rawitsch, Ricky Carter and Gary Stager. And content also came from participants who were experts in different disciplines.

Twenty Things is the Foundation for Constructionism

Fred Martin

March 10, 2021

I was a graduate student and then researcher in Seymour Papert's Epistemology and Learning research group at MIT from 1986 to 2001. I was part of the team that created the series of Programmable Bricks that led to the launch of the transformational LEGO Robotics Invention System kit in 1998.

When I joined Papert's team and we started working on our first Programmable Brick, I hadn't realized that the vision for what it should do had been shared fifteen years earlier, when Papert and Solomon published *Twenty Things to Do with a Computer*.

It takes a profound act of imagination to remember what the computational world was like when *Twenty Things* was written. Computers were emerging from the large, refrigerator-sized devices that lived in machine rooms, consumed and produced data via punched cards, and were touched only by trained operators.

At large research universities, it was becoming common to interact with computers with a teletype machine, where you would type statements on a keyboard, which would appear on a roll of paper and as they were echoed by the computer. The computer would interpret your statements and print results on the roll in real time—sort of like a text chat, but on paper. Video display terminals were also becoming available, which were the same idea, but with the text scrolling up a display screen instead of being printed on paper.

MIT itself was one of the leaders of this work—it led the development of Multics in the 1960s, one of the earliest multi-user operating systems which allowed multiple users to interact simultaneously with a single computer.

Computers and Cybernetics

Reading *Twenty Things* now, what jumps out is the idea of connecting the computer to the world. Twelve of the twenty ideas are based on this. If interacting with a computer via a keyboard was new in 1971, it's hard to imagine how *out there* it must have then seemed to be connecting computers to devices—and providing kits for doing so to children.

Indeed, "educational robotics" is both normalized and popular now. Inspired by LEGO's Robotics Invention System product, there are now many, many robotics construction kits. There are also kits for domains such as e-textiles, which have much more cross-gender appeal than robots do.

Looking deeper into *Twenty Things* is the idea of building robotic creatures. It's literally idea #1. This first turtle is a different version of the turtle we commonly associate with Logo (a device for making drawings). Idea #1 is inspired by biological systems. The idea that we can build mechanical systems based on animals in our world goes back thousands of years. It got its modern name—cybernetics—thanks to Norbert Wiener, who launched the field in a landmark 1948 book, *Cybernetics: Or Control and Communication in the Animal and the Machine*.

The idea that we and other animals have control systems in our bodies also inspired W. Grey

Walter, an American-British neurophysiologist. In the 1950s, he invented a series of vacuum tube-powered floor robots that he reported upon as if he were a biologist discovering new life forms, giving them names like *Machina speculatrix* and calling them "tortoises."

As recounted in *Twenty Things*, Papert's robot turtles were so named "in honor of a famous species of cybernetic animal" made by Walter. Per Cynthia Solomon, those early MIT robots closely more resembled upside-down office trash cans than turtles, and children were always sitting on them in the lab.

Beginning with #1 Make a Turtle, the ideas of cybernetics run throughout *Twenty Things*. Here are other examples which become evident when we recognize the pervasiveness of cybernetic thinking in Papert and Solomon's work:

- #10 Make a Movie, where we experiment with our persistence of vision by using a video display to show a series of images that appear to move across the screen
- #12 Play with Semi-Random Musical Effects, where we make a list of notes that comprise a musical mode (e.g., a major or minor scale), select random notes from the list repeatedly, and recognize that our musical sense might characterize the resulting tones as being "spooky" or otherwise.
- #16 Try C.A.I. (Computer-Aided Instruction) and Psychology, where we create software that interacts with us by giving us randomized math problems and discovers, by keeping track of user responses, which problems are harder than others.
- #17 Physics in the Fingertips, where we balance rods of various lengths on our fingertips or the palms of our hands, or think about how we fling a yoyo—and then use that knowledge to design and program a machine to do the same
- #18 Explain Yourself, where we build a device to measure how quickly we can respond to stimuli, and determine variations and consistencies in different individuals' reaction times

In all of these, we are invited to create computational systems that help us understand our bodies and minds.

This is an idea which Papert would later describe as "body syntonicity" in *Mindstorms* (1980)—that by using the knowledge of our bodies, which we inhabit every moment of our lives, we may make sense of abstract ideas of things-in-the-world.

Microworlds and Languages for Them

Another theme that runs throughout *Twenty Things* is the idea of learning about a domain, or "microworld," by giving names to computational representations of the ideas embedded in it —that is, learning by writing procedures.

The Logo language, which was inspired by Lisp, is itself *a language for making languages*. Throughout *Twenty Things* are examples of this:

- In #2 Program the Turtle to Draw a Man, procedures are defined to DRAW a line, draw a pair of lines in a VEE-shape, and then draw multiple vees in the shape of a stick figure.
- In #3 Turtle Biology, individual sensors are named FRONTTOUCH and BACKTOUCH, and then an overall behavior is designed by moving FORWARD and turning RIGHT when a touch sensor signals contact.
- In #11 Make a Music Box and Program a Tune, the SING primitive plays a note which is specified via its position in the Western 12-pitch scale and a duration. Octaves are signified with an exclamation-point "!". The sample song has its melodic phrases organized into named subprocedures. These phrases are then assembled and played from a main procedure—which concisely presents the structure of the whole song.

In computer science, the idea of making a language to represent, make sense of, and script actions in a specific microworld is now known as creating a *domain-specific language*, or DSL. The idea of DSLs was emerging at the time when *Twenty Things* was written (it got its name later).

Logo is ideal for making DSLs because Papert and Solomon knew that creating a language that facilitates representation of ideas provides a powerful way of knowing. In writing procedures, learners are declaring what is important about a domain; they are finding what is worth naming and then doing so. Then, the procedures become the building blocks for building applications (projects) in the domain.

The Foundation of Constructionism

Taken as a whole, *Twenty Things* is the practical manifesto for the educational philosophy which Papert later termed "constructionism." All the ideas are there: a collection of wonderful artifacts which can be made by children using computers; connecting computers to the world to cause actions in it (and sense the world); creating computational representations and giving names to those artifacts (i.e., making a DSL); and learning by debugging.

Also part of *Twenty Things* is the powerful idea of using knowledge of one's own body to gain understanding of the more abstract world—body syntonicity.

This message takes on more importance as we look towards the future of learning in a world increasingly mediated by screens and virtualization.

Papert and Solomon's work makes us remember that experiences which engage all of our senses matter deeply, and that we must continue to invest in this kind of hands-on learning.

References

Papert, S. (1980). *Mindstorms: Children, Computers, and Powerful Ideas*. Basic Books.

Wiener, N. (1948). *Cybernetics or Control and Communication in the Animal and the Machine*. MIT Press.

Life in Logoland

Marian B. Rosen

I met Logo in January, 1983 at a workshop for Ladue School District (Missouri) teachers. I then taught myself Logo by reverse engineering the sample programs and reading the documentation that came first with the version for the Texas Instrument 99A and later with Sprite Logo for the Apple IIe. It changed my life. I spent the next twenty five years being one of Ladue's technology coordinators and enjoying an international group of mentors and friends that formed what I fondly think of as Logoland.

I met Seymour Papert for the first time in August, 1984. What Seymour said and what I heard may have been two different things. But I have two memories from that meeting. First there was his theory on what happens to the natural curiosity of children. And secondly there was the power of programming in a constructivist environment.

About curiosity—I heard Seymour say that when children are young, they explore their environment without having to read or ask an adult for answers. Think of babies who throw objects from high chairs, watch grown-ups return them, and then throw them again. Watch toddlers with different sized pails filling and un-filling them with sand and six-year-olds spinning gears. They are tinkering and learning. But at some point, children have questions about things they cannot physically handle and they need to ask questions that require reading. At this point they are put into a system of formal learning with adults as gatekeepers. Seymour challenged us to imagine a world in which a child could talk to the computer, ask a question, and get it answered with pictures and sound and even video. I heard him suggest that in the summer of 1984 when I was a first-grade teacher who taught reading. My 128K Apple IIe could not handle four color graphics and words on the same screen and had no sound except for a few tones. The internet was unknown, and search engines had not been invented. Was he crazy?!

By 2020 Seymour's prediction of a world in which vast numbers of kids have daily access to devices that can answer questions and connect to the web has happened. Instantly available photos, videos, and sound files have changed—or certainly should have changed—the way we teach. One example: Our second graders did a report on animals. They would pick an animal, research it in books in the library, word process a report and then when they were almost finished we would allow them to go on to the internet and find one or two photos to insert in the report. Essentially we were saying, "Eat all your vegetables, and then you can have dessert." But when Google Images arrived we changed. Now the kids looked at hundreds of photos and used them to create questions about habitat, diet, social patterns, sleep habits, size, color, etc. We were rewarded with much better reports.

There have been unexpected consequences to having such easy access to information on the internet. We did not foresee the need to teach people how to evaluate the truth and completeness of what they see. This has, of course, become a huge problem in our politics. But questions arise even within the limited domain of second-grade animal reports. A child had asked Seymour, "How do giraffes sleep?" and he loved the question. He used this example as the lead-in to his 1984 fantasy of a computer that could answer a young child's question with photos and videos. Currently, if you ask Siri to show you pictures of sleeping giraffes, you will be shown photos of giraffes lying on the ground with their necks curled and their heads resting on their rumps. Charming! But in fact giraffes rarely sleep this way because it makes them vulnerable to predators. They need as little as thirty minutes of sleep a day and they sleep for just a few minutes at a time while standing up. Sleeping baby giraffes are so cute that they dominate the photos and videos on the web. It is actually hard to find a photo of a giraffe sleeping while it is standing. After all, it essentially just looks like a giraffe. We are at the mercy of the gatekeepers who attach descriptors to the great databases of online photos and videos.

Returning to the first time I met Seymour… I had gathered up the courage to ask him why, since teachers had messed up math for many kids, he didn't also fear that they would mess up Logo for many kids? His answer was that the kid and the computer could have a relationship without the teacher. Students could direct their own learning. The computer would give feedback. I myself was a classic example. As mentioned earlier I taught myself a lot of Logo by reverse engineering a few programs. I was hooked. I stayed up all night without realizing I was staying up all night. I experimented and let the computer tell me what I had done right or wrong. I fell in love with the error message "I don't know how to …" Like many people, when frustrated, I typed in a curse word "xxx" and hit return only to have the computer tell me that it didn't know how to "xxx." And then I would write a procedure to teach it how to "xxx." The metaphor of learning and teaching was built into the language itself. I felt as if I were standing on the shoulders of people who understood me and thought like me.

Now my challenge was to package up my experience in ways that busy teachers could buy into. Ladue School District administration fully supported me in this. One of my first jobs was to create a curriculum for gifted sixth graders. I had free rein. I asked Seymour what I should do. He, of course, rubbed his chin and said, "I'll be interested in what you decide." So, I decided that we should write software. I wanted to demystify the black box of the commercial games they were buying for their home computers. The kids designed games, tested them on each other, and wrote documentation. I never knew for sure where this would take us. In one memorable instance it led to list processing. The kids knew that when their commercial games asked them for their names they could type in dirty words and the computer would then address them in those terms. They did not want the users of their games to be able to do that. So I introduced list processing and they made an Obscenity Checker. I pretended that I couldn't look at their code while we were in school but I checked it when they weren't looking and the list was blood curdling. When the time came for me to try out their product, they had thoughtfully included the word "Heck" in the list of banned answers so that I could participate even though we were in school. I typed in "Heck" as my name and the message came back: "You can't use that word! You should be ashamed of yourself! You deserve to be kicked in your dairy air [sic]!"

I was offered a full time job of Gifted Education but I declined saying that Logo had shown me a way to give all kids, not just the intellectually gifted, real experiences in dynamic, self-directed, creative learning. I now would work with all the kids and all the teachers. Between 1986 and 2008 we co-created a full computer learning environment for kindergarten to fifth grade. We used word processing, the internet, and the multimedia aspects of Logo (LogoWriter and later Microworlds) for our creative projects and report writing. The most beguiling reports had animation effects created by turtles. Bones connected to form a skeleton and then sang "Dem Dry Bones;" a hamburger went through the digestive track and turned into poop; flowers grew; Mayflowers sailed; sloths millimetered their way across the screen; hearts pumped blood through circulation systems; planets flew in orbits; maggots turned into flies… Logo unleashed imagination and creativity in ways nothing else had.

However, there were two areas in which I felt Logo was limited. The tools for composing music just weren't good enough so we supplemented our curriculum with Morton Subotnick's Making Music software. Also, I wanted kids to collect and analyze data. For this we used Chris Hancock's excellent data visualization software, Tabletop Jr and Tabletop Sr. Today, only a remnant of this software exists in a game called Zoombinis. It is a shame to have lost such a powerful tool for children to analyze and visually understand data.

Tabletop Jr allowed even kindergarteners to ask three kinds of questions and to code the answers on little characters which could then be sorted on axes or in Venn diagrams. The three types of questions were Boolean (yes/no), multiple choice (up to five possible answers), and questions which required a number as an answer. I remember a third grader who did research on how many four-leaf clovers each of his classmates had found. The range was from zero to twenty-four. The vast majority of answers were zero or one, but there were three kids who insisted that they had found eighteen, twenty-one, and twenty-four. Outliers? or just plain liars? On further questioning we discovered that each of those kids had the same story to tell—there was a special place they knew of where they could always find four leaf clovers. This led to a call to the Missouri Botanical Gardens and finding out that indeed there is a genetic component to four-leaf clovers and that they grow in patches. We had done authentic research in the second grade.

Yet the core of our curriculum was neither music nor data, but programming in Logo. To make it palatable to busy teachers who had to give kids standardized tests, we found ways to connect it to math. This wasn't hard to do, of course. All we had to do was look at the topics in the official math curriculum and devise projects that would help us teach those topics. I had already worked with hundreds of people before I stumbled upon Cynthia Solomon and Seymour Papert's paper *Twenty Things to Do with a Computer*. When I read the paper I was amazed how many things we had done that were listed there. Apparently the ideas of the paper are so intrinsic to the Logo language itself that we had re-created the projects without being conscious of the paper's existence. It seems to me that this is a true tribute to the importance of Logo as Mathland.

First graders drove turtles around and were estimating distances, learning inverse function operations, and experimenting with angles. My first grade faculty had created a curriculum around holidays and seasons of the year. We used Logo to draw parts of Johnny Appleseed's hat, turkeys, snowflakes, Abraham Lincoln's hat, valentines, wigwams, tepees, flowers, and spider webs.

Second graders programmed castles using ninety degree turns.

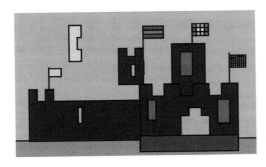 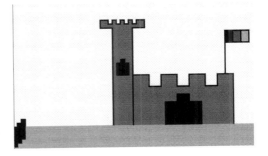

Third graders used mirror symmetry to create aliens…and animated them.

Third graders also made quilts. To make a quilt you first programmed the lines and colors for a patch, and then connected four patches together to make a quilt. Using rotations, slides, and flips some kids found as many as twelve or more ways to connect four patches.

Fourth graders took a dive into Cartesian coordinates by programming a word of their choice using only SETPOS, SETX and SETY. Some kids made four versions of their procedure by reversing the positive and negative signs on their coordinates as in the second example.

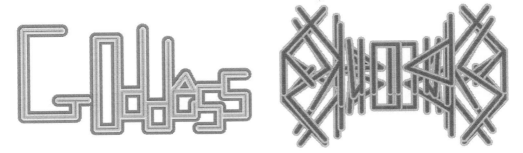

They completed a project based on pattern blocks. I gave them a set of procedures for drawing the blocks but they figured out wonderfully complicated radiating patterns using those shapes. Some kids programmed in spaghetti style—an enormously long list of commands. Others found the pattern and refined it into a single line of code using REPEAT. E.g., *repeat 6[Brhomb.l fd 30 tri.l rt 60]* lays down the circle of blue rhombuses and green triangles in the middle picture.

Fifth graders explored rotational symmetry and produced hubcaps and African baskets. They learned to use the Rule of 360 and variables to draw all polygons and then use their polygon tools to draw geometric pictures.

Fifth graders also did a unit in LEGO TC Logo. They invented scores of smart LEGO machines including a Morse code sender and receiver; a carwash; a machine that sorted objects and delivered them to bins; a gondola that rode along a string and lowered a claw to rescue objects below; and many more.

I retired in 2008. The faculty kept our curriculum going for another four or five years. But slowly the competing demands of newer technology made inroads. The glitzy side of Seymour's vision of students interacting with the internet took over. Programming disappeared from the daily curriculum. This is apparently true in most school districts. In my retirement I teach at an after-school Hebrew School. The kids are interested in Minecraft, have dabbled with Scratch in clubs, and some of the older ones think they want to code in HTML. During the pandemic I combined Zoom with Lynx (a browser-based version of Logo quite similar to MicroWorlds) and started working with a handful of kids on beginning turtle graphics.

I started my Lynx/Zoom experiment by introducing FD, BK, RT, LT, and REPEAT. I also added SETC, SETBG, SETPENSIZE, and RANDOM. The kids played for hours experimenting with wrapping lines of color around the screen in various directions. They tried holding an angle constant while going randomly forward thousands of times. Or holding the distance constant while turning randomly. They made flashing backgrounds. They used different pen sizes. They tried random everything they could think of. I wanted to take control and suggest that they needed to understand what was happening by slowing down and analyzing what was really causing the flashing swirling graphics. Then I remembered two things. First, I didn't have to get them ready for any standardized tests—we could play. Second, I could look at their faces rather than at their screens. They were excited, engrossed. So I let it happen and I limited myself to an occasional question or showing them something I have done that is more controlled. The experiment is progressing and they have begun figuring out how to control their designs and also started to explore regular polygons, spirals, symmetry, etc.

I do not know for how long or where this experiment is going. But I do know that it is magic and these sophisticated children have never seen anything like it. They are delighted by the core lessons of programming—debugging, breaking a project down into smaller chunks, finding patterns, and having an idea and bringing it to life.

I do not know when or if the public schools will ever implement Logo coding/programming. I wish they would. I know about the environment that needs to be around Logo.

- A mix of media—computers and hands on manipulatives
- Easy to use and find resources—cheat sheets, books of ideas, color charts
- An emphasis on collaboration and sharing
- Use of the "Ask three before me!" rule which makes sure kids teach each other and frees up the teacher from being the only source of information
- A project based on a simple set of commands but which ensures success for the timid and yet has no boundaries for the adventurers
- Enough time for play
- A finished product

In many ways this environment is generic and necessary for all forms of authentic learning. But I have been a teacher for fifty years and Logo is still enshrined in my heart as one of the very best ways to teach and learn.

The First Thing I Did with a Computer

Bryan P. Sanders

Setting: California. 1983. Elementary school.

I was a nine-year-old student when Governor Brown worked out a deal with Steve Jobs to put Apple II computers in classrooms. Teachers worked out schedules for each student to have weekly classroom minutes for Lemonade Stand, The Oregon Trail, and Apple Logo at the single workstation. Bragging rights went to the kids who had $50 in lemony assets or who managed to ford the river. But that traveling triangle that drew shapes on the screen had me wondering and staring from across the room.

We had computers at home starting in 1977. Bally Astrocade, Atari 800, and then the Apple II. Zork, Castle Wolfenstein, Lode Runner, Olympic Decathlon—those are burned into my DNA. I felt expert at moving sprites with a joystick or the WASD keys, but Apple Logo was a complete mystery to me.

After our teachers made sure we knew how to turn the Apple II on and off, as well as how to load programs, they let us be. The curiosity of working freely on a computer with no discernible objective left me stumped for weeks. I thumbed through the spiral-bound book of commands on the desk. Soon I confidently made boxes and circles and triangles.

Drawing flowers was a crowning achievement. Kids started asking other kids how to write commands to make art with a computer. Kaleidoscopic wild creations started to emerge on the screen every day. There was noticeably less talk about profits in rainstorms or how to avoid dysentery.

Setting: California. 1984. Next school year.

Ewoks and Jedi. You couldn't avoid them. Together with some friends, I negotiated to stay inside at the computer a few times a week during recess. We wanted to program a choose-your-own-adventure Star Wars game in BASIC that would allow us to explore new story plots and outcomes. We found some books on BASIC and taught ourselves. Writing fiction and line commands together felt unfamiliar and exhilarating, as though we were explorers of an ancient future world.

Months went by. We must have saved our program thousands of times to that 5.25" floppy. We read somewhere that we could also draw graphics with BASIC. Those abstract polygons with Logo from the previous year started having a reason to exist. Line by line, we saw the project through to completion and proudly stood by as our peers and our teacher played our game and witnessed the graphic finale.

And for all the love and care we had in making our Star Wars fan fiction game, nobody kept the floppy or even the computer. I have ten boxes filled with art and schoolwork my mother kept from those days, but on this one you'll just have to believe me. It happened. And I was there.

That was the first thing I did with a computer. Thank you, Logo. Thank you.

Twenty Things and Onwards

Stephen Heppell

Twenty Things came out while I was an undergraduate. As part of my degree I was trying to build working models of the UK economy. I attempted creating one through programming—punch cards and batch processing saw me cycling to the data center in the small hours of the night to utilize the precious gaps in the vast computer's run-time, before returning days later to collect the output of my hopefully clever programming! It was, in truth, a pretty poor model. A group of us had also built an alternative model of the UK economy using plumbing materials with pumps, water, piping, valves, and flow regulators; it was a far better predictor of economic behavior. At the time I assumed this was because of the leaks.

Graduation led me eventually into school teaching, which was a joy, and I found that I was that comparatively rare person for the time—a trained teacher who could make computers do things. Which begged the question, of course, about what things we might want to do.

So what did we want to do? In *Twenty Things*, Seymour and Cynthia noted that it was strange that the idea of computers in education should so often reduce to "using bright new gadgets to teach the same old stuff in thinly disguised versions of the same old way." Strange, and indeed sad. It seemed glaringly obvious back then that, in education, these clever boxes might at least be utilized to do the things we were failing to do, or better, to attempt the things we had never been able to contemplate doing before.

There is of course an inverse relationship between policy makers' understanding of technology and their panic to ensure it can only be used to do that "same old stuff" in the "same old way," as they eventually try to lock down and limit potential.

But comfortingly, over the years it became apparent that there is a useful little space for subverting the gravitational drag back to doing those same old things. Running Ultralab for a quarter of a century, tasked with blue sky innovation and with the budget to do it, we had spotted that: "With new technologies, between denial and adoption is the space for innovation and that is where radical progress is made." This became known as Ultralab's Law[1] and many of us have spent fruitful careers in that fertile space.

It is a big space. Educational systems seem to take an eternity to notice that something new is afoot. Initially, as we saw with slide rules, calculators, smart phones, and even the internet, Educational systems greet technical innovation with denial. *It is not for us.* Phones are banned, TikTok has nothing to do with learning, and so on. An innovation's potential contribution is simply denied... and the door for subversive innovation and radical progress opens!

Eventually, a terrible realization dawns for policy folk—these things are unstoppable and already ubiquitous—attention turns instead to prescribing the *right sort* and to severely limiting what might be then achieved. Draconian rules are introduced. Sometimes they are characterized as an existential threat to education. In the worst case, a special limited *educational version* is embraced... and the door for subversive innovation and radical progress closes.

In the EURIT '86 conference at Twente University, Netherlands we argued against feeble cut-down "educational spreadsheets" with their 96 rows and tiny capacity (Heppell, 1987). We showed a video of a seven-year-old comfortably manipulating and asking *what if* questions about a fully-functioned spreadsheet application (Multiplan on a 128K Macintosh) without any difficulty at all. The higher education conference audience was stunned. As ever, education undervalues the capability and potential of children. To put a sense of perspective onto this anecdote, that little seven-year-old today is a forty-two-year-old teacher. But today, spreadsheets have a controlled and defined place in the primary curriculum in England. They appear safely corralled into Key Stage 3 Computer Science where they can't threaten maths or science. The spreadsheet is a thing to understand, not a thing to understand with. An artifact not a tool... but Ultralab's Law says not to worry, shed no tears, move on to the next space between denial and adoption. Find progress there instead.

Another of the *Twenty Things*, in fact the first listed in Seymour and Cynthia's paper, was to build a turtle, and in 1997 the team at Ultralab found ourselves as one component of the ambitious European i3 project. The pan-European i3 idea was to build distributed expertise in conjoined research labs across the continent, with each doing something a bit blue sky and joining into a kind of virtual MIT. We won't dwell here on the impact of European bureaucracy on creativity and ingenuity (!) but it is fun to recall that in the end we built an AI report generator to automate the entire production of the plethora of required EU reports, whilst we got on with the research! It worked well; clearly nobody ever read the reports! However, our research component was to build an intelligent robot (the éTui[2]) which could be taught, rather imperfectly, and to do this in conjunction with young children as co-creators. At that time there was a broad consensus in education that very young children could not reflect on their own learning.

Our intention was to refute that by creating a teachable toy, but with imperfections so that in noting its failure to learn, children might reflect on their own strategies and successes. Metacognition for tiny ones. Of course, we'd had plenty of teaching time with various Logo turtles and we immersed the kids in every controllable toy on the market and our own éTui simulator. The further we got into the process, the less AI we included. In *Twenty Things* there is discussion of the language used to offer simple commands to the turtle. Our little éTuis could be programmed in many ways: by moving them around, by lines and bars on the floor, by touch, by flashing lights at them, and more. The little éTuis weren't smart; the kids demonstrably were. As they watched the éTuis struggle with discovering a way out of a maze they would say "Oh you silly thing, that's not how I'd do it" and right there was our reflective learner.

Kids were inspired co-creators. They recognized few limits. At one point, discussing the size and weight of the ideal éTui with the children (we were imagining pocket sized), one commented that "I don't care how big it is, as long as I can teach it to carry me to school." Children's limits and parameters are always broader than you expect! We'd had the benefit of a regular link to Jony Ive and his team, then still at Apple. An enduring memory of his team was their *never say die* attitude. At the time of our éTui development they also had a project for which they needed a soft rubber-like material which sadly didn't exist. Can't buy it? No problem they said, and boldly dived into chemical engineering to invent it. Clearly for them too, the limits and parameters were broad and always surmountable. The child in them had survived.

A further great insight from the project was about age. We were working largely with pre-school children. But one Friday evening I took a sackload of éTuis into a busy pub in the City of London. I just switched them on and stood back. Within ten minutes the floor was filled with wealthy city brokers on their knees, talking animatedly about learning. Learning really is for everyone.

At the end of *Twenty Things* we are reminded that "If every child were to be given access to a computer, computers would be cheap enough for every child to be given access to a computer." Towards the end of the '90s, alongside pals from Intuitive Media, we were fortunate to be at the heart of a project, Tesco SchoolNet 2000 which gave all UK kids access to computers though computer labs that we built in the very many Tesco supermarkets around the nation. It grew to a Guinness World Record as the (then) largest *Internet Learning Project* in the world with millions of Tesco carrier bags and their huge fleet of lorries carrying marketing to encourage participation by everyone.

Children were presented with regular challenges—laying down some useful insights into the importance of asynchronous, distributed learning as we did so. Children of all ages did the same challenges with a beautiful bell curve of participation between four and eighteen years old. Of course the eighteen-year-olds did more and did them differently, or were themselves in mixed age groups. *Stage not age* was apparent in outcomes.

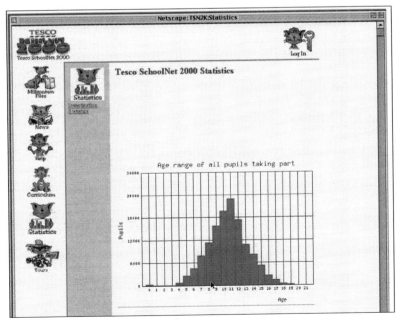

In one challenge, "Find the most famous person where you live and ask about their schooldays" we gave great support in terms of introductory letters, safety advice, and more. But the children found their celebrities SO willing to chat to our cub-reporters. A-list movie stars and national sports heroes poured out a mix of shocking and laugh-out-loud memories. Real scoops, real news. But the news media didn't take up or repeat a single story. Somehow the fact that children had secured the scoops meant journalists had no interest. I still dine out on some of the more salacious stories! Sadly, when every child WAS given access to a computer lab, many adults still failed to see or appreciate the potential thus revealed. That doesn't matter as long as a few do. Validation doesn't need unanimity, it just needs enough to constitute an audience.

A constructivist model of learning confirms that some audience is an important component of effective learning. Children enthusiastically watching their Logo turtles stepping out a recursive spiral always had an element of theatre. With Tesco SchoolNet 2000, although the professional journalists provided no audience at all, it didn't matter because the project was showcased in the vast Millennium Dome in London, and again online. Simply standing in the Dome, watching the children enjoying adults exploring their SchoolNet project work, was a daily reaffirmation of the role of audience. Technology gave the children agency in attaining an audience. It was enough.

Of course, these are just a few personal snapshots of so very many projects over the fifty years since *Twenty Things…* and although the plural of anecdote is not data, these many projects have had substantial scale and longevity. So, what might be taken away from a lifetime of meandering in that space for subversive innovation and radical progress?

Four conclusions stand out:

- When that space for subversive innovation and radical progress opens up, seize it. And don't be dismayed when it closes. That is your cue to move on. Stay resilient and agile.
- Keep those supposed limits and constraining parameters very broad indeed. We learn from the children that usually, everything is surmountable. If we retain a childlike streak, that will hold true. It will certainly be hugely enjoyable too.
- Children are inspired co-creators, given access to knowledge and agency. If you want to see dramatic progress though, stand back and embrace fully learner-led projects. There will always be plenty of adult naysayers, but their cynicism is overwhelmed by the weight of progress the children evidence.
- Finally, and this is a reminder of the fierce bravery contained in *Twenty Things*, be recklessly ambitious for your projects. Looking back at our own projects over the many years, it is clear that the ones which left the whole team tossing and turning at night, sleepless for the apparent risk in what we had committed to do, were the projects just about brave enough to keep pace with the children once they were immersed in the work.

Seymour and Cynthia gave us *Twenty Things to Do with a Computer*. With today's technology you can do pretty much anything, so assemble your own *Twenty Things to Do with* Children and make sure that each one of those new things terrifies you afresh!

References

Heppell, S. (1987). The use of business software as a content free teaching tool: emulation or assimilation? (Paper 3a). In J. Moonen & T. Plomp (Eds.), *EURIT 86: Developments in Educational Software and Courseware: Proceedings of the First European Conference on Education and Information Technology*. Pergamon Press.

Notes

1 Ultralab's Law - naec.org.uk/ultralab/ww3/about/aboutultralab/contentpanels_view?pageIndex=8
2 éTui - rubble.heppell.net/archive/etui/default.html

Purple Constructionism

Nettrice Gaskins

Constructionism is a process in which people create their own unique ways of knowing with prototypes, devices, and tools that others can use and critique (Papert, 1991). Seymour Papert and others who study constructionism usually look at machines that compute as materials for making. Making music using computers enhances an artist's material agency through creative production, entertainment, fabrication, and so on. This transfer of music production to computation can also take place where students learn how to make things.

Musicians, as early adopters of technology, did really interesting things with computers. Prince took the polyrhythmic patterns of Black music such as funk, R&B, gospel, and jazz and amplified those sounds using the Linn LM-1, the first computer to use digital samples of acoustic drums. This machine was a staple of 1980s pop music production. The song "777–9311" from The Time's album *What Time Is It?* was produced, arranged, composed, and performed by Prince and is known for the musician's innovative use of the Linn LM-1 (Brett, 2020).

"777–9311" and Prince's use of the Linn LM-1 played a critical role in engaging high school students at Boston Arts Academy through meaning making—interpreting situations, events, and objects through knowledge and experience—and making things, which evokes the idea of constructionism. MIT's Mitchel Resnick (Madda, 2016) talked about this process:

> *There can be a problem if you go to the other extreme where you focus on process, and not on creating something meaningful. Once you make something, it's something you can reflect upon, share with others.*

The students were given permission to spend their afternoons in the STEAM Lab where they were challenged to come up with a project that was meaningful to them (Gaskins, 2021). They chose to make MIDI sound controllers using 3D printers, soldering and circuitry to create the musical interfaces, and then programmed circuit boards to operate the devices. They wanted to use the devices to compose their music. None of these students knew how to do any of these things at the start. Making the devices was a challenge for them, as was the experience of failing creatively with computers and electronics.

It was Prince's innovation with the Linn LM-1, especially in "777–9311" that helped the students persist. His rhythm programming in this and other songs generated an iterative feedback loop that the students could emulate. While listening to the song while they soldered components, they discovered that it helped them focus. They requested that the song be played repeatedly, which brought them closer to what they were making through "call-and-response participation" (Smitherman, 1977), a process in which statements (calls) are quickly followed by answering statements (responses). In the lab, the students worked in response to the Linn LM-1 drumbeat, following the looping rhythm with the movements of their hands. Research shows that this type of engagement enables students to learn (Cazden, 1988).

This example demonstrates how to help students empower themselves by using cultural referents such as music to impart knowledge, skills, and attitudes. The presence of music and computers altered the nature of the learning process in the STEAM Lab, shifting the balance between transfer of knowledge to students and the production of knowledge by them. The MIDI sound controller project linked music and innovation through Prince and digital fabrication in a learning lab and this touched on Papert's work. Constructionism holds that learning can happen most effectively when learners are active in making physical objects in the real world. Making and using drum machines played a part in mediating a change in the way students were learning. Students who completed making their MIDI sound controllers were able to perform with them during senior music recitals the following year.

High school music majors create MIDI sound controllers in the STEAM Lab at Boston Arts Academy. Photo: Nettrice Gaskins.

References

Brett, T. (2020). Prince's Rhythm Programming: 1980s Music Production and the Esthetics of the LM-1 Drum Machine. *Popular Music and Society, 43:3,* 244-261.

Cazden, C. B. (1988). *Classroom Discourse* Heinemann.

Gaskins, N. R. (2021). *Techno-Vernacular Creativity and Innovation: Culturally Relevant Making Inside and Outside of the Classroom.* MIT Press.

Madda, M. J. (2016). The Maker Movement Isn't Just about Making and Electronics: EdSurge Talks to MIT's Mitch Resnick. *Edsurge News May 23.* edsurge.com/news/2016-05-23-the-maker-movement-isn-t-just-about-making-and-electronics-edsurge-talks-to-mit-s-mitch-resnick

Papert, S. (1991). Situating Constructionism. In I. Harel & S. Papert (Eds.), *Constructionism* (pp. 1-11). Ablex. papert.org/articles/SituatingConstructionism.html

Smitherman, G. (1977). *Talkin and Testifyin: The Language of Black America.* Wayne State University Press.

My Rules

Jennifer Orr

In the interests of full disclosure, before I pretend to any expertise, I need to note that I am an elementary school teacher with no real knowledge of coding or computer programming. I enjoy playing around and I love watching students play around. Even with first graders, my students are often far more capable than I am very quickly. Papert and Solomon state that their *Twenty Things to Do with a Computer* gave "a glimpse of the proper way to introduce **everyone** of whatever age and whatever level of academic performance, to programming," and I completely agree. I can't do all twenty of the things in their paper, but I've had some fun trying.

I will take some credit for my students' skills. My skill may not be in programming, as it is in making the space for students to do so. I have some cardinal rules for myself and a few for my students that I think are crucial for giving them the space to learn, the space to tackle Papert and Solomon's *Twenty Things*. This isn't just true for programming either. These rules, at least the ones for myself, are useful again and again as a teacher.

Rules for Me

1. Show students what I don't know

Young children have great faith that the adults in their lives know everything. That can make for quite an endorphin rush when your students believe everything you say. It took me too many years to realize that showing my students all the things I don't know is not a weakness, but a powerful model. If *I*, the grown up and the teacher, don't know how to do things, it must be okay that they don't. It frees them to take more risks and to ask more questions.

2. Celebrate questions

If I want my students to ask questions, I have to encourage them and make sure I'm not inadvertently discouraging them. Asking a question is a risk, it sets one up to possibly look foolish or unintelligent. Even young children often learn, especially at school, that they should know things and not need to ask. Responding to students' questions with enthusiasm helps ensure that more questions are asked. Turning their questions over to the class, rather than answering them yourself, is even better. That way the questioner sees the value of their question and everyone gets involved in problem solving to answer it.

3. Similar to showing what I don't know is modeling mistakes

Again, in my first years of teaching, I tried to hide when I made a mistake, or I tried to play it off. Now I highlight my mistakes for my students. I point out what I did and how I addressed it (or opted not to address it if that is the case). Seeing adults make mistakes and realizing it isn't a big deal (most of the time, at least) gives students the freedom to make mistakes. Learning doesn't happen without making mistakes, so this is exceptionally important for them.

4. Celebrate mistakes

In addition to highlighting my mistakes for students, I celebrate theirs. Students make mistakes because they are stretching beyond what is comfortable so that is definitely worth a celebration. Also, most mistakes are made with some strengths showing. Noticing how a student stretched, or pointing out the strengths within their error will encourage students to continue stretching and building on those strengths.

5. Play (maybe this one should be at the top)

It is easy, as a teacher, to get caught up in the Planning and Pacing Guide and Expected Outcomes and Standards, Benchmarks, and Whatnot, and lose sight of the children in front of us and all they can do. Giving them time to play with the tools is something I have to literally write in my lesson plans and force myself to do. I never regret it. The things children learn through their own explorations are often far more complex and advanced than I would be able to teach them. Given the space and time to play, students are motivated and engaged on their own terms.

6. Remove barriers to entry

The more I restrict access to tools, the less students learn. When it comes to programming, this means that I don't have any prerequisites for getting their hands on tools. Whether it's BeeBots or the Scratch website or a micro:bit, if students want to give it a try, they can. Before school, for indoor recess, or during any free time we have, these tools are available to them. When we, as adults and authority figures, raise barriers to learning, we turn kids away. My goal is to turn the tools over to the students, and for them to have complete ownership of them.

7. Learn from students

When students have complete ownership, they become the teachers. As soon as I see them do something new, I ask them to teach me how to do it. Since I've already shown them how little I know, they are ready to be my teacher! This has the added bonus of pushing them to explain their process, often resulting in revisions and improvements.

8. Enlist students as teachers

As often as possible, I turn things over to the kids. We bring their work up on the projector or put the tool under the document camera and give them the microphone. They are often better teachers of their peers than I am. They understand each other well and can respond to questions and explain things in ways that make a lot of sense. That benefits the one teaching and their students.

Rules for Students

1. Get up, walk around the room, check out what other students are doing

Some kids will immediately get up to see what happened as soon as they hear a classmate's gasp or chuckle. Other students have learned too deeply that you don't get up in school without permission. I engage with those who get up, discuss what they see, and get excited with them. Then I encourage other students to get up and walk around. Some students are too engrossed in what they're doing to get up and that's fine too. But it's important to me that students know they *can* get up and check out what else is happening around the room.

2. No touching another person's tools

This rule came out of watching students follow rule number one and then ask a classmate how to do whatever they saw. Often the result was that the classmate would go with their friend back to their computer (or BeeBot or KIBO or whatever) and do it for them. No one benefits from that. Student A, who discovered how to do something cool and is seen by Student B, is welcome to go with Student B back to their tool and walk them through the process. Student A can explain while Student B implements. That forces Student A to explain what they did, pushing them to think it through more carefully than they might have done on their own, and it forces Student B into more of an understanding through action than they would get just from watching someone else do it. Both students end up with more and stronger skills as a result.

One Final Rule

Reading Papert and Solomon's *Twenty Things to Do with a Computer* now, fifty years after it was written, is both a treat and painful. Everything they suggest remains important and valid today, which is amazing. Unfortunately, it is a paper people still need to read because it is not common understanding. Papert and Solomon are encouraging practices that would grow students as problem solvers and thinkers as well as programmers. Building those skills is the goal of my rules as well.

One final rule that is often hard for me: *Get out of their way. The kids have got this.*

Radical Ideas: Joy and Empowerment

Ken Kahn

I met Seymour less than two years after *Twenty Things* was published (AI and Logo memos felt like publications to me despite the lack of peer review). I was a few months away from becoming a graduate student in the MIT Artificial Intelligence Lab. My dreams were largely focused on creating AI but I soon became drawn to the Logo Group where I would spend a fraction of my time in the following six years.

What excited me most about *Twenty Things* is that many of those "things" were AI activities. The idea of giving children the power, joy, and creativity of computer programming was a radical idea that appealed to me. And not just any computer programming but AI programming seemed even more challenging and exciting.

Seymour and Cynthia wrote "But while reading the paper you need not (and should not, it is a distraction) think about how the commands we describe will produce their effects." I like this attitude even though it does run counter to the standard view of computer science education with its emphasis on learning low-level foundations first. For a long while I've advocated *middle-out* programming where one starts with high-level commands/components (the middle level) and builds very capable impressive programs (the upper level) while being careful to support those learners that are interested in how the middle level is realized in terms of lower-level components, perhaps to edit or create their own.

I also fell in love with turtle geometry. I attempted to marry it to AI by exploring higher-level constructs whose foundations are turtles. I explored programs that treated turtle programs as objects that other programs can manipulate in various ways. Ten years after reading *Twenty Things* I explored how turtles could be used to map concurrent logic programs onto the nodes of parallel computers. Thirty years later I became fascinated with how NetLogo supports agent-based modeling and embarked on a large-scale project to support a higher-level way of defining and composing NetLogo agents and behaviors.

In my graduate studies in AI I learned about natural language parsers and generators, knowledge representations, dialogue systems, and more. I wanted to enable children to be able to use these powerful ideas in their own creations. I built toy worlds in Logo where children could make a sort of *blocks world* where they could create a dialogue system for placing and animating shapes in a scene. Pattern matching was used to interpret commands and a very simple grammar could be defined to generate responses.

At the same time, I was learning about AI programming languages that go beyond Lisp to make AI programming easier and more intuitive. So I started building a child-friendly version of these ideas in Lisp Logo—a very capable version of Logo that was easy to extend. I was also learning about *actor* languages where computation was thought of as actors or objects passing messages to each other. This led me to implement Director as an AI-oriented big brother to Logo. I saw a programming language for children based on message passing as the next generation in the Logo family of languages that took Logo's *Little Man* metaphor of computation (now the *Little Person* metaphor) to the limit.

Sometime in the mid-1970s Danny Hillis wrote an unpublished paper called "Ten Things to Do with a Better Computer." It was directly inspired by *Twenty Things* and described ten new, and more challenging, things. As I remember it, the ten things were all AI projects. It was full of good ideas that inspired me (and sadly seems to be lost to history).

Twenty Things also inspired me to try my hand as a cartoonist. Guy Steele in the AI Lab often drew cartoons and taped them to his office door. The characters looked like ball lightning and I found the cartoons to be very funny. The cartoons were full of inside jokes about Lisp, computers, AI, etc. As Seymour and Cynthia wrote in *Twenty Things* turtles might have "touch sensors, light sensitive cells, and sound detectors." My cartoons involved turtles with different sensors encountering each other. Each turtle knew of the others only via its solitary sensory device. For example, a turtle with a sound detector bumps into a turtle with a touch sensor. The touch sensor turtle says, "Who's there?" and the sound turtle says, "I heard something, is there someone here?" The light sensor turtle watches this all unfold. These cartoons are now lost and ill-remembered, which is probably no great loss since they weren't all that funny.

An Eternal Source of Inspiration or What the Bulgarian Turtle Told Achilles This Time

Evgenia (Jenny) Sendova

But there is a world of difference between what computers can do and what society will choose to do with them.—Seymour Papert

Prologue

Scene 1 – Enter the Narrator

It was not long ago that I took part in a discussion on "innovations in education." The moderator was very surprised when I said that a good innovation in contemporary education would be for students to go to school with love—as was the case with the so called "cell schools" (the first and only schools in Bulgaria from the fifteenth to eighteenth century) and in more recent times in the schools that the Research Group on Education of the Bulgarian Academy of Sciences ran as an experiment from 1978 to 1999 in 2% of the Bulgarian schools (Sendov, 1987). These days not only in Bulgaria but also around the world, innovations are often associated with technology such as multimedia, interactive boards, smartphones, etc. and the innovativeness of a school is measured by the number of laptops and not by what the teachers or the students have *chosen to do with them.*

In an attempt to recreate the atmosphere of a series of educational discussions from the period 1980–1996 on the difference between the constructivism and constructionism, on the essence of Logo (of which *Twenty Things to Do with a Computer* is an essential part), and on the experience of implementing Logo mainly as a philosophy and a culture—I'll start with a dialog between Achilles and the Turtle with an occasional intervention by the Cat, the mascot of Scratch.

Scene 2 – Enter Achilles and the Turtle

Achilles and the Turtle are characters we know not only from the famous Zeno's Paradox but also from the essay by Lewis Carroll "What the Tortoise Said to Achilles" (1895) and the book *Gödel, Escher, Bach* by Douglas Hofstadter (1980), in which the author promotes the idea that in the history of human civilization the division between science and art is in fact superficial.

Turtle: Do you remember twenty years ago I was telling you about Logo and its implementation in the Bulgarian setting?

Achilles: Logo is a Greek word! Of course, I know what Logo is! It has several meanings—*word, thought, principle, speech.*

Turtle: You are right! And every sense is applicable to Logo—but many people today associate *Logo* with me mainly!

Achilles: With YOU!!! Remind me!

Turtle: Because I embody a robot which can draw geometric figures on the screen with the commands for moving FORWARD and turning RIGHT.

Achilles: I have heard about something called "turtle geometry" and I was wondering why some people refer to it also as "geometry of FORWARD and RIGHT."

Turtle: Because if you think of it, these two commands are sufficient for me to draw figures as simple as a line segment and as complex as a fern.

Today we are invited by Jenny Sendova to celebrate fifty years of the CS article about a number of things to do with just a turtle like me.

Achilles: By CS article, you mean an article about computer science?

Turtle: No, my dear miseducated friend! I mean Cynthia (Solomon) and Seymour (Papert), the authors of this fundamental article! They are illustrating MY geometry first with a physical robot-turtle (the floor turtle) and then with what they call a "display turtle"—a small triangle.

Achilles: A triangle? Why on earth, a triangle? Did Kandinski make your portrait?

Turtle: I wish he did but in fact, my original Logo image exposes and emphasizes my new role as a drawing instrument (which some more modern environments hide behind cats, bees, and other animals).

Achilles: That is true. I remember your dialog with primary teachers who told you once: *We don't work with turtles, we work with other animals!*

Turtle: But Logo people know that under any "mask" it's me, the turtle, which can draw figures and become different characters if needed.

FORWARD 50

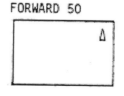

The turtle advanced 50 units in the direction it was facing.

Act 1

Scene 1 – Drawing a Man (Thing #2)

Achilles: I have heard that in drawing, nothing is better than the first attempt.

Turtle: Maybe for Picasso this might be right, but in programming we say that if a program works when first executed, there is certainly a bug in it.

I very much liked the second of the twenty things—the man. You can draw it in so many ways. Our friends CS (from now on short for Cynthia and Seymour) decided to use it to introduce the notion of *procedure* and *subprocedure* by decomposing their model of a man into the elements of a V shape. They also introduced the notion of *procedure with inputs* to make man's figures in different sizes (Fig. 1).

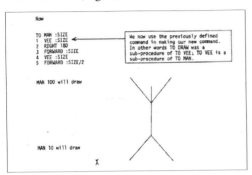 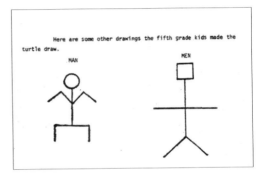

Fig. 1. *Thing #2 of the CS article as proposed by CS (left) and performed by children (right)*

Scene 2 – Geometric Human Figures

Achilles: I see that it is not only a natural task for children, but one that allows for various solutions even if you decide to draw the same figure as the one proposed by the authors.

Turtle: Here is how students from the Academy 21 Century in Assenovgrad (Sendova & Grkovska, 2005) created human figures (Fig. 2).

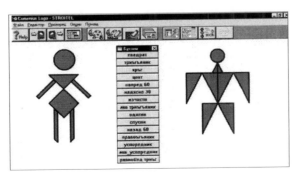

Fig. 2. *Work of 11-year old students in Comenius Logo (the buttons' names are in Bulgarian)*

In a number of situations they had to calculate angles and lengths of segments (requiring a more advanced math). But they proudly would refuse hints from the teachers murmuring, "I prefer to use MY mind." When building their compositions the children used two typical programming styles—top-down (designing a preliminary sketch and decomposing it into simpler geometric figures) and bottom-up (trying out various combinations of given geometric elements).Turning the turtle to angles with different signs brought them quite naturally to a new understanding of *symmetry about an axis.*

Achilles: I am curious to learn if the authors of the boy and the girl in Fig. 2 were limited in the number of shapes to use?

Turtle: No, the authors were a girl and a boy (eleven-year olds) led by their own aesthetics.

Scene 3 – Visual Modeling à la Pencho Balkanski and Sonia Delaunay

Turtle: Look at these models in the style of the renowned Bulgarian artist Pencho Balkanski (Fig. 3) by fourth graders from Sts. Cyril and Methodius School (Sofia) who participated in a competition dedicated to the artist.

Fig. 3. *The original by Balkanski "Girls from Rhodope Mountains", 1982 (left) and Logo variations by 10-year old children (right)*

Achilles: This visual modeling is impressive. Have you tried something similar with university students?

Turtle: Yes, of course. One of my favorite artists to model was Sonia Delaunay because of her love of geometric shapes. I introduced her models for Diaghilev's ballet to teachers-to-be (fourth-year students at Sofia University). The goal of the course was to present the students with an educationally rich environment supporting active and exploratory styles of learning. Visual modeling always enjoys great interest among students. After having worked on a program generating variations of certain famous paintings (Fig. 4) they would often share their enthusiasm for learning to look at abstract art with new eyes.

Fig. 4. *Students' computer variations of Sonia Delaunay's models*

Scene 4 – From One Step to 3D Animation

Another dimension (pun intended) is achieved by Pavel Boytchev in his article "Turtle Metamorphoses (from FD 1 to 3D animation)" (2003). His early attempts to build a 3D character resulted in a wire-frame model (Fig. 5, left).

Fig. 5. *Modeling the movements of humans, android, a robot-warrior and a mutant in 3D*

Achilles: Could he animate the wired man?

Turtle: Pavel says that although it is not hard to build and animate such a model, it becomes very difficult if one wants to put some flesh on the bones. For example, in a wire-frame mode, if wires are drawn by a turtle there are no problems to draw them relative to each other, this is one of the key features of turtle graphics. However, if the drawn parts are more complex, it is not clear how to handle it. The problem becomes even harder if some parts are not drawn by the turtle, but with other tools.

Scene 5 – Enter the Cat

Cat: I can also draw the man offered in the CS article! The kids don't care about turtles, they want to draw with me. They even like it when I bump into the screen edges or move randomly because the figures I draw become funnier! Here is the man an eleven-year old Scratch fan managed to draw (Fig. 6)!

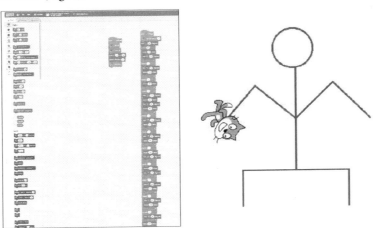

Fig. 6. *The first version of the man's figure using a chain of commands*

Turtle: What is this? No procedures or subprocedure—just a long chain of blocks, containing REPEAT 1 [*something*].

Cat: The important thing is that he got the man! And he did not have to change my size, he likes me as I am. I myself wonder sometimes how they see the drawing under me. To make you happy here is another version of the program with subprocedures for the body parts (Fig. 7).

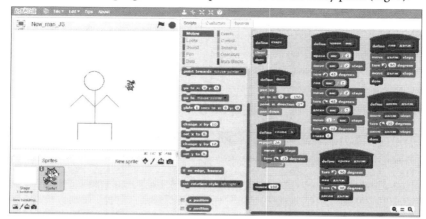

Fig. 7. A second version of the man's figure above using subprocedures and an input for the size

Scene 6 – The Dance of the Triangular Village People

Turtle: This is something else! I am sure that it was the teacher who encouraged the real Logo style.

Cat: You bet! And he challenged his fifth graders to draw a "triangle man" and make several "horo" dancers (Fig. 8).

Turtle: I notice that it is only the program generating the dance of couples (Fig. 8) that uses the REPEAT command. The authors of the other horo-dances have procedures for the elements of their dancers, combined in a "man" superprocedure, but the main "horo" procedure invokes "man" at several places followed by the commands for positioning you (in my role) for the next dancer.

Cat: You are difficult to please! I myself am happy with the variety of approaches and results!

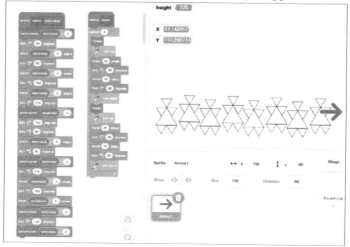

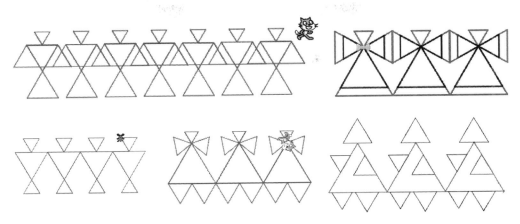

Fig. 8. *Triangular variations of the traditional Bulgarian "horo" dance, by fifth graders from Bulgarsko Shkolo, Sofia*

Intermission – time for a coffee break

Act 2

Scene 1 – Modeling the Pendulum in the Spirit of Logo (Thing #17)

Turtle: Let us talk about one of the physics models in #17 of the CS article—the pendulum model.

Achilles: From what I saw there, after directing the turtle appropriately, you could draw a line segment with a number after FORWARD (so that your trace disappears) and do the same symmetrically about the negative y-axis.

Turtle: In the first Logo version used in Bulgaria this was the simplest possible model but after drawing the segment and waiting for some time I had to erase it. A very interesting process of stepwise refinement and enrichment while creating a pendulum model was experienced in Geomland (Sendova & Sendov, 1999), a Logo-based mathematical laboratory, which I don't inhabit but the Logo spirit is there! The setting was fourth-year math teachers-to-be at Sofia University. The first task was to start with the simplest model—the rod represented by a connected vector which changes its direction while oscillating about a fixed axis (Fig. 9).

Fig. 9. *Modeling the pendulum as illustrated in Geomland*

Before demonstrating the process of constructing and editing the program, let me remind you about the special OBJECT primitive in Geomland, which is like MAKE extended with an automatic

69

visualization of the geometric objects and an automatic maintenance of the relationship among the newly constructed objects and those used in its construction.

Achilles: Slow down, please! So, in the pendulum case, if we define the deviation angle as an OBJECT, any time we change its value, the objects depending on it will change automatically?

Turtle: Precisely! Let's start:

```
OBJECT "T POINT 0 84
OBJECT "ang 60
MAKE "length 100
OBJECT "V VECTOR 270+:ang :length
OBJECT "P SEGMENT :T :V
```

The rod is constructed as a directed segment P representing the free vector V whose direction makes an angle of 270+:ang with the X-axis and whose length is 100 (Fig. 9, left).

So, what command do you think should be executed to make the rod oscillate with an amplitude of 60°?

Achilles: Let me think—you said that once the deviation angle *ang* is defined by the OBJECT command, it is enough to just change it so as to move the whole rod, right? So, let me try this:

```
OBJECT "ang :ang-10
```

It works, even though I had to execute it several times *by hand*!!! But I suspect you expect me to organize the whole pendulum-like movement. I am not only the *Fastfoot*, you can easily call me the *Fastmind*! If the amplitude is 60°, then the rod should be displaced gradually, first by 120° and then again, in the opposite direction to return in its initial position. So, what about the following two commands:

```
REPEAT 10 [OBJECT "ang :ang-12 WAIT 5]
REPEAT 10 [OBJECT "ang :ang+12 WAIT 5]
```

Turtle: All right! That is almost the same thing the students tried initially. You somehow remembered that the positive direction in classical math is counterclockwise. But in Logo everything is "no threshold" first, and "no ceiling" afterwards. So, the positive direction was clockwise—natural for the children (although today's clocks…). What you would get if you also made the rod leave a trace (TRACED "P) is what you have in the middle of Fig. 9.

Achilles: Am I not great! I solved the problem so fast! Give me another one!

Scene 2 – Introducing an Endless Oscillation

Turtle: You have not acquired the Logo spirit yet! The students were first challenged to achieve an endless oscillation.

Achilles: I am not fond of endless processes since according to Zeno of Elea I can never reach you if I give you a small advantage. However, if *Geomland* has the usual WHILE command, a possible solution would be:

```
WHILE "TRUE [REPEAT 10 [OBJECT "ang :ang-12 WAIT 5]
    REPEAT 10 [OBJECT "ang :ang+12 WAIT 5]]
```

Turtle: True, but not elegant to my taste, neither to the taste of the professor! Picking up his gauntlet they came up with the next algorithm:

```
WHILE <a key is not pressed>[Keep moving in the chosen direction until
    the amplitude is reached and then change the direction]
```

For the purpose the students introduced the parameters `maxang` for the amplitude (the maximum deviation angle) and `anginc` for the angle increment:

The enrichment of the procedure looked as follows:

```
MAKE "maxang 60
MAKE "anginc 10
OBJECT "ang :maxang
...
WHILE NOT ReadKey? [(IF (ABS :ang)>=:maxang[MAKE "anginc NEG :anginc])
    OBJECT "ang :ang+ :anginc WAIT 5]
```

Achilles: I must admit I am impressed! Did the students figure out immediately that the angle deviation has a sign?

Turtle: Not really! The improvement might look purely technical from a programming point of view but it reflected a better understanding of the nature of the pendulum—the fact that it deviates only to a certain angle. The latter approximation was preceded by a version in which the pendulum behaved more like a clock-hand—moving endlessly clockwise (I did skip this step not to bother you with all the intermediate tiny steps since you are not called *Fastfoot* in vain).

Achilles: Don't tell me that the professor was still not satisfied!

Turtle: Yes and no. Of course, there were students ready to attack another problem. But let me emphasize that the original Logo paradigm of letting the learner take the initiative for further explorations does not work properly in a strictly fixed time interval (which in the case of the school setting is also very short). Therefore, when teaching in a real school it is important for the teacher to sharpen the students' feelings of being unsatisfied with their latest achievement. Thus, it was part of professors' endeavor to promote the Logo philosophy and culture by cultivating among the future teachers the need for improvements and refinements in the process of problem solving.

Achilles: So, if I was one of these students, I would not rush for a new problem, but rather think of further ideas for improvement, e.g. How to make the rod move towards the axis no matter what the initial deviation was? How to prevent the rod from moving if it was in equilibrium initially? How to model the slowdown effect?

Turtle: Yes, the students did ask or answer these questions playing with several ideas about modeling the slowdown effect. First, they tried to express the input of `WAIT` as directly proportional to the deviation without taking into account that the inputs of `WAIT` are natural numbers and its values should not be zero at a zero-angle deviation. After some adjustments the students defined the time *t* of `WAIT` as follows:

```
OBJECT "t (ABS ROUND 0.15*:ang)+2
```

Achilles: Bravo! So, the lecturer was finally satisfied, I guess.

Scene 3 – Improving the Pendulum Model

Turtle: The visual effect was satisfactory, but the trace of the rod still matched a uniform motion rather than an alternate change between a moderating and an accelerating one (Fig. 9, middle). So, the next, even more ambitious step, was to make the consecutive positions of the rod with an angle increment decreasing by absolute value.

Achilles: Oh, Zeus! This is becoming a really endless process…but students are normally good in investigating functions, aren't they?

Turtle: You point to the root of the problem. While the students are used to drawing graphs of functions, it turned out to be relatively difficult for them to construct a function with given properties. Eventually they produced the final (for that particular session) version of the code:

```
MAKE "angincmax 8
MAKE "angincmin 1
MAKE "maxang normalized RANDOM 360
OBJECT "ang :maxang
OBJECT "V VECTOR 270+:ang 100
OBJECT "P SEGMENT :T :V
MAKE "k (:angincmax - :angincmin)/:maxang
OBJECT "anginc "angincmax - :k* (ABS :ang)
MAKE "d (NEG SIGN :ang)
WHILE NOT ReadKey? [(IF (ABS :ang)>=:maxang[MAKE "d (NEG SIGN :ang])
    OBJECT "ang :ang+:d*:anginc WAIT 3]
```

This code with the trace left (Fig. 9, right) made it clear that the model was a more realistic approximation of the pendulum. But as Logo people often say: *Wait, there is more.* So, further ideas for explorations included applying trigonometric functions when describing the increment of the deviation, modeling a marionette performing exercises at the end of the rod to a musical accompaniment, etc. The informatics instruments were naturally involved in the process of modeling and tuned so as to provide the necessary counterpoint to allow important mathematical ideas to stand out sharply.

Achilles: From what I already read, the latter idea reminds me of several more of those twenty things to do with a computer. But I think I understand the main educational property of all these projects—some effects can be obtained by extremely simple means; extra efforts will produce more exciting effects!

Turtle: The main message of this example is that in order to provide learners with an environment supportive of the style of "doing" science, software designers should develop continuous computational media providing a whole range of tools and examples—from easy sketches to means enabling you to create the tools you need. Such a continuity reflects the Logo spirit of refinement and enrichment of the program, and might be best achieved by integrating a direct manipulation interface with full (and text based) programmability.

Scene 4 – Pendulum Harmonics in 3D

Finally, I would like to show you some screen shots of *Pendulum Harmonics* developed by Pavel Boytchev—a model of the movement of a dozen of pendulums with specially calculated periods. The magic is due to the rational ratio of these periods. If the pendulums are released together, then sooner or later they will be become perfectly aligned (Fig. 10).

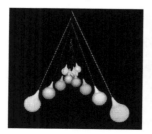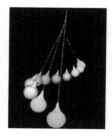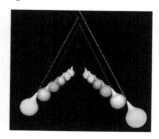

Fig. 10. *Pendulum Harmonics (youtu.be/PyvWjtdL3I4)*

Intermission

Act 3

Scene 1 – Can a Computer Play and Compose Music? (Things #11 and #12)

Turtle: It sounds amazing that even the first programmer Lady Ada Lovelace thought of the computer as an engine (the so-called analytical engine) and wrote in her scientific memoirs that it "might compose elaborate and scientific pieces of music of any degree of complexity or extent" (quoted in Howe & Kassler, 1980).

Achilles: Everybody thinks they know what music is, but I wonder if there is a more formal definition?

Turtle: A somewhat simplified definition would be that music represents well-ordered tones, so composing music means *extracting order from chaos*. The whole point is to find out what well-ordered means. There are three basic musical structures under this notion—melody, harmony, and rhythm. Different cultures (or even different styles within a specific musical culture) might have different musical organization or different emphasis on these structures. What music has in common is that it obeys some structure. And it is a lack of any structure that irritates me in so-called computer compositions, which are either a sequence of random notes, or sequences of notes each entered by an individual member of the class.

Achilles: But this could sound very chaotic.

Turtle: If we want to imitate the oriental[1] RANDOMSONG in the CS article in Comenius Logo, we could use the following procedure:

```
TO PENTATONIC
   OUTPUT [277 311 470 415 466]
END

TO DURATIONS
   OUTPUT [100 200 300 400]
END

TO ORIENTAL :N
   IF :N=0 [STOP]
   SOUND LIST PICK PENTATONIC PICK DURATIONS
   ORIENTAL :N-1
END
```

Achilles: And if I want to use all the twelve keys of the chromatic scale, instead of PENTATONIC, I'll use a procedure whose output is a list with numbers corresponding to all the twelve keys of the chromatic scale:

```
TO CHROMATIC
   OUTPUT [262 277 294 311 330 349 470 392 415 440 466 494 523]
END
```

Then I'll edit the ORIENTAL procedure appropriately:

```
TO WELL_TEMPERED :N
  IF :N=0 [STOP]
  SOUND LIST PICK CHROMATIC PICK DURATIONS
  WELL_TEMPERED :N-1
END
```

Turtle: You get the point. Now you have illustrated the notion of a well-tempered piano. But what is missing is the internal structure, which is required for every musical form.

Scene 2 – Enter a Musical Structure

Achilles: If we assume that music is *extracting order from chaos* in the system of music elements, it would be natural to model the process of modeling (miniature) music forms by consecutive approximations of an initial set of rules (Sendova, 2001b). When looking at several children songs I would suggest starting with the following rules:

- The tunes are 8-bar periods in C major
- The measure is 4/4
- The first tone belongs to the tonic triad
- The last tone is the tonic (C in our case)
- The tonal range is one octave

Turtle: This is a good start. Next you could add four rhythmic groups: (i) four quarter notes; (ii) two quarter notes and a half note; (iii) two half notes; and (iv) a whole note—and have these four groups occur with probability 1/3, 1/3, 1/6, and 1/6 respectively.

Achilles: In principle, I don't like to obey rules, but the tunes obeying just these rules still sound very chaotic, except at the beginning and the end. What if we add some more rules, as follows:

- The tune ends with a cadenza (the three last notes to be selected among a set of possible cadenzas)
- The adjacent notes are close enough

Turtle: What do you mean by "close enough"?

Achilles: This is still to be determined. We could start with "close" meaning at most one second, and if the tunes sound too monotone we might redefine it as "at most one third."

Turtle: I am afraid that *complete chaos* and *complete order* are equally dull to the human ear. Still, I am thinking of a couple more rules:

- The 8-bar period is divided in two phrases
- Each phrase ends with an appropriate type of cadenza (semi-cadenza)
- The set of measures includes 7/8
- The biggest possible interval between adjacent notes is a fourth
- The user can interact with the program and accept or reject the generated phrases

Achilles: Have you seen and heard tunes based on this last set of rules?

Turtle: Yes, in August 1990, there was a workshop with teachers in Hartford, led by Brian Silverman, where Jenny S. worked with David Almond, a teacher in music in Kingswood Oxford School on *Algorithmic Melodic Constructions: Computer-aided Compositions of Melodies Modelled on Simple Children's Songs* (Sendova, 2001b). Of course, I was well-trained to choose Bulgarian folk rhythms, and here is one of my favorite results (Fig. 11).

Fig. 11. Ruchenitsa (Bulgarian folk dance in 7/8) generated by a Logo Writer program

Achilles: O-o-oh, a Bulgarian song composed on American territory. Was this the first computer-generated composition in the world?

Scene 3 – A Short History of Machine Compositions

Turtle: The first serious experiments (1957) in modeling the process of compositions are based on investigating the local relationships of the tones. The American mathematicians Brooks, Hopkins, Neumann, and Wright wrote a program based on generating sequences of tones which are Markov chains of order (*n*-1) (Brooks et al., 1993). Hiller and Isaacson deal with formalizing some rules of the strict counterpoint (1959). Significant achievements in the modeling of the macrostructure of tonal music are in the works of Zaripov—his programs generate pieces in the three-part music form ABA (Zaripov & Russell, 1969).

Achilles: And in Bulgaria?

Turtle: In fact, the first experiments in Bulgaria in this area are of the same age as the CS article (Dimova & Kolarova (Sendova), 1971). Jenny S. together with her mentor Stefka Dimova, modeled the process of composition and 4-voice harmonization of 8-bar tunes based on algebraic formalization. It might be interesting to note that a simple bug (due to a mistake in the documentation of MINSK-2 computer) in the program for music composition took months to find. Much effort was dedicated to overcoming the then existing limitations in terms of memory and runtime. It was much more natural to build a microworld with typical music objects and operations, which Jenny S. accomplished in 2000 as part of her PhD thesis (Sendova, 2001a).

Achilles: Is it just on the traditional musical principles that one can build a model of a musical composition?

Turtle: If you could incorporate some basic principles of the traditional music in your program, why not try to formulate an original theory, which you could then experiment with? Some musicologists claim that music imitates the nature—it follows various patterns, such as alternating between chaos and order, new and old things, accents and pauses, harmony and disharmony—just like nature.

Achilles: Some scientists had an idea to use a language designed to model the behavior of an ant colony in a musical context (Brooks & Ross, 1996). I wonder if there are mathematical formalisms which are used in biology?

Turtle: There have been numerous experiments to find a musical correspondence between various recursive structures, e.g. curves, related to Lindenmayer systems for describing the growth of biological organisms (Mason & Saffe, 1994). When using fractals as a music generator, the idea is to achieve compactness and repeatability of the structure. You can find the opposite as well—recursive phenomena in musical pieces—thus it is natural to look the connection between music and mathematics in both directions (Johnson, 1996).

Achilles: I'd like to hear the opinion of experts in programming about it. To the best of my knowledge, there was an idea to create a musical language in the frames of a programming language similar to C or Lisp.

Turtle: According to James Moorer (involved in algorithmic composition since 1970) once the musicians reach certain freedom in programming, they need the full potential of an extendable language. Dijkstra (1972) mentions that Lisp (and I think Logo for that matter, too) is a language which has helped prominent figures in a number of areas.

Scene 4 – The Marriage of Logo and Music

Achilles: When did you hear about music in a Logo context for a first time?

Turtle: It was at the Logo '86 conference at MIT. I heard Gary Stager propose that the marriage of Logo and music may provide Logo programmers with new challenges and is an excellent instructional tool for teaching components of the traditional music curriculum. His experience confirmed the findings of Jeanne Bamberger of the 1970s that a child's use of Logo and music mirrors the learning process itself.

Achilles: So, who profits more from the marriage of Logo and music?

Turtle: According to Gary, "this marriage encourages the process of procedural thinking by breaking a problem down into its component parts and natural learning takes place through exploration and experience." In his classes he had observed "children discovering and learning important mathematical concepts: counting, addition, subtraction, seriation, symmetry, similarity, transposition, positive/negative integers, decimals, seriation, time, velocity, randomness, and recursion. On the other hand, several fundamental Logo topics had been used when working with music, including procedural writing, inputs, commands, operations, the editor, and list processing" (Stager, 1986).

Scene 5 – What Does Scratch Offer as a Marriage Partner?

Achilles: What about children's creativity?

Turtle: Today it is troubling to see how often educational software designers trivialize the notion of creativity by claiming that children can easily become composers, poets, artists, or filmmakers—just by using their imagination and by rearranging the elements of a story, a poem, a famous painting, or the bars of a musical piece. Even when students program a famous musical piece nobody brings their attention to its structure!

Cat: Come on! Why do children need to complicate their lives with structures! See how joyful these programs are that children have done to perform *Ode to Joy* by Beethoven. They can google the notes, they can build scripts with sound blocks that play in sequence (Fig. 12 – left), what more do they need! They can even create multiple scripts which when played together in order, create chords (Fig. 12 – right).

Fig. 12. Examples of fragments of Ode to Joy in Scratch (Veselinova, 2020)

Scene 6 – Adding to the Intrigue

Turtle: Let me show you a couple of examples of how we integrated music as part of *Informatics for Beginners* (Nikolov & Sendova, 1989).

Achilles: I see a music text in the standard notation (Fig. 13). Does the problem say that students have to code it in Logo for the computer to play it?

Fig. 13. The main theme of the Ode to Joy by Beethoven as part of a Logo problem for fifth graders

Turtle: If the students can read music notation, they will figure out that this is a fragment of the *Ode to Joy*. The trick here is for them to recognize the specific structure which is reflected in the following procedure:

```
TO JOY
    THEME1 THEME1.1
    BAR1 BAR1.1 BAR1.2 BAR2
    THEME1.2
END

TO THEME1
    PLAY [A1 A1 B1 C2 C2 B1 A1 G1 F1 F1 G1 A1 A1 G1 G1]~
    [4  4  4  4  4  4  4  4  4  4  4  4  4  4. 8  2]
END
```

```
TO BAR1
   PLAY [G1 G1 A1 F1][4 4 4 4]
END

TO BAR2
   PLAY [F1 G1 C1 A1][4 4 4 2]
END
```

Achilles: But here not all the subprocedures are given. You can't run JOY!

Turtle: That is exactly what the problem is about—to complete the program by adding the missing procedures. They do this by editing the existing ones, recognizing that THEME1 represents the first four bars. They should figure out that THEME1.1 and THEME1.2 could be obtained by editing THEME1.

Achilles: Thus, they would realize that music is also a language with a structure and although the specific elements could be denoted differently, this structure could be reflected in the Logo description as well!

Cat: I don't feel any joy without a dancing cat! Besides you could make all the instruments involved dance—like, the guitar could jump on the cymbals, wouldn't it be fun?

Turtle: OK, fun, but not fun for fun's sake! We, the Logo people, say—It's hard, it's fun! What about this other problem, with the framed music fragment (Fig. 14)?

Fig. 14. *Language and mathematics (Logo) for 6th graders [(Nikolov & Sendova, 1984) Problem 3]*

Cat: What is this? Why are the notes combined with the dancing men? At least someone is dancing!

Turtle: It is a part of the *Coding of Information* lesson in the same textbook. The idea was borrowed from *Gödel, Escher, Bach* (Hofstadter, 1980) where I saw it for the first time. The problem reads: *A great composer has coded his name. Who is he?*

The tricky thing here for Bulgarian students (sixth graders) is that Bach in Bulgarian is written with three letters (phonetically) as БАХ. Besides, we use the Italian names for the notes (do re mi…) It is thanks to the Logo notation that the students could solve the problem: B A C H.

Act 4

Scene 1 – Can the Computer Learn Grammar? (Thing #15)

Turtle: Let me share with you several examples of language phenomena related to grammar, poetry, and humor structure by illustrating how the classes in Bulgarian and English language and literature could be enriched and motivated (Sendova, 2008).

Achilles: Some grammar rules could be modeled very easily in one language and not as easily in another. Take for example the rule for the plural form of a noun. In Bulgarian it depends on the grammatical gender of the word, on its type (animate/inanimate), whereas in English you just add an "s" to the noun, or in Logo language:

```
TO PLURAL :NOUN
    OUTPUT WORD :NOUN "S
END
```

So, if you give the command PRINT PLURAL "DOG you will get DOGS; similarly PRINT PLURAL "CAT will result in the word CATS.

Turtle: A good first try! But what if you put BOY and LADY as inputs?

Achilles: So, you are saying that in this case my program PLURAL will produce BOYS (correct) and LADYS (incorrect) which means I have to change it appropriately.

Turtle: Yes, if the word ends with *y* you have to check if the preceding letter is a vowel and if it is, delete the *y* and add *ies*. Or, translated in Logo language, the refined description could be as follows:

```
TO PLURAL :NOUN
    If (LAST :NOUN)="Y [OUTPUT PLURAL_ENDING_IN_Y :NOUN]
    OUTPUT WORD :NOUN "S
END

TO PLURAL_ENDING_IN_Y :NOUN
    IF VOWEL? LAST BUTLAST :NOUN [OUTPUT WORD :NOUN "S]
    [OUTPUT WORD BUTLAST :NOUN "IES]
END

TO VOWEL? :L
    OUTPUT MEMBER? :L [A E I O U]
END
```

Achilles: I guess that you can describe other special cases as subprocedures in the main PLURAL procedure.

Turtle: The important lesson is that the informatics tools used could be made as natural as possible for a given context and could be given to students as we did in *PhiloLogo*, a specially designed microworld for language explorations (Sendova, 1988). Even better, such tools could be developed by the students themselves and then used as an extension of the original Logo language.

Of course, the refinement and the enrichment of the rule behind the PLURAL procedure, could not be done with the ambition to cover all the exceptions—one has to be aware of the *reasonable price* of such a process. Although the corresponding rule for plural forms in Bulgarian (or other Slavonic languages) is much more complicated, the steps of refining an initial simpler rule are similar. To discover situations in which a specific rule does not hold is not a failure, but a chance for the students to improve that rule—often in the spirit of the modeling in natural sciences. It is in this very spirit that Andee Rubin (as quoted by Goldenberg (1989)) considers a computer program as an "unambiguous materialized model-like hypothesis."

Achilles: Grammar rules make sense, although native speakers are not always aware of them and have to rediscover them when teaching the computer to speak correctly. But what about rules in poetry?

Scene 2 – Rules in Poetry

Turtle: You might be surprised that a well-known poet finds poetry without rules to be like "a tennis match without a net."

Achilles: But it is very tedious for students to learn the traditional meters such as iambs, anapests, or dactyls.

Turtle: Even Vladimir Mayakovsky, the famous Russian poet, in his essay "How to make poetry" (1959) writes that in his works he has never had to know what iamb or dactyl were: "These things take 90% of the textbooks in literature but only 3% in my practice." Still, when describing his difficulties in a poem about Sergei Esenin, he uses a format structure description of the kind (**ra** shows the stressed syllable):

ra-ra-**ra**/ ra-**ra**/ ra-ra-**ra**/ ra-**ra**/

and tries to find the most suitable words and phrases fitting the structure.

Achilles: So, can you use a similar formal description of a poetic structure by means of Logo?

Turtle: Actually, you can. Take for example "A Chant for Childhood," a poem by Kenneth White, whose poetry combines the influence of the old Eastern poetry with modern lyrics. If you describe the rhythm of each verse symbolically by reflecting the number of words, syllables, and the stress as sequences of **DA** and **di** (where **DA** stands for a stressed syllable), here's how the first verse of the translation in Bulgarian will look:

Пръч/ки от бре/зи/те	DAdi_di_diDAdi	Rituels des bouleaux	*Birch rites*
Тре/во/ля/ци пус/ти	didiDAdi_DAdi	bruyères désertes	*Empty moors*
Не/бе/са су/ро/ви	didiDA_diDAdi	cieux écrus	*Raw skies*
Сняг не/ве/ро/я/тен	DA_dididiDAdi	neige incroyable	*Incredible snow*

Achilles: In what language was the original written—English?

Turtle: No, it was in French (Psalmodie pour l'enfance), which I found only recently (Duclos, 2006). As you might guess, the first column is the Bulgarian translation. It is interesting to compare its rhythmic representation with the original one in view of the difference between the law of the stress of the words—the stress in Bulgarian and English being free, and in French on the final syllable.

Achilles: So, how do you proceed with the Logo procedure of generating verses *a la* White?

Turtle: If we are interested only in the melody of the verse, we could reduce the rhythm figures of the whole poem (of four verses) in three basic meters: (1) **DA**dididi**DA**di. (2) didi**DA**di**DA**di, and (3) **DA**di**DA**di**DA**di, and describe the rhythm of the original poem symbolically as:

1-2-2-1__1-2-1-1__2-1-1-3__1-1-1-2

If we then enter the structure as a list of elements corresponding to the number of the rhythmic group, the Logo procedure might look as follows:

```
TO VERSE :STRUCTURE :RHYTHM
    IF EMPTY? :STRUCTURE [STOP]
    PRINT RUN ITEM FIRST :STRUCTURE :RHYTHM
    VERSE BUTFIRST :STRUCTURE :RHYTHM
END
```

Then, in order to get poems as close to the original as possible we could give the command:

```
VERSE [1 2 2 1 1 2 1 1 2 1 1 3 1 1 1 2]~
    [DAdididiDAdi][didiDAdiDAdi][DAdiDAdiDAdi]]
```

where DAdididiDAdi is the name of a procedure generating a phrase of the corresponding rhythm by combining randomly chosen words from lists provided by the students.

Achilles: So, whose work is the generated verse then?

Turtle: Our experiments with students and teachers have shown that we should not be too skeptical about the so-called computer works, since they are neither purely made by the computer, nor random. In the poetic models, we always specify the structure of the poem and the sources the computer is to choose from. Thus, an important application of computer-generated works is that they are a sort of "invitation for an intellectual dance" (Goldenberg & Feurzeig, 1987) in which the best verses contain word combinations unexpected from humans, which could be used as a source for further processing according to taste.

Achilles: What I am getting from this is that you create a model of a given poem by observing certain patterns and stick as close as possible to the original. Then you generalize your finding by creating procedures which might generate the original, but also other poems in the style of the author. Depending on the types of poetic structure that the teachers would like to consider, they might encourage the students to explore various structure ideas, e.g., rhymes of the type ABBA, or verses following the structure found in Eastern poetry (e.g. haiku, cinquain, tanka, sedoka, sijo, and related genres).

Achilles: O-o-h, I first heard of cinquain while exploring language in Logo style inspired by the book of Goldenberg and Feurzeig (1987). The structure is very easy (1-word theme, 2-word description, 3-word action, 4-word feeling, 1-word summary). You can see it with the cinquain I wrote myself:

runners
brave athletes
vainly chasing turtles
sad heroes of paradoxes
fast-footed

Turtle: It is clear that poetry is not *your own heel*! But what you might find funny is that we have tried to model even humorous forms—aphorisms and dull jokes—based on two famous theorists on humor, Sigmund Freud (1916) and Marvin Minsky (1985).

Scene 3 – Modeling Aphorisms

Achilles: How could you mix up something which is AI with "dull"?

Turtle: Freud investigates the so-called "dull jokes," or more generally "nonsense that wants to pass for wit" and they are easier to model. When modeling short humorous forms, we try to capture what is invariant in a concrete piece and then try to generate computer variations of it. Let me start with Logo model of aphorisms in the style of Georg Lichtenberg:

The horse started resembling a donkey – like a translation from German to Dutch.

Achilles: I get the first one as conveying the idea of how much can be lost in translation—the author compares *pairs* of objects, the first object being similar in a certain sense to the second, but going beyond it.

Turtle: Precisely! We encouraged the students to use an associative list containing the *pair of similar words* from the original aphorism but enriching it with their own *pairs of similar words*, e.g.

[[horse donkey][masterpiece kitsch][wine vinegar][watermelon pumpkin]].

Then they create a procedure generating variations of the original aphorism:

```
TO APHORYSM :LIST1 :LIST2
  MAKE :PAIR1 PICK :LIST1
  MAKE :PAIR2 PICK :LIST2
  OUTPUT (SENTENCE "The FIRST :PAIR1~
  [started resembling]~
  LAST :PAIR1 [- like a translation from]~
  FIRST :PAIR2 "to LAST :PAIR2)
END
```

Achilles: Let me try it with appropriate inputs:

```
PRINT APHORYSM [[horse donkey][masterpiece kitsch][wine vinegar]]~
[German Dutch] [English Greek][Russian Bulgarian]
```

I'll run it twice:

The wine started resembling vinegar – like a translation from Russian to Bulgarian.
The masterpiece started resembling kitsch – like a translation from English to Greek.

Turtle: Of course, the success of the joke depends on many factors, but the important thing in such an activity is that students grasp the structure of the genre, that they understand what is fixed and what can be modified so that the sense of the aphorism remains the same. Still, they are surprised by the great variety of aphorisms generated by the above Logo procedure, especially if they have created long enough associative lists.

Achilles: Do you know aphorisms of a similar structure but based on semantically distant words?

Turtle: Here you are—an aphorism by Carl Sandburg on poetry:

Poetry is the synthesis of hyacinths and biscuits.

Achilles: So, I can slightly edit the APHORISM procedure by providing it with an input which is an associative list of words which differ semantically, e.g.

```
[[hyacinths biscuits] [diamonds puddles] [stoves orchids] [perfume glue]]
```

Turtle: Yes, the very activity of making lists *of semantically close* or *distant words* (which does not have corresponding semantic categories), could be an interesting learning activity in a language context.

82

Scene 4 – Modeling Dull Jokes

Achilles: Creating new semantic categories of words might be interesting indeed, but what educational value could you find in modeling dull jokes?

Turtle: By the way, there are aspects of the dull jokes related to AI and education. Although Minsky is not optimistic that it is possible to define a humor grammar, he argues that humor has a practical function in the learning process—that is related to how jokes have a way of subverting the censors in our mind that protect us from illogical thoughts. The most productive forms of thought are just the ones which are most vulnerable to errors.

Achilles: This probably means that if we confined ourselves to cautious, logical reasoning, we would be less open to new ideas. Give me a classical example of a dull joke.

Turtle: Here is one by Freud:
Life is like a chain bridge.
In what way?
How should I know?

Achilles: From what I learned so far, a possible Logo procedure for generating variations on this joke would look like as follows:

```
TO NONSENSE
    OUTPUT (SENTENCE SOMETHING [is like a] SOMETHING_SIMILAR)
END
```

Here the subprocedures SOMETHING and SOMETHING_SIMILAR could be defined as follows:

```
TO SOMETHING
    OUTPUT PICK [Life Death Love Destiny]
END


TO SOMETHING_SIMILAR
    OUTPUT PICK [[chain bridge][running river][slipping moment]~
    [boundless sea] [flower field]]
END
```

As you can figure out, the SOMETHING procedure generates a word randomly picked from the list [Life Death Love Destiny] which contains the word *Life* together with other words I have suggested. The SOMETHING_SIMILAR procedure generates a phrase randomly picked from a list suggested by me (or potentially, by the students) but which does contain *chain bridge* after the original being modeled. Thus, each execution of NONSENSE would output one of the twenty possible sentences, including the original one, e.g.

Life is like a running river.
Love is like a chain bridge.
Death is like a slipping moment.
Love is like a flower field.

The last two lines of the original nonsense could be varied by means of the same mechanism and added to the NONSENSE procedures in a super procedure DIALOG:

```
TO DIALOG
    PRINT NONSENSE
    PRINT PICK [[How come?][What do you mean?][In what way?][How is  that?]]
    PRINT PICK [[How should I know..][I wonder myself...][God knows...]
END
```

83

Turtle: Your NONSENSE could be made more flexible by letting Logo combine randomly the adjectives with the nouns thus allowing for somewhat unusual combinations, e.g. *running sea, chain moment, flower bridge,* etc.

Achilles: So, in this case I could say that AI generates *natural stupidity*.

Intermission

Act 5

Scene 1 – Enter Recursion: Polygons and Spirals (Things #6 and #7)

Turtle: Practically every book on Logo starts with amazing drawings I can draw with just two commands FORWARD and RIGHT (and of course, a great informatics tool called recursion).

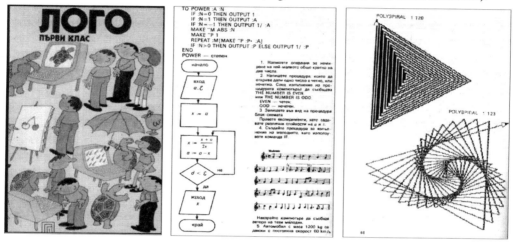

Fig. 15. *The first Logo book in Bulgarian (Nikolov, 1983)*

In the early 1980s, V. V. Davydov, a famous Russian psychologist, visited a school in the country (Blagoevgrad), a day earlier than he was expected. When entering the school, he smiled and said: "I know that you would show the best you have to a guest, but I want a realistic picture." The teacher looked at me slightly embarrassed, but I encouraged her to carry out her plan for the day. The lesson was exploring procedures for drawing spirals with parameters (the angle of the turtle turn and the size of the initial segment). The self-similarity of the construction naturally led the fifth graders to write a recursive procedure (Fig. 16).

```
TO SPIRAL :SIZE :ANGLE
   FORWARD :SIZE
   RIGHT :ANGLE
   SPIRAL :SIZE+5 :ANGLE
END
```

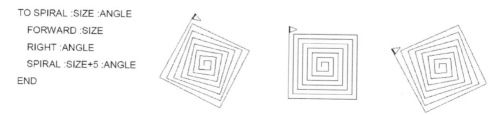

Fig. 16. *Looking for patterns while experimenting with a Logo procedure for spirals (Sendova, 2013)*

By experimenting with various values for the ANGLE parameter the students found interesting patterns. They were able to create spirals with the shape of regular polygons, and to produce switching spirals with a fixed number and direction of branches. They introduced a parameter for the increment of SIZE and explored another rule of augmenting it (SIZE*2). (Although they didn't know at the time that they were getting the graphical representations of arithmetic and geometric sequences, this was an excellent introduction for constructing a better understanding of these notions). Then the students decided to check what would happen if they fixed the first parameter (SIZE) and increased the ANGLE. The latter idea was born with the help of the teacher who was thus preparing the ground for experiments in science with processes depending on several parameters. The visitor was genuinely surprised, and the teacher and I felt happy that he could experience the creative atmosphere typical for the *Language and Mathematics* classes without doubts about it being staged for his benefit.

Scene 2 – The Cat Comes Back!

Cat: I can also draw beautiful figures in Scratch like POLY and POLYSPI (Fig. 17).

```
TO POLY :STEP :ANGLE
1   FORWARD :STEP
2   LEFT :ANGLE
3   POLY :STEP :ANGLE
END
```

```
TO POLY :STEP :ANGLE
1   FORWARD :STEP
2   LEFT :ANGLE
3   POLY :STEP+5 :ANGLE
END
```

Fig. 17. *Logo procedures for Things #6 and #7*

Here is one I got with POLY, using the angle 150 (Fig. 18). (Not quite sure though why 150…)

Fig. 18. POLY 100 150 *in Scratch*

Turtle: The trick here is not only to play with numbers and say: "It's beautiful, let me try with other numbers."

Students should be encouraged to find a pattern that helps them to conduct experiments on the inputs so that they generate something they want, e.g. the number and type of rays of a star-polygon. For instance, in the case of a spiral generated by stars with twelve rays, they could give ANGLE the value of 5*360/12 (without even bothering to calculate it).

Achilles: How did you figure it out?

Turtle: Some teachers would say: "Because I am smart!" But I prefer to reach the answer together with my students. I give them a procedure for drawing simple N_gons, then we play with the procedure:

```
To N_STAR :N :TURNS
   REPEAT :N [FORWARD 100 RIGHT :TURNS*360/:N]
END
```

And then they find a lot of interesting relations between number theory and geometry. After performing a number of experiments with different values of N and TURNS they figure out that for the N_STAR procedure to generate a star with N rays, they have to take TURNS to be mutually prime with N. They might find different possible solutions and decide which of the possible values of TURN would make the rays sharper, and which make them flatter.

But you, Cat, hide part of the beauty of the figures you draw!

Cat: I am sorry, Turtle, but if you don't like my Cat appearance, I can act like a bee (Fig. 19):

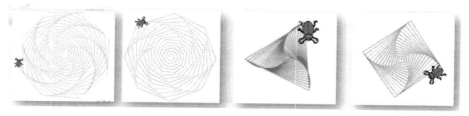

Fig. 19. *Experiments with* POLYSPI *in Scratch*

And I can modify the POLYSPI procedure by adding a figure at each corner of the spiral and (if needed) erasing its trace (Fig. 20):

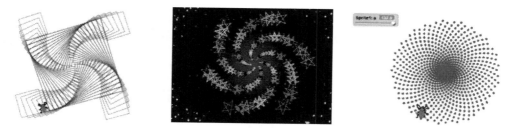

Fig. 20. *Variations on* POLYSPI *in Scratch*

The sunflower (Fig. 20, right) took me the longer time to model—I had to discover the angle at which the sunflower seeds would be spread like in nature!

Scene 3 – Modeling Ferns

Turtle: I know that children are crazy about colors, sounds, and animation but in my youth, I was absolutely happy to produce plants such as the fern. At the time my geometry was also called the geometry of FORWARD and RIGHT (НАПРЕД and НАДЯСНО in Bulgarian). See my work (Fig. 21):

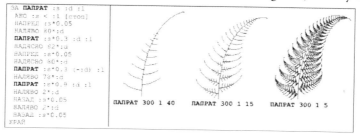

Fig. 21. *Modeling a fern with the Bulgarian version of Comenius Logo (Sendova, 2017)*

Of course, I have done it in other environments as well (Fig. 22).

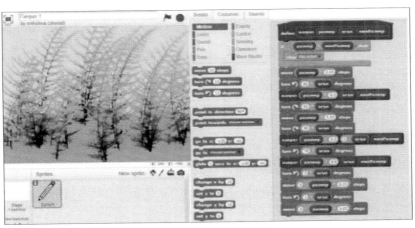

Fig. 22. *Modeling a fern in Elica Logo with a 3D turtle (Boytchev, 2003) (top left), in Imagine (with high school students from Stara Zagora) (top right), and in Scratch (Sendova E. et al., 2018) (bottom)*

Epilogue

Scene 1 – Together Again: Achilles, Cat, and Turtle

Achilles: To prove to you that I am fully inspired by the twenty things of CS, here is a procedure I came up with:

```
to things_inspired_by_20_things :list_of _things :pages :limit
    If :pages> :limit [output :list_of _things]
    things_inspired_by_20_things fput new_thing :list_of _things
    :pages+1 :limit
end
```

But let me ask you this: With five decades using computers in modeling a vast range of activities—from composing and harmonizing 8-bar tunes, to the mechanism of cell differentiation, and four decades of implementing the educational spirit of the CS article in a Bulgarian setting—what would you describe as the *Logo spirit*?

Turtle: For the members of the informatics team at the Research Group on Education (RGE) at the Bulgarian Academy of Sciences, the fundamental aspect of a computer microworld was its being an environment facilitating discovery learning—experimentation, hypothesis generation,

87

testing, and open-ended explorations. Furthermore, we wanted the microworld to be a medium where the learner's understanding of the phenomena (specific for the domain) is enhanced during the process of learning via programming. An excellent example of a microworld is the Logo Turtle geometry (the turtle being *the object to think with*). And what is associated often with explorations in appropriately designed microworlds is the so-called *Logo spirit*. It goes beyond the principle learning by doing and combines it with discussing and reflecting about what we have done. This spirit is not dependent on the programming language itself, but rather on the philosophy and the culture we associate with the word Logo.

We have frequently found that actually trying out a certain idea in the form of a program can provide new insights. Experimenting with the formalization of this idea brings out further insights, providing a real understanding, which, in turn, possibly provides for a new formalization and new ideas.

Cat: What was the role of the teachers then and what should it be now, under such different circumstances?

Turtle: Take a deep breath and listen to my favorite story.

Scene 2 – Ten Rules for Creative Teaching

Turtle: The leader of the Research Group on Education, Blagovest Sendov, has pointed out what a crucial mistake it would be to think that teachers could be replaced by good text books or well-programmed computers. In essence, they are creative personalities and should not be told what to do. In this regard he made an interesting observation concerning the biblical Ten Commandments—that they are "do nots", e.g. "Thou shalt have no other gods before Me!" The only exception is "Honor thy father and thy mother"! And it is this approach, the freedom to choose and act, subject to only a few fundamental, necessary constraints that appeals to man's creative nature. Thus to recommend to teachers exactly what to do in every circumstance would stifle their creative abilities. I would dare to tell teachers only what they should *not* do, and so avoid deviation from the basic principles I have derived from the Logo community and my personal experience with teachers and students alike. Here are my ten rules (Sendova, 1990) and the corresponding cartoons, drawn originaly by Todor Kolarov (Sendova, 1987) and remade by Yovko Kolarov.

1

You should not lead children to predetermined solutions. (In informatics there are often no right answers but rather right paths.)

2

Eureka!

εὕρηκα!

You should not deprive children of the pleasure of solving problems by themselves.

3

You should not let children become discouraged.

4

You should not show a Logo facility that is new to chidlren unless they see a need for it. (Or, as others put it, programming should not be a goal, but a tool.)

5

You should not be afraid of cooperation with children as equal partners and certainly not afraid of learning from them.

6

You should not automatically reject an unexpected result obtained in the process of programming but rather analyze and explore it.

7

You should not think of programs as being right or wrong but rather as artifacts that could be developed and improved.

8

You should not let students be afraid of making mistakes. Moreover, it may well be that the approach of debugging is one of the most profound educational ideas of twentieth century.

Fig. 23. *Scanned fragments of Ten Rules with added translations. Artist: Todor Kolarov (Sendova, 1987)*

Words of Thanks

Acknowledgments to Gary Stager for the invitation and the great initiative, to Cynthia Solomon for being such an inspiration during the years with all her activities, and to Artemis Papert for sharing pictures and her love for turtle art. Special thanks go to Sylvia Martinez for her editorial help in making this essay sound more like a "horse" than a "donkey."

My deep appreciation goes to the international Logo community for keeping the Logo spirit alive through all these years with the Eurologo and Constructionism conferences and related books and journals.

My special gratitude to the pillars of the Bulgarian Logo culture—Roumen Nikolov, for creating the first Logo text book and the first Logo version in Bulgarian; Bojidar Sendov for designing and leading the development of Geomland as a mathematical laboratory for exploration in Euclidian geometry in a Logo spirit; Darina Dicheva for co-authoring a number of informatics textbooks in Logo style; Iliana Nikolova for leading a Logo center at the Faculty of Mathematics and Informatics at Sofia University and a project for adapting Comenius Logo for the Bulgarian Schools; Ivaylo Ivanov and Vesela Ilieva for developing educational resources for the primary school in Bulgaria; and finally to Pavel Boytchev who created Elica (a 3D Logo environment), the Logo tree project, and a whole dynamic ecosystem in which versions of Logo emerge and communicate with a variety of programming languages, virtual educational environments, educational video-clips, games, films, and exhibitions with artistic value. It was his idea to present this dialog like a play with acts and scenes.

The biggest THANK YOU goes to the numerous teachers and students who proved that they *can* do twenty things (and many more) with a computer thanks to a teacher and friend such as Seymour Papert—a genius and dreamer with the curiosity of a child.

References

Boytchev, P. (2003). *Turtle Metamorphoses (From FD 1 to 3D Animated Characters)*. Proceedings of 9th European Logo Conference Eurologo 2003, Porto, Portugal, 50-61.

Brooks, F. P., Hopkins, A. L., Neumann, P. G., & Wright, W. V. (1993). *An Experiment in Musical Composition*. In S. Schwanauer & D. Levitt (Eds.), Machine Models of Music. MIT Press.

Brooks, S., & Ross, B. (1996). Automated compositions from computer models of biological behavior. *Leonardo Music Journal, Vol, 6*, 27-31.

Carroll, L. (1895). What the Tortoise Said to Achilles. *Mind, 4*(14), 278-280.

Dijkstra, E. W. (1972). The Humble Programmer. *Comunications of the ACM, 15*(10), 859-866. dl.acm. org/doi/pdf/10.1145/355604.361591

Dimova, S., & Kolarova (Sendova), E. (1971). Modelling of Creative Processes in Music. *Vselena'70 Вселена'70, Nauka i Izkustvo, Sofia (in Bulgarian).*

Duclos, M. (2006). *Kenneth White – Nomade intellectuel, poète du monde.* micheleduclos.files.wordpress. com/2014/12/livre-ellug.pdf

Freud, S. (1916). *Wit and Its Relation to the Unconscious.* Sofia (in Bulgarian).

Goldenberg, E. P. (1989). Linguistics, Science, and Mathematics for Pre-college Students: A Computational Modeling Approach. *Proceedings, National Education Computing Conference NECC'89*(June 20-22), 87-93.

Goldenberg, E. P., & Feurzeig, W. (1987). *Exploring Language with Logo.* MIT Press.

Hiller, L. A., & Isaacson, L. M. (1959). *Experimental Music.* Mc Graw-Hill.

Hofstadter, D. R. (1980). *Gödel, Escher, Bach.* Vintage Books.

Howe, H., & Kassler, M. (1980). Computers and Music. In *New Grove Dictionary of Music and Musicians* (Vol. 4, pp. 613). Macmillan.

Johnson, T. (1996). *Self-Similar Melodies.* Two Eighteen Press.

Mason, S., & Saffe, M. (1994). L-Systems, Melodies and Musical Structure. *Leonardo Music Journal, No.1*, 31-38.

Minsky, M. (1985). Censors and Jokes. *The Society of Mind, Simon Schuster, NY.*

Nikolov, R. (1983). *Logo. An Experimental Textbook for 5th Grade.* RGE, Sofia (in Bulgarian).

Nikolov, R., & Sendova, E. (1984). *Language and Mathematics (Logo), An Experimental Textbook for 6th Grade.* RGE, Sofia, (in Bulgarian), 71.

Nikolov, R., & Sendova, E. (1989). *Informatics for Beginners (Part 1).* Narodna prosveta, 92 (in Bulgarian).

Sendov, B. (1987). Education for an Information Age. *Impact of Science on Society, 37*(2), 193-201.

Sendova, E. (1987). Ten Rules. *Informatics-Mathematics Journal, RGE, Sofia (in Bulgarian)*, 87-92.

Sendova, E. (1988). *Logo for Philologists (Teachers' Handbook).* RGE, Sofia.

Sendova, E. (1990). *Are There Rules for Creative Teaching Informatics, T.H.E. Journal, December/January, vol. 17, No. 5, 68-71.*

Sendova, E. (2001a). *Computer Microworlds and Models for Integrating the Learning and Creative Processes.* PhD Thesis, Sofia].

Sendova, E. (2001b). *Modelling Creative Processes in Abstract Art and Music.* Eurologo 2001, Proceedings of the 8th European Logo Conference 21-25 August, Linz, Austria.

Sendova, E. (2008). Materializing Model-like Hypotheses in Language, Poetry and Humor by Means of a Computer Microworld. *Cognitive Studies | Etudes cognitive* (8), 273-285.

Sendova, E. (2013). Assisting the Art of Discovery at School Age: The Bulgarian experience. In P. Sanchez-Escobedo (Ed.), *Talent Development Around the World* (pp. 39-98). Merida, Yucatán.

Sendova, E. (2017). Constructionism as an Educational Philosophy and a Culture - a Tribute to Seymour Papert. *Proceedings of the Forty-sixth Spring Conference of the Union of Bulgarian Mathematicians Borovets. April 9-13*, 29-51. math.bas.bg/smb/2017_PK/tom_2017/pdf/029-051.pdf

Sendova, E., & Grkovska, S. (2005). Visual Modeling as a Motivation for Studying Mathematics and Art. *Educational Media International, 42*(2), 173-180.

Sendova, E., & Sendov, B. (1999). *Harnessing the Power of Programming to Support Explorations in Euclidean Geometry* (Vol. 9 No.3/4, 183-200). International Journal of Continuing Engineering Education and Life-Long Learning.

Sendova E., Nikolov, R., & Boytchev, P. (2018). A Glance Backward with Nostalgy and Forward with Optimism (or do we need to start from Scratch when introducing children to programming) *XI National Conference "Education and Research in the Information Society".* sci-gems.math.bas.bg:8080/jspui/ bitstream/10525/2957/1/ERIS2018-book-p16.pdf

Stager, G. (1986). Logo and Music – A Powerful Tool for Learning. *Logo'86 Proceedings*, 247-249.

Veselinova, E. (2020). Let's compose my musical masterpiece in… Scratch, or my variation of the "Ode to Joy". *EU Code Week Blog.* blog.codeweek.eu/lets-compose-my-musical-masterpiece-in-scratch-or-my-variation-of-the-ode-to-joy/

Zaripov, R. K., & Russell, J. (1969). Cybernetics and Music. *Perspectives of New Music, 7*(2), 115-154.

Маяковский, В. (1959). *Полное собрание сочинений* (Mayakovsky, Vladimir, Complete works), 447.

Notes

1 Using the term "oriental" is increasingly controversial, especially when referring to people. There is disagreement about whether the term is racist when applied to things like food, rugs, or in this case, music. In this context, we made the editorial decision not to replace the term since Logo procedure names are by their very nature, arbitrary labels, and it appeared in this context in the original *Twenty Things* memo. Feel free to substitute another collection of letters as the procedure name if you wish.

I Learn How to Code and Lengthen My Reach #makingliberation

Susan Klimczak

"I got technology at learn 2 teach. . . I learn how to code and lengthen my reach"
From rap written by youth teacher Cypress Wilson

Is it possible to *make liberation* while exploring turtle geometry and coding? Exploring turtle geometry and TurtleStitch has really ignited my excitement and imagination as I work with the young people of color in Boston ranging from teen youth teachers in the Learn 2 Teach, Teach 2 Learn program, to younger children in the online STEM Explorers after-school program at the Gallivan Community Center.

TurtleStitch can also inspire teachers like me to fall in love with computers and coding all over again. Sarah Magner, a master teacher at the Flint Hill School in northern Virginia, shared with me that educators as well as youth need "moments for playing, the opportunity to learn in a way that we don't get an opportunity to do in our jobs." So, Cynthia Solomon and I have been meeting online weekly for Tea & TurtleStitch with educators from across the US and around the world!

These are some stories from our experiences about using computers, code, sewing machines, and online environments in new and exciting ways.

What is TurtleStitch?

TurtleStitch (turtlestitch.org) is a free online software application, built in Snap! Adults and youth are drawn to collaborate with code, computers, and a sewing machine as they create digital embroidery designs. The computer communicates with a computerized embroidery machine (like my sturdy little Brother SE600) using a USB drive loaded with files from TurtleStitch.

TurtleStitch is a whole activity. It is not just coding. It is a mix of art, design, and technology. It involves computers and coding, working with machines and materials, and making products. It affords a rich playground of exploration for beginners as well as experts. The struggle of thinking up a design, embroidering it, and especially creating something you use or look at everyday provides an environment of ups and downs and ups, capturing what Seymour Papert referred to as hard fun!

It also provides opportunities for falling in love with materials, for falling in love with what you create—and for falling in love with yourself as a learner and thinker. This love is often disregarded and de-emphasized in the teaching/learning experience of both educators and learners. It is a good and affirming thing to show your love and encourage learners. Everyone should be encouraged to not be afraid to show their love!

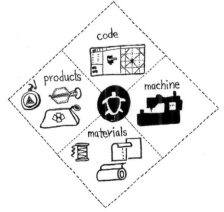

My Own Journey Falling in Love with TurtleStitch

My experience coming to TurtleStitch is rooted in my family culture and personal history. I grew up sewing and doing hand embroidery in a Polish working class family. I studied electrical engineering (the only woman in my class), learning to code in Fortran on punch cards! For the past twenty years, I have been engaged in the participatory design of learning and teaching with Boston youth of color in a makerspace that holds the first Fab Lab built outside of MIT. This is where I first met Cynthia Solomon, who helped our Learn 2 Teach, Teach 2 Learn STEAM (Science, Technology, Engineering, Art + Design, and Math) program youth in the early days.

Three things attracted me to TurtleStitch.

I was particularly drawn to approaches to computers that combined high and low technology through the work of MIT Media Lab researchers Leah Buechley and Jie Qi. They worked with our young people to sew circuits with conductive thread and create circuits on paper with craft materials. So the idea of learning and teaching coding and debugging through TurtleStitch immediately captured my imagination.

The social and creative learning opportunity to explore TurtleStitch with Cynthia Solomon over the past few years has excited and sustained my interest. The tremendous power and momentum that relationships and social learning play between educators is also too often overlooked or ignored. I certainly would not have progressed as far in my understanding of and work in organizing education with TurtleStitch without such a wonderful collaborator.

Finally, the potential for imagining and creating meaningful products featuring TurtleStitch designs is inspiring for both educators and learners. For me, it wasn't enough to just stitch the designs—I wanted to make them real and useful in the world.

For instance, I love the moon, enjoying its phases and movement through the sky. So I decided to celebrate the moon by combining the digital embroidery of my TurtleStitch design with "analog" embroidery with thread and beads. I then used a computer to design and lasercut a frame, which is hand-painted. It hangs above my desk at home, reminding me of the loves of my life—coding, embroidering, fabricating, and of course, the moon!

Cynthia and I also used TurtleStitch to make teaching aids. Seeing physical examples of actual stitches helps new TurtleStitchers design their code. These hang on the wall where we can grab them and toss them to young people as they learn.

Last year, I saw an article about Temari, balls with bells inside that Japanese grandmothers make for their grandchildren by wrapping thread in designs that look like TurtleStitch designs (Jobson, 2013). I imagined combining this with my childhood love of embroidery samplers in a way that could demonstrate the range of a TurtleStitcher's coded designs. Obviously a ball can't be laser cut with wood. Instead, I lasercut a cube with windows to display 6 different designs. I also put a little sleigh bell inside, just like Japanese grandmothers do. The sound reminds me of the many bells that have called me to meditation and mindfulness over the years.

Code Conversations between Educators and Youth

In *Twenty Things to Do with a Computer*, Seymour and Cynthia write that "transactions between children and computers" are a kind of "conversation." Cynthia and I recently taught TurtleStitch on Zoom with a group of 8-year-olds in a STEM Explorers program for the Gallivan Community Center in Mattapan, Massachusetts. We and the children were playing with text, stars, and regular polygons when Paul, who loves Minecraft, created a square using stars and the word "minecraft."

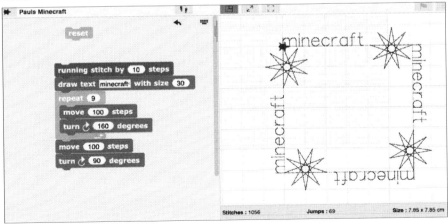

Paul's family also raises chickens. To our surprise and delight, the Lady Buffington chicken "liberated" herself from the pen, wandered into the house and flew up on the table. She looked at the computer and started pecking at the keys—she actually changed the TurtleStitch code! We all joked that Lady Buffington loved TurtleStitch so much, she wanted to learn to code, too. Paul and his sister Joybella joked that we should make a new design called "chickencraft," instead of "minecraft."

Cynthia and I continued giggling about this after class. We decided this idea deserved to be made real. Cynthia designed a simple chicken on TurtleStitch using the spiral and triangle procedures the children had been working with. I modified Paul's code and lasercut a frame for the digital embroidery. We not only sent Paul his original TurtleStitch design, turned into an case for the new earbuds he received for his birthday, we also sent him our improvisational "chickencraft" design as our response and as documentation of the chicken-human coding experience!

It was so much fun to have this "conversation" and see the delight on Paul's face after he received both his earbud case and "chickencraft" in the mail. The chickens and their new babies have become regular attendees at STEM Explorers. Though Lady Buffington died a week after this happened, we sent up blessings that she is teaching TurtleStitch coding to all her friends in chicken heaven!

On a more serious note, the Reggio Emilia approach lifts up the importance of documenting "traces of learning" ("The Power of Documentation in a Reggio-inspired Classroom," 2018). This "conversation" is an active example of lifting up a memorable social and emotional coding moment that was meaningful in the life of Paul and Joybella.

Playing with Teachers and Setting up Coding as a Way to Foster Creative Curiosity

My experience is that teachers are often apprehensive about incorporating computing into their classes because their imagination about good teaching is so aligned with the "expert" model. They often think that they must be experts in coding before they can begin teaching it. Creating learning environments where educators are able to take the time to play and nurture their own creative curiosity and love of coding is important. This can help them make a shift to exploring a new role as master learner with young people. Being adventurous in confronting mysterious bugs in the code together and discovering how to fix or feature them can be empowering

An exciting thing that happened during the pandemic is that people have been trying out different ways to learn, collaborate and play together using computers on platforms like Zoom, Google Hangout and Jitsi. People who live in different places in the US and beyond are now comfortable gathering together.

In the spirit of trying out new ways to use computers, Cynthia and I started a Sunday morning meetup called Tea & TurtleStitch. The timing allows educators from Europe, Africa, and the US to get together and play together with TurtleStitch. We were interested in the insights educators could discover from their own experiences about what children need in education, especially about the kind of creativity that is too often missing in public education today. My hope is that experiencing the power of play—rather than just instruction—will empower educators to advocate for educational change. The method Cynthia and I have developed—which builds on her experience teaching children Logo—is to help the teachers make blocks of code with input variables. These blocks allow them to explore the possibilities of different turtle geometries such as polygons, spirals, star polygons, star spirals, and arcs. They spend time experimenting and getting curious about what different inputs produce and how they can repeat the blocks in different ways. Here is an example of a spiral code for regular polygons with inputs side, turns, and number of sides and one design that a teacher produced during the tinkering time:

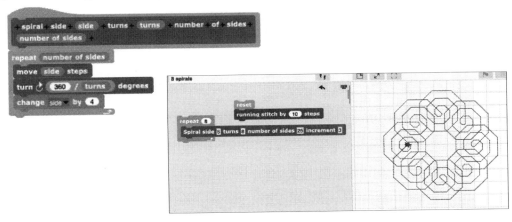

This gives teachers an opportunity to be curious about what will happen and to serendipitously explore the geometry of the spirals that appeal to them, rather than have a singular end goal of producing a specific spiral out of a specific regular polygon. I want teachers not only to use their computers to gain TurtleStitch skills, but to change how coding is taught so that a way opens to "introduce everyone of whatever age . . . to programming," as Seymour and Cynthia put it in *Twenty Things to do with a Computer.*

The Power of Using Computers to Show Off

Young people at Learn 2 Teach, Teach 2 Learn make their TurtleStitch designs into everyday products they want using hand sewing and regular machine stitching. Necklaces, earbud cases, backpack tags, zipper bags, and upcycled clothing are some of the things they have created to show off their TurtleStitch designs.

In fact, I was delighted to see youth teacher Makenda recently. She was proudly wearing the earbud case on her belt that she had designed with code and sewed eight months ago! She obviously loves and treasures it. I am delighted that she chooses to show off her coding skills and I imagine her joy when friends ask her about it and she says, "I made that!" (with a computer!). It is a tangible thing that reminds her to think about how she knows and what she knows.

Everyday use of TurtleStitch designs in products like these are examples of the necessary "public entities" of constructionism and collaboration with computers. When their friends and families ask about these products, young people have more opportunities to explain and appreciate their learning process.

LET'S SHOW OFF

When people look at us, do you believe they see
our knowledge, our accomplishments, our ambition?

All they see are the colors, nothing more
from the color of our hair to the skin that we wear.

Instead of taking offense, LET'S SHOW OFF...

Put them in a state of convolution when the words
Flowing from your mouth are words of wisdom.

For once, let's show them we can create.

We too can transcend above the world.

SO LET'S SHOW OFF!

Let's diminish the misconception of us and the life we live.

Let's not retaliate against the ignorance of the others
with violence because that will only hurt them physically
and that is morally unjust

Let's retaliate with our knowledge
because that will get us a home, one without bars.

This will get us a dream and help us prevail to the stars!

SO LET'S SHOW OFF!

Let's help them not to misconstrue, but to see depth
in the real you.

Break barriers, pave paths, you lead the way and
you change the world.

Poem by a Learn 2 Teach, Teach 2 Learn Youth Teacher
Jammy Torres Age 17

From the beginning of their work together, Seymour and Cynthia wanted to make constructionism available to *everyone* and saw constructionism as an approach that could "help kids from all racial, social, and economic backgrounds improve their learning and thinking" because "there is hope for *every* child" (Harel, 2016). A close collaborator, Gary Stager, in a tribute to Seymour said, "From his early days as an anti-apartheid dissident in 1940s South Africa to his work with children in underserved communities and neglected settings around the world, social justice and equity was a current running through all of Papert's activities" (Stager, 2017).

For our teen youth teachers of color, the act of "showing off" what they learn is also an act of resistance and a call to change. I think this is best demonstrated by a poem written by former youth teacher Jammy Torres that hangs in the Learn 2 Teach, Teach 2 Learn makerspace: This practice of showing off things that young people make with code can actually disrupt the prejudice, low expectations, and negative attitudes from people and media that they face daily in their lives. As Jammy says, it "helps [others] not to misconstrue but to see depth in the real you."

Showing off products can be one small step toward liberation. I remember one day many years ago, a teacher walked into the makerspace and asked what we were doing. One of her math students, who regularly slept through class and rarely completed homework, showed her something very complex that he had made at Learn 2 Teach, Teach 2 Learn. She was surprised at his ingenuity and the depth of his understanding and wanted to know what was happening in our makerspace that inspired him in a way her class did not. She started using the power of hand-on project-based learning in her math classroom and a few years later won a Teacher of the Year award at her school. Showing off products can be one small step toward liberation through an education so it works for all our young people.

Closing with Technologies of the Heart

These are some of the things that have made me fall in love with coding and the many expressive things that we can do with computers when we combine it with a practice of what my mentor Mel King calls the "Technologies of the Heart." His vision is that these technologies should bring out the best in us, bring out the best in our relationships with each other (and computers!), and bring out the best in our communities and our planet.

To answer the question posed at the start, yes, #MakingLiberation with computers is possible! I have witnessed how TurtleStitch can help youth and teachers experience the joys of geometry and see the creative potential and meaningful use of math through coding and sewing patterns. I've seen children be empowered by expressing themselves through design. I've seen teachers struggle to experience and discover new ways of teaching and learning with code. And I've seen the immensely positive impact that young people showing off what they have made can have. Try it and you too will "lengthen your reach," just as youth teacher Cypress raps about!

References

Harel, I. (2016). A Glimpse into to the Playful World of Seymour Papert. Edsurge News. edsurge.com/news/2016-08-03-a-glimpse-into-the-playful-world-of-seymour-papert

Jobson, C. (2013). A Huge Collection of Embroidered Temari Spheres by an 88-Year-Old Grandmother. Colossal. thisiscolossal.com/2013/12/temari/#:~:text=Temari%20balls%20are%20a%20form,-Year's%20day%20as%20special%20gift

The Power of Documentation in a Reggio-inspired Classroom. (2018). Compass School Blog. thecompassschool.com/blog/power-documentation-reggio-inspired-classroom/

Stager, G. (2017). Seymour Papert - Father of the Maker Movement. Invent to Learn. inventtolearn.com/seymour-papert-father-of-the-maker-movement/

The Best Day Ever

Cathy Hunt

In the early 1980s, when the dinosaurs walked the earth, I was in primary school.

My Dad had a keen interest in electronics. He was so clever, always tinkering or building something, publishing technical work on radars amongst other things. And he was an early adopter when it came to technology. Dad bought a computer home from work, and I remember the excitement, how he spoke of "potential" and the future and changing lives. Together, we guessed at what we could do together. We wondered, if the computer had legs or could fly, what that might mean. If the computer wanted to help, could it do good? If it could make art, what it might draw?

We were the first kids to have a computer in our neighborhood. Since I'd always been told that my grandmother was the first woman to drive a car in Melbourne, it just made sense to me. The novelty meant that in those early days, it was like having a new baby in the house. Family and friends, old and young, would come by to marvel at the blinking green cursor. Sometimes, a friend of a friend would ask to come and visit, students from the university popped in, a guy who Dad got chatting to at the hardware store... and everyone hoped to be the chosen one when it was time to insert a floppy disk into the mysterious abyss.

Of all these fond memories of our friendly IBM PC, it is the Grade 1 Bring Your Parent to School Week that stands out. In hindsight, I feel like the concept may have been significantly misinterpreted, since as far as I know, no one discussed Dad's "important job" at all, because he offered to bring his computer in for show and tell. It was, according to six-year-old Me, "The Best Day Ever."

Unlike other parents who came to school toting a briefcase at best, my dad pulled into the loading zone with a rented trailer. He'd taken a day off work. With this kit and commitment he appeared a little like Batman to me as he exited the car in slow motion. The helper students, who had almost dislocated their shoulders volunteering with vigorous hands up, flocked to the car to carry in equipment and be a part of the spectacle.

A computer on campus! Surely this was the greatest day at school ever. As far as I was aware, I had never been a part of anything as important as this. My friend Kelly, who had her finger on the pulse as the weekly classroom monitor, told me so. Then she asked if she would get to use the keyboard first due to her associated importance as my best mate.

Despite the hype, to be honest the computer just looked big and heavy, like a refrigerator, wrapped in swarths of bubble wrap. Some students worried that there were no visibly flashing lights or dials; hopefully it had not been broken in the journey. The principal herself came out to the car park to supervise the enthusiastic cast of thousands, escorting the precious still-not-beeping-or-blinking cargo to the security of the classroom. Once we got there, sweating and grunting, there were no tables trusted to take the weight. But technical difficulties were "all part of the experience, kids" and before too long a wooden picnic table appeared.

Dad plugged in cords and pushed buttons and spent the whole morning getting our dream machine fired up with Logo. Intrigued teachers dropped in and out of the classroom between servings of instant coffee and finally we were all set to play with The Turtle on our computer by lunch time.

The Turtle. It was everything we'd hoped it would be.

With the turtle, we made circles. Big and small. All different colors. We made diagonal lines race across the screen again and again, and we screeched with delight as they filled the screen. We made spirals and looked to our protractors to change them and suddenly they were patterns. There were mistakes, there was raucous laughter, and then periods of intense frustration. We solved problems, and when we couldn't, we told the turtle very definitely that she was wrong and that we didn't say to do that! But the turtle remained calm, and quietly righted itself when we made changes to our code.

And so we learned.

I can't remember those first lines of code, I can't see the images we created in my mind's eye, and I have nothing that I can hold in my hand to remind me of the lessons that day. But the memories, the moments of magic, the mischief, and the madness—they've stayed with me always.

And I continue to learn from Papert's work.

When I reflect on my first experiences of Logo as a student, it's now flavored by twenty years in the classroom. Through this lens, it's obvious that Solomon and Papert's more procedural guides such as *Twenty Things* reveal a depth of understanding born of observing children's responses to objects they find, and how they spark curiosity. Reading their work as a teacher and an artist, computers become "found objects" for children, at times props for make-believe and play, full of possibility and wonder. Hardware softens, offering intrigue to the hand and eye, challenging what is known, and calling to the imagination. Metal and plastic, bits and bytes… it all becomes the means for children to express themselves, give voice to their ideas, make visible their thinking, feed their soul. And there is an opportunity for mutuality, for learners big and small to be together in the moment.

While the warmth of a responsive adult presence is not detailed in the step-by-step instructions Papert presents, the space to work into is there.

With no teaching in his computing experience, when Dad came to my Grade 1 classroom he felt this space, and worked into it.

With no computers in their teaching experience, our Grade 1 teachers saw this space, and they worked into it.

As Solomon and Papert suggest, it's not about what you learn, it is about a genuine interest in how learning happens. Perhaps the nature of a how-to guide doesn't immediately speak to the heart in the way that some other mediums may do, but this set of concrete examples swiftly gives way to a new language, a creative empowerment. I see Logo as a touchstone to his foundational belief in the value of children engaging in "hard fun."

I imagine that Cynthia Solomon and Seymour Papert both had the hearts of artists. Just as the Impressionists relied on the invention of the paint tube to develop a new visual language created *en plein air*, Logo provided twenty-six kids in the Western suburbs of Victoria with new tools to communicate and create *in plain sight*. Perhaps in both cases, you need only to know how to describe what you want in an appropriate language. Transcending art, computing, or labels, Solomon and Papert's contribution to education began a movement that advanced our understanding of the world. And all these years later, as an educator I see their legacy when our children have the same reaction to the turtle as I did.

The Best Day Ever indeed.

Section 2 —
Intellectual Timidity

Why then should computers in schools be confined
to computing the sum of the squares of the
first twenty odd numbers and similar so-called
"problem-solving" uses? Why not use then to
produce some action? There is no better reason
than the intellectual timidity of the computers-
in-education community, which seems remarkably
reluctant to use the computers for any purpose
that fails to look very much like something
that has been taught in schools for the past
centuries. This is all the more remarkable since
the computerists are custodians of a momentous
intellectual and technological revolution.
Concepts from the sciences of computation --
"cybernetics", "information theory", "artificial
intelligence" and all its other names — have
deeply affected thinking in biology, psychology
and even the philosophy of mathematics. Machines
from its engineering branches are changing our way
of life. How strange, then, that "computers in
education" should so often reduce to "using bright
new gadgets to teach the same old stuff in thinly
disguised versions of the same old way.

—*Twenty Things to Do with a Computer (1971)*

The Computer Programs the Child

Audrey Watters

"When people talk about computers in education," Seymour Papert and Cynthia Solomon wrote in 1971, "they do not all have the same image in mind. Some think of using the computer to program the kid; others think of using the kid to program the computer." This dichotomy—who or what programs whom or what—appears throughout Papert's writing. He observed in *Mindstorms* in 1980, for example, that "in most contemporary educational situations where children come into contact with computers the computer is used to put children through their paces, to provide exercises of an appropriate level of difficulty, to provide feedback, and to dispense information. The computer programming the child." Papert's vision—and Solomon's as well—was different. Instead, "the child programs the computer. And in teaching the computer how to think, children embark on an exploration about how they themselves think" (1980, p. 19). But some forty years after the release of *Mindstorms* and now fifty years after the publication of Papert and Solomon's essay *Twenty Things to Do with a Computer*, it seems clear that in most contemporary educational situations where children come in contact with computers, the computer still programs the child.

Indeed, a more apt title for an essay extolling the capabilities of digital devices today might be "Twenty Things Computers Do to Children." Computers surveil children. Computers discipline children. Computers data-mine children. Computers recommend books and lessons and college majors and career paths. Computers—or at least, the vast technology and education technology industries that peddle computers—profit from children. Despite the fervent belief of Papert and Solomon that computers marked a "momentous intellectual and technological revolution"—a revolution that could upend teaching and learning as we know it—computers circumscribe behaviors and potential rather than unlock imagination and intellect.

Even in those cases where children are ostensibly learning to program computers, the language used to describe these ventures often underscores the prevailing belief that computers are there to do things to children—this or that product teaches the child to code, that is, rather than the other way around. Moreover, these educational computing endeavors are often subsumed under quite naked corporate interests. Learn to code with Google. Learn to code with Microsoft. Learn to code with Disney. Computers brand children, shaping their intellectual experiences—not so as to turn them into epistemologists, as Papert hoped, but to turn them into "users" and hopefully into loyal customers. Much of the "learn to code" movement is not interested in the kinds of exploration that Papert believed the computer could unlock, the kinds of playful inquiry that Papert and Solomon's list of twenty things highlighted. Rather, the monied interests behind this movement today are keen to develop a workforce with certain, specific technical skills rather than, say, a citizenry that can think.

The computer programs the child.

Computers in education remain largely in the mode that Papert and Solomon described in 1971: "using bright new gadgets to teach the same old stuff in thinly disguised versions of the same old way." This is a testament, no doubt, to the conservative streak in schooling, but also to the lasting influence of programmed instruction, the predecessor to computer-assisted instruction.

Programmed instruction was the methodology developed by B. F. Skinner and his students for use with the Harvard psychology professor's teaching machine. The principles of programmed instruction will sound eerily familiar to those of "personalized learning" software today: a student moves through the exercises at his or her own pace, ensuring that a concept is mastered before moving on to the next. The lessons are thus perfectly tailored to each student's level of understanding, and as such mistakes are minimized—all in the service of the positive behavioral reinforcement that Skinner believed essential for learning. In the 1950s and 1960s, the goal was the teaching machine would program the child; today computer software promises the same.

It's commonplace to dismiss Skinner and behaviorism as irrelevant and outmoded. The latter was supplanted by cognitive science, or so the story goes. But clearly behaviorism's influence remains, not only in educational technology but in computing more broadly. Our digital devices nudge and cajole us, encouraging us to scroll and click. The behaviorist bent of computing isn't new; it's not something dreamed up in the innovation labs of Silicon Valley or Stanford University. The behaviorist bent could be found the cybernetics of the 1950s and 1960s; indeed Papert and Solomon mention the Pavlovian conditioning of dogs in their essay—"by ringing bells and delivering meat powder"—as an example of the kinds of tasks that computers in 1971 could perform. And Skinner, for his part, would argue that conditioning a dog and conditioning a child to learn are not dissimilar. The computer now rings bells and dispenses educational pellets to children.

The historian Ellen Condliffe Lagemann (1989) has argued that "one cannot understand the history of education in the United States during the twentieth century unless one realizes that Edward L. Thorndike won and John Dewey lost." That is to say, policies and practices privilege the data collection and analysis that comes from standardized testing rather than the inquiry and civic-mindedness of democratic education. I'd add to her assertion that one cannot understand the history of education technology in the United States unless one realizes that B. F. Skinner won and Seymour Papert lost. Layered on top of the standardized testing and the fetishization of data is an educational machinery that programs the child. Even in the face of all the learn-to-code brouhaha and the proliferation of makerspaces, multiple-choice testing has triumphed over democratically oriented inquiry. So when we hear technologists champion "personalized learning," it's far more likely that what they envision draws on Skinner's ideas, not Dewey's and not on Papert's.

To say that Skinner won and Papert lost doesn't mean that we should surrender. Educational institutions, beliefs, and practices are socially constructed after all, not set in stone. But as we think about what it means to make the ideas expressed in *Twenty Things to Do with a Computer* more of a reality for more children—intellectual inquiries in which children learn to understand and manipulate powerful scientific and philosophical ideas, we must recognize that the computers themselves are not the solution. Computers have become, in many ways, part of the problem.

When Papert (1993) described his work as "guided by the Robin Hood-like idea of stealing technology from the lords of the laboratories and giving it to the children of the world," it's worth considering what those laboratories were doing and building with computers. These were weapons of war, of surveillance, of control. It should be no surprise then that the ways in which children experience computers echo this—the computer monitors, disciplines, and programs the child. And no list of fun activities in and of itself can so easily counter that.

References

Lagemann, E. C. (1989). The Plural Worlds of Educational Research. *History of Education Quarterly, 29*, 185.

Papert, S. (1980). *Mindstorms: Children, Computers, and Powerful Ideas.* Basic Books.

Papert, S. (1993). *The Children's Machine: Rethinking School in the Age of the Computer.* Basic Books.

Where Have All the Metaphors Gone?

Gary S. Stager

Metaphors have a way of holding the most truth in the least space. —Orson Scott Card

Metaphors orient our stance, shape our priorities, and guide our practice. They govern who has agency in the educational process. Over the past fifty years, there have been prominent metaphors used to define and describe the pedagogical implementation of digital technology. Reviewing a few of these metaphors may refresh our memory, serve as a basis for dialogue, or inspire emergent strategies.

Over time, educational technology has come to mean anything with a battery or power cord. A once proud intellectual community has long since been replaced by a bazaar peddling new wine in old bottles. Entrepreneurs continuously reinvent digital flashcards, surveillance systems, and what *Twenty Things* described as "using bright new gadgets to teach the same old stuff in thinly disguised versions of the same old way."

> Even before the publication of Twenty Things, Seymour Papert was predicting the morass that would come to be known as educational technology.
>
> The phrase, "technology and education" usually means inventing new gadgets to teach the same old stuff in a thinly disguised version of the same old way. Moreover, if the gadgets are computers, the same old teaching becomes incredibly more expensive and biased towards its dumbest parts, namely the kind of rote learning in which measurable results can be obtained by treating the children like pigeons in a Skinner box (1970). [1]

Early Metaphors for Computers in Education

Cynthia Solomon's 1986 book *Computer Environments for Children: A Reflection on Theories of Learning and Education* explores how the perspectives of four men shaped the earliest visions of educational computing. Solomon used two metaphors to describe the philosophical stance guiding the design of educational computing environments.

> As a first strategy in exploring the many ways computers have been used in education, I focus on two images of the computer: (1) the computer as an interactive textbook in control of the user and (2) the computer as an expressive medium under the control of the user. As examples of the computer-as-textbook, I chose two different approaches. Patrick Suppes, of Stanford University, developed a system to provide students with sequenced drill-and-practice exercises, whereas Robert Davis, of the University of Illinois, using the Plato system, imbued the computer with a Socratic style of interaction. With regard to the computer as expressive medium, I again chose two approaches. Tom Dwyer and his colleagues at the Solo Works Laboratory at the University of Pittsburgh developed a variety of programming activities around BASIC, and Seymour Papert and his Logo group at the Massachusetts Institute of Technology developed new mathematics and new technology for children (Solomon, 1986).

There is not much serious discussion about distinct visions of computers in education today. Educators may organize around the products they consume or flaunt their certification in the use of those gadgets, but there is too little care given to a unifying view of how learning occurs or the role technology may play in facilitating that vision. Quite simply, we need a language to organize, plan, and realize our philosophical ideals.

The three metaphors Robert Taylor introduced at the dawn of microcomputers in school were the computer as tool, tutor, or tutee (Taylor, 1980). The first two are still used. The computer may be used to get work done or to teach you something. Solomon and Papert depart from both of these approaches. Therefore, Taylor invented a third metaphor to describe the approach described in *Twenty Things*, the computer as tutee.

> *To use the computer as tutee is to tutor the computer; for that, the student or teacher doing the tutoring must learn to program, to talk to the computer in a language it understands. The benefits are several. First, because you can't teach what you don't understand, the human tutor will learn what he or she is trying to teach the computer. Second, by trying to realize broad teaching goals through software constructed from the narrow capabilities of computer logic, the human tutor of the computer will learn something both about how computers work and how his or her own thinking works. Third, because no expensive predesigned tutor software is necessary, no time is lost searching for such software and no money spent acquiring it.*

> *The computer makes a good "tutee" because of its dumbness, its patience, its rigidity, and its capacity for being initialized and started over from scratch. Students "teach" it how to tutor and how to be a tool. For example, they have taught it to tutor younger students in arithmetic operations, to drill students on French verb endings, to play monopoly, to calculate loan interest, to "speak" another computer language, to draw maps, to generate animated pictures, and to invert melodies.*

> *Learners gain new insights into their own thinking through learning to program, and teachers have their understanding of education enriched and broadened as they see how their students can benefit from treating the computer as a tutee. As a result, extended use of the computer as tutee can shift the focus of education in the classroom from end product to process, from acquiring facts to manipulating and understanding them (Taylor, 1980).*

Clearly defined categories and delineated philosophical differences help educators justify their pedagogical practice.

Mucking About

Thomas Edison shared a great fondness for tinkering and learning-by-doing. He called his collaborators muckers. Mucking had its origins in perfecting bricks that could withstand transport through rain and snow without absorbing moisture while remaining porous to reduce furnace gases. Muck was the term used to describe the countless binding agents tested (Edison Muckers, 2010). "Mucking about" is what scientists and craftsmen do. Solomon and Papert admired David Hawkins who also recognized the value of mucking. His 1965 essay "Messing About with Science" (1965, 2002) influenced a great number of progressive educators.

Papert continuously sought to find ways of describing the powerful ideas of *Twenty Things* and subsequent work in a fashion comprehensible to the laity. He loved playing with language and traded in parables. *Muck, mud, messing, mucking* was just the sort of wordplay Seymour enjoyed. In 1984, Papert offered an endearing metaphor of computing that should be universally understood—the computer as mudpie.

I would like to think of the computer as a clapping hand, as a mudpie, as the pencil that you use to scribble on the walls and get into trouble with (because you want to get into trouble too, it's a highly charged thing to do). This is the kind of use of the computer that I think is radically, deeply important for changing the conditions of learning. Needless to say, I am not talking about the computer as a "teaching machine." We all recognize the popular image of the computer being used to teach or to program the child, and I would like to emphasize the absurdity of that...

... Now, putting the computer in the hands of the child, and allowing the child to dance with it, or to play with the computer like a mudpie, could mean that the child will learn certain concepts in a natural way. He or she wouldn't need to be "taught" it. The height of perversity is not to allow children to use the computer to acquire concepts in a natural way, so that they can go on not acquiring the concepts, and then come to school where we try to use the computer to improve the process of artificially teaching things that they didn't learn in a natural way. This is contradictory and perverse, and yet, generally speaking, it is what we do. Why? When computers first appeared on the scene they were exotic, expensive, fragile, hard-to-use devices that one had to keep in air-conditioned rooms. There were not very many computers, and so we could give children access to them for only ten or twenty minutes at a time, and then we would make the children go away. Under those conditions there was very little that anyone could do with the computer, except something called "drill and practice," where the computer says: "What is 17 times 8?" and you say, jokingly, "32." And it says, "No, try again." (Papert, 1984).

"Computer as Mudpie" continues to make several powerful arguments still relevant today. (The emphasis is mine.)

That way of using the computer does not demand particular access to it. *But I would like to consider the computer in a very different way: as mudpie. You can make a mudpie when you want to and play with it as your personal desires direct you. You do not practice mudpie ten minutes a day, because your schedule says that now it is mudpie time. In other words,* **I am talking about a world in which children have free access to a computer.** *They can decide where to go with it, and what they want to do with it. They can play with it without adults standing over their shoulders.* **They can take possession of it, rather than be possessed by it** *(Papert, 1984).*

It is sadly the case that critics of computers in education often are correct to conclude that learners benefit very little from educational technology. This is especially true when technology is used to minimize student agency or reinforce the dominance of the front of the classroom. By the late 1960s, Seymour Papert and Arthur Luehrmann were asking the question[2], *"Does the computer program the child or the child program the computer?"* (Luehrmann, 1971, 2002). So much of what computers are used for in schools today hardly justifies their presence. Learning to program and programming to learn is perhaps the best way computers add value to an educational context.

Computer as Material

When people talk about computers in education, they do not all have the same image in mind. Some think of using the computer to program the kid; others think of using the kid to program the computer. But most of them have at least this in common: the transaction between the computer and the kid will be some kind of "conversation" or "questions and answers" in words or numbers. —Papert & Solomon, Twenty Things

In 1987, Seymour Papert and New York City public school teacher George Franz found a particularly evocative way of communicating the powerful ideas of *Twenty Things* and anticipating the maker movement twenty years in the future. In a middle school science classroom, students were encouraged to invent all sorts of clocks.

> *While some students were speaking the language of Logo in order to achieve their goal of making a timer, others were speaking the language of a chisel, or of a battery and electric motor, or of a ball rolling down an inclined plane. Most of these languages were new to the children. What was important was that the students were learning to speak the languages of many different materials in the classroom in an attempt to create their clocks from ideas in their minds. When the students let their imaginations go, they found a variety of odds and ends for different explorations and investigations. The emphasis was on inquiry and learning, not on the type of material used. The computer was just one more material, alongside candles, crayons, ammeters, and rulers. The computer did, however, add dimensions not present in other materials, allowing students to go beyond the capabilities of the clocks constructed with the more commonly found materials (Papert & Franz, 1987).*

In this enormously important and underappreciated article, "Computer as Material: Messing About with Time," Papert and Franz make explicit connections between the ideas of Robert Taylor, David Hawkins, Jean Piaget, John Dewey, Eleanor Duckworth, and Susan and Nathan Isaacs, as well as tacitly share the ideals of other progressive movements, most notably the Reggio Emilia Approach. However, the article does not seek to minimize the power or significance of the computer by making it equal to non-computational materials. The computer adds precision, flexibility, and extensibility to making things. The things you make may be then used to make other things or integrated into other inventions.

> *The computer clocks, as compared with those made from other materials, were unique in several aspects. First, these clocks could be extremely accurate. As we have noted, some students calibrated them to tenths of a second. This high degree of accuracy is clearly unparalleled when compared with the other types of clocks the students made, and the students appreciated this accuracy when they wanted to time their LEGOmobile's speed precisely.*

> *Second, it was quite simple to adjust the speed of the LOGO clocks by changing the number following the WAIT command. Thus, it was relatively easy to match the handmade LOGO clock to the clock on the wall or the wrist. By contrast, calibrating the sand clocks meant ripping them apart and changing the size of the hole through which the sand flowed. Only painstaking trial and error showed exactly how much larger or smaller the hole had to be. This was true for the other non-computer clocks as well. Further, the LOGO clocks were more adaptable and could be easily connected to other ongoing projects in the classroom (Papert & Franz, 1987).*

"Computer as Material" concludes with wise and timeless advice for computer use in schools:

1. *Seek out open-ended projects that foster students' involvement with a variety of materials, treating computers as just one more material, alongside rulers, wire, paper, sand, and so forth.*
2. *Encourage activities in which students use computers to solve real problems.*
3. *Connect the work done on the computer with what goes on during the rest of the school day, and also with the students' interests outside of school.*

4. *Recognize the unique qualities of computers, taking advantage of their precision, adapt-ability, extensibility, and ability to mirror individual students' ideas and constructions of reality.*

5. *Take advantage of such new, low-cost technological advances as temperature and light sensors, which promote integration of the computer with aspects of the students' physical environment (Papert & Franz, 1987).*

Constructionism vs. Instructionism

Constructivism is the idea that knowledge is something you build in your head. Constructionism reminds us that the best way to do that is to build something tangible—something outside your head—that is also personally meaningful (Papert, 1990).

By the mid 1980s, Papert had deduced and named two opposing views of education, constructionism and instructionism. Hence, there would be two types of educators, constructionists or instructionists, based on their own mythopoetic belief of how learning occurs. Constructionists center the learning process on the learner, while instructionists behave as if learning is the result of having been taught. Since educators are human and complex, there are elements of instructionist and constructionist in each of us. However, a choice of stance tends to dominate and define one's pedagogical approach.

All my work is focused on helping children learn, not on just teaching. Now I've coined a phrase for this: Constructionism and Instructionism are names for two approaches to educational innovation. Instructionism is the theory that says, "To get better education, we must improve instruction. And if we're going to use computers, we'll make the computers do the instruction." And that leads into the whole idea of computer-aided instruction.

Well, teaching is important, but learning is much more important. And Constructionism means "Giving children good things to do so that they can learn by doing much better than they could before." Now, I think that the new technologies are very, very rich in providing new things for children to do so that they can learn mathematics as part of something real (Papert, 1980s).

I once saw Papert address a large audience to which he was trying to make the point that constructionism does not preclude instruction, it just does not favor it. Seymour was struggling a bit to eliminate any confusion while unsuccessfully fiddling to turn on the projector in front of him. Suddenly, a member of the audience hopped up on stage and pointed to the on/off switch. Papert flipped on the projector and proclaimed, "Now, that's a good use of instruction!"

Instruction is a technique used within a much broader palette of ways to prepare a learning environment in which learners construct knowledge through projects, interact with materials, and collaborate with the computer, peers, or members of a community. Simply improving instruction is inadequate for realizing substantive educational progress.

I am asking what kinds of innovation are liable to produce radical change in how children learn. Take mathematics as an extreme example. It seems obvious that as a society we are mathematical underperformers. It is also obvious that instruction in mathematics is on the average very poor. But it does not follow that the route to better performance is necessarily the invention by researchers of more powerful and effective means of instruction (with or without computers).

> *The diffusion of cybernetic construction kits into the lives of children could in principle change the context of the learning of mathematics. Children might come to want to learn it because they would use it in building these models. And if they did want to learn it they would, even if teaching were poor or possibly nonexistent. Moreover, since one of the reasons for poor teaching is that teachers do not enjoy teaching reluctant children, it is not implausible that teaching would become better as well as becoming less necessary. So, changes in the opportunities for construction could in principle lead to deeper changes in the learning of mathematics than changes in knowledge about instruction or any amount of "teacher-proof" computer-aided instruction (Papert, 1991).*

One of the great gifts bestowed upon me by the at-risk students in our prison project[3], was that the kids would not tolerate much instruction before tuning out or walking away. Once my fragile ego recovered, I realized there is almost never an instance when more than a minute or two of instruction is necessary before asking students to do something (Stager, 2006).

While engaged in project work, a teacher might visit with individual students as a consultant, throw a well-timed obstacle in their way leading to an epiphany, grab a group of kids for an impromptu demonstration—if necessary, encourage kids to seek wisdom from their peers, or gather the entire group's attention to seize a teachable moment with another moment of instruction.

My suggestion for teachers interested in developing a more constructionist learning environment to embrace my mantra, "Less us, more them." Anytime you think you should intervene in an educational transaction, ask yourself, "Is there less that I can do and more that they can do?" Shifting as much agency as possible to the learner(s) ensures the greatest learning dividends.

A practical exercise to try is, if you are lecturing for forty minutes, try twenty. Twenty minutes? Try ten. Ten minutes? Try five. As an educator and researcher, I am obsessed with the question, "What is the smallest seed I can plant that generates the largest blossom and most beautiful garden?" I am often reminded of the likely apocryphal tale of the night Frank Sinatra went backstage after a Luciano Pavarotti concert and humbly asked, "Maestro, how do you end your notes so beautifully?" Pavarotti replied, "You close your mouth!" Now, that is the sort of learning story Papert relished. It is sage advice for educators as well.

What happens in an educational setting is dependent on one's stance. Educational computing policies are no different. Are you an instructionist or a constructionist?

We are prisoners of our own metaphors, metaphorically speaking. —R. Buckminster Fuller

WP/DB/SS – IT/ICT – Apps? Let's Call the Whole Thing Off

After Logo reached its zenith in schools in the mid-1960s, conservative forces and an edtech industry hell-bent on selling lots of software eroded interest in the hard fun of *Twenty Things*.

By the early 1990s, I was joking that all schools did with computers was word processor/ database/spreadsheet (WP/SS/DB). This new metaphor was uttered so frequently and rolled off the tongue with such alacrity that it became one syllable. Integrated "office" suites of software were de rigueur.

To many, the creation of a generation of fifth graders with fabulous secretarial skills was quite attractive. Edtech made a quick shift from a liberal arts to a vocational focus. Computers were now instruments of efficiency in schools as they were in industry. One could certainly argue that the use of WP/SS/DB tools could be used in the spirit of *Twenty Things* for creativity and knowledge construction, but alas that was not to be. Quickly, the SS/DB part of the triad largely disappeared from widespread classroom practice, eliminating even more computational potential. The very same mathphobia and sclerotic nature of math instruction that made Logo so critical had not only rendered programming too difficult, but sidelined its less potent successors, spreadsheets and databases, as well.

Word processing revolutionized every sector of the economy. If it enjoyed even a fraction of that impact on classroom practice, the resulting progress in student writing, research, collaboration, and publishing would have been seismic. Alas, that too was not to be. Despite schools' overwhelming emphasis on literacy, there is little evidence that word processing has had the qualitative or quantitative affect it should have on student writing.

This history of the hype, boom, and bust cycle for word processing may be predictive of what will happen with the democratization of digital video editing. Making movies is clearly consistent with the vision set forth in *Twenty Things*. However, as developers seek to make video tools "simpler," they sacrifice power and flexibility. The tools become more opaque and paradoxically, harder to use. TikTok-style videos may be popular, but fewer and fewer kids seem to be learning filmmaking, especially in school. Students use the Internet, often under odious rules and surveillance, but few publish online, learn markup languages, or are taught to design on web platforms like WordPress. The only exception is specialized magnet or vocational programs.

Despite millions of powerful computers in the pockets of children and tablets in the backseats of minivans, companies like Apple have shown no interest in creating software environments like Logo, or even HyperCard, uniquely suited for programming and having agency over the "device."[4] *Twenty Things* offered a vision for how the democratization of access to powerful constructive technology may be used in infinite ways. Sadly, such experiences remain alien to most kids in school.

By the mid-1990s, the vague and vulgar terms of ICT or IT became catchalls for educational technology. The emphasis on information retrieval, storage, and distribution supported the dominant activity of school—talking, while maintaining a patina of legitimacy by situating computers as tools of the workplace. Creative expression, experimentation, computation, individuality, collaboration, design, making things, and changing the world are always marginalized by schools concerned with compliance, language arts, and math instruction. The focus on rhetoric, information delivery, and regurgitation is justified by the ISTE Standards, an unnecessary, unenforceable, and unimaginative set of ambiguous pronouncements embraced by schools and governments around the world more concerned with the illusion of modernity than the power of children.

The ISTE Standards not only reinforce the most traditional and instructionist tendencies of schools, but even when they advocate for high-minded objectives like *students as knowledge constructors, innovative designers,* or *computational thinkers,* actual computation or programming is invisible. One needs a microscope to find language about computer programming or examples of students engaged in computation in any of the standards documents or example videos created by ISTE or its adherents. Computer science does not appear once in any of the 26 ISTE Standards or its 100 sub-standards. There is much talk of leadership, but no acknowledgment of any guiding vision such as that set forth by Papert and Solomon. There is plenty of rhetoric about digital citizenship without any assertion of student rights, access, or democracy. Computers are simply viewed as instruments for doing school or having school done to children.

ISTE is not alone in co-opting the spirit of *Twenty Things* while disarming its powerful ideas and justifying inaction. Lavish web sites, curricula, and books make pronouncements about "learning in the digital age" while disempowering children. These products espouse a great deal of emphasis on social implications of computing, problem solving, and off-computer activities at times over many years of piecemeal instruction (Stager & Martinez, 2017). A school can embrace a K-12 computing/computational thinking/design/problem solving/digital citizenship curriculum without the need for pesky computers or ever teaching a single student to have agency over the machine. Don't believe me? Take a gander at *Computer Science Unplugged* or DQ Institute's "world's first global standard related to digital literacy, digital skills, and digital readiness, the IEEE 3527.1™ Standard for Digital Intelligence." (Bell et al., 2009; DQ Institute, 2020) Hilariously, even pronouncements that every child "should code" are often unaccompanied by a personal computer, Internet access, or learning to program.

Computer Literacy

Although "literacy" is a profound intellectual trait, the educational industrial complex uses the term to denature or dumb down powerful ideas. Digital literacy, media literacy, even financial literacy are terms used to describe the teaching *about* a set of concepts without the necessity for meaningful experiences. This is similar to the way in which *Music Appreciation* is a music class where the only person making music is the teacher. Learning in such classes tends to be passive. The modification of strong terms such as literacy or citizenship is an instructionist tell. Perhaps the most enduring example of the phenomenon is *computer literacy*. Far too many children are being taught to memorize the parts of a computer or the vocabulary word, "algorithm," all in the name of satisfying a computer literacy curriculum.

Papert wrote, "When ideas go to school, they lose their power" (2000). Arthur Luehrmann is credited with coining the term "computer literacy" around the time *Twenty Things* was published. Computer literacy was defined in terms that even today remain aspirational and out of reach for too many students.

> *Computer literacy must mean the ability to do something constructive with a computer, and not merely a general awareness of facts one is told about computers. A computer literate person can read and write a computer program, can select and operate software written by others, and knows from personal experience the possibilities and limitations of the computer (Luehrmann, 1980).*

Luehrmann goes on to make constructionist arguments while defining computer literacy.

> *Any course in computer literacy ought to spend four-fifths or more of its time and effort on performance objectives, such as the ones in this latter group. Going further, I would argue that it is intellectually improper to inculcate beliefs and values about a subject that do not arise out of the student's direct experience with the content of that subject. If I were writing about mathematics or reading and writing, there would be little disagreement about this point (Luehrmann, 1981).*

Personally, I find it amusing to look back on the days in which computer-using educators engaged in verbal skirmishes over the virtues of children learning to program computers in BASIC or Logo. Many of my Logo-advocating friends and I sought to vanquish our opponents and drive BASIC into the sea. In hindsight, those debates look positively quaint, yet were imbued with a level of sophistication, subtlety, and reason that I long for in edtech today. Today, the advocacy of *Twenty Things* is imperceptible against the instructionist ballyhoo of Class Dojo, Mathletics, Pear Deck, BrainPOP, and the weaponization of technology against students serving Zoom detention.[5]

> *Computer literacy is the ability to do computing. —Arthur Luehrmann (1981)*

Words for Learning

Those of us on the side of children need to be heard. The stories we tell expand our collective imagination and fuel our progress. Papert loved parables and metaphors. The turtle may be one of the most enduring metaphors of all. It is a metaphor for ourself. Papert introduced images of the pencil lab, a jet engine connected to a stagecoach, time-traveling surgeons, and a land where the diet is entirely comprised of suet as ways of explaining the education system's reluctance to change.

Papert searched for examples of powerful learning in popular culture and played with etymology in an effort to help readers understand that things do not need to be as they seem. He even proposed that his book *The Children's Machine* (1993) be titled, *A Word for Learning*.

For Solomon & Papert's vision to endure, coherent oppositional perspectives are necessary so that one may choose a path for educating children. The current metaphor-less morass causes inaction and fossilizes bad practices. Regardless of your stance, although you might guess my preference, I urge you to pick a lane and develop a language for talking about how learning occurs best. Clear comprehensible communication, dialogue, and debate are the imperative building blocks of progress.

A metaphor is not an ornament. It is an organ of perception. Through metaphors, we see the world as one thing or another. —Neil Postman

References

Bell, T., Alexander, J., Freeman, I., & Grimley, M. (2009). Computer science unplugged: School students doing real computing without computers. *The New Zealand Journal of Applied Computing and Information Technology, 13*(1), 20-29.

DQ Institute. (2020). *What is the DQ Framework?* dqinstitute.org/dq-framework

Edison Muckers. (2010). What is a Mucker? edisonmuckers.org/what-is-a-mucker

Hawkins, D. (1965). Messing About in Science. *National Science Teachers Association, Science and Children, 2*(5), 5-9. colorado.edu/ftep/sites/default/files/attached-files/ftep_memo_to_faculty_42.pdf

Hawkins, D. (2002). *The Informed Vision: Essays on Learning and Human Nature.* Algora Press.

Luehrmann, A. (1971). Should the computer teach the student, or vice versa? AFIPS '72 (Spring),

Luehrmann, A. (1980). Computer Literacy: The What, Why, and How. In R. Taylor (Ed.), *The Computer in the School: Tutor, Tutee, and Tool.* Teachers College Press.

Luehrmann, A. (1981). Computer literacy—What should it be? *The Mathematics Teacher, 74*(9), 682-686.

Luehrmann, A. (2002). "Should the Computer Teach the Student..."—30 Years Later. *Contemporary Issues in Technology and Teacher Education, 2*(3), 397-400. learntechlib.org/p/18864

Papert, S. (1970). Teaching Children Thinking. IFIP World Conference on Computers in Education, Amsterdam,

Papert, S. (1980s). Constructionism vs. Instructionism. [Speech transcript]. dailypapert.com/constructionism-vs-instructionism

Papert, S. (1984). Computer as Mudpie. In D. Peterson (Ed.), *Intelligent Schoolhouse: Readings on Computers and Learning.* Reston Publishing Company.

Papert, S. (1990). *A Critique of Technocentrism in Thinking About the School of the Future* (2). (M.I.T. Media Lab Epistemology and Learning Memo, Issue. papert.org/articles/ACritiqueofTechnocentrism.html

Papert, S. (1991). Situating Constructionism. In I. Harel & S. Papert (Eds.), *Constructionism* (pp. 1-11). Ablex. papert.org/articles/SituatingConstructionism.html

Papert, S. (1993). *The Children's Machine: Rethinking School in the Age of the Computer.* Basic Books.

Papert, S. (2000). What's the Big Idea? Toward a Pedagogical Theory of Idea Power. *IBM Systems Journal, 39*(3&4), 720-729.

Papert, S., & Franz, G. (1987). Computer as Material: Messing About with Time. *Teachers College Record, 89*(3). papert.org/articles/ComputerAsMaterial.html

Solomon, C. (1986). *Computer Environments for Children: A Reflection on Theories of Learning and Education.* MIT Press.

Stager, G. S. (2006). *An Investigation of Constructionism in the Maine Youth Center* [Ph.D., The University of Melbourne]. Melbourne, Australia.

Stager, G. S., & Martinez, S. L. (2017). Thirteen Considerations for Teaching Coding to Children. In S. Humble (Ed.), *Creating the Coding Generation in Primary Schools: A Practical Guide for Cross-curricular Teaching*. Routledge.

Taylor, R. (1980). *The Computer in the School: Tutor, Tool, Tutee*. Teachers College Press.

Notes

1   Nicholas Negroponte has said that Papert began discussing the content of the paper, "Teaching Children Thinking" as early as 1968. This text was published several times, including in Robert Taylor's book (1980).

2   While this question is most often attributed to Seymour Papert, it is equally possible that it originated with Arthur Luehrmann. Of course, they may have come to the same idea contemporaneously or borrowed it from someone else.

3   From 1999–2002 Seymour Papert created an alternative school inside a troubled prison for teens. I was one of the collaborators as well as principal investigator of the Constructionist Learning Laboratory at the Maine Youth Center. This work was the subject of my doctoral thesis.

4   Environments like Scratch, Snap!, and Turtle Art will run on a tablet, occasionally with UI compromises. Google's App Inventor has promise but receives little advocacy.

5   Dear incredulous readers of the future. In 2021, these were actual products and practices popular in schools.

Hitchhiking to Logo's Mathland

Molly Lynn Watt

I met my first turtle, a painted turtle, living in a glass bowl in Miss Crane's kindergarten. I stared at her under the fake palm tree and wondered, is she alive? Years later, in a wooded area I watched a snapping turtle almost motionless expelling eggs like ping-pong balls into a sandy hole. In the mid-seventies I wandered into the MIT Logo Lab to meet up with my husband, Dr. Daniel Lynn Watt. Beside him on the floor sat a large domed robot he called a turtle. Nearby was the first computer I'd encountered with a tiny triangle in the middle of the screen he likewise called a turtle. Turtles in any form captured my imagination. Each in her own way sat motionless, blinking as if waiting, but for what? I love watching, waiting and letting wonder grow.

In 1976 Dan took sabbatical leave from teaching fifth grade students in the Massachusetts Brookline Public School System to work with someone he admired by reputation. Dr. Seymour Papert and his MIT Logo Group were working on developing an artificial intelligence language called Logo. Dan said the group was building a mathematically rich sandbox to install in computers for classrooms worldwide. They dreamed children would, by playing in it, learn to speak mathematics as naturally as they learned, for example, to speak English, with no threshold upon entering this Mathland sandbox nor ceiling to cap their learning. There were no computers in schools at the time. I had not met Papert. This was my first inkling Papert's work might be of interest to me. But I was busy with my mixed-aged classroom of thirty-six students in grades 1–3, a humming mix of kids, exploring with buttons, marbles, Cuisenaire rods, attribute blocks, building blocks, needles, thread, yarns, looms, live turtles, dead birds, sprouting seeds, and much more stuff available in brightly painted recycle bins. I was busy, with no time to be curious about Papert's ideas. But Dan had started his campaign of, "Papert's ideas about education are very much like yours." I buried myself in responding to each daily journal entry of my thirty-six students. I was thinking about provisioning my classroom for the next day, not thinking about some distant future of what I assumed, erroneously it turned out, would be mechanized programmed instruction. Nor could I dream I would be part of steering schools toward offering more project-based learning by leading workshops on educational uses of computers for teachers and administrators. Dan and I sometimes called the computer our Trojan Horse for open education.

What were my ideas about education? I believed a person of any age is able to learn by engaging with curiosity and passion and real stuff making something that mattered. Able to make good choices. Able to resolve problems encountered, involve others as allies, enjoy learning while doing hard stuff. The role of teachers was provisioning the learning environment with rich materials, offering powerful challenges, time to experiment, and maybe doing a bit of coaching along the way. Students of any age need to be poets, mathematicians, and architects, rather than only learning about poetry, math, or architecture. These ideas guided my work with kindergarten students in the same way they guided my mentoring master's degree students or teachers with twenty years in the classroom or officials in departments of education.

In hindsight, Dan was right, I was using an idea Papert popularized later with his terrific metaphor of no threshold, no ceiling. A good curriculum is one where you can immediately do something without climbing over a steep threshold and then just keep extending explorations. Without a ceiling to stop you, there is no end to doing or knowing. The writings of John Dewey, Carl Rogers, Jean Piaget, Maria Montessori, the German kindergarten movement, and the English Primary Schools brought me new insights that enriched and enlarged mine as I continued to evolve my own teaching practice. But since first teaching my younger brothers to write when I was eight years old, I realize I've used this idea. What did my brothers need to write? They needed to write, GIRLS KEEP OUT, and worked with great deliberation to form each letter I taught them to make for their sign. When with gleeful satisfaction they taped it to their bedroom door, my mother and I were barred from entry. They were immediately writers using the power of literacy. I did not stop their impetus to teach them the alphabet first.

During my early days of teaching, I was profoundly influenced by participating in three professional development workshops as a learner. The first, Workshop for Learning Things, was facilitated by Dr. Alan Leitman and funded by the US Department of Education. Leitman invited teachers of young children into his open space warehouse. When I entered, it was as if I were back in Miss Crane's kindergarten, but for the adult me. I spied a potter's wheel and clay. Stained glass and soldering gun. Leather scraps and tools. Pinhole cameras and film. Printing press and type fonts. Soapstone and carving tools. Everywhere I turned was crammed with stuff. There were no manuals or instructions. Some participants immediately started making things. Others were wandering and observing. I itched to try my hand at creating something, and after I finished my leather handbag, I kept returning.

Eventually I joined the staff. My job description: invite participants for a cup of tea and conversation. No schedule. Sometime during the evening workshop, we settled into a cozy corner and talked for a while. Maybe about their job, or project, maybe others joined us and they asked each other about what they were making, why, how, could they take a look. Sometimes they asked for or offered ideas. I used what I call my Beginner Mind, not setting myself up as an expert, but I had ideas, knew a few things and could help connect people and resources. These conversations were part of Leitman's plan. As teachers talked with each other, they gained new insights about their work. I watched some teachers, over a few months of participating, shift their ideas by 180 degrees, from *teaching by prescribing* to *teaching by provisioning*. Would this have happened without conversation? I cannot say, but I suspect not. Since then, I include informal talking and describing to others as integral to educational events I lead. Extricating participants from the urgency of finishing, to the quiet of reflecting, is one way learning leaps forward and finds its perch.

Three magnificent insights many participants took away were: wandering around can be useful, not a waste of time; if you want to learn, do not keep your eyes on your own work; working with others can be more productive than learning alone plus more fun.

My second inspiration for teaching was participating in a month-long, hands-on, workshop required for teachers employed to teach K–4 classes at two private schools in Cambridge, Massachusetts, The Shady Hill School and the school where I taught, The Cambridge Friends School (CFS). Our school faculties were inspired by the Director of Shady Hill, Ed Yeomans' report on his visit to the British Primary School Movement. His slides showed densely populated classrooms of forty-five students, guided by a single teacher. Breathtaking displays of collaborative and individual projects artfully and meticulously realized and installed throughout the school environment. All students apparently flourished in these classrooms despite the diversity of the school population. This was our dream for our students.

The August Workshop was for teachers committed to changing their classroom practices to emulate the British Primary Schools the next month in September. The CFS faculty decided on this change by consensus. The Civil Rights Movement was in full motion. We took a long look at the school mission for our diverse student body, a mix of races, cultures, and economic status. Was every student succeeding? No, if we were honest it was not happening. Our traditional classrooms tended to reify society's hierarchies, we intended to do better.

An overarching idea used in the British Primary Schools was that schools needed to provide students opportunities to participate in projects they could not do if they stayed home. There were many exciting reasons to be in school every day. Learning music and performing a concert. Using data collection, or maths, to create schoolwide—or town-wide knowledge about say the town's animal population, by counting all dogs and cats and horses and pigs owned and graphing the data in several ways. Or hatching monarch butterflies and painting murals to record the life cycles they observed. Or writing a play from a favorite story like *Mary Poppins* and producing it for the town's citizens to enjoy. Each project involved students in acquiring and using knowledge and many skills. And afterwards students experienced the authentic reward of people engaging with them about their project and showing appreciation for their careful work and knowledge—not praise nor blame for a grade given.

Roy Illsley, a school head from Leicester, England, and leader of the August Workshop, challenged us to undertake a learning project for ourselves; we were not to use the time to prepare specifically for teaching in September. I don't remember him offering project examples. I didn't think of forming a group. I embarked on what I came to call, The Build the Elusive Compass Problem. I had a vague idea of wanting to make a compass, perhaps because I have trouble with direction, or was not allowed to study physics in high school due to gender. This was before personal computers, the internet, google, or smart phones. I did not have a compass to experiment with. In the workshop's temporary quarters there were no books or other resources. Someone suggested getting a magnet. I could not find one nor did I know why I might want it. I was trapped in my own bewilderment, wandering around, in this case, unproductively. Was I waiting for a teacher to step in and rescue me? I never thought of changing or revising my project goal. This was not a predetermined experiment with a fill-in-the-blanks high school lab sheet. I never made any progress on building a compass, but had I learned something in my bewilderment? Yes. Was it what was intended? Maybe not. Was it useful? Yes. I learned when someone is stuck, needing some knowledge or a tool they may not even know exists to move forward on their project, tell them that piece of knowledge or hand them the tool or connect them to someone who can! And I've tried to do this ever since.

My third inspiration was derived from my experience as a trial teacher for effectively implementing Elementary Science Study (ESS) kits into classrooms, before disseminating them widely. Funded by the National Science Foundation (NSF), ESS was conceived after the Soviet Union sent Sputnik to circle planet Earth revealing to the US citizens our national gap in educating scientists, and general lack of national preparedness. This became an urgent concern and embarrassment, perhaps a national scandal. In the mid-sixties Dan, with his shiny new PhD in engineering from Cornell University, was recruited to be a scientist by the ESS project. I loved the kits from the get-go: batteries and bulbs, can you make the bulb light? Straws and pins, how high can you build a structure? Sink and float, can you predict which will sink and which will float? Students were drawn to the stuff, loved the challenges, recorded data, made conjectures all the while talking and laughing and figuring stuff out. They were being scientists, not just learning about science. I was given some sheets of mimeographed challenges and a list of supplies. But what was not provided was a little summary of the science knowledge being explored by the students. Many teachers, like myself, had little science education from teacher training institutions or liberal arts education. My formal science education stopped at high school chemistry and college biology. The Build the Elusive Compass Problem was banging on my Beginner Mind. I knew not all explorations lead in productive directions. I did not know which directions to nudge a student toward for a no ceiling exploration. What were powerful ideas in engineering, in physics, I hadn't a clue. I remember feeling angry by not knowing. I felt the kit designers were withholding the science knowledge because they held, what I considered an erroneous idea, that teachers might be tempted to shortchange productive student explorations by telling them what to do or what the science was showing them. I considered strong science and strong pedagogy must proceed hand in hand. The science explorations developed for the kits continues, half a century later, to be the foundation for many elementary school science programs, but now, with glossy ancillary material, goals, grading rubrics, and science knowledge spelled out, well, they probably are a bit *too* slick and *too* teacher dominated. But dig deep and you'll find the same excellent science explorations developed by ESS, ones students never forget being engaged with.

In the mid-seventies I found myself gaining a bit of fame, or notoriety, as an open education classroom teacher of self-directed students doing amazing things with lots of raw materials. Research by the US Department of Education shows one way teachers improve their teaching is by seeing another teacher, somewhat like themselves, teaching in a way they don't. They think: *that looks like the students are doing good stuff, maybe I can give it a try*. I worked on that study conducted by Education Development Center, Inc (EDC) and may have over-simplified but this is why curriculum development projects and training courses were lining up teachers from across the United States to visit a real classroom and see how fill-in-the-blank can be implemented well. My inner-city classroom fit the bill with more than half my students on free breakfast and lunch. We had a steady stream of visitors. Dr. Deborah Meier once told me, if you want to improve student learning, let students guide visitors and explain the how, what, and why of everything. My students were the visitor guides. Even fifty years later, informed by layers of new research on how children learn, the hubbub in my classroom at Lincoln School was all I could hope for my students and a great deal more.

Dan was deeply involved with Logo at MIT, I with kids in open classrooms. I was being trained by Dr. Thomas Gordon to lead Leadership Effectiveness Trainings (LET) and working with Dr. Tom Lichona, author of *Raising Good Kids*, and Dr. Carol Gilligan, author of *In a Different Voice*, and a dozen others on what makes a democratic classroom. It was a time of political turmoil and busing in Boston to address school segregation. Students commuted from Roxbury on the METCO bus to our school. The women's movement was taking on society, and I was trying to establish a sexual harassment policy in the Brookline Public Schools. It was a heady time of political awareness and personal engagement. But at social events I noticed men, my friends, mostly white and educated, talking with excitement about computers. The rest of us talked about causes, GEDs, fasting once a week to feed the world, kids, clients, therapies—everything except computers. Suddenly I wondered, what if, as I read, the computer really is the biggest mind extender and human connector ever conceived? Maybe today I need to spell it out, but then, computers resided where primarily white men dominated—the university, big business, and government. Who else had access? Well, business offices and secretaries and data entry clerks.

I realized I was prejudiced against computers in education. But I realized I must engage with them, to see a different trajectory in our society. I was on a mission to include ordinary citizens of every demographic, age group, and especially females. This was my first glimmer that Dan and my professional paths might converge in a new way. The MIT Logo Group's pilot teaching and research project sent Dan back to the Brookline Public Schools, to the same elementary school he was on leave from and I continued to teach in, the Lincoln School. Some of my former students, thrivers in my hands-on classroom, were selected for Dan's minds-on project using the General Turtle Logo computers. I was curious, and what I saw convinced me. Skipping over the lack of aesthetics in the print-out, I saw students excited on this adventure to somewhere unknown. They were proud of teaching the turtle how TO STAR, TO BOX, how TO DAN including Dan's beard, and saving their procedures. They taught the turtle, any mistakes by the turtle were theirs in writing directions, not the turtle's. They knew how to revise the directions, to fix a bug, to change the size or angle, and could immediately watch the turtle to check the change. They were captivated and ran their procedures for each other again and again with great delight. These kids knew they were in charge.

I'd transitioned into a Logo enthusiast. Theoretically, that is, because it wasn't until around 1980 that Apple IIs were ready for classrooms. But classrooms weren't ready for them. I saw something I could do, a role I could play, but I wasn't ready yet. I liked Logo, but I didn't know Logo nor did I speak mathematics, yet.

At the end of his sabbatical, Dan was in too much demand to go back to his fifth-grade teaching. He was opening up the world of Logo Mathland for students, teachers and superintendents in ever broadening geographic spheres through workshops and curriculum and articles and lectures and international conferences—he was getting schools ready for Mathland via computers. Dan moved his office to TERC, in Cambridge, Massachusetts and I moved my job 100 miles down Route 2, now assistant principal of a K–6 school of 450 students in Amherst, Massachusetts. We got together on weekends, but not so I could learn Logo. But I bought an Apple II, a black Apple adapted for school use by Bell and Howell with plug-ins for overhead projectors and tape recorders and other now forgotten electronics. I moved my Apple to a table in my office of glass, determined to learn to program Logo, and believing it a good thing for students to see adults learning. No published reference books, nor idea books, I clutched a handful of xeroxed pages from Dan giving things to do with Logo.

I polled my staff, no one in the school owned a computer, nor had it registered on anyone's wish list. But at my door stood a sixth-grade student. He said, Hi, I'm Daniel Van Blerkom, I see you have an Apple II. I nodded. I have one, too. My ears perked up. Actually, he continued, there's a little club of boys from the school. All of us have an Apple. You can join, you don't have to be a boy, just have to have an Apple. Tempted as I was, I could not join the club meeting in the bedrooms of sixth-grade students even for this worthy cause. But sixth-grader Daniel and I met in my office of glass from time to time to make a go of Logo instead of the right/wrong quiz question programs he'd been making in BASIC. We both had that invaluable tool for learning I call Beginner Mind. As young as he was, Daniel knew something about learning. I continue to use his instructions to this day.

Daniel's Four Instructions for Learning
1. Try anything that comes to your mind.
2. Hang around and watch what other computer users are doing.
3. Write down everything you find out and everything you do.
4. Write down all your questions until you get the answers.

Daniel and I got together to muck around in Mathland from time to time, and in the spring, he and I offered the Fort River School teaching staff their first hands-on computer awareness workshop. We managed to scrounge a small bunch of computers for the afternoon, and invited teachers to come with Beginner Mind. We got started with a quote to ponder from Papert's emergent manifesto, *Mindstorms: Children, Computers and Powerful Ideas* (1980) about teaching the turtle to draw in Mathland. Then we introduced the little turtle triangle on the computer monitor that their small group would eventually have the opportunity to teach to draw something. We asked them to watch as I taught Daniel to draw a square as he played the turtle, and paced my instructions out on the floor. For our demonstration I was restricted to four English-language Logo commands: FORWARD, BACK, RIGHT TURN, LEFT TURN. Then we moved our preliminary model of teaching the Daniel-Turtle to draw a square, onto the computer to teach the Logo turtle by typing in the commands. We watched to see if it worked, or needed fixing—size, angle, typing mistake. We revised until we had a procedure we liked and named it SQUARE and saved it to use over and over again. We broke into small groups to work on this challenge, then closed the afternoon with a discussion of how did it go?

The afternoon was an overwhelming success. The teachers found value and hard thinking in doing this simplest of tasks, teaching the turtle to draw a shape. They marveled at the different ways each group went about programming and what bugs they ran into. They reflected on their own learning and on the mathematics involved. But there was a criticism from a few—it was very wrong of me to have a student present when teachers were learning. Teachers need to be regarded as people with authority who know. Au contraire, I asserted. Students must always see their teachers as learners engaged with content. I'd learned this in that long ago August workshop. I shared the values I'd found in the years I lugged my floor loom into my kindergarten and I had counted out the warp and strung it, chose the colors to make patterns and much more, and then the kids wove on it. But being a learner with your students was even more important if computers were to be integrated into classrooms. Most had never used a personal computer until the workshop, how could they know? Schools don't have time to wait for everyone to take a year off to learn, and it was highly unlikely we would learn this alone, I reminded them of my essential tools: Beginner Mind and Daniel's 4 Instructions. If the computer is to be a thinking tool for everyone, everyone needs to be able to use it for something that matters. We must work with our students and learn together. And if some students are more adept at using the computers, we must enlist them as allies in supporting others in the class. Good programmers like to demonstrate and debug!

That summer Proposition Two and a Half eliminated my position in a tax cut, and the new administration in Washington cut Dan's NSF funding. Surprise, we were both unemployed with two daughters in college. We transitioned a bit bumpily into our new roles as independent contractors. Or as I prefer to call it, our fifteen years as Missionaries for Logo and Computers in Education. (My positive use of the term missionaries is due to my happy childhood on the campus of a theological seminary.) Dan and I each wrote monthly columns for national magazines, Dan in *Popular Computing*, me in *Teaching and Computing*. The Banks Street Writer word processor—developed informed by research on how students learn coupled with how professional writers write—was out of the beta versions I had trial taught with and was now firmly ensconced in schools. One of its innovations was the blank page with a blinking cursor waiting, but for what? (Does this remind you of the Logo turtle?) The first stage of writing is free writing, and it was waiting for a flood of words. The last phase of publishing is the time to experiment with spacing on the page and fancy fonts, hmmm, I found this very compatible with what I was teaching in Logo workshops. And there were more software packages offering inquiry and cooperative learning projects. Dan and I were building an international following among educators. We were in demand individually and as a pair.

I was invited by the assistant superintendent of the Hamilton-Wenham, Massachusetts School System to offer a three credit, graduate course in Logo for teachers working on master's degrees from Lesley University. I was pleased and immediately agreed. Then I asked around for advice. No one at Lesley, nor TERC, nor EDC, nor the MIT Logo group had taught such a course nor knew anyone who had. Some I asked were highly indignant, claiming Logo cannot be taught, period. Somehow many who knew Logo had limited views of what constitutes teaching.

Like other school systems, Hamilton-Wenham had no computer labs, and just a handful of computers distributed throughout the system. We managed to create a lab every Thursday after school for thirteen weeks by begging, borrowing, and lugging. I brought mine from home. The first thing was not playing turtle. The first thing was opening up each computer and inserting the precious 16K memory boards into each computer's mother board so it would just barely have the 64K of memory needed to operate Logo. Our texts were Papert's *Mindstorms* (1980) for theory, Dr. Harold Abelson's book, *Logo for the Apple II (1982)* for tech support (edited by Dan), and Dan's galleys for his forthcoming *Learning With Logo* (1983) for projects and challenges. All three authors worked with the MIT Logo Group and all became bestsellers, and all are still treasures sometimes available on eBay. I met Dr. Brian Harvey at the MIT Logo Lab who once told me he thinks of each Logo procedure as a script for a play. We played turtle to start projects and put on procedure plays to see if our scripts worked. The teachers loved naming their procedures whether for their friend, JOEY, or their favorite flower, DAISY. These were friendly afternoons as we built through the weeks into variable inputs and recursion. Even when everything went awry, we got everyone on board to debug, or on a couple of occasions we phoned Dan as our debugging lifeline.

But the assistant superintendent who hired me sat in on each session. After class she unfailingly asked, when will you get to programming? I always drove home a bit defeated. If the teachers who had resisted this required course for their master's degrees were now loving it and seeing connections for using Logo in their varied teaching situations, if they felt they were learning mathematics and learning about learning and appreciating debugging and experimenting—what was wrong with the way I was evaluating the situation, weren't the teachers doing what I hoped and challenged them to do?

At the end of one of these Hamilton-Wenham days, Dan invited me to join him and others from the MIT Logo group at a party. It was held in the home of Dr. Gloria Rudisch, the pediatrician for the town of Brookline, and she was my friend. Her office was across the hall from my exuberant classroom and she often stopped by to enjoy the projects kids were generating. I was still feeling a bit down when I arrived, Gloria was busy hosting, Dan was circulating, and I knew no one else. I plopped down in an empty chair. The man beside me smiled and said, "What do you do?" I said, "I teach Logo to teachers." He followed up, "What do you do when you teach Logo?" I told him about playing turtle by teaching someone to walk a shape with just four commands to get them started when he interjected, "Do you know what I would do if I were teaching Logo?" I shook my head. "I would draw a house with the most beautiful door I could make. When admired, I would say, you can have it if you can get it." That was the beginning of my respect for superprocedures, subprocedures, the total turtle trip theorem, and again, walking around to see what others were doing. Later Dan said, did you know you were talking to Gloria's husband, Dr. Marvin Minsky, credited with being the father of artificial intelligence?

Long before Papert's book, *Mindstorms* was published in 1980, Dan and others frequently referred to the powerful ideas embedded in Logo, informed by Piaget's learning theories and artificial Intelligence. No one spelled these ideas out for me. I embarked on an informal survey assembling a list because I needed to know. I realized by not knowing I was reproducing what I had criticized the scientists developing the ESS kits of, withholding the very knowledge from classroom teachers the curriculum was developed to explore. Expecting every teacher to come up with these was not only unreasonable but ridiculous. I built the list over the next while, eventually landing on a tidy twenty. These powerful ideas informed all my future work with Logo including three major collaborations with Dan. When writing *Teaching with Logo: Building Blocks for Learning* (Watt & Watt, 1986), we took teachers along as we support five students with diverse passions. We follow their easy entrance exploring and building their first shape, placing it inside a superprocedure, and embellishing it with complex recursions and variables into something quite extraordinary. When founding and leading The Logo Institute for teachers as learners and observers of their own learning we spent three weeks in a residential immersion Logo learning community or *samba school*. We wrote a proposal to the NSF to fund The Logo

Action Research Collaborative (LARC), a national pilot network of teacher researchers studying the multiple learnings by their students by studying how they taught the turtle to draw a shape by studying the procedures they wrote. Our energy initiating and carrying out these projects was a huge boost to catapulting Logo into classrooms.

By now *Welcome to Logo*, my K–6 workbook series was published (Watt, 1986). The publisher gave them as samples to all their clients, not selling them, so no royalties, but classroom teachers began to find me. But my progressive education and Logo community joined in criticism of the project. Without peeking inside, they proclaimed workbooks bad, apparently equating all workbooks with some kind of right-answer programmed instruction or just plain busy work. I stand by my work. I issued the same open-ended challenges to engage students from the start that I continue to issue, and gave students the tools they needed to carry out personal explorations without needing other instruction. Usually, in those days the one computer sat at the back of the classroom while the teacher worked with a small group elsewhere. The workbooks were translated into Spanish and used in Mexico and I've heard translated into Hebrew (others saw copies, but I never did, and rumors abound of pirated versions).

All this activity created a kind of buzz. Dan and I were involved from the start of Apple's entry into classrooms and the phenomenal pressure for schools to incorporate educational computing into every classroom overnight. We were ready because we had classroom experience, teacher training experience, and curriculum development informed by learning theory experience. We were ready because our children were adults and we were free to travel. We were ready because we had a sense of world-wide community and sought adventure. Our travels meeting committed and deeply dedicated educators world-wide were perhaps the most exciting fifteen years of our lives. We worked in the Pierre Indian Learning Center with Lakota, and Anglo teachers in South Dakota. We worked in high schools in Chicago with almost all African American teachers. We worked on Mackinaw Island in Michigan, where no motorized vehicles are allowed. We worked in Puerto Rico in classrooms without doors or windows. We worked in New Orleans as it prepared for Mardi Gras. We worked near the Pacific in California and near the Atlantic in Nova Scotia. We worked in almost every state and province, plus England, Italy, China, Australia, and Bermuda often repeatedly and sometimes for a few weeks. In every place we worked, children and teachers loved the turtle metaphor and it transcended cultural differences to carry them to Logo's Mathland.

By now Logo was taking hold throughout the world. We'd worked tirelessly and were both exhausted and exhilarated, and we'd loved every minute. Somehow more than fifteen years had flown by and we realized many people had written excellent materials, many teachers knew Logo and other materials, and other good curriculums existed. We wanted to spend more time in our beautiful airy home on the banks of Gregg Lake in the shadow of Mount Monadnock. We needed to find substantial projects nearer home when Dr. Dennis Littky, the principal of the Thayer School in Winchester, New Hampshire showed up. His public school served a working-class community and was beginning to gain national recognition. His was the first school to join Ted Sizer's Coalition of Essential Schools Movement dedicated to equity, democracy, and the role of teachers as coaches and many practices we embraced, plus exhibitions not grades, were the closure for all projects, something like the British Primary Schools. Littky invited us to introduce the uses of computers into his school. He offered us a half-time shared job, on site from 8 am to 6 pm just one day a week. Our first task was setting up a computer lab, seeking volunteers from the students to assist us and then be in charge the days we were not. We paired with each teacher to bring powerful uses of the computer to augment their curriculums in these grade 6–12 classrooms. We deepened our knowledge and respect for the many ways a computer can be a tool and mind extender from the get-go. We renewed our respect for its power to engage students and teachers immediately, and what it asks of a teacher to incorporate something so awkward and buggy!

I found work as an adjunct for the continuing education department at nearby Keene State University. My courses were Computers in Education and The Logo Computing Language. I was bringing something to my adult learners mostly struggling to complete graduate degrees while working and raising families, some on welfare, one waiting to hear if he was accepted for a doctoral program at Harvard, or Keene State Faculty needing to get their professional development credits. And I found a true colleague. Dr. Tony Stavely, a professor of psychology, who was passionate about the list processing capabilities of Logo. This was the topic of his writing. Neither Dan nor I were as interested in this aspect of Logo as in turtle geometry. The three of us started a Monadnock Logo Users Club meeting monthly in homes. Long story short, the three of us founded the aforementioned residential three-week Logo Institute and are forever grateful to Keene State University and the teachers who took a chance on us coming from nearby and as from as far away as South Africa.

I was intent on creating a *samba school* atmosphere, written about by Papert in *Mindstorms*, where mixed ages and mixed skills work for months creating a costumed dance performance for the annual carnival in Rio. For the Logo Institute I needed to choose the first community challenge well. I wanted to welcome everyone to participate from the first hour of day one, women and folks from diverse backgrounds, those who had never used a computer alongside those teaching in BASIC and Pascal to advanced high school students, no threshold, no ceiling, the institute would be our challenge. I wanted to create a culture of respect and equal worth, employ the powerful ideas in Logo and use exhibitions, not grades, as closure. We needed to lead three weeks, teaching in ways we hoped teachers would teach in their own classrooms. Remember the research referred to earlier conducted by EDC for the US Department of Education, it also found many teachers emulate the way they are taught, and think, *I can do that!*

I thought about our New Hampshire community, and one way we celebrate an event as a community is to make a quilt. Each person decorates one square, and then a group fastens it to a backing and ties it together, like subprocedures and superprocedures. It's an art many women are especially familiar with. We opened the Logo Institute with a quilt challenge, each team programmed a design inside identical square procedures, then we threaded it together into a superprocedure. Embedded in this challenge were many powerful ideas—procedure, subprocedure, naming , experimenting, variables, recursion, total turtle trip—plus we used this project for our institute tee shirt, our first exhibition proudly worn by each of us.

We called on Daniel's Four Instructions, Beginner Mind, and offered three daily and simultaneous courses: Turtle Geometry, List Processing, and Creating Microworlds Using Tool Procedures. As folks worked through the days and nights on their chosen projects, we interrupted from time to time to offer pop-up demonstrations for something several folks asked about, a choice to gather around. We posted butcher sheets in the corner where anyone could post a question and anyone could offer a response. We grew a poster of helpers and what they could help with as people became more skilled. These were our main methods, plus serendipity. I think we were all good human beings who took time and showed empathy and people liked us. On the Saturday following the last Friday, we held a one-day conference, an opportunity to demonstrate, try out, practice leading hands-on workshops, give talks they would eventually deliver to their to school board, or share some dazzling phenomenon. Guests were welcomed, former institute attendees returned. I think Sizer, Littky, and Papert would be proud of our samba school, the conference was our big exhibition.

This may seem the natural ending for this chapter, but there is one more essential story to share. In 1984 Dr. Sandy Dawson of Simon Fraser University located in Burnaby near Vancouver,

British Columbia offered Dan a series of public lectures plus a summer school teaching position. Dan was reluctant, the beautiful lakeside summer was popular with friends and family, our Logo Institute, and a daughter planning to marry in August. Dawson was persuasive, Dan said, only if Molly can come give lectures and teach a course of her own. Dan had a doctorate, I did not. Dan's dilemma solved, a summer at home. But Dawson surprised us with a parallel offer for me to hitchhike along with Dan to Vancouver. He had the advanced course, I had the introduction course. But dilemmas immediately reared their heads, a university course demands syllabi, grading rubrics, final exams. Syllabi were easy using Papert's *Mindstorms*, Abelson's *Logo for the Apple II*, and Dan's *Learning with Logo* for texts. But what about grading? We each worked on our separate courses. My rubric was something like this:

20% class attendance

20% Daniel's Four Instructions

20% engagement with Logo learning challenges posed for the class

20% participation and support of each other's Logo project development

20% class reflection on learning process, and role of teacher facilitator

I started boldly—we are all educators. As an educator I believe everyone can learn and make good choices, otherwise I would not be a teacher. Everyone here is interested in what is taught and the many ways students learn. In this course it is important to all of us to share your stumbling places and the bugs you encounter. These may be even more valuable to your classmates than seeing perfectly completed projects. Knowing what is hard, or misunderstood, or remains un-debugged will help us facilitate the learning of our students. If everyone fulfills the rubrics, it is possible for everyone to earn an A. The classroom was a hubbub from day one, and at the end, I was confident each had earned an A. But the Simon Fraser administration were not as confident. I was called up to defend the unheard of situation of all students achieving success. I shared my rubric, the student's work, and my grades stood. There I was with Beginner Mind—still a beginner programmer facilitating powerful uses of Logo's mathematical sandbox inhabited by a digital turtle, and the communities I facilitated were thriving.

I've enjoyed one heck of a trip toward Logo's Mathland, and I am deeply indebted to my traveling companion, Dan, for picking up this hitchhiker on the adventure he started on first. I am ever grateful to the many who gave me a hand and offered trust along the way. I'm excited by the next generations following the exploration and pioneering days I described, Constructing Modern Knowledge (CMK), Lifelong Kindergarten, the Logo Foundation, and many more. I'm proud feeling I may even have contributed a tiny bit of my DNA. This fall I watched a dozen painted turtles lined up by size on a tree branch, slide off into the river—who knows where they are going? I love watching, waiting, and letting wonder grow.

References

Abelson, H. (1982). *Logo for the Apple II*. McGraw-Hill, Inc.

Papert, S. (1980). *Mindstorms: Children, Computers, and Powerful Ideas*. Basic Books.

Watt, D. (1983). *Learning With Logo*. McGraw-Hill Book Co.

Watt, M. (1986). *Welcome to Logo*. D.C. Heath and Company.

Watt, M., & Watt, D. (1986). *Teaching with Logo: Building Blocks for Learning*. Addison-Wesley.

When You Wake Seymour Papert in the Middle of the Night

Gary Stager

Back in the late eighties, there was a Logo conference held in Los Angeles. After a wild night reminiscent of Martin Scorsese's 1985 film *After Hours*, longtime Papert collaborator Brian Silverman and I found ourselves locked out of the friend's home where we were supposed to spend the night.

Ever the problem solver, Brian suggested, "Seymour always has a big room. We can sleep there."

So, we drove back across town and woke Seymour before 5 AM. Despite our discourteous invasion and before we went off to sleep, Papert offered a bit of profundity that withstands the test of time.

One of the people we had been partying with earlier in the evening was teacher-turned-software developer, Tom Snyder. Brian remarked something along the lines of, "Tom is a good guy." Seymour disagreed and said that he viewed the world of educational technology as a triangle with Alfred Bork, Tom Snyder, and himself (Papert) in each of the vertices. Papert went on to say that each of the three men held a stance that views technology as benefiting one of three constituents in the educational system.

Alfred Bork was notorious for saying that teachers had low SAT scores, were not very bright, and any future teacher shortage would be corrected by replacing teachers with teaching machines. Today's online testing, "personalized instruction," and other dystopian systems concerned with delivery, testing, surveillance, and accountability are manifestations of Bork's fantasies.

Tom Snyder was a fledgling educational software designer in the late 1980s trying to make payroll and in need of a catchy marketing niche. He looked around and found that most classrooms had one computer. So, he decided to make software for the "one computer classroom." In this scenario, the teacher is the actor, the classroom a set, and the computer is used as a prop for engaging in whole class or small group problem solving. Oddly, this practical marketing slogan born from a shortage of computers more than thirty years ago remains an enduring metaphor for classroom computer use today. The "interactive" whiteboard is one such recent example.

Snyder's vision is compelling to creative educators who enjoy being the center of attention, but along with that spotlight shifts the locus of control away from the learner. When the best way to use thirty computers in a classroom is to turn twenty-nine off, the shortage of the primary vehicle for intellectual and creative pursuits limits the potential of learners.

Since the late 1960s, Seymour Papert believed that every child would and should have at least one *personal* computer with which to "mess about" with powerful ideas, create, and collaborate.

These three points of view articulated by Papert in the middle of the night describe how technology is predictive, and in an educational setting always grants agency to one of three actors: the system, the teacher, or the student. Papert's disciples see the greatest benefit arising from granting maximum agency to the learner. In purely arithmetic terms, the greatest return on investment (ROI) redounds to those who embrace Papert's vision.

Technology is never neutral. An incredibly clever teacher might be able to pull the use of some technology a little bit between the vertices in the triangle, but that doesn't change the equation. Educators need to decide upon whom they wish to bestow agency. I'm in Papert's corner. It is best for learners and enjoys the greatest return on investment.

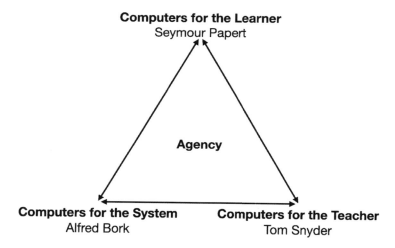

Parents, educators, and citizens investing in educational computing need to plant their feet and point their practice towards a specific vision.

A choice must be made.

2020 Things to Do with a Computer

Dale Dougherty

When I read *Twenty Things to Do with a Computer*, I thought that all of the twenty things were, in spirit if not in substance, the kind of things the maker movement has embraced in education. Yet when I got to the "Epilog: How to Make Those Things Happen," I changed course, realizing that "making it happen" in education is still just as challenging as it was back then. A lot has changed over fifty years, but the core challenge that Papert and Solomon address remains unchanged.

How can that be? Computers are everywhere, just like televisions and telephones, which are now just another form of computer with interactive interfaces. The problem isn't the technology, per se. It's our relationship as users, not producers. If the challenge was once to get computers for children to use in school, that challenge has been met, not entirely but mostly. However, Papert and Solomon were not just concerned about getting computers into schools; they wanted education systems to embrace the liberating use of computers to transform student learning from passive to active, from repetitive to creative, from memorization to realization.

Only inertia and prejudice, not economics or the lack of educational ideas, stand in the way of providing every child in the world with the kind of experience of which we have tried to give you glimpses.

I'm afraid they'd be disappointed that, despite us having technology everywhere, inertia and all forms of prejudice continue to block changes. In fifty years, there have been so few fundamental changes in how students learn in school. Yet today there are probably more people than ever trying to make such changes happen.

The 2020 Experiment

In 2020, the computer became the school, as the pandemic forced the education system to undertake the largest experiment in the history of education, for which no one was prepared. With school campuses closed, teaching and learning only existed on a computer, via a video conferencing application. The *only* experience of school was through a computer. What have we learned from this experiment?

"One of the most fascinating research outcomes of the Zoom pandemic teaching mode has been kids' absolute refusal to turn on their cameras or to unmute themselves. And it's making our teaching workforce crazy," Pam Moran told me. Pam is an educator with a thirty-two-year career that culminated in serving as superintendent for Albemarle Public Schools in Charlottesville, Virginia. She added: "Have people not ever considered that when those same kids were sitting in class, they were turning off the screens and muting themselves? It just was inside their heads." That tells us about everything we need to know about how computers are used in education today. Of the twenty things that Papert and Solomon write that you might do with a computer, none of them were being done in schools.

The pandemic also exposed inequities that are even more damning as students in low socio-economic status lacked computers and internet access at home during the pandemic. One Laptop per Child, another MIT project rooted in similar beliefs about how computers could help students direct their own learning, developed inexpensive laptops, but adoption met with the usual bureaucratic resistance. Administrators tend to think even more today of computers as something closer to mainframes, managed by them, rather than widely distributed laptops connected to a network. Despite the fact that technology is cheaper than ever, we are hesitant to put it in the hands of children to give them more control over their future. School budgets are spent on learning management systems like Google Classroom, so-called smart boards, and video conferencing systems like Zoom.

Students see the computer itself as extending the kind of control that school has over their lives, not as a tool that invites them to be creative—to play, explore, make choices, and do things they want to do. In some school districts, students were required to login by 8:15am in the morning and the number of hours of instruction via Zoom was mandated by the district.

The challenge to give students access to technology to support self-directed learning in a playful, open context is much the same in 2021 as it was in 1971.

"Have a Go"

The last line of the Epilog reads, "If every child had access to a computer, computers would be cheap enough for every child to be given access to a computer."

Today's computing technology is certainly cheap enough. I was reminded of a trip I made to Cambridge, England in March 2015 for a Raspberry Pi Day celebration. Raspberry Pi is one of these small microcontrollers that is inexpensive and can be used by a student to build her own computer, connect up devices, and create many powerful applications. Papert, I think, would realize that Raspberry Pi could give every child access, but it isn't just access or ownership.

The occasion was the third birthday for Raspberry Pi, and its founder, Eben Upton, gave the opening address. "We must do a better job of developing our own talent," he said. "Certainly, we want to see more girls get into coding but look at it this way, we also have only about 5% of boys. That's a rounding error." He believes that more people should learn to code. "Having ideas is not a contribution," he said. "Implementing ideas is how you make a real contribution."

For me, the best session was in a breakout room. UK teacher Sway Humphries led a session titled "The Pi in Primary." Once Ms. Humphries learned about Raspberry Pi, she thought it would be good for her school. She requested that her school buy them for class, but she was turned down "because they thought Raspberry Pi was too new and not yet proven." Undaunted, she brought her own in, and began working with the kids. Word began to spread with children asking her what this "Cherry Pie" was. Through her participation in an Hour of Code challenge, she won a pack of Raspberry Pis for her class, and that really got things started. "I gave them to the kids and said: 'Have a go. See what you can do,'" she related. They began building their computers. Getting them up and running was a proud achievement shared by the group.

Ms. Humphries introduced four of her ten-year-old students and asked them to share their experiences. One boy said that when he heard students talking about Raspberry Pi, he thought they were talking about brownies and cupcakes for a bake sale. Quickly, he learned otherwise, but he added: "The first time I saw a Raspberry Pi, I thought—that's not a computer." Others described their experience as "exciting, fun and scary." The Raspberry Pi would change their minds about computers and what they were used for.

The students described how, in a school computing lab, they were taught Word and Power-Point—how to use computers. (The kids were no doubt unaware that the building they were in was named after Bill Gates.) "Once you learned how to use those (Microsoft) programs," said one of the students, "there's not much more about it to learn." In contrast, the Raspberry Pi was "fun to use and hard to use," said another. None of them felt that they understood computers until they began working with a Raspberry Pi. One student said that he didn't know how to code but he was learning and he could see that it was possible to do many things with it such as math, music, and games. That led to the defiant remark by one of the ten-year-olds: "People who think we are too young to code are WRONG."

Papert and Solomon estimated that the cost of a time-sharing computer would be about $30 per year per students. Today, students could each have a powerful microcontroller for about the same price and have a lot more fun with it. By 2019, over thirty-five million Raspberry Pis had been sold and in March 2020, the Raspberry Pi Foundation reported sales of 640,000. Upton, quoted in Tech Republic,[1] said that the coronavirus had created the demand: "It used to be sustainable to have a shared family computer, but now every family member needs to have one to work or learn."

Maker Educators

By 2021, Ms. Humphries, now Grantham, had gone to work for the Raspberry Pi Foundation to develop curriculum. Her story is similar to what I have heard from many maker educators that I have met over the years. They got involved themselves. They bought equipment and supplies at their own expense. They created a makerspace as best they could. They introduced the toolset, skillset, and mindset to children directly. They did it because they wanted to encourage the kind of playful, creative experiences that making offered and that engaged students. These teachers became champions of the maker movement, recognized as maker educators, and began helping provide training and resources for other teachers.

The maker movement can be seen as a grassroots movement, one of the only such bottom-up, distributed efforts to change education. However, the shift towards maker education has not been accompanied by support from the top down in the education system. The dominant mode of teaching and learning remains entrenched in schools, reinforced not relieved by the pandemic.

Maker educators are rowing against the current. Progress was slow but it is happening, although not in a straightforward fashion. The spread of makerspaces throughout all levels of education is certainly one of the unexpected bright spots and a sign of hope. We have seen what children can do in a makerspace and how some flourish who struggle in the more academic tracks.

Enough educators saw the opportunity to re-engage children in learning that this distributed network has had its own impact. Individually and in small groups, they pushed back against a bureaucracy that expected so-called twenty-first century skills to emerge from a nineteenth century one-size-fits-all approach to education. Makerspaces as well as maker programs were also casualties of the lockdown.

With distance learning, the computer took on a role that seemed like another version of educational television but now with two-way communications. I remember taking an eighth-grade math class in which fifty or more students sat in desks and in front of a pair of wall-mounted television sets, which in my memory are black and white. A single remote teacher at a chalkboard taught a math course broadcast to classes like mine around the state. This was then how to use technology to improve the quality of student instruction. It was no doubt an efficient use of technology but it was a terrible way to learn.

As superintendent, Pam Moran did more than most administrators to support maker education. I recall her telling me that her schools did not have a makerspace—the entire school was a makerspace. At the heart of this approach was listening to the children and helping them grow. Today, she works with "people who are taking the risk to move away from schools as institutions of testing to become homes of opportunity." A home of opportunity, she explained, "really builds out everything that we believe is essential for a child to be successful in life—sustaining their curiosity, their sense of believing in themselves, finding friendships and meaning and relationships with other people of being able to feel like that they have value because they do." This is not something that technology itself provides. Caring adults in roles as teachers, mentors and coaches are necessary to understand and support children's growth and development.

131

Tested to Death

Our current framework of standardized testing started about twenty years ago, when the No Child Left Behind legislation was passed in 2001. All students in America would be required to take standardized tests to measure student achievement. Testing would point out which schools and which teachers were failing their students. The big fallacy of NCLB was that we could not know which schools were underperforming without data generated by standardized testing; we already knew which schools struggled but we didn't know what to do about it, even if we had the data. This led to blaming teachers and principals, holding them accountable, while we ignored the underlying causes of poverty and inequitable funding.

No Child Left Behind started under the George Bush administration, and continued into the Barack Obama administration, where it was revised and repackaged in 2015 as Every Child Succeeds. As a consequence of these programs, the emphasis on standardized testing changed how teachers were expected to teach. Now they taught to the test, changing how they taught and what they taught their students. This meant that school was less engaging for students and they lost a real connection to learning. "The reality is we have tested the kids to death," said Pam Moran. "We have weighed them in every way that's possible, and they are not getting better as a result of a testing environment." We continue with standardized testing without seeing any improvements.

Educational technology, developed by Silicon Valley startups, also promises to improve student test scores. Like educational television, these apps are a fundamental misuse of computing, because they are tied to curricular goals not to expanding student learning experiences. Students (and teachers) are treated as consumers of educational applications.

Connecting Students

In the 1990s during the Clinton administration, Net Day was organized to raise money and mobilize communities to connect their schools to the internet. In the local district where I live in California, two high schools raised money for information technology. These schools at different locations in the same county raised money but one of them only had enough money to buy computers for a lab but could not afford to wire the campus. The other high school used its money to wire the campus but did not have enough money for computers.

The big difference in technology from fifty years ago is not the computer itself, it is connectivity. Not only are computers connected but all devices, and most people through such devices. Being disconnected has even greater impact now, as the pandemic has demonstrated. But this was true before the pandemic. Connectivity also impacts life outside of school.

Michael Kim, a teacher at Oakland Charter High School in Oakland CA, held a virtual "creative tech event" for his students and invited community members to come see the projects that students created and hear presentations from the students. One student gave a presentation that was critical of the Zoom-based lectures but she said that what she missed most was connecting with other students at school. She meant the social side of education, which is not about being in class, but being beside your peers in person. Students feel this loss deeply.

Learning from 2020

Will schools learn from the 2020 school year to improve the learning experience for students? Will maker programs resume and makerspaces re-open? Or will there be even more inertia and prejudice behind the "standardized" model of learning?

I would hope that schools might realize that connected computers offer a nearly unlimited number of choices for learning—the opposite of standardization. These choices could give children the freedom to learn in ways that fit their needs and their goals. For some children, learning remotely is a new skill they've learned, and they could continue to develop it to take courses from many different teachers. Take, for instance, computer science. A given school may or may not have a course in computer science. If they do, and they have one teacher offering the course, the student may wish to learn from a different teacher, even one that is remote. Will school even allow students to make the choice of an equivalent class?

How can we take advantage of this connected world to help students learn from each other and other people around the world? Students can connect beyond the school to students in any geography.

The changes that are happening in education are coming from outside the education system. Places like Outschool are providing access to additional learning opportunities. And while learning pods might seem like something by and for the upper middle class in America, more people should embrace them, and see how these small group associations are positive, providing both new ways to learn together as well as the social side of education. They aren't really that different from clubs at school or outside organizations like youth scouting.

Another positive is how some small groups of maker educators have begun offering educational workshops directly online. These are *a la carte* options for education that bring additional costs. But these options are important alternatives.

One example is CodeJoy, a series of a live-online, interactive workshops, developed by Kelsey Derringer, a maker, writer, and educator with more than fifteen years experience teaching, along with Matt Chilbert. Both live in Pittsburgh but they are conducting sessions for children across the country. They teach robotics and coding on an interactive platform that allows the student or teacher to write programs in the cloud that control devices on their desktop. A robot on one student's desk could respond to a command sent by another student. Or students could control the motors on a robot on the teacher's desk. Their workshops are engaging and fun. Kelsey and Matt have a vision that this platform could be used in schools by teachers who are teaching remotely or in-person.

Shree Bose is a highly accomplished young woman who is currently in medical school at Duke University. She won the Grand Prize in the Google Science Fair, and then went to Harvard. While an undergrad at Harvard, she co-founded a company called Piper Learning that built kits that turned the Raspberry Pi into a home computer for children. Having recently returned to the company, Shree told me about a new product, Piper Make, that is based on the Raspberry Pi Pico and uses Google Blockly to provide a web block-based coding platform. It combines an inexpensive computer that connects to sensors and an easy-to-learn visual coding platform. Shree understands what her product could mean to children: "what I'm really excited about is the fact that we're going to have users who create things that we have never thought of," she said.

At Duke, her bioengineering lab is full of students doing projects with Arduino or Raspberry Pi. They are building medical devices with technology that can be used by kids. "I see the medical challenges that could be solved with technology," she said. "I want to see kids getting started, getting them to a point where they understand that these things can be coded and can be used in ways to solve really big problems, like ventilators during the pandemic."

There are many more examples of maker educators doing what they can. The shared idea of maker education is what kids get to do with computers and technology, not what it gets to do to them. Yet we know that these kind of experiences are available to too few children. Reaching every child? We must make it happen.

Notes

1 TechRepublic: Raspberry Pi sales are rocketing in the middle of the coronavirus outbreak - techrepublic.com/article/raspberry-pi-why-sales-have-rocketed-in-the-middle-of-the-coronavirus-outbreak

Intellectual Timidity

Eleonora Badilla-Saxe

I don't remember the first time I heard or learned about many important concepts for my life in general, or specifically for me as an educator. But I do remember very clearly when I was inspired by Seymour Papert. I know what and when I learned from him and his collaborators, not only about computers in education but about the future of learning.

And I remember very well the first time I tripped on the idea of intellectual timidity in education in general, and specifically in computers in education. It was in 1990 when I had access to the paper he and Cynthia Solomon wrote in 1971, *Twenty Things to Do with a Computer*. It was many years after it was written and I was already part of the intellectually timid community of education in Costa Rica. It resonated with me very profoundly because I was already feeling very uncomfortable and unsure about the role I should play with colleagues and students.

A couple of years before, personal computers started to be introduced in public elementary rural and inner-city schools throughout the country. It was a politically revolutionary decision of a small developing country in a time when the few computers where found in education in first world countries were placed in mostly private high schools.

It was a radical and risky decision for Costa Rica, and as the major newspaper put it, we were in good hands, with the advice of Seymour Papert and his team from the MIT Media Lab.

IN GOOD HANDS
Minister of Education Francisco A. Pacheco, Seymour Papert, and children.
La Nación front page, February 1989.

We were proud to be pioneers in introducing computers in education in the elementary educational system of our country, in public rural and inner-city schools.

I was, initially, the pedagogical director of the program and very committed to learning about constructionism and the use of computers in education to allow children to program the computer and not the other way around. I participated in workshops with Papert and his team,

135

and read most of the documents available at the time. It was a whole new vision of education opening to my eyes and mind.

One of the best ways that lead me to understand the powerful ideas underlying constructionism was the opportunity I had to translate many of Seymour Papert's talks into Spanish. I had time alone with him before each talk. He told me the main ideas he would develop during the address and then he spoke and I translated. Or maybe, more accurately, I interpreted into Spanish. That is how I constructed my understanding of his ideas.

Interpreting Papert into Spanish - 1989

And that's when I started reading Solomon and Papert's paper *Twenty Things to Do with a Computer*. But on the third paragraph I stopped—*educational timidity*? The simple but profound and powerful idea triggered many questions in my mind. Are we shy in education? Is this why I am so uncomfortable about my role within an educational community? Even my country, Costa Rica—taking a very radical and risky decision to introduce computers into a system—is timid? The next sentence helped me answer my question. Papert and Solomon continued saying that education "seemed remarkably reluctant to use the computers that fails to look very much like something that has been taught in schools during the past centuries." And I saw, back then, that we were doing exactly that with the bold political decision of introducing computers in education—making them to look very much like we have been doing in our educational system, which by the way, we were very proud of at the time.

I felt even more uncomfortable than before, and now I see why. I was facing cognitive dissonance, trying to deal with conflicting beliefs or ideas. That is, the educational community in my country would be reluctant to accept the use of computers in ways that looked different than what we already have been doing; innovation would be neutralized by the power of the system.

I shared my concerns with Mitchel Resnick, who at the time was a graduate student and Dr. Marilyn Schaffer, visiting researcher, both at the MIT Media Lab, and with Papert himself, amongst other people, like Dr. Alberto Cañas, at the time director of IBM's Latin American Education Research Center, located in Costa Rica.

My understanding from those conversations was that we should take the opportunity to use the computers as Trojan Horses, to bring innovation into schools, and to do so, we must give teachers things to do with them that seemed like traditional schools. But then again I was troubled by the phrase in Solomon and Papert's article, that we would be "using bright new gadgets to teach the same old stuff in thinly disguised versions of the same old way."

Anyway, thinking of the computers as Trojan Horses to bring innovation into the educational system gave me hope. So, I went on to review twenty things that could be done with the computers we had.

As Papert and Solomon said, in spite of the computers we had, we should focus on what we could do with them. We did not have a physical turtle, but we had the LogoWriter programming language version and each teacher and student had it installed in floppy disks. The computers were IBM Personal System/2 without a hard disk, one for each pair of students. Compared to today´s available digital technology, it might seem that we didn't have the resources to transform the computers in education program into a Trojan Horse to bring innovation into the educational system. But looking back little more than thirty years, I think the technology was enough, for the time being. Our main challenge for provoking transformation was the intellectual timidity of our educational community.

Intellectually, we had access to Solomon and Papert´s *Twenty Things to Do with a Computer* and also to what I consider its sequel, Papert´s 1980 book, *Mindstorms: Children, Computers, and Powerful Ideas.*

There were (at least) mathematics, geometry, and biology fundamental concepts underlying the programming of the LogoWriter turtle, that could have be evidenced if serious reflection had followed the implementation. But, as Solomon and Papert had predicted, computers were used to replicate activities that looked "very much like something that has been taught in schools during the past centuries." They both were right fifty years ago, and their ideas are still valid in 2021; in the midst of the COVID–19 pandemic, computers in education (with exceptions of course) are used to transmit information (this time using streaming), as we have been doing in education for the past centuries.

In the meanwhile, what happened to the Trojan Horses in the educational system in Costa Rica? New and more powerful computers with hard discs, local area networks, access to internet, and cloud computing were gradually introduced. Different versions of Logo from MicroWorlds to Scratch were brought in, as well as programmable bricks to give behaviors to physical creatures (from LEGOLogo to Crickets and Arduinos). And in spite of Papert's urging to give one computer to each child (OLPC), and although some have been given to a percentage of students, in general computers are kept in laboratories within the schools. Teacher preparation has been a fundamental component of the experience. And as a country we have failed in providing high-speed connection to families, communities, teachers, and students.

So it seems that the Trojan Horses have not yet passed the gates of the educational system. And as the pandemic has proven, in education we were not ready to face the challenges of the world in the twenty-first century.

Why? The short and powerful answer is the idea Solomon and Papert proposed fifty years ago—intellectual timidity of educational systems.

In another sequel to *Twenty Things to Do with a Computer*, Papert elaborates more on the idea of intellectual timidity. In his paper "Why School Reform is Impossible" (1997) he answers the question with a profound statement—because complex systems cannot be formed or reformed—they evolve.

Fifty years after we need to accept that there is a twenty-first thing to do with computers in education. We must provoke change to a complex system; not reform it. In Papert's words:

The central issue is analogous to one that has played a central role in theories of biological evolution: How do features of the system whose functions are mutually dependent come into being without a guiding designer? Attempts to change the medium and leave the content (e.g., use computers to teach the same math) or change the content but keep the medium (e.g., National Council of Teachers of Mathematics standards or 'The New Math' performed in the old medium) do not create a new equilibrium—in fact they make a 'camel' in the sense of 'a horse designed by a committee.' (Papert, 1997).

We have designed camels instead of Trojan Horses in an effort to bring change to education. The time has come to surpass intellectual timidity—to understand how this complex system behaves, and instead of trying to reform it, find the most sensible of its interactive connections and relations to bring the urgent change that is needed.

References

Papert, S. (1980). *Mindstorms: Children, Computers, and Powerful Ideas*. Basic Books.

Papert, S. (1997). Why School Reform is Impossible. *Journal of the Learning Sciences*, 6(4).

Seeking the Magic: One Teacher's Evolution Story

Carol Sperry

Seymour Papert's and Cynthia Solomon's brief paper *Twenty Things to Do with a Computer*— simple in construct but revolutionary in ideas—was a seminal work in progressive educational thought.

My intention is to illustrate how people interested in teaching and learning can be attracted to constructionism, learn to have agency, foster creativity, and join in an expansive and productive relationship with their students. As Papert and Solomon say in the early part of their paper, "We are convinced [our suggestions] give a glimpse of the proper way to introduce <u>everyone</u> of whatever age and whatever level of academic performance to programming, to more general knowledge of computation and, indeed… to mathematics, to physics, and to all formal subjects including linguistics and music." The spirit of *Twenty Things* expresses itself in an exhortation from page 33 that states, "neglect all complications, try something."

So, here is the story of my evolution to constructionism.

If I had known that the trajectory of my life was about to change, I might have taken better notes. As it was, I skipped the first day of the August 1981 Logo workshop but managed to turn up for the second. I felt intimidated and now prepared to be bored.

I was at The New York Academy of Sciences, on the recommendation of Mrs. Tessa Harvey, the assistant superintendent of New York City's Public School District 3, where I taught fifth and sixth grade at P.S. 75. I told Ms. Harvey that I considered myself more of a poet than a computer person but she stood firm and assured me that "Computers are the ultimate poetry." I was bewildered by that remark, but I trusted the source, and I wanted my students to have access to computers. So I signed up, cynically thinking I could mindlessly take the course and then be rewarded with a computer or two.

Some history: When I left university and started teaching, I was immediately uncomfortable with my role. I had attended Catholic school from kindergarten through university. The teaching was always authoritarian—we were viewed as empty vessels that had to be filled, usually with simple facts. I don't remember anything from those years except for one or two nuns who were especially kind. I did love school, though I'm not sure why. Perhaps the boredom provided some quiet and comfort from a hectic home life. So, I sat through every class and dutifully did what they told me to do. However, not a single lesson stands out in my mind, not a single lesson that I took in. I think the phrase, "took in," is apt since it is a more accurate description of what was happening. I certainly wasn't really learning very much. Real learning must be deeper than what I experienced. I did excel in the things I enjoyed, such as reading and writing stories. But I "took in" only a minimal understanding of other subjects, such as computation (the beauty of mathematics was never presented to us), some smattering of history, a bit of geography, and hardly any science. And I was taught to teach in this same way. In every classroom, desks were lined up, the teacher's desk almost always in the front of the room, the same pictures on every classroom wall. Textbooks were open and children were copying or (supposed to be) listening and almost always forbidden to make any noise. There was no spontaneity and certainly no fun. It was a difficult time for me because I was doing what I was told to do, what everyone said was correct, what I, myself had done in school, and I had to admit, I turned out pretty okay, right? But I wasn't happy, and it certainly didn't feel right.

I got a job teaching in what they then called a special school for the emotionally disturbed. It was a public school and the kids there had problems that spanned the spectrum of mental illness and disability. The circumstances were odd for a public school. It was housed in the basement of a synagogue. There was no principal but there was a psychologist-director. The teachers were mostly young and inexperienced, but we all had a deep passion and regard for our students. We didn't have much pedagogy to go on and so we actually devised our own curriculum. I immediately felt released somehow and excited about the possibilities.

A colleague and I brought in art supplies and took it from there. We built things with the kids and engaged them in conversations about everything. We tried all kinds of activities because there was no one there to tell us whether we were right or wrong. We tried everything we could think of to unlock whatever it was that imprisoned the minds of our children. There was one student who rarely spoke so I tried to engage him by teaching him some Spanish. I was hoping he might feel the lure of having a secret language. It didn't work, but it is a good example of how we approached our challenges. Many of the kids thrived and many at least found school to be a safe and happy haven. We were impressed with what our children had to offer, if only we listened closely enough. This was a beginning for me. If such an open and organic learning experience worked so well for these kids, why not for all kids? I was beginning to understand the true meaning of learning and teaching and found that it could include intellectual freedom, spontaneity, imagination, and even fun for both students and teachers.

After five years at the special school, I was asked to be an acting guidance counselor at P.S. 75, and was later asked to teach there. The principal assigned me to the so-called "traditional" part of the school, and soon I felt the old unease of the top-down, sit quietly, and do-as-I-say approach. I had no validation for my itchy impulses to break out and practice learning and teaching as a cooperative venture with my students, one where we could forge a relationship with each other and the material we were covering. What I did have was an "official file," with many reports about rules broken and boundaries crossed. There was hope, however; I fell in with a group of teachers in the opposite part of the school. They had been to London to explore what was called the Open Classroom method. This meant that their students could expand out of their classrooms and into the hallways in order to accommodate project-based explorations. I was drawn to the freedom and dynamism of this idea and my own classroom began to change.

Then came the workshop organized by Seymour Papert and a collection of his associates from MIT and the constructionism universe. On my first day there, people were milling about and there seemed to be a buzz in the air. My memory is more about how I felt than the specifics of what actually happened, so I'll describe the impressions that I remember best. It seemed I was dropped into a band of merry (mostly) men, surrounded by books and papers and a variety of computers. I say merry because the atmosphere seemed loose, friendly, and welcoming. The chairs in the room were casually laid out and there were no desks in straight, constricting formation. In fact, it reminded me more of my own classroom with its layers of projects, pictures, papers, and books. The only person in the room that I knew was Michael Tempel, a former colleague at P.S. 75 and one of the leaders of the workshop. He was an open-classroom adherent, who, with his fifth and sixth grade students had constructed a pond in their classroom, inhabited by a variety of flora and fauna collected from the park ponds near our school. Michael had encouraged me to attend this workshop and I trusted him. I looked around. In one corner, someone was teaching a group how to juggle and, I started to think, "Hey, this looks promising."

Seymour gave the group copies of *Mindstorms*, which had been published the year before. Two astonishing weeks followed, filled with heady ideas, down-to-earth activities, and engaging learning stories. I realize now that much of the substance of the workshop had origins in *Twenty Things to Do with a Computer*. But it was all new to me then. I didn't sleep much during those weeks, my mind felt constantly in an uproar, percolating with ideas, and new connections. I was struck by the philosophical power of concepts, simple and complex, such as naming, recursion, syntonicity, debugging, and began to wonder at the unauthentic separation of disciplines. The ideas were both small and big. There was an *okayness* with not understanding that I had not experienced before. No question was considered too trivial for consideration. No idea was treated with disrespect. This was different. In a complicated world replete with, but often enhanced by ambiguity and nuance, here was a group who embraced these ideas and aspects of life and learning in depth and with verve.

Best of all, there was validation from Seymour and his colleagues that my instincts about teaching and learning were viable, valuable, and in synch with the goodness, graciousness, and joy of expansive learning. In *Mindstorms*, Seymour says: "Only rarely does some exceptional event lead people to reorganize their intellectual self-image in such a way as to open up new perspectives on what is learnable" (p. 43).

That sentence hit me like a lightning strike. Something happened to me. My entire way of thinking was upended. It felt like it came from inside out. I guess you could say, my mind was blown. And it stayed that way for the remainder of the workshop.

The delight in mastering a computer as a tool for learning and change is hard to equal. I vowed to bring this experience to other teachers, to help them throw off old constraints, to help them abandon deadening curricula, and to bring their own personalities and passions into the learning equation. I knew that this would be especially tricky in public school, where teachers had little autonomy unless they seized it for themselves, usually behind closed doors.

I scored two computers for my classroom. We had objects to think with, but also objects to think about—where would we put them, how would we share them. And so we took it up at our morning class meetings. My kids decided we would put the computers in the back of the room, and they would pair up and spend about fifteen minutes a day on their projects. Throughout the day, I had mini-lessons with individuals or the entire class and then, more or less, turned them loose. We decided that at the end of each week, pairs could discuss the ups and downs of pairhood, seek input into working out a shaky relationship, get advice about forming a new one, or consider the wisdom of joining pairs to gain new ideas and more time on task. In a magnificent display of childhood fairness and concern, this improbable set-up actually worked out. The conversations this situation provoked were rich in thinking about thinking and learning, about how to get along, how to care for others, and what to do when things did not go your way.

I remember instances when, amazingly, kids would give up their own precious time on the computer to help out a classmate who was just minutes away from finishing a project or discovering a new element of Logo. The discussions and projects that emerged were many and varied, some very simple, and others actually beyond my own scope. The freedom they had to think and create with such a robust and evocative tool inspired an admirable degree of energy and perseverance that everyday school could not accomplish. Limits melted away, the dynamism was unmistakable. It became natural to absorb the pedagogical philosophy that so strongly underpinned the use of Logo as a way to make palpable the power and efficacy of the construction of one's own learning.

A note about this class—my students were from one of the most diverse districts in New York City. They were rich and poor and in between. They had a broad range of abilities and school histories. At one point, we counted over thirty different ethnic groups in our class. We had our problems, but we all worked to figure how to handle them and the computer presence fit right into what we had already built together.

Soon I began to give workshops to interested teachers. At that time, many teachers, especially women, were intimidated by computers to the extent that their hands would freeze over the keyboard. Learning how to get through this brought them a new feeling of agency. My own experience with these kinds of fears made me want to create powerful, dynamic workshops that would begin a revolution in their thinking about teaching and learning. I had that opportunity a few years later when, after some time at The Computer School in New York City, I was asked to direct Project Mindstorm at Gardner Elementary School in San Jose, California. I gathered a group of like-minded educators, some experts in their fields. They also had qualities in common that I think are necessary for successful learning: flexibility, comfort with ambiguity and nuance, generosity of spirit, willingness to make mistakes, curiosity, and kindness. Together we endeavored to create an atmosphere of intellectual exploration and adventure.

I firmly believe that each workshop should be different and reflect the interests and passions of the teachers, and the culture of the community and the school. Gardner had a group of dedicated, talented teachers, some who were delighted to have computers, some who were very successful just the way they were, and some who didn't trust this whole project at all. I commiserated. All teachers see new ideas come and go, some of which might create a frisson of excitement, but most are abandoned as soon as possible. How could this project touch their passions?

I thought about Seymour, the toddler who fell in love with gears, which led him to a love for mathematics. But we forget that Seymour fell in love with a lot of things: poetry, flying a plane, cooking, music, art, human rights, the names of flowers, puzzles, the samba school, prismed eyeglasses, rivers... I could go on but I think the point is he was interested in everything and the connections of things and the emotions aroused when deep understanding is developed. I believe that is the magic and it is something that we can all develop if we are open to it. I wanted this for my own workshops.

Most of the Gardner teachers were intent upon learning things that they could immediately apply to the children in their classes. I realized, however, that they must create something personal to achieve the intellectual excitement I experienced in my first workshop. This kind of activity was strange to them, almost threatening. They were used to transferring what they knew to their students, rather than allowing their students to discover or follow their own paths to a specific end. They were expecting the same for themselves. They wanted to be told what to do and how to do it. They wanted to get it right. I believe that in constructionist classrooms there are times when there is a tension between how much to tell and how much to let students discover. Teachers new to this method are especially vulnerable. They fear they will deny their students certain knowledge or abilities. It is quite reasonable to feel this way at first, especially if your own education has been traditional or authoritarian. Eventually, they learned to trust me and the process. They were convinced to give up some control, let go, pursue something they, themselves, desired. This kind of learning is built, as is all real learning, on relationships, in this case the one between me and the teachers and between them and the new material they were encountering.

One teacher proposed that she make a birthday card for her fiancé. She worked for the entire two weeks on that project of love and in the end had learned much more Logo than if I had directed her in her effort. Another teacher recreated patterns that she used in weaving. The psychologist was determined to make an interactive personality test. Two teachers made a book of their own cartoons. Stories were written and illustrated, the turtle morphed into many personalities, made videos, and learned to dance. The satisfaction was tangible. Having experienced the freedom and elation of constructing something, the teachers could more readily imagine the same for their students.

And they did!

I stayed with the project for two years. During that time, I saw many original ideas develop that were relevant to the lives of the students and their teachers. One second-grade class decided they wanted to contribute to the construction of the new light rail planned for the city of San Jose. They had discussions about where the line should run, how long it should be, how to create shelters along the way that would best serve the public. They considered what size the shelters should be; how would they shield people from the sun and rain; how would they accommodate the elderly and disabled; and what was the best way to celebrate the cultures of the city in the decoration of those shelters. They worked in pairs and in groups for many weeks and eventually created a portfolio that they presented to the city council.

One fifth grader who had learning issues and was not happy in school, developed a way of making pictures with the period key. There was no plan involved, he seemed to work it all out in his head and then create impressionistic pictures of boats, airplanes, farm scenes, even portraits. No one could figure out how he did it, but it became a crowning accomplishment for him and gave him confidence to broaden his attempts at learning.

One teacher, after reading *The Wizard of Oz* to her class, invited a parent to accompany the children on piano while they sang all the songs from the musical. The class decided to recreate the story on their computers, programming the characters, the scenes, and the music. Another class learned good urban planning while they plotted out blocks for cities of their own making, taking environmental, practical, and design issues into consideration. Another class put together a motorized circus, not unlike Alexander Calder's effort housed at New York City's Whitney Museum.

I remember walking along with a group of kindergartners on their way to the computer lab. They had been animating nursery rhymes. One little boy turned to his friend and said, "It's fun, it's hard, it's Logo." It sounds like an ad but it really happened. About a week later, I was with a group of my students as they presented their work to the San Jose school board. To my surprise, a fifth-grade presenter said almost the exact words, "It's Logo and it's hard and fun." Seymour boiled those stories down to "hard fun," and I think it illustrates profoundly how willing students are to engage in learning that relates to them, fascinates them in some way, and challenges them.

Perhaps this should be the mantra for our way forward after the pandemic: "It will be hard but it's up to us to make it fun." To comfort the skeptics, perhaps we can call it rigorous fun or gritty fun. After a year of virtual school, I can already hear the call for "back to basics," and "Oh, the kids have missed a whole year of work," as though learning is a linear endeavor and every student learns exactly what is offered by the curriculum for that specific day. The cry for standardized testing is loud and clear already. Perhaps the parents who have home-schooled have figured out what good teachers have always known, that they already understand what their kids are capable of—no testing necessary.

As a believer in constructionist teaching and learning, I've grown accustomed to all the criticisms. As a practitioner of constructionist teaching and learning, I have witnessed proof that these criticisms are bogus. Every teacher is capable of incorporating constructionist ideas into her practice. Every teacher is capable of finding allies (parents are essential) to this way of thinking. Allies are capable of helping to change policy. Success brings more allies and better policies. Perhaps it is unreasonable to require activism from overworked teachers but I think it is crucial. In the meantime, teachers, perhaps you can close your classroom doors once in a while.

What would Cynthia and Seymour say?

References

Papert, S. (1980). *Mindstorms: Children, Computers, and Powerful Ideas.* Basic Books.

Bad Design is Violence: Powerful Ideas and Powerful Politics in Constructionist Education

Paulo Blikstein

"The computers-in-education community [...] seem remarkably reluctant to use computers for any purpose that fails to look like something that has been taught in schools for the past centuries." — Papert & Solomon 1971

It's been fifty years since Seymour Papert and Cynthia Solomon wrote a short but foundational paper called *Twenty Things to Do with a Computer*. Rarely do we see a piece that is simultaneously so visionary and concise. Over the span of forty typewritten pages, Solomon and Papert suggest activities and ideas that were later developed into entire research programs, programming languages, and products. They cover computational biology, animatronics, digital music, robotics, and many other fields, embedding in their exploration a variety of topics, from differential geometry, feedback, and physics, to randomness, recursion, and poetry.

Nevertheless, the conciseness of the paper is deceptive, some of the most powerful messages are surreptitiously incorporated in the examples therein. Some combine science and the arts in very creative ways—today, we would call them STEAM activities. Others involve sophisticated projects using different technologies and materials—we might refer to them now as maker education or project-based learning. The *Twenty Things* also implicitly include self-explanation and reflection—which have since been proven crucial to deep scientific sensemaking. Thus, even though the paper does not read like an academic one, it is dense with knowledge from education, psychology, and cognitive science—disguised as a mere list of activities.

A naïve reading of the paper would be that it is simply about "things to do," or even about computers or digital technologies. Instead, I believe it is about something else—*a powerful political message about educational design using contemporary technologies*. It is about what happens when—instead of inert, oppressive, or surveillance technologies, embedded in overly-scripted curricula—you give children powerful and expressive tools, and design creative contexts for their exploration, full of emancipatory possibilities.

Powerful Ideas: The Lost Dimension of the Technology-in-Education Debate

As Papert pointed out when commenting on the subtitle of his book, *Mindstorms: Children, Computers and Powerful Ideas* (1993), too many critics focused on the "children and computers," and many forgot the "powerful ideas" part. Conversations about powerful ideas have indeed lost centrality over the past decades as computers-in-education became enmeshed in a myriad of political and academic debates. Educational technologies have inspired—sometimes rightfully so—discussions about cost, test scores, learning gains, opportunity cost, and professional development. Those are important questions, but they somehow made us stop asking what ideas are powerful enough to justify the effort of bringing these technologies to schools, what radically new possibilities these technologies might enable, and whether in doing so they might enact valuable educational goals.

Note that these elements are somewhat independent; there might be powerful ideas that do not achieve what society considers valuable educational goals. There will not always be perfect alignment between what scientists and researchers find powerful and what the more extensive societal discourse considers worth including in national standards. *When there is alignment, however, magic happens.* Examples abound: the powerful ideas in computing had already been exhaustively researched for forty years before they became mandatory (in many countries) in K-12 education in the early 2010s. The power of making, design, prototyping, and engineering was well known before maker education was incorporated into national curricula, and we were aware of the powerful ideas in statistics and data science decades before they entered the educational policymaking wish list.

This points to the fact that promoting powerful ideas and the designs that convey them is also a political act, and a long game that takes decades. Specific designs of educational technology can produce kits, tools, social contexts, and artifacts that could, in the hands of children, enable them to mobilize powerful ideas to subvert the logic behind different types of oppression. We often forget that youth are excellent at turning the tables and repurposing technologies and artifacts in surprising ways—and well-designed tools can augment these subversive uses.

Instead, our conversation often focuses too much on signaling the dangers of new technologies instead of perceiving the possible spaces for creative, subversive, and radical experimentation. Granted, modern technology can be dangerous and oppressive when used in harmful ways. But we often forget that books and pencils (as well as their predecessors) were also once novelties in education and seen as hazardous to our memorization or calligraphy skills—or other, now-defunct abilities. And yet, at some point (and it took centuries every time), we realized that there was no way to produce meaningful education without them, both because they enabled powerful modes of agentic, civic, and cultural participation and because much of the knowledge was encoded in written form. Another risk of introducing books into education was that, arguably, they can also be used for manipulation—but then, any powerful medium can (and will) be used by multiple political stakeholders for advancing their agendas. The point, thus, is not to isolate children from all technology, but to give them the tools to inhabit this new world critically.

It is seductive to argue for isolating youth and keeping them safely restricted to an imaginary world where the old ways would suffice. But when we see technologies as pillars of new literacies, in the broader sense of the term (see diSessa, 2001; Wilensky & Papert, 2010), isolation is not an option. Once a critical mass is achieved, knowledge production, civic participation, and learning become too entangled with the new infrastructure. The *Twenty Things* paper reminds us that, even within this new ecology, there are ways to design new materials and pedagogies to enable students to critically venture into understanding contemporary issues.

Today these new tools, materials, and practices are not just nice-to-haves. For children and youth to begin understanding and taking action around current societal challenges (such as gun violence, climate change, racism, or inequality) we need to provide them with the most potent available tools for sensemaking and activism.

To counter the anti-vaccination propaganda online, children could use automated techniques to extract the contents of millions of social media posts and, using Natural Language Processing and other tools, show that they are based on non-credible sources. Students could put up a fight against social media algorithms by designing browser extensions that reveal how companies manipulate users' timelines or use similar data science tools to expose racial bias in news coverage or police violence.

The Powerful Politics of Design

Nevertheless, the fear of contemporary technologies is not unjustified. Just when we were starting to overcome, at least in some countries, the lack of access to computational technology and connectivity, a handful of (mostly) Silicon Valley companies were working hard to find new ways to profit off of the widespread use of technology. Unfortunately, as we naively enjoyed their "free" services, those companies built one of the most insidious data-driven technocracies in history (see Surveillance Capitalism, Zuboff, 2015). As a result, we ended up with the worst possible type of computational ubiquity, which is used for surveillance, monetization, and control, reviving the debate about the politics of technology in a world with a renewed awareness of issues of oppression and inequality (see, for example, Joerges, 1999; Winner, 1980 and more recently Selwyn, 2010, 2013; Selwyn & Facer, 2013; Vakil, 2018; Watters, 2021; Williamson, 2016)

Still, we cannot forget that the politics of technology can go both ways. The same programming language employed to develop surveillance algorithms can also be used to disable those systems. Winner's foundational article about the "politics of artifacts" (Winner, 1980) has come under attack because it placed too much emphasis on the politics of the physical artifacts as opposed to the enabling systems that augment their oppressive potential. Thus, technologies (embodied in artifacts or processes) need to be enacted within a system that enables and amplifies specific political uses of technologies (Latour, 2004; Woolgar & Cooper, 1999). It is an essential reminder that challenges the wholesale critique of educational technologies about their inefficacy (Tyack & Cuban, 1995) or oppressive properties (as Winner himself did later).

In their intent to overgeneralize or overlook the centrality of "enabling systems" (Woolgar & Cooper, 1999) many critiques of technology in education are flawed. Critics might look at a set of materials that are *today* used for oppression and control (software, computers, microcontrollers, networks) and assume that they have always been and must always remain part of an inescapable set of socio-technical artifacts designed to oppress students. Unfortunately, this technocentric reading that ignores history, intention, and ever-evolving contexts, became almost a new genre in educational scholarship; it is almost too easy to look at any technology and see horrible uses for it, while it is a lot harder to design justice-oriented, ethical, and subversive versions of them.

Also, there is a history to inventions; the intentions of the designers matter as much as how others might try to co-opt these artifacts for their purposes--think of Santos Dumont's airplane or Nobel's dynamite. We can create technologies that seed specific uses, possibilities, classroom cultures, and interactions. But while the design of these artifacts may be about empowering children, over the years, different micro and macropolitical regimes might want to interfere with the original intent and direct them towards different (or opposite) purposes. Coding and educational robotics were initially conceived as tools of radical resistance to instructionist education. But over the years, there have been many attempts to co-opt and fit them to other, much more conservative goals such as curricular compliance, preparation for the job market, or simply commercial profit. This is why these wholesale, ahistorical critiques miss the mark— and also why Papert, Solomon, Edith Ackermann, and others spent a good part of their later careers reminding us of their original ideas—they were never just advocating for computers in classrooms, but for technologies embedded in student-centered, justice-oriented, emancipatory cultures, curricula, and systems.

In that sense, *Twenty Things* is also a strong political statement because it presents subversive examples that upend the conventional materialities of schools—the examples offered by Papert and Solomon simply do not work in a regular classroom! They tell students to investigate topics that are not found in any national standards. They suggest ways of learning that are anything but compliant. And they are a great example of why Holbert would say, decades later, that constructionism is "a pedagogy of disrespect" (Holbert, 2020). Constructionism is ultimately about challenging how we think about teaching and learning, pushing back against the status quo, and using technology in empowering ways. When a robotics kit gets coopted and starts to be used in a scripted, uncreative way, it's time for designers to step in, again, and remind everyone that the point was not to "build robots," but to learn the powerful ideas that were mobilized in the construction of robots.

The original Logo designs and the puzzle-solving (masquerading as coding activities) type of programming are both about coding, but they are entangled in completely different enabling systems. Moreover, these enabling systems are dynamic and evolve/devolve. This is why our work as designers and educational activists never ends—it is not just about creating a given technology and considering that it will forever conserve its favorable properties—we need to spend a lifetime fighting other enabling systems that will try to recruit said technologies to other purposes—especially if they are successful.

Tasks and Mediations Co-evolve—It Is Not Just about Tools

The fact that both technologies and contexts change points to another important lesson from *Twenty Things*—tools, tasks, and mediations co-evolve. Many of the projects proposed by Papert and Solomon would be trivial today because the tools have since improved and diversified. As tools evolve, tasks become more straightforward or even trivial. In 1971, the only tool available was Logo, and some of the features that made it powerful are less relevant in today's world of parallel processing, networks, machine learning, and other new ways of programming and interacting with computers. Today, we have laser cutters, biomaking, 3D printers, e-textiles, and a myriad of other tools, not to mention the renaissance of different forms of *making things* stemming from research into non-dominant communities (e.g., Blikstein, 2020; Buechley, 2013; Buechley & Perner-Wilson, 2012; Calabrese Barton & Tan, 2018; Holbert et al., 2020; Tzou et al., 2019).

Now we do not have just twenty things, but most likely *two thousand things* to do with this plethora of tools. And in this new tool- and idea-rich world, we can be far more inclusive. We can consider new types of technologies and materialities from all over the world, such as the sophisticated techniques from indigenous communities (Barajas-López & Bang, 2018), African-American culture (Gaskins, 2021), or the communities that are experts in recycling in Brazil (Blikstein, 2008).

This work is not only possible but urgently needed. The diversity of tools and activities matter more than ever. It is not only because of how they can tap into different practices, ways of being, and epistemologies, but also due to the fact that they can create a whole host of possibilities for how computing, science, engineering, and making, broadly conceived, can be used in the world—and transform it (see for example, Tissenbaum et al., 2021).

Conclusion: Bad Design Is Violence

Not long ago, many people naïvely imagined that we just need to tell people the facts and they will understand, for example, climate change or vaccines. But facts can be fabricated, data can be cherry-picked, statistics can be manipulated. Offering pre-packaged truths about climate change to students will not foster the sensemaking practices that will enable them to survive this information deluge. Instead, they need to be engaged in collecting, analyzing, and making sense of data.

Similarly, some were quick to say that we needed to teach kids about the dangers of social media. But analogously, directly telling students about these risks does little to alleviate the problem: when it comes to understanding the algorithms of social media, we need youth to build their own AI software. The answer to both challenges is to create tools and experiences that let them investigate and build the phenomenon themselves.

Thus, the constructionist agenda, as Mike Eisenberg beautifully articulated (*Seymour Papert Tribute Panel*, 2013) is not so much about coding or computers but about using new tools to bring a variety of powerful new areas into the reach of children—not just because they are in the national standards, but because youth cannot take action to change the world without a sophisticated understanding of what is around them, and powerful tools to make the change happen. Paulo Freire (1974) would say that education is ultimately about using knowledge to go from the consciousness of the real (the here and now) to the consciousness of the possible, or the *inéditos viáveis* (the viable unprecedented).

In our complex world, we need to give children the best possible cognitive partners for this challenge. Today, these tools might look different from the Logo of 1971, but will likely share its ethos. They will have to cover a wide range of topics, enable different ways of learning, and work across diverse social settings—on top of honoring and elevating local cultures and epistemologies.

The design of those tools will be a gargantuan task. My concern is that we will be seduced by the instant gratification of armchair technology critique, and not fully engage in the much harder task of design and creation. Academics often fall in love with critique (granted, there is plenty of educational technology that is ill-conceived). But we cannot settle for just pointing out everything that is oppressive, unjust, wrong, and ineffective. We have the moral responsibility to get our hands dirty and create new tools, designs, and environments. Refusing to do so will have well-known consequences. We will leave the space open for the worst version of educational technology and their canned, scripted, elitist, and disempowering solutions, and thus deny children valuable tools to augment their presence in the world. Nothing will stop the influx of new technologies into schools—the question is what types of technologies will be there.

Creating empowering tools and embedding them in generative activities is a risky, time-consuming, labor-intensive, and subtle job. But not doing it, or doing it badly, or settling for pure armchair critique, is a form of violence, or a way to enable the violence of others onto children. It is misleading to read Papert and Solomon's *Twenty Things* as a static list of technology-in-education activities—it is much more useful to see them as their best attempt at this crucial political job, a brilliant snapshot of what was possible in 1971. The way we see those possibilities has crucial implications not just for what you can do with technology, but for the kind of society we want to live in, and the educational systems that we will design to bring that future about.

Acknowledgments

Thanks to Nathan Holbert, Sylvia Martinez, and Alicja Żenczykowska for helpful comments, edits, and ideas.

References

Barajas-López, F., & Bang, M. (2018). Indigenous making and sharing: Claywork in an Indigenous STEAM program. *Equity & Excellence in Education*, *51*(1), 7-20. doi.org/10.1080/10665684.2018.1437847

Blikstein, P. (2008). Travels in Troy with Freire: Technology as an Agent for Emancipation. In P. Noguera & C. A. Torres (Eds.), *Social Justice Education for Teachers: Paulo Freire and the Possible Dream* (pp. 205-244). Sense Publishers.

Blikstein, P. (2020). Cheesemaking Emancipation. In N. Holbert, M. Berland, & Y. B. Kafai (Eds.), *Designing Constructionist Futures: The Art, Theory, and Practice of Learning Designs* (pp. 115-126).

Buechley, L. (2013). Plenary talk at FabLearn 2013. In: FabLearn 2013. Stanford University.

Buechley, L., & Perner-Wilson, H. (2012). Crafting technology: Reimagining the processes, materials, and cultures of electronics. *ACM Transactions on Computer-Human Interaction (TOCHI) 19*(3), 21.

Calabrese-Barton, A., & Tan, E. (2018). *STEM-rich maker learning: Designing for equity with youth of color.* Teachers College Press.

diSessa, A. A. (2001). *Changing minds: Computers, learning, and literacy.* MIT Press.

Freire, P. (1974). *Pedagogy of the Oppressed* (M. B. Ramos, Trans.). Seabury.

Gaskins, N. R. (2021). *Techno-Vernacular Creativity and Innovation: Culturally Relevant Making Inside and Outside of the Classroom.* MIT Press.

Holbert, N. (2020). Constructionism as a pedagogy of disrespect. In N. Holbert, M. Berland, & Y. B. Kafai (Eds.), *Designing Constructionism Futures: the art, theory, and practice of learning designs.* MIT Press. doi.org/10.7551/mitpress/12091.003.0018

Holbert, N., Dando, M., & Correa, I. (2020). Afrofuturism as critical constructionist design: Building futures from the past and present. *Learning, Media and Technology, 45*(4), 328-344. doi.org/10.1080/17439884.2020.1754237

Joerges, B. (1999). Do politics have artefacts? *Social studies of science, 29*(3), 411-431.

Latour, B. (2004). Why has critique run out of steam? From matters of fact to matters of concern. *Critical inquiry, 30*(2), 225-248.

Papert, S. (1993). *Mindstorms: Children, Computers, and Powerful Ideas* (2nd ed.). Basic Books.

Selwyn, N. (2010). Looking beyond learning: Notes towards the critical study of educational technology. *Journal of Computer Assisted Learning, 26*(1), 65-73. doi.org/10.1111/j.1365-2729.2009.00338.x

Selwyn, N. (2013, May 23-25). *Discourses of digital 'disruption' in education: A critical analysis* Fifth International Roundtable on Discourse Analysis, City University, Hong Kong.

Selwyn, N., & Facer, K. (Eds.). (2013). *The politics of education and technology: Conflicts, controversies, and connections.* Springer.

Seymour Papert Tribute Panel. (2013, June 27). IDC 2013 : The 12th International Conference on Interaction Design and Children. vimeo.com/69471812

Tissenbaum, M., Weintrop, D., Holbert, N., & Clegg, T. (2021). The case for alternative endpoints in computing education. *British Journal of Educational Technology, 52*(3), 1164-1177. doi.org/10.1111/bjet.13072

Tyack, D. B., & Cuban, L. (1995). *Tinkering toward utopia: A century of public school reform.* Harvard University Press.

Tzou, C., Suárez, E., Bell, P., LaBonte, D., Starks, E., & Bang, M. (2019). Storywork in STEM-Art: Making, materiality and robotics within everyday acts of Indigenous presence and resurgence. *Cognition and Instruction, 37*(3), 306-326. doi.org/10.1080/07370008.2019.1624547

Vakil, S. (2018). Ethics, Identity, and Political Vision: Toward a Justice-Centered Approach to Equity in Computer Science Education. *Harvard Educational Review, 88*(1), 26-52.

Watters, A. (2021). *Teaching machines: The history of personalized learning.* MIT Press.

Wilensky, U., & Papert, S. (2010). Restructurations: Reformulations of knowledge disciplines through new representational forms. In J. Clayson & I. Kalas (Eds.), *Proceedings of the Constructionism 2010 Conference.* Paris, France, Aug 10-14.

Williamson, B. (2016). Silicon startup schools: technocracy, algorithmic imaginaries and venture philanthropy in corporate education reform. *Critical Studies in Education, 59*(2), 218-236. doi.org/10.1080/17508487.2016.1186710

Winner, L. (1980). Do artifacts have politics? *Daedalus,* 121-136.

Woolgar, S., & Cooper, G. (1999). Do artefacts have ambivalence: Moses' bridges, winner's bridges and other urban legends in S&TS. *Social studies of science, 29*(3), 433-449. doi.org/10.1177/030631299029003005

Zuboff, S. (2015). Big other: Surveillance capitalism and the prospects of an information civilization. *Journal of Information Technology, 30*(1), 75-89. doi.org/10.1057/jit.2015.5

Thou Shalt Not Write Curriculum

Peter Rawitsch

An Apple II Plus computer was delivered to my first grade classroom in the fall of 1982. It arrived with a pile of floppy disks from MECC. The green images on the black background were spellbinding. Who knew that munching words could be so much fun? Even my students liked it.

A couple of months later a Terrapin Logo Language binder (with a manual and the accompanying Logo disk) appeared in my school mailbox (Grammer & Goldenberg, 1982). This was something totally different—just a triangle on a screen. Every journey begins with a single step. Mine began with *FD 100*.

I brought the school computer home on many weekends so I could learn the Logo. I learned about Seymour Papert and *Mindstorms* (1980) from Harold Abelson's bible, *Apple Logo* (1982).

I set up the computer in my classroom as a learning station where the children could explore the keyboard and teach the turtle *tricks*. Eventually I got a grant from my P.T.A. so I could purchase a clear, inverted popcorn bowl shaped robot to tether to my hardware. Now the kids were really hooked.

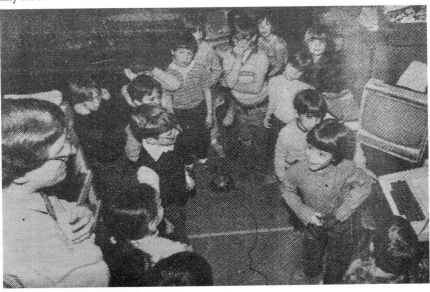

Then I broke my Third Commandment of Learning: Thou shalt not write curriculum.

In my excitement to share this amazing tool where children were in control of their learning and could create knowledge, I agreed to develop a curriculum plan for using Logo in grades 1–5. I believe Logo died in my school district about three years later. My sin.

However, I kept it alive in my classroom with LEGO Logo bricks and LogoWriter, while the rest of the world seemed to move onto "learning games" and activities that didn't require much thinking.

Looking back on those years, I came to realize that Logo was not meant for the one-size-fits-all factory school model. It was meant for self-directed learners who were interested in creating things with a computer.

I was probably looking through various Logo bibliographies in preparation for teaching a graduate-level Logo course when I stumbled across Seymour Papert and Cynthia Solomon's *Twenty Things to Do with a Computer*. I must have found a copy of it online. Its historic significance was striking. It was written eleven years before I started teaching the computer *TO BOX*.

It is wishful thinking that no one used their first nineteen ideas as lesson plans or teacher-led projects. Hopefully they honored student independence and voice and allowed anyone who was interested to think up their own things to do.

I retired after forty-two years of teaching in public schools. I spend my time now as an activist for racial and educational justice. Here are some of the things I am doing with a computer.

1. Meet on Zoom to educate people on racial justice issues and to build alliances.

2. Attend school board policy meetings remotely to monitor local decision making.

3. Write speeches to give in-person at board of education meetings.

4. Create and post educational justice memes on social media.

5. Share an online petition to end preK–fifth grade school suspensions.

6. Send e-mails to social justice organizations to get support for the petition.

7. Read and share articles and blogs about racial and educational justice.

8. Think of more things to do.

Learning Logo did not make me a better activist. But it helped to affirm my belief in the right of every child to be free to learn.

References

Abelson, H. (1982). *Apple Logo*. Byte Books.

Grammer, V. C., & Goldenberg, E. P. (1982). *The Terrapin Logo Language for the Apple II*. Terrapin Inc.

Papert, S. (1980). *Mindstorms: Children, Computers, and Powerful Ideas*. Basic Books.

The Wider Walls

Bill Kerr

The room was humming harder as the ceiling flew away
—*Whiter Shade of Pale, Procol Harum, 1967*

Seymour was very good at finding a great pithy expression to describe a learning event. For example, he described the turtle as "an object to think with." Another such expression is "wide walls" to express a diversity of doing, but I'm less certain about who coined that one.

I wasn't aware that the concept of wide walls (as distinct from the expression) was there from the start. I thought there was a transition as the baton passed from Seymour to Mitch Resnick. Not only did the turtle become a cat but, in my mind, the philosophy also changed from "low floor, high ceiling" (*Seymour*) to "low floor, wide walls" (*Mitch*).

Being a long way away in Australia, perhaps I missed some nuance. Maybe someone closer to MIT can fill me in. In reading *Twenty Things*, I can see the wide walls were there from the beginning: floor turtle, screen turtle, turtle graphics, game making, movies, music, robots, light displays, poetry, physics, curiosity about self, even making fun of Computer Aided Instruction.

Nevertheless, we owe a lot to the Scratch team for continuing to lower the floor (block coding), opening the windows (remix and a web site where it is so easy to share) as well as wider walls (easy to code multimedia and extensions to music, the micro:bit, Makey Makey and others). The user interface, with its color coding of blocks into categories has always been brilliant.

What attracted me to computers in the first place was Seymour's book *Mindstorms* (1980) with its intention of making maths more accessible to those who struggle with textbook maths or maths in general. Start by drawing a square using your body. Build further from that simple starting point by changing the angles, changing the number of repeats, and introduce variables. This approach was both more interesting and could bring maths to more students.

Regarding the importance of tinkering, Seymour was also there early on in a collaborative article with Sherry Turkle, "Epistemological Pluralism and the Revaluation of the Concrete" (1991). Ostensibly, this was directed at the needs of girls but in reality, it was about those who tinker or the bricoleurs. It's better to initially allow sloppy code (spaghetti) and for design to iterate through stages. If a teacher insists on getting it perfect from the start then that is a sure way to kill motivation in many students. If only the standards-based curriculum designers, remote from the classroom, who separate the what from the how, understood that. This was pointed out by Mitch Resnick in a recent exchange with Mark Guzdial in the comments at Mark's blog.[1] There are those who understand how the wider walls can work and those who, through not understanding, put up barriers to them working.

Artbotics

In my research, I came across a thesis by Jennifer Cross (2017) where she designed a course called Arts & Bots. Taking this cue, I wrote a submission for a new course in my current school and called it Artbotics. Rather than robotics, we can have Artbotics, with the Hummingbird Bit. Let us create a provocative, tangible sculpture and then add robotic actuation and sensing.

This reframing of robotics makes a difference. The Artbotics word hit a nerve since there is an ongoing desire for school administrations to introduce more creative middle schooling curricula. I see Artbotics as another expression of wider walls, integrating different subjects in the curriculum into a whole which students find more meaningful.

As Seymour pointed out, the computer has a protean nature and can be used as a multimedia hard fun machine. It is also true that the division of knowledge into different subject domains, although useful in some ways, has always created artificial distinctions too. Maths can be Arty. Art can be Mathy.

In Central Australia, where I live, there is a famous indigenous art movement called Papunya Tula. One of its core motifs is dotted circles. I had a go at simulating parts of that work using Snap! and the local gallery in Alice Springs agreed it was worthwhile. Since this book is in black and white, I invite you to see the simulations at my blog, with a link to the Snap! program where you can do your own.[2]

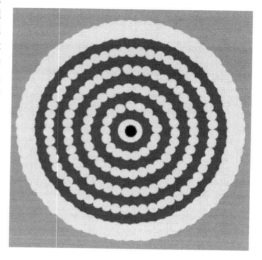

By making art a real part of the plan we soften the traditionally hard cultures of the STEM subjects and broaden the appeal of the whole mix. It has to be real and it can be real because digital by its nature does embrace everything. A program such as Scratch is multimedia with built-in icons, backgrounds, sounds, music, and speech with all of them editable. The coding is there too, of course, and the purpose of the coding is to bring the multimedia to life.

As well as art, storytelling needs to be in there too. I managed to rewrite all my introductory Scratch projects as short stories rather than lessons in technique, e.g. weird animals where the dog meows and the cat barks. This serves as a good model for later when I ask students to create their own stories.

One of the best expressions of the wider walls concept is a 2005 article by Mitch Resnick and Brian Silverman about how to evaluate construction kits. We need those design principles now with all the new construction kits (and this also applies to the new microcontrollers and new software) that have become available. A key principle here is that a little bit (of programming) goes a long way. By using the KISS principle, new users will make a fast start and the possibility is there to transition rapidly to projects they really want to do, not just can do.

When it comes to learning principles, the value of tinkering and iteration (iterate, iterate, iterate …) as well as curriculum integration also fit under the rubric of wider walls.

You can see the same KISS principle designed into TurtleArt (by Brian Silverman and Paula Bontá). Its variety of coding blocks is restricted yet you can make beautiful art readily. There are beautiful TurtleArt examples on the website gallery.[3]

From Bits to Atoms

What I've really been looking for is a pithy expression to describe the ongoing evolution of the creative use of computers in education. In reading *Invent to Learn* (Martinez & Stager, 2019) I was struck by the three game changers assertion, the game changers being coding, physical computing, and fab labs. Could there be a pithy expression to describe these?

Possibly "wide walls," although a good try, lacks a bit of oomph, requires too much explanation and can only be stretched so far. Can we set the world on fire with wider walls? Perhaps. As my students explore more I do feel the room humming harder… but I am still not satisfied that it is an adequate descriptor.

Jay Silver takes this a step further when he situates his invention, Makey Makey, within the larger context. He designs tools which enable a sensual re-experiencing, a re-seeing, of the everyday world. With Makey Makey you can make an orchestra which is played by pieces of fruit, rather than a keyboard. Digital meets the banana. It began with Seymour's insight that the turtle could be "an object to think with" and has now further developed, in Jay Silver's words, into conceiving the whole "world as a construction kit" (Silver, 2014).

The world as construction kit has a very long history. Indigenous Australians used to live off the land and made all their tools, as well as their food and medicine, directly from nature. When they looked at the natural environment, they saw a construction kit. The part of this argument that I like is that our perception is a variable: we can design new tools, like Makey Makey, which change the way we perceive the computer/keyboard. Insofar as modern consumerism can kill off self-reliant productivity this new way of perceiving is a good thing.

Wouldn't it be desirable for many more of us to become more maker orientated, particularly if the developments in modern technology lower the entry barriers? From STEM to STEAM then moves on to STEAM for the 99%. STEAM for the 99% means bringing all of the subjects to a broader audience. This may be achieved through diverse cross curricular subjects which go under names like Artbotics, Digital Wearables, Culturally Situated Design Tools,[4] and Unruly Splats.[5]

When the computer is used as a dynamic (programmable) multimedia fun machine it becomes the best tool available for wholesale curriculum integration. In other words it's time to merge the computer into the world with all its junk. If that isn't wider walls, then what is it?

References

Cross, J. L. (2017). Creative Robotic Systems for Talent-Based Learning (Publication Number CMU-RI-TR-17-30) [Doctoral dissertation, Carnegie Mellon University]. Pittsburgh, PA. kilthub.cmu.edu/ndownloader/files/12248549

Martinez, S. L., & Stager, G. (2019). Invent to Learn: Making, Tinkering, and Engineering in the Classroom (2 ed.). Constructing Modern Knowledge Press.

Papert, S. (1980). Mindstorms: Children, Computers, and Powerful Ideas. Basic Books.

Resnick, M., & Silverman, B. (2005). Some Reflections on Designing Construction Kits for Kids. Proceedings of the 2005 Conference on Interaction Design and Children, 117-122.

Silver, J. S. (2014). Lens x Block: World as Construction Kit [Doctoral dissertation, Massachusetts Institute of Technology]. 1derful.org/phdthesis.php

Turkle, S., & Papert, S. (1991). Epistemological Pluralism and the Revaluation of the Concrete. In I. Harel & S. Papert (Eds.), Constructionism (pp. 161-191). Ablex Publishing Corporation.

Notes

1 Mark Guzdial's blog - computinged.wordpress.com/2020/12/29/the-goal-of-the-first-cs-course-should-be-to-promote-confidence-if-were-going-to-increase-diversity-in-cs-paying-off-on-a-bet/
2 Dotted circles revisited - billkerr2.blogspot.com
3 TurtleArt gallery - turtleart.org/gallery
4 Culturally Situated Design Tools - csdt.org
5 Unruly Splats - unrulysplats.com

Let's Kill the Pencil

Gary Stager

The recent period of horrific health and economic crises caused by COVID-19 might have at least one educational benefit. Students are "working" from home and like everywhere else in the past two generations, their communication is now largely via computer generated text, not manual handwriting.

Whenever I visit a school, I scan the environment, observe social interactions, and look for learning artifacts. Even while strolling around spectacular schools—the sort of institutions blessed with phenomenal facilities, grandiose grounds, well-stocked libraries, makerspaces, and performing arts centers—I sense reason for concern. The lower primary classrooms have examples, presumably of exemplary student work, adorning the corridor walls. Sadly, the displayed work fails to match the grandeur, quality, and expectations of the school. Por qué?

Thanks to the technology of choice, the pencil, your average elementary school student will spend an inordinate amount of time filling a cleverly designed worksheet with two or three banal sentences. I truly lament the lost opportunities for children to create work commensurate with their creativity and intellect. The prophylactic barrier is the pencil.

How many learning disabilities are created by a six-year-old's confusion between their ability to express oneself and their physical prowess at etching letters with a primitive writing stick? The development of a child's fine motor skills is much better suited to typing than handwriting. Few other intellectual pursuits require muscle development. The hysterical argument that handwriting is needed for fine motor skill development is as circular as it is preposterous. Surely, this development is possible without handwriting and if not, handwriting ability seems an unworthy objective.

Word processing is the undisputed winner of the computer age. No serious writer under the age of a presidential candidate uses a writing stick for more than writing "not my fault" in Sharpie. **Writers "write" on computers.** Period. Full stop. Fin!

I harbor no doubt that the pencil has retarded literacy development. It spawned the five-para-graph essay, inauthentic "writing" assignments, and has made life unpleasant for teachers sifting through piles of student chicken scratch. The pencil has fundamentally limited the quality and volume of student writing. This is indisputable.

You learn to write by writing. When you waste several *years* teaching kids, not one, but two different styles of ancient stick scratching, you severely diminish opportunities for students to say something with coherence, persuasion, beauty, or personal voice.

Word processing makes it possible to write more, better, and quicker, while the editing process is continuous and fluid. You may still turn in X number of drafts to satisfy an assignment, but each of those drafts is the product of countless micro-drafts. Best of all, word processing eliminates another useless and ineffective subject of bygone eras, spelling instruction! Bonus! #winning

Students composing text (writing) with word processing software should dramatically increase the quality and volume of written communication. There should be no need to remind them to attend to errors revealed by spelling or grammar checkers. Continuous correspondence should be a staple of childhood and last a lifetime.

It boggles the mind that as far as I know, no research has been done anywhere to study the benefits or consequences of introducing writing to young children without handwriting, in other words on a computer rather than with a hand-sharpened sliver of lead. As Papert and Solomon say in *Twenty Things to Do with a Computer*, there may be no greater example of "the intellectual timidity of the computers-in-education community, which seems remarkably reluctant to use the computers for any purpose that fails to look very much like something that has been taught in schools for the past centuries."

Nostalgia is a Powerful Narcotic

Spare me the academic papers by tenure-track weenies at East Metuchen Community College seeking to "prove" that handwriting instruction raises test scores. This will only force me to send you reams of scholarship on butter churning as an effective weight loss strategy, bloodletting as an indicator of entrepreneurship, or phrenology as a symptom of mindfulness.

I am sorry, but publishers of handwriting workbooks and providers of D'Nealian professional development may have to go and get themselves some of those clean coal jobs or find some other way to torture young people. I hear that The College Board may be hiring!

If schools never widen their gaze beyond reading, writing, and 'rithmetic, the pencil is still the wrong tool. Writing and mathematics are done with computers everywhere, but school. In a drawing or painting class, pencils might be handy. However, imagine if the only tool provided in art class was a shovel. That would limit artistic development in the way the pencil remains an obstacle to learning everything else.

If you feel nostalgic about handwriting, offer a calligraphy elective. Now your school will have an art class! The high-falutin' handwritten International Baccalaureate a concern? Relegate penmanship to an 11th grade PE unit.

The only time I use a pen or pencil is when asked to autograph a copy of a book I composed on a computer. Banking is online, so no more check writing excuses. You can teach kids to sign their name on a greeting card for their great-grandmother in a session or two and then say, "Aloha!" to Eberhard Faber. Spend the rest of elementary school learning how to think and engaging in work that matters. Their lumbrical muscles will thank you and their intellectual development will no longer be limited by a Number 2 drawing stick.

Teachers, it's time to say goodbye to your little friend… Pencils R.I.P

Whatever Happened to the Revolution?

Geraldine Kozberg

Geraldine (Gerry) Kozberg founded the St. Paul Logo Project, which provided teacher education in Logo programming and philosophy to thousands of teachers in St. Paul and beyond, and was a leader in the Logo community. She left us in 2018. This article was originally published in *Logo Update*, the newsletter of the Logo Foundation (1996), as a series of two letters written a decade apart in 1986 and 1996.

In the halcyon days of the early 80s, the technology was new and euphoria high. Logo would transform our schools. From all over the world, the Logo community converged on MIT. Logo 84. Logo 85. Logo 86.[1] We were ready for *Star Wars*.

At the final session of Logo 86, however, Brian Harvey and Bill Higginson stunned the audience with the question, "Whatever happened to the revolution?" *Logo Exchange* asked me to respond to Brian and Bill, an open letter of sorts. Here are parts of that letter:

Dear Brian and Bill,
Your presentation at Logo 86 was stunning. It was a piece of theater, a *New Yorker* postscript, a witty, sophisticated, calculated statement on education in general, and Logo in particular.

You speak of revolution. You ask, "Whatever happened to the revolution?" It depends. It depends on definitions and perspectives.

Nikolai Lenin: From a Lenin-like view of revolution, we know that we have the weapons. We know how to teach; we have the tools and the resources. We do not have what Lenin called an "intolerable level of discontent." People bitch a lot, but not enough to upset the status quo.

Martin Luther King: From the teaching and life of Martin Luther King, we know that revolutions are not created by the masses, rather by the small committed minority. We have a small committed minority within the Logo community. We do not have a critical mass.

Stephen Jay Gould: From the theoretical mind of Stephen Jay Gould, we understand cultural change in terms of "transformation." Change is preceded by a slow accumulation of stresses that the culture resists until a breaking point is reached, moving the culture to the next higher level of transformation.

Learning in a computer culture in 1986 is learning in a changing culture. I would say we are a culture in transition, not revolution. We experience resistance, but the more things change... the more things change!

Logo teachers see change. What do they see? They "see" students thinking. The following learning behaviors—there are eight—were culled from teacher observations and anecdotal reports.

Students talk to themselves and to others. The act of languaging one's thoughts is a form of verbal mediation, a way of mediating and clarifying understanding.

Students move. Heads, hands, shoulders move with the turtle. Syntonic learning appears to be firmly related to how children process their worlds.

Students draw upon mental images. Memory is grounded in words and images. Visual imagery facilitates the storage and retrieval of information and instruction.

Students regulate their work. Casual explorations with the turtle give way to conscious control. Self-correction and evaluation are related to the sense of empowerment and control that we see in mature learners.

Students look for and create patterns. Pattern recognition is a basic strategy of organization and comprehension at the meta-cognitive state of learning awareness.

Students use Logo procedures as building blocks. The process of breaking problems into meaningful pieces of deconstruction has long been associated with formal problem solving.

Students compose and create. Artists describe the process of composition as impressionistic and generative. Ideas seemingly emerge, one idea triggering or guiding the next one, the subconscious driving the conscious.

Students present. Young people enter the adult world of presenters with confidence and poise. The work they present is their own.

These behaviors tell us something. Collectively, they give us an extraordinary new way of looking at learning. It may not be a revolution, but a new culture is emerging.

We call it a Logo culture. We are too close to it to fully understand it. The impact on learners and learning environments involves complex relationships. We have yet to tease out the nuances and subtleties. This is what I see:

Stronger Learners... stronger in the sense of learners who use their intuition, who claim ownership of their learning, and are thus free to risk in order to learn more. I see students using learning modalities that are not tapped by the present curriculum.

Real Work... a work intensity that is satisfying and worthwhile; a work ethic that encourages co-learning. Gender roles and age differences are blurred.

Expanded Vision... in the shape of new visual forms that expand our vision and guide us toward a clearer understanding of our changing world. Throughout history, artists have operated at the edge of social and cultural change. The fluid rhythms and transformations of Logo images are visual expressions of a new aesthetic.

Thank you, Brian and Bill, for pushing us to new levels of consciousness and concern. I leave you with the words of the poet, Robert Frost: "I bid you a one-man revolution."

Sincerely, Geraldine Kozberg

The above letter is dated August 10, 1986. Ten years have passed. My enthusiasm and support for Logo has not diminished. I still see stronger learners, real work, and new visions, but the realities of our schools are harsh and compelling. There has been no revolution. The promise of systemic change is yet to come as the power of Logo waits its turn.

It is time for another letter. This one is addressed to you, the larger Logo community.

Dear Friends,

Whatever did happen to the revolution? The conditions for revolution were not present: There was no intolerable level of discontent, no critical mass, no breaking point in the larger culture; some cracks, perhaps, but no breaking point.

Revolution? In my school district we talk about test scores, violence, poverty, immigration. Technology? We talk about computers and the Internet. We buy computers and we inventory them.

The Logo community has been unable or unwilling to confront the larger social issues that are tearing at public education. In 1981, I wrote: "Logo is one part of a larger change effort designed to serve as an intervention in learning and learning environments." For the most part, this has not happened. The problem is not the technology, certainly not Logo. The problem is one of equity. Logo is for all kids, but the kids who need Logo the most have no access to it. They are relegated to educational games and instruction in the basic skills.

Logo remains the province of a small, somewhat special group of schools, teachers, and students:

- Teachers who are sophisticated learners themselves
- Students identified as gifted and talented
- Middle class and upper middle class populations
- Private and suburban schools

Logo is for all kids. That does not mean all kids are the same, or that the Logo experience is the same for all kids. Rather it talks to the power of Logo as a language of learning, an instructional process appropriate for a wide range of learning behaviors.

Which brings me to my second point, learning and learning environments. We have not done a good job of helping teachers understand the learning process, not Logo, but learning itself. We have not paid serious attention to the social determinants of achievement, focusing instead on cognition and the technology. For some students, social and behavioral skills may be a prerequisite to classroom participation and learning.

Papert taught that the context for human development is always a culture, never an isolated technology. School is a social institution and Logo understands the principles of learning within the culture of the school. Learning takes place in a social context. Learning is grounded in our social and cultural histories. Why, then, doesn't Logo learning transfer? Why doesn't the integrated learning of Logo pervade the culture of the school?

In Czarist Russia, Jewish children were not allowed to attend the public schools. When Marc Chagall was thirteen, his mother bribed a local school official and Chagall entered the secular, academic world. In his autobiography, Chagall remembers a wondrous time in his geometry class of "... lines, angles, triangles, squares ... They carried me far away to enchanting horizons. And during those hours of drawing, I lacked only a throne."

Or Piet Mondrian, the Dutch artist. When we examine the structural evolution of Mondrian's work, we begin to understand the deconstruction of the process into its most elemental forms. Reconstruction takes on different forms. What could be more relevant for today's young people than the visual learning of Chagall, Mondrian, Logo?

The findings of Logo studies in Saint Paul suggest that improved achievement is more likely to occur at the lower end of the scale. Kids at the top already have their set of "gears" to work with. Kids at the bottom are still looking. The odds are that when they find their "gears," the learning process will be strengthened. It may be that Logo facilitates the development of natural learning systems, and especially for those youngsters who have not had the freedom to make learning connections in their own unique ways.

On Monday, we begin our 15th year of continuous Logo teacher education in Saint Paul. I hope the next fifteen years will concentrate on issues of equity and the dynamics of learning. Some will argue that I am asking too much of Logo. Not so. I would ask why have we denied access to Logo for significant populations? I would ask why have we lost the educational context to technocentric commercial interests?

Logo takes on social and political perspectives as schools search for solutions that will act upon the forces that create and maintain inequity in public education.

At the end of the year, we plan to open five Logo centers in Cambodia, a small country halfway around the world, ravaged by war and social upheaval. Phnom Penh... Battambang...

Siem Reap... Takeo... Ratanakeri. Strange and exotic sounds that translate into people and places.

Phnom Penh, a city of one million. The Logo center will be housed in a high school serving 6,500 students in three shifts.

Siem Reap, a rice village, site of the ancient ruins of Angkor Wat, on the edge of the jungle hiding Pol Pot and the Khmer Rouge guerrillas.

Ratanakiri, a remote mountainous province bordering Laos and Vietnam, accessible only by air. Electricity was installed last year.

Our challenge will be to apply the lessons of the first fifteen years: helping teachers understand the learning process, learning environments, and why Logo is for all kids.

I end this letter with a story: In old Cambodia, the people tell of three monks who were looking at a banner flying from the top of their temple. The first monk said, "The banner is moving." The second monk said, "No. The wind is moving." The third monk said, "It is the mind that is moving."

I heard this story in 1988 in a makeshift temple in a refugee camp on the Thai-Cambodian border. The image of "the moving mind" helped me transcend the suffering and deprivation of the camp, and moved me to focus on the wonder of the human mind and spirit. The mental image of the mind in motion has stayed with me. It is a fitting metaphor that helps me understand Logo and learning in a computer culture.

Love,

Gerry

Gerry Kozberg at a 1986 Logo Summer Institute in St. Paul, Minnesota

References

Kozberg, G. (1996). Whatever Happened to the Revolution. Logo Update, 5(1). el.media.mit.edu/lo-go-foundation/resources/logoupdate/Logo_Update_v5n1.pdf

Notes

1 Logo 84, Logo 85, and Logo 86 were international conferences held at MIT.

Section 3 —
Personal Computing

Only inertia and prejudice, not economies or the
lack of good educational ideas, stand in the way of
providing every child in the world with the kind of
experience of which we have tried to give you some
glimpses. If every child were to be given access
to a computer, computers would be cheap enough for
every child to be given access to a computer.

-*Twenty Things to Do with a Computer* (1971)

A Dreamer Given Sight

David Loader

Many were the dreamers whose eyes were given sight
when the Spirit filled their dreams with life and form.
Deserts turned to gardens, broken hearts found new delight,
and then down the ages still she flew on.

From such a powerful image, beautifully described in Bishop Light's verse "She comes sailing on the wind" I draw my inspiration for this essay. No matter whether you call it—Spirit, inspiration, revelation, or an *aha* moment, Seymour Papert's work provided that for me. He showed me how my dreams could take form; I would like to share the story of how that happened.

We all dream of how things could be better. There are dreams of marriage, family, or a new home, or even larger dreams of a new society, like that of Martin Luther King Jr., "I have a dream that one day, this nation will rise up …"

The possibility of a dream coming true is what drives people to get out of bed in the morning. Dreams stir and challenge us. Dreams can worry and depress us when we cannot see a way forward. Sometimes we need help to achieve the ends we seek in our dreams, from a partner or even a team of people. Sometimes what we need to achieve our dream is a disruption to a way of working and thinking, a disruption that is as big as a move from candles to electricity or horses to machines or pens and paper to computers. These were not just technology changes, they were radical changes in our thinking and ways of acting. Furthermore, such changes cannot occur without an enlightenment, a revelation, and a seer to guide us. For me to find a way forward for my dream of changing schooling, I needed Papert to help me with the theory and the insight, and computers to make it happen.

Papert provided me with a penetrating analysis of how young people learn, of how this learning can be facilitated and thus of how schools could be transformed. To dreamers like myself, who could see what was wrong with how young people were being taught but could not clearly see a way to rectify this, Papert brought sight, power, and new delight. Papert was

David Loader and Seymour Papert

a quiet, unassuming person whom I was fortunate enough to meet a few times, but his insight and inspiration stayed with me throughout my career. His insights were transformational in my thinking as a school principal. It was Papert who powered a brave new experiment in learning in a land distant from his own.

I cannot speak about many of the other revolutions that Papert inspired but I can speak with authority about how he helped transform one school, which then influenced a state and, finally, a whole country—Australia.

It began thirty-one years ago in 1990 when, with the help and support of many dedicated and wonderful people, I required all students in two Grade Five classes of Methodist Ladies College (MLC), Melbourne, Australia, to have laptop computers. By 1996 all 2,000 of the school's students, from Years Five to Twelve, together with their teachers, were required to bring a laptop to school. This was a Papert-inspired world first.

Some Personal Contexts

School days were not happy days for me. I felt suppressed and silenced, my views were not important. I remember one teacher's way of addressing students: "Be quiet and get back up on your perch!" The class work and the teachers were all *out there* in a place where, try as I might, I could not reside. I was told to learn this, to do this, to be this. I felt little better than an item produced in a factory. At school I had no voice, I lost confidence and developed low self-esteem. But one thing that school did give me was resolve. I wanted to change the teaching and learning process. So, I became a teacher, then a school principal with a burning desire to make schools better places for young people. I wanted to move from formal teaching driven by teachers, to learning driven by the learner. I wanted curriculum that was immediately accessible to young people and not some inherited curriculum from the industrial period. Consequently, I was attracted to Papert's constructivist approach, building knowledge and the importance of play in learning.

> *Constructionism is built on the assumption that children will do best by finding … for themselves the specific knowledge they need; organized or informal education can help most by making sure they are supported morally, psychologically, materially, and intellectually in their efforts. (Papert, 1993, p. 5)*

I saw educational potential in computers, where students could use the computer programming language Logo, to drive turtles and create machines that could be manipulated for learning purposes and for concrete modeling of abstract ideas. I liked Papert's understanding of cognitive development and, like Papert, rejected the idea of more passive accumulation of knowledge. Later I was to learn that Papert stumbled on computers in his first days at Massachusetts Institute of Technology (MIT) and had an epiphany. "These are the *children's machines* for learning," he said. He saw that these machines could help young people to understand abstract ideas and solve difficult problems. Serendipity was important to me too!

Thinking and Practical Friends

In the 1980s, Professor Cliff Hooker of Newcastle University introduced me to the programming language Logo, showing how it could be used by young people to understand difficult concepts. I was fascinated but could not at that time understand how I could apply this knowledge, as my school had very few computers. As well I did not have sufficient theory base to support such a change in learning. The school curriculum was already too full, and teachers were constantly being pressured to do more in the time available. Teachers were not keen to add more to their curriculum or to their workload.

Dr. Elizabeth (Liddy) Nevile, herself an initiator and inspirer, who was then at the Australian Council for Educational Research (ACER), introduced me to computers that were being used for student learning, and to some new thinking about what was happening overseas in the artificial intelligence laboratory at MIT. I was intrigued and wanted to know more. Then Liddy introduced me to Papert's work. I read some of his writing and was stirred by it. I was familiar with the schools-are-bad-places-for-kids literature but struggled with what should replace current schools and their programs. Papert's understanding of cognitive development and computers stimulated an epiphany of my own; now I could see a way forward.

Papert was building on the work of Piaget, who regarded children as active builders of knowledge, little scientists developing theories and knowledge and continually testing them against the real world. Papert was also drawing on Dewey and others, who argued that children learn by doing, not repetition. I had learned from Piaget and Dewey and now I was learning from Papert! This was exciting, and I tried to share my excitement with others. At the same time, I was reflecting on Martin Buber's work around I-Thou and I-It, about relationships and about the *between*. Standing on the shoulders on these great thinkers, I could see that my amorphous dream was not idle fantasy. Others too were trying to change how young people could learn, be valued, and be given agency and that the impossible could be possible; schools could be saved through transformation.

While these ideas were circulating in my head, Liddy again provided the insight that I needed. She had seen what was happening in the USA and decided to set up a computer classroom in a Melbourne museum, not a school—a story in itself. She showed me students working independently on computers. I wondered, why not give every MLC student one of these computers and thus transform the learning process? But in practice this meant that students would need more than one computer. They needed to use them in the classrooms, in specialist rooms like science labs, and at home. Surely this was an impossible dream. But then, by chance I discovered that Toshiba laptops existed. Excitingly, these laptops could go everywhere. I discovered later that they would even be found under students' pillows! The computer industry discovered later that laptops are ideal for school students.

I wanted to give students power over their learning. But I needed more than theory and computers, I needed to convince staff and the community that this could work. I chose a group of teachers from the secondary school whom I thought might buy the idea—they did not! Some of the selected teachers laughed at the idea! By chance, I told my sad story of failure to the Deputy Head of Junior School, Steve Costa. Steve was familiar with Papert and Solomon's paper and their practice at MIT. He said, "I will do it. I will introduce computers into the Junior School." And he did! Steve changed how Year 5 classes operated at MLC and that, together with the work of some inspired and dedicated teachers and leaders in Year 7, led to a whole school transformation.

In 1990 at MLC, we made this brave and difficult step of making laptops compulsory for three Year 5 classes (eighty-two students) and invited Year 7 students to voluntarily participate. Sixty Year 7 parents (two classes) also bought laptops. The program was considered a success by students, parents, and staff. Now there was no looking back; in 1991 it was decided that all students in Years 5, 6, and 7 would have laptops. In 1992 this increased to Years 5 through 8, so that by 1996 there were more than 2,000 laptops in use in the school, with every teacher and every student in Year 5 or above having their own laptop.

There is not space here to speak in detail about how we went about convincing parents and the Board of the school; a challenge and another story in itself. Having gained their support, I needed to find practical and technical support for my theoretical ideas. I had the support of Liddy—and then I found Dr. Gary Stager! I met Gary, a larger-than-life personality, a self-styled "educational terrorist," at an international conference on computing in Sydney. I invited him to MLC and subsequently he provided ongoing support for us in those early years, both with the philosophy and with the practice.

Gary was always enthusiastic, insightful, unconventional, and totally committed to Papert's thinking and to Logo. His experience was invaluable. His energy and innovative ideas, including an infamous pajama party in-service training, contributed much to the program's success in those early days. Central to the successful implementation were the teachers; they were excited by the possibilities and, in parallel with the girls, worked on developing their skills. Older teachers led the way with a new-found energy for their teaching. One teacher was so excited that she constantly used the computer and, unfortunately, developed a repetitive strain injury. In this new classroom, students also became teachers and ambassadors for the program in their homes and the community. They saw themselves as leaders showing the way forward. In-house technical support was also critical; more than technicians, they were real problem-solvers, modeling learning!

There were also computer suppliers who helped support us, particularly Bruce Dixon, whom we met at the end of our first year of compulsory laptops. Bruce provided the laptops for our second year, 1991, and helped sort out warranties and insurance. But he did more than that as he understood both Logo and schools. The computer manufacturers, while keen to sell to us, saw their role as designing computers solely for business, which meant that we had to have business machines not school machines.

David Loader, Steve Costa, Gary Stager, Seymour Papert, and Bruce Dixon (Left to right)

A School Transformed

The introduction of laptops thirty-one years ago was not a publicity stunt, as some of my peers described it, but an educational assertion that a basic education in an emerging digital age should go beyond the so-called basics of the three Rs. Drawing on Papert's work, Liddy Nevile and I argued in *Educational Computing: Resourcing the Future* (1991) that the introduction of laptops represented a paradigm shift from teaching (teacher-focused) to learning (student-focused)—a new approach to pedagogy that focused on each student taking more responsibility for their own learning. Students could now progress with the traditional curriculum at their own pace and not be locked into the class's speed. Students found this liberating and, as well, both teachers and students found more space in the day to play. This gave us the chance to broaden the curriculum by introducing Logo and later LogoWriter.

Logo is an easily learned computer coding language that gave students power over their computer and increasingly over their world. At that time, every student was programming, not an elite few students or computer nerds. We also introduced LEGO blocks, to give students concrete materials with which to model and even to build simple robots, and we had access to leading thinkers like Brian Silverman of LogoWriter, and Steve Ocko of LEGO.

Students were playing and learning and there was a real buzz in the classrooms that visitors noted. Students were supporting each other; now the classroom had many teachers! Visitors came to see technology in the classrooms, but it was not about technology. These were classrooms that were developing valuable personal dispositions in girls, such as confidence, initiative, inquisitiveness, persistence, collaboration, and even intelligence. Despite the critics' dire predictions, the school's academic results did not drop, even though our girls were disadvantaged because academic outcomes were determined by paper and pencil tests when the students' learning had been all keyboard-driven! Today we would invoke Carol Dweck's theory of growth mindsets, not then formulated, to support our programs of growing knowledge and intelligence.

Given that all MLC students had to undertake external exams to access University, the old curriculum had to be taught but it was done in a different way. A technology-based classroom was born, where in addition to pens there were computers as student tools, where text was supplemented by graphics, music, and even robotics as a medium of expression and where students were given greater autonomy. With the coming of the internet, the classroom walls were further expanded, with students able to access teachers and other students outside their school.

Regrettably for many schools, machine-centrism is still the case; they have introduced computers without understanding their potential for good. These schools know nothing of the writing of Papert. They have utilized the computer's power to continue to suppress students, by using these computers to teach students more and more stuff; this is a modern version of treating students as empty vessels to be filled! It is not about giving agency to students for their learning.

Radical Change

To many educational leaders, radical educational changes are unthinkable because they may lose their job if they fail. "Play safe and do what you have been doing for years" is their philosophy. As a result, no change comes, and the media continues to report that standards are slipping. Playing safe may mean you keep your job as a principal, but at what expense for students?

There is current practice, best practice, and next practice. The greatest of these, we are told, is best practice. Best practice is good only as long as there have been no major disruptions in the technology, such as the Pony Express to the telegraph, handwriting to word processing, maths tables to electronic calculators.

Compared to other aspects of life, the schooling process remains astonishingly primitive. At best its tools, such as subjects, textbooks, and examinations, are crude efforts to link schooling with the larger society. The more telling criticism of the current didactic school model is that it creates a response on the part of the student of dependence or resistance. Instead of the old transmission model of knowledge, we need a more experiential, self-directed model of learning, where the learner is an active participant, the curriculum arising from interactions with the real world. Schooling needs more than best practice; it needs radical change through next practice. The capacity to learn something new has become a more critical skill than simply knowing what is currently known.

Papert was a thought leader in powerful ideas, ideas that were radical at the time and unfortunately continue to be so for far too many people. Sadly, I do not believe that Seymour Papert's books are on the reading list for teachers in training in university today. The future for many educationalists is a nostalgic nod to the past, not a grasping of what the modern world can contribute.

Reflection

I was probably fortunate that I had no background in computers and knew nothing of Alan Kay's 1968 vision for personal computing, a Dynabook, nor of the existence of schools like Bank Street College in New York in the 1980s. I was not merely copying any fads but trying to solve particular problems that I was facing in my school. MLC classes were large, not all students were motivated by the existing teaching, and the curriculum and the class-instruction model was derived from the industrial batch processing model. I wanted a more personal, more intrinsically motivational, and more collaborative learning setting. Personal computing had the potential to address some of what I saw as fundamental problems with education.

Regrettably, schools, including MLC, are powerful forces of inertia. Schools have managed to subvert the real potential of computers, using them to facilitate old curriculum and old pedagogy. Schools today are back to where they were in the 1980s but with media-enhanced presentations for the benefit of teachers.

MLC of the 1990s was an inspirational start, but the change has not gone far enough. What is retained and needs to be mined is the inspiration and insight of our elders—Papert, Buber, Piaget, Dewey, and many more—to produce the radical new school that we need.

Papert and Solomon's ideas are even more important today than they were for me in 1990. It is my hope that their spirit continues to fill others' dreams with life and that their ideas will fly on into the future.

References

Loader, D., & Nevile, L. (1991). *Educational Computing: Resourcing the Future*. Incorporated Association of Registered Teachers of Victoria.

Papert, S. (1993). *The Children's Machine: Rethinking School in the Age of the Computer*. Basic Books.

Personal Computing

Gary Stager

One, the rich countries of the world ought to be providing laptops for every child in the world. Two, my vision is that a laptop computer will become so inexpensive, that every country will be able to afford to give them to the children. — Seymour Papert (USINFO Webchat Transcript, 2006)

An Irresponsibly Brief History of Personal Computing in Schools

By 1971, Seymour Papert, Cynthia Solomon, and Alan Kay were confident that personal computers and computing would become increasingly affordable, accessible, powerful, and ubiquitous, even if this seemed like science fiction to the rest of the world. Alan Kay, who is credited with inventing the personal computer, was so inspired by what he saw children do with Logo in 1968 that he sketched the "Dynabook" on a paper napkin on his flight home, fully intending it to be a children's machine. The original Dynabook sketch bears an uncanny resemblance to the modern laptop or tablet computer. In other words, the desire to invent a programmable computer *for children* is foundational in the development of the personal computer.

A decade later, the rise of the microcomputer energized their educational vision and was simultaneously fueled by it. The software company Solomon and Papert had a hand in starting, Logo Computer Systems, Inc. (LCSI) produced Apple Logo, the first, if not one of the first, piece of licensed software for the Apple II. There were versions of Logo available for every new microcomputer on the market. The public appetite for children using computers was awakened and Logo was seen as an integral part of that vision. If a school owned a new microcomputer, there was a very good chance they had a dialect of Logo on it. Logo even made software ubiquitous by pioneering the site license for software.

In 1986, LCSI lowered the bar for kids programming computers, certainly in school, by creating LogoWriter—a programming language that added word processing and multiple turtle animation to the Logo environment. This allowed student project development in language arts and social studies. Teachers were much more comfortable in those domains than mathematics or computer science. The genius of LogoWriter (and its descendants) was that storytelling, the dominant comfort zone in many classrooms, was an invitation to use all the mathematical problem solving and thinking skills found in Logo in service of "the curriculum." An argument may be made that this quickly popularized Logo yet simultaneously led to its marginalized role in the world of educational computing. While many children subversively engaged in powerful programming, creativity, and mathematical thinking in service of traditional curricular fare via LogoWriter projects, one might further argue that this approach was biased towards school's dumbest parts. For too many adults, quick, easily produced products meeting basic curricular expectations were good enough. This was especially true in light of the increasing emphasis on what Alfie Kohn calls the "bunch 'o facts" model of education. Sadly, this shift in using Logo to produce "school" products came at the expense of the less visible process skills or computational fluency made possible by Logo programming.

The full benefits of improved Logo software environments could never be realized by students competing for time on the one computer at the back of the classroom or the biweekly excursion to the school's computer lab. That would change in 1989, when David Loader, principal of Methodist Ladies' College (a PK–12 girls school in Melbourne, Australia) committed to every one of his students in grades 5–12 owning a personal laptop computer.[1] This was not just a technology play or marketing gimmick. David saw the growing portability, power, and availability of **personal** computers as a way to "liberate children from a failed system" (words David used in a parent newsletter). The laptop would be one element in making learning more meaningful, personal, and consistent with the unforeseen challenges his students would face in the 21st century. The laptop would be an instrument for change making the visions of Dewey, Piaget, Papert, and John Holt become a day-to-day reality in his otherwise conservative girls school. Under Loader's leadership, every child would use their personal laptop for the purposes of knowledge construction across the curriculum. Within two years, close to 1,000 kids and their teachers were creating interdisciplinary projects by programming in LogoWriter, the predecessor to MicroWorlds or Scratch, with their own laptops. AND he achieved this with his existing teaching staff! It is critical to note that going 1:1 was never considered a pilot program or experiment. David and his colleagues knew that they were on the right side of history. Kids should and would have their own portable personal computers to break down the artificial boundaries between school and non-school learning. Finally, modern learning could naturally occur anywhere anytime.

David Loader's pioneering leadership on behalf of 1:1 computing came more than two decades after Alan Kay and Seymour Papert began dreaming aloud about the "children's machine" or "personal computer." I earned my first laptop when I began leading professional development at David's school in 1990.

David Loader believes in the capacity of children and the competence of teachers more than any school leader I have ever met. He invested heavily in supporting teacher dreams for improving their classroom or the entire school. Research & Development was the norm in his schools. Every tradition, brick, and bit of conventional wisdom was there to be challenged. His teachers were encouraged to rock the boat, knowing that David would support and defend them. David's visionary leadership hardly ended with inventing 1:1 computing. As a principal, he publicly fought for the rights of children to be free from the sorts of coercive and constrictive forces being imposed on schools. He embraced any idea that might bear fruit and trusted his teachers to experiment, lead, or even tell him when something was a terrible idea.

He is an author of deeply candid and personal books about school leadership, and as a community leader was a true public intellectual, never one to shy away from a good fight. David's first book, *The Inner Principal* (2006), is a classic. Loader was the architect of Papert and Solomon's realized dream of a computer for every child, although his career as a school leader was filled with equally momentous and seemingly audacious achievements. *Twenty Things* was possible in David Loader's schools because his efforts were embedded within the context of constructionism and a faith in the remarkable capacity of children and teachers.

Almost immediately, we knew that going 1:1 mattered when teachers began demanding structural changes to the daily schedule, curriculum, assessment, class sizes, and physical spaces to support project work inspired by the affordances of the laptop. The original "laptop teachers" at MLC suddenly enrolled in post-graduate studies, enjoyed remarkable job mobility, became school principals, and even started their own education-related companies. However, the real indicator of progress came when students began decorating their laptops with stickers and glitter paint. They appropriated and personalized their personal computers. In the process, they seized ownership not only over the computer, but over the work created within. It was not uncommon for students to transfer the programming skills they learned within the classroom context and employ them in service of much more personal, expressive, and fantastic projects created in their free time. The implications of this shift exceed the scope of this book.

Over the course of the '90s, upwards of 100,000 Australian students had laptops and the idea began catching on all over the world. By the end of the decade, the Henrico County school district in Virginia provided a laptop for every student, making it the first large scale implementation in the United States. Despite Henrico's embrace of instructionism, the district demonstrated the feasibility of 1:1 computing in North America.

During the winter of 2000, the governor of Maine, Angus King, was blessed with a budget surplus and called an impromptu press conference announcing that the state of Maine would provide a laptop to every 7th and 8th grader in the public school system. His friend Seymour Papert spent the next year or two building support for the initiative that continues to exist to this day. King loved Papert but continued to view computers through school-colored glasses and education principally as a vehicle for economic development. Although I fear that Maine never truly understood or embraced the challenges of *Twenty Things*, it is not insignificant that a rural state has continued funding 1:1 computing for two decades.

> *I guess this week the question to ask in Maine is "Why should every seventh grader have a laptop computer?" The short answer is, well, every seventh grader should have a laptop computer because everybody should have a laptop computer. And why? Again, the short answer is "Well, I have one."*

> *I couldn't get to do a quarter of the things I do without it and everybody I know with very, very few exceptions engaged in any sort of intellectual creative work, writers, artists, historians, mathematicians, they have and use these things, so it seems obvious that it's the prime instrument for our days for intellectual work.*

> *Now you might not think that the work of kids is intellectual. If you don't think that, that's why we're in such trouble, it is and ought to be and so they want to have this instrument and having said that we turn to the longer answer, including why is it that anybody would resist this? Why would it occur to anybody to deprive them of this intellectual tool since many of the people who are to deprive them of the intellectual tool themselves would protest vehemently if we tried to deprive them of their computers (Papert, 2000).*

Around the time of the Maine Learning Technology Initiative, the charismatic leader of Quebec's largest English-speaking school district became impatient with the pace of progress and yearned for something better for the students he served. Early in the new century, Ron Canuel put laptops in the hands of thousands of students in the Eastern Township School Board. While Eastern Township did not embrace the computational specifics of *Twenty Things*, under Ron's leadership they became a model of internet-era computer access that trusted teachers and children against the increasingly hysterical, paranoid, and surveillance-focused backlash against young people and screens. Canuel, like Loader and others, were school leaders who viewed Papert and Solomon's visions of truly personal computing as a vehicle for wholesale school reform, teacher improvement, and child empowerment.

Not long after laptops arrived in Maine, MIT Media Lab founder Nicholas Negroponte and his friends Seymour and Cynthia launched the One Laptop Per Child (OLPC) initiative, a plan to put a personal computer in the hands of every child on earth. OLPC went beyond simply buying computers for students in the world's wealthiest countries and sought to design and manufacture a computer cast in the spirit of *Twenty Things* and constructionism that would be affordable by any nation on earth. Arguments persist between critics of OLPC, its advocates, and its millions of users across Latin America, South America, and Africa. Yet one piece of OLPC's legacy is undeniable—it drove down the price of personal computers. Prior to Negroponte announcing the goal of developing a $100 computer, the tech firms of Japan and Silicon Valley swore that a sub $1,200 computer was impossible. If you or your child has an iPad, Chromebook, or $300 PC today, you can thank OLPC for lubricating the wheels of progress.

In *Twenty Things*, Solomon and Papert stressed the affordability of universal personal computing. Although that goal may have seemed far-fetched or unattainable fifty years ago, opponents of the computational empowerment of young people still choose to argue on the battlefield of cost. Thirty-five years ago, Cynthia Solomon impressed on me that sound educational decisions are never based on price. Papert long argued that computers appear expensive due to the accounting trick of comparing them to pencils but can represent just a few percent of per pupil spending when amortized over several years. This reality has been proven by schools, districts, and states embracing 1:1 across the globe.

I hail from the United States of America, the richest nation in the history of history. We can certainly afford to provide every single school child with a laptop, a cello, and a well-stocked classroom library. Failure to do so has much more to do with failure of leadership, imagination, and will than it does funding.

What Part of *PC* Don't You Understand?

Papert, Solomon, and Negroponte proposed that the cost of computing goes down when students maintain and repair their own computers. Nicholas Negroponte argued that "It's absolutely critical the kids own their own laptops, that it's given to them by the state, and they own it. The reason it's important is the same reason that you have never washed a rented car because it doesn't belong to you. If it's your own car, you take more care" (ABC News). This has certainly been the case in every 1:1 school I have been associated with.

Again, ownership of your very own personal computer is more than symbolic. There is a pride of ownership felt by children entrusted with a powerful tool and that influences the pride and care shown in the work created with their laptop. Show me a school where computers are broken or neglected, and I can predict that they are used for passive tasks in which students are not invested.

When MLC embarked on universal personal computing for students, the maintenance and repair of more than 1,000 laptops was handled by a nice older woman named Louise. If a kid's laptop was broken or not operating properly, they went to see Louise who assured them that everything would be fine and then called the vendor to repair or replace the computer. Before long, Australian schools (using the right vendor) were experiencing over 90% of computer repairs being completed the same school day.

Personal computers are robust and reliable, yet schools insist on complicating matters and increasing the cost of ownership. They employ technicians who disable functionality, tell teachers how to teach, surveil students, and inhibit what Papert described as the computer's "protean ability to take different forms—and, if you use it right, to become a kind of mirror in which you can see reflections of yourself" (Papert, 1985). In the wrong policy environment, a $1,000 computer becomes a piece of sculpture. The computer we give a child should be capable of doing everything our adult brains value, and more than we can imagine.

More students would enjoy learning more with more computers if they were personal and focused on knowledge construction, not curriculum delivery, testing, surveillance, or school photo-ops. Students can save their work on their own laptops and be responsible for maintaining backups in any way they wish, just like they keep track of their textbooks or gym clothes. There are countless free options for sharing work online unless we oppose sharing. It sometimes seems as if we give students computers just to catch them breaking a rule and confiscate their "device." Of course, there should be reasonable measured consequences for any misbehavior or infraction, but one cannot argue that the computer is necessary for education and societal participation and then deprive a child of it for breaking a rule that may not have been necessary in the first place. If a child commits a crime with their computer or anything else, call the police. Otherwise, take a deep breath and be guided by why we chose to become educators.

Extensibility

I was with Dr. Papert when he was asked, "Are you really suggesting that every child should have a personal computer?" His reply was quintessential Seymour. "No, I'm suggesting that every child should have at least two computers." The vision of *Twenty Things* included more than advocacy for children owning and programming their computer, it laid a foundation for the maker movement four decades in its future. Children should not only control their computer(s) but use their computer to make and control a variety of creations outside of the computer.

> *In our image of a school computation laboratory, an important role is played by numerous "controller ports" which allow any student to plug any device into the computer. The ports are protected by fuses and suitable interfaces so that little harm will be done if anyone carelessly puts the main voltage into a computer output port. The laboratory will have a supply of motors, solenoids, relays, sense devices of various kinds, etc., etc. Using them the students will be able to invent and build an endless variety of cybernetic systems.* — Papert & Solomon, Twenty Things

By the late aughts, the maker movement had captured the imagination of the public, media, and even schools. It spoke to a basic human impulse to create, invent, and solve problems by combining timeless craft traditions and materials with new digital technologies.

In the mid 1980s, Seymour Papert, Steve Ocko, Mitchel Resnick, Brian Silverman, and others at the MIT Media Lab helped LEGO develop the first robotics construction kit for children, LEGO TC Logo. Now, children could bring robot ballerinas, kinetic sculptures, and other interactive creations to life using the child-friendly LEGO building blocks augmented by motors, lights, and sensors. These inventions were then programmed in Logo. Like building with LEGO, programming a robot only involved a handful of commands used in infinite combinations. Projects created by kids with LEGO and Logo made authentic engineering experiences accessible to children just as Logo had created mathematical opportunities.

In 2005, the Arduino microcontroller was released. Arduino (available in various forms) is a small, powerful, low-cost "brain board" that allows all sorts of sensors, actuators (motors, buzzers, lights), and even networks to be programmed by novices and professionals alike. The plethora of ways in which Arduino and the proliferation of similar boards could be used generated a great deal of excitement. For about $25, seemingly anyone could create an intelligent gadget to do real work or just make you laugh. At a Maker Faire, you could find microcontrollers embedded into machines of all sizes; some solved serious problems while others were used in a more whimsical fashion. The fact that you were no longer limited to using LEGO as building materials dramatically expanded the range of potential projects, while also contemplating use by children, particularly in schools. One also needed to know more about electronics to safely connect an endless assortment of components.

Despite its groundbreaking power and affordability, the major weakness of Arduino were the languages used to control it, primarily a dialect of C. Some children (and their teachers) were of course capable of learning enough C to program Arduinos, but they rarely could start from a blank screen and create. Most Arduino projects begin with finding someone else's program online and modifying it to meet your needs. Such remixing is fine, but the finicky syntax of the Arduino Integrated Development Environment (IDE) made debugging difficult and was never designed for children learning mathematics. The needs of adult professionals and hobbyists were the rightful focus of Arduino development. The power and functionality one can purchase for the price of a burger and beer is mindboggling but comes at the expense of using the boards in a classroom context. Remember, the goal of *Twenty Things* was to democratize these experiences by making them accessible to all. New hardware is sensational, but software matters!

Half a dozen years after the Arduino, the BBC micro:bit was released as a microcontroller development board specifically for children. Adults are welcome to use them, but the intent was accessibility, flexibility, and power for young people. The micro:bit could be used for electronics and robotics projects like the Arduino, but also features a small 5X5 matrix LED display, two buttons, speaker, microphone, compass, and light and temperature sensors. Micro:bits can communicate with one another via radio, meaning that they work together as colonies of creatures searching for food or as a remote control to control another machine with a micro:bit on board.

The micro:bit may be used as a programming platform or embedded inside other inventions. The low cost of the micro:bit (approximately $15 as I write this), flexibility, and their ability to work together means that students can not only use micro:bits in authentic projects, but they can afford to leave those inventions together to perform a repetitive task or just inspire their classmates. Imagine a hallway display that tells you whether you need to wear a jacket at recess based on outside temperature data (reported from a second micro:bit) or building a remote control to drive a vehicle you also create and program.

When chips are as cheap as chips, you don't need to disassemble a project at the end of each class period.

Rather than a reliance on soldering, most micro:bit projects may be wired with alligator clips and easily repurposed. The millions of micro:bits currently in circulation and the extensibility of their design have inspired developers to invent a range of peripherals allowing for even more functionality. The ingenious Hummingbird Bit Robotics Kit, invented by Tom Lauwers, allows students to build and program anything with an easy-to-use micro:bit based robotics platform, arts and craft supplies, and recycled materials such as cardboard.

Best of all, the micro:bit and its sibling, the Circuit Playground Express, may be programmed in block-based languages, including Scratch, Snap!, and Microsoft MakeCode. These environments eliminate syntax errors and lower the threshold for empowering programming and engineering projects. Mathematical thinking and computer science concepts are supported in this software designed specifically for young people.

Enthusiasts of teaching computer science often point to videogames as projects that motivate students. Many of us embrace the rule, "You can play any game you program" when trying to manage recreational computer use in schools. The problem is that many of these projects feel like denatured school versions of youth culture. After all, commercial videogames are insanely complex and developed by large teams with diverse expertise and large budgets. Even when computer games are created by kids, gameplay is compromised by being on a computer. That has recently changed with the advent of the block based MakeCode Arcade programming software and low-cost handheld computers sharing the same architecture with the micro:bit. Now for $30, kids can not only design videogames, but can carry them in their pocket, and play them anywhere. Such games now have the aesthetic feel of the games so many children love.

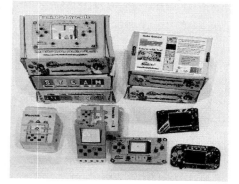

Forget about making games to teach children multiplication or spelling or any of those old-fashioned basic skills. The really basic skill today is the skill of learning, and the best use of games is to leverage their tendency to enhance it…

I have found that when they get the support and have access to suitable software systems, children's enthusiasm for playing games easily gives rise to an enthusiasm for making them, and this in turn leads to more sophisticated thinking (Papert, 1998).

The micro:bit, the Circuit Playground Express, and a variety of programmable MakeCode Arcade devices allow learners of all ages to create wearable eTextiles, robots, interactive art installations, modern toys, experiment laboratory instruments, games, and at least twenty new things to do with a computer.

PC All the Way Down

The OLPC XO was designed to be serviceable by children. In some schools, kids have been taught to repair computers dating back four decades, yet such opportunities remain rare. If you think that kids owning and repairing their own PCs is controversial, how do you feel about students building their own computer? It drove Seymour Papert absolutely crazy that kids could not build their own computers. The hardware industry's stranglehold on the supply chain made making your own computer unfeasible. You can assemble your own PC, but there has been little economic incentive to do so.

The Raspberry Pi computer changes everything. This roughly $40 computer, about the size of a playing card, runs Linux or Windows, uses very little power, and does everything a standard PC can do. It browses the web, runs applications, and has extension ports for receiving sensor input and actuator control, like an Arduino or micro:bit, albeit at the expense of some simplicity. Best of all, the Raspberry Pi can be connected to any USB keyboard, mouse/trackpad, and monitor and you have your own computer with power likely to exceed the PCs your school might buy at a much higher price. Students can take their Raspberry Pi computer home and connect it to a TV, even an old composite model, as well. Now, families who cannot otherwise possibly afford a computer can join the digital economy.

The recycling and reuse of what would otherwise be e-waste is attractive to young people passionate about saving the planet by going green.

A variety of Raspberry Pi models offer different functionality at even lower prices. That game you designed in MakeCode Arcade can be downloaded to a $5–10 Raspberry Pi Zero, placed in a cardboard or wooden box with an old display, and voilà! a video game cabinet featuring games created by students can reside in the school cafeteria!

There is no way Papert and Solomon could have predicted that computers would be cheap enough to literally give them away for free. I recently received a copy of HackSpace, that had the new Raspberry Pi Pico, a board useful in Arduino-like physical computing projects attached to the magazine cover. Clearly, there are no credible excuses left for depriving children of computers and computational materials.

For more information about Arduino, the BBC micro:bit, Raspberry Pi, and the maker movement, read *Invent to Learn: Making, Tinkering, and Engineering in the Classroom* (Martinez & Stager, 2019).

Free board on magazine cover

Instrumental Computing

One of my favorite memories of the past decade was meeting two fifth grade boys at a conference in Vermont. They identified as makers and what they made was a marimba out of a wooden frame using PVC pipe as the resonators. Their marimba displayed a nice bit of carpentry, but that was far from the most impressive part of the project. The boys explained that the way that they tempered the instrument to play the notes of a Western musical scale was by finding a formula online that uses the frequency of the pitch you wish to reproduce and the diameter of the tube being used to determine its desired length.

The boys said that while they were capable of performing those calculations, they weren't sure that all of their classmates could, and they wanted them to participate too. This displayed either a great deal of empathy, hubris, or both, but that doesn't matter much. What the boys did next took my breath away. They wrote a program in Scratch that asks users to enter the desired audio frequency and tube diameter, then the program tells you where to cut the tube.

When most people think of computer programming, they imagine the product of their efforts will be a computer program. In this case, the student program resulted in a marimba. Computer programming was literally instrumental in creating an instrument.

I waited for a pause in the action after the students played their marimba for countless adoring educators who complimented their talent and ingenuity. I grabbed the pile of lookup tables they printed from the web containing musical pitches and corresponding numerical frequencies and asked a question. "This is about music, right?" The boys nodded in agreement. "Why can't I type F# into the computer and be told how long the tube should be?" In unison, the boys exclaimed, "Oh," then grabbed their laptop and ran away. Some days later, their teacher reported that they had improved their program to accommodate my suggestion.

I often meet loving, well-meaning teachers who gush with pride while telling me all about the wondrous things their students can do "even though I don't know anything." Sometimes I reply, "You know what would be really good? If you knew something. Then you could ask good questions, understand their thinking, point them in the direction of resources, or throw a well-time obstacle in their way leading to an encounter with a powerful idea." The fact that I program in Scratch provides an essential expertise used to determine that these students could be challenged within their zone of proximal development to push their project farther. I knew that solving the problem of communicating with the computer in musical parlance, rather than numerical values was possible, but more importantly I knew it was possible for the kids to write that program. My simple question led the boys to challenge themselves to solve a problem they eagerly embraced.

The Technology Ecology

> *[The computer is] not merely a tool, it's much more than a tool. It's a medium of thinking like writing isn't just a tool. Writing is a way of thinking. And when you say somebody's a literate person it's not that that person has mastered a tool (Papert, 2004).*

Schools and governments around the world are mandating multi-year, in some cases K–12, computing or computer science standards, yet I have seen little evidence that the corresponding curriculum represents time well spent. Too much focus is spent on vocabulary, ethics, or *about* computers while students are denied rich experiences with the power of computing. A child with a personal laptop should be able to use a programming language designed for learning (e.g. Logo, Scratch, Snap!, Lynx), a micro:bit-based robotics construction kit, web browser, and word processing software for their entire school career. Add something like Tinkercad for designing fabricated objects and some media editing software and you're ready to tackle any project. Emerging software like Wolfram Language is also terribly exciting. Build your own computer and you're positively omnipotent.

Some might wonder how a half-dozen software environments could be used to learn, create, collaborate, and publish for as many as thirteen years, but only if you are thinking in terms of atomized school objectives with a "Computer Appreciation" mentality. We should refrain from teaching about hardware or software and use those materials to learn everything else. That perspective leaves you with infinite possibilities and a fear of insufficient time for students to learn all they can.

Imagine an educational technology ecosystem in which children build their own computer with something like the Raspberry Pi, create a server out of another, automate classroom or home appliances, program videogames on their personal computer, post programs online for others to download to their handheld gaming systems or remix, control robots they invent, 3D print toys, make films including musical scores they compose, share experimental data with scientists, sell their poetry anthology, and oh yeah, do some schoolwork too. One of the biggest ideas of *Twenty Things* is that we can do so much (more) with just a few good constructive materials.

For fifty years, those of us on the Solomon/Papert team have been dismissed as reckless utopians for advocating the outrageous notion that every student should own a personal laptop. Providing something of value to "other people's children" is particularly controversial with affluent parents whose own kids have multiple phones, tablets, and smartphones. Providing reasonable access had been a long hard slog until 2020. When the COVID-19 pandemic struck and schools were forced to move online, laptops magically rained down from the sky into the waiting arms of students. Imagine how much better and less instructionist "Zoom School" might have been if the educational leaders who miraculously found sufficient funds to purchase computers during a crisis had an educational philosophy ready to support their use? Any coherent vision and accompanying pedagogical strategy would have been welcome. *Twenty Things* is among the best and most imaginative roadmaps for educating children during such moments of profound uncertainty.

References

ABC News. (November 21, 2005). World News Tonight [Television]. *Person of the Week: Nicholas Negroponte.*

Loader, D. (2006). *The Inner Principal: Reflections on Educational Leadership.* Constructing Modern Knowledge Press.

Martinez, S. L., & Stager, G. (2019). *Invent to Learn: Making, Tinkering, and Engineering in the Classroom* (2 ed.). Constructing Modern Knowledge Press.

Papert, S. (1985). Different visions of Logo. *Computers in the Schools, 2*(2-3), 3-8.

Papert, S. (1998). Does easy do it? Children, games, and learning. *Game Developer, 5*(6), 88.

Papert, S. (2000). *Millennial Lecture at the Muskie Archives.* dailypapert.com/bates

Papert, S. (2004, July 11, 2004). *Sunday Morning* [Interview]. Australian Broadcasting Corporation. dailypapert.com/seymour-papert-on-abc-radio-sunday-profile/

USINFO Webchat Transcript. (2006). *Professor Papert Discusses One Laptop Per Child Project.* United States Department of State. dailypapert.com/professor-papert-discusses-one-laptop-per-child-project/

Note

1   In 1990, Coombabah State Primary School in Queensland also embraced 1:1 computing. Many of the mentors and teacher educators involved with MLC also worked with Coombabah. Collaboration between this public school and the private MLC was common. I began working with both schools in mid-1990. A collection of papers, articles, and books related to the early days of 1:1 computing in schools may be found at dailypapert.com/laptops.

Kid Power

Dennis O. Harper

My first encounter with computers was in 1966 when I lucked into a job with Lockheed Propulsion Company (LPC) while attending the University of Redlands. LPC provided both the Launch Escape Motor and the Pitch Control Motor of the emergency escape tower atop the Apollo command module, using propellant made of polysulfides. I started out as a card keypuncher that, in those days, was the vehicle to input data and code into computers. I moved on to testing the propellant and then entering the data that would be analyzed to determine the best fuel for future NASA efforts. Simultaneously, I was honing my programming skills at my university's trusty PDP-11 computer.

I was hooked on programming and mathematics (my major) and after graduation began the career I had always dreamed of—teaching. My first job was teaching mathematics at an East Los Angeles high school for three years starting in 1968. My first experience with combining computer science with mathematics took place from 1973–75 at a German high school near Frankfurt. One of my student's father worked for the Opel automobile factory and agreed to take the students' code (PL1) to his office, have it key punched, and then entered into Opel's computers. Even with those archaic I/O tasks, those kids created some amazing math-related projects.

After teaching mathematics, studying educational systems, and after visiting more than eighty countries, I became convinced that there must be a better way to teach mathematical concepts. During my travels, a 1978 Apple computer advertisement caught my eye, and my wife and I decided to return to the United States to see what this new personal technology had to offer education. In 1980 I read *Mindstorms* and, as many others had, found in it something personal given my background. *Mindstorms* affirmed my thoughts about teaching mathematics to both students and teachers, and I became fascinated by the potential uses and benefits of Logo and the microcomputer.

I began working on a PhD that would emphasize the use of Logo in educational programs in developing nations. After completing a 1983 Logo study at the National University of Malaysia (Harper, 1985) and finishing my degree, I became concerned that Logo use was moving ahead of teacher training and that not much was being said about the role of K–12 students themselves helping educators infuse Logo into the learning process. As luck would have it, MIT hosted three intensive meetings organized by Seymour Papert, Cynthia Solomon, and other Logo colleagues. Beginning with LOGO '84 and continuing for two more years with LOGO '85 and LOGO '86, these meetings brought a worldwide community together at Logo's unofficial home.

Lessons learned from those three events led me to write *Logo Theory & Practice* (Harper, 1989) . A large portion of the book expanded on the *Twenty Things to Do with a Computer* paper produced in 1971 by Papert and Solomon. Hundreds of projects were detailed. In addition, Seymour Papert gave his permission to include an updated version of his theoretical paper "Computer Criticism vs. Technocentric Thinking" (Papert, 1990) first presented at LOGO '85.

Kids as Change Agents

Attending these early Logo events was intimidating—at first. Being at MIT and surrounded by some of my heroes resulted in me being a fly-on-the-wall during the first summer event. As a supervisor of teacher education on the faculty of the University of California Santa Barbara,

I began to expand the inclusion of Logo into my teaching mathematics curriculum for both elementary and secondary courses. These preservice teachers often worked with Logo during their student teaching assignments.

Starting at the LOGO '85 event I finally felt confident joining in on some of heady conversations. By 1986 I was even disagreeing with some of the prestigious attendees—including Seymour Papert. A major discussion question during these times was why Logo was not being used (or even on the radar) of most teachers. Teacher preparation and lack of funding were the prime culprits. Much discussion centered around solving these challenges.

Regarding teacher professional development, the solution seemed to be establishing Logo summer and holiday workshops for teachers, Logo books and articles for teachers, and journals dedicated to Logo aimed at teachers. Even I fell into the *train the teachers first* strategy when I established the International Logo Exchange (ILX) that reported on how teachers throughout the world were integrating Logo into their lessons. All ILX and Tom Lough's Logo Exchange journals are still available online.[1]

Eventually, my argument became that Logo advocates would achieve greater scalability if we would give workshops, books, and resources first to K–12 students and then have them pass along this information to their teachers. In this way, students and educators would become allies in reforming the education system. At the very least, a hybrid model could be delivered where both students and teachers came to Logo professional development events.

Papert and others agreed that when they worked directly with students they learned more about Logo's strengths and weaknesses, in addition to how children think, as compared to working only with their teachers. Nevertheless, they didn't see how education systems could change enough to give students real agency. Ten years later, in 1996, they began to see.

I left UCSB in 1987 and spent six years as a professor at the Institute of Education in Singapore, Helsinki University in Finland, and the University of the Virgin Islands. During those years I continued teaching Logo classes as well as math education and establishing distance learning graduate education courses throughout the Caribbean. I made a decision in 1992 to return to the US and get serious about using lessons learned from the past twenty-six years to conduct rigorous research in the area of K–12 students as change agents. I also decided I could not do this as a university professor and needed to once again return to my K–12 district roots. In August 1992 I accepted a position as technology director at the Olympia School District in Washington State.

As the only adult responsible for technology in a district with 10,000+ students, I was afforded an opportunity to see what kids could really accomplish. In addition to providing Logo and general professional development for teachers, teams of what we called Student Technology Leaders (STLs) built and then maintained the district's network and website. STLs from each of the twenty schools were on the district's tech committee as well as numerous other curriculum committees.

Things really ramped up in 1995 when the US Department of Education established the Technology Innovation Challenge Grants. The STLs and I submitted a proposal to establish the STL model in 150 schools in Washington State, Kansas, and the US Virgin Islands. We received a five-year $3.8 million grant and were on our way. The program was called Generation Y (later changed to Generation YES in 2000).

Starting on July 17, 1997, MIT hosted another five-day event called 2B1 focused on bringing computers to children who live in technologically isolated places.[2] For the first time in eleven years, I was back at the MIT Media Lab—but this time I came with some of my Student Technology Leaders. These STLs participated seamlessly in all parts of the event including giving presentations, working with graduate students in the Media Lab, and joining in the discussion with Seymour Papert and other adult leaders. At the end of the event, an eighth grade STL named Ryan Powell interviewed Seymour Papert. Here is what Papert said in that interview:

> Well, as for the Generation Y project itself, all I can say is the obvious—it's great. It is one of the rare times when the US Department of Education is really funding a great project and I think it is by far the best project funded by them. But I would like to put it in a bigger perspective. Taking this personally, I see it in the perspective of the last 45 years I have been on a crusade believing that school will change and that school as we know it with teachers who are supposed to know everything teaching a lot of kids who are supposed to know nothing—this isn't going to last. But people often ask why do I think this can change? One hundred years ago John Dewey said about the same sort of criticisms that I'm making and that didn't have much effect. There has been one education reformer after another trying to cause it to change, predicting it will change.
>
> What's different now? Well two things are different now. One thing is that we have a techno-logical infrastructure. Without these computers it couldn't change very much because it is designed to fit the previous kinds of knowledge technology like chalk and blackboard and print and paper and that sort of stuff. With a new kind of knowledge technology we can have a new kind of learning. But there is another factor. In my last book, The Connected Family, I call this factor Kid Power and this is in line with the philosophy of the Generation Y project. (Papert, 1997)

This 1997 Papert interview transcript relates to the 1971 Papert/Solomon paper in one important way. In the 1997 interview Papert is saying that education reformists have failed to change education very much. The 1971 paper also refers to this lack of change when it says:

> How strange, then, that 'computers in education' should often reduce to 'using bright new gadgets to teach the same old stuff in thinly disguised versions of the same old way.'

Another quote from the 1971 paper conveys the same message in the above 1997 interview regarding continuing to use knowledge technology in the classroom in the same old ways (blackboards, print, and paper) when the paper questions why there is a lack of change. Papert and Solomon conclude:

> There is no better reason than the intellectual timidity of the computers-in-education community, which seems remarkably reluctant to use the computers for any purpose that fails to look very much like something that has been taught in schools for the past centuries.

While both the 1971 paper and the 1997 interview transcript pinpoint clinging to old ways as a deterrent to change, Papert takes this a big step forward in the interview when he concludes there are "two things" that are now different that could lead to significant change: (1) new kinds of knowledge technologies and (2) Kid Power. Let's take a look at these two things in turn.

Change in Knowledge Technologies

The twenty-six year gap between the two documents certainly saw many technological advances. The twenty ways to use primitive computers listed in the 1971 paper pale in comparison to the technology found and millions of ways one could use computers in 1997 when Papert now felt the technology was sufficient to "lead to significant change." As schools today in 2021 try to create the *new normal* we see that the 1997 technology pales in comparison to what we have now and there are literally billions of things to do with a computer.

We know that Papert was correct in 1997 when he stated that the technology of the day could now change education. It is certainly true in 2021. So why has so little changed? I'll take a look at answering this question after we examine Papert's second factor for education reform.

Kid Power

There is no mention of Kid Power in the earlier 1971 paper. Previously, I discussed how Professor Papert and myself came to see Kid Power as a key factor in education reform. This led to Papert coining the phrase Kid Power in his 1996 book and the 1997 interview above. Although knowledge technology was well on its way in 1997, Kid Power was in its infancy. Papert said in the interview "I see it in the perspective of the last forty-five years I have been on a crusade believing that school will change and that school as we know it with teachers who are supposed to know everything teaching a lot of kids who are supposed to know nothing—this isn't going to last."

To this day, adultism is still the norm in most K–12 schools but things have been changing. Generation YES[3] has now spent over $30 million dollars on research and development efforts since receiving the US Department of Education grant in 1996, that Papert spoke so highly of twenty-five years ago. Many others have written about and conducted Kid Power research or synonyms such as youth voice, youth engagement, student leadership, student as change agent, youth infusion, etc.

Not long after the Papert's 1997 interview, Dan Tapscott's popular book *Growing Up Digital* emphasized the danger of ignoring Kid Power.

> *Unless we boomers have a change of heart about youth, their culture, and their media, the two biggest generations in history may be on a collision course—a battle of the generational titans. An older generation, mistrustful and threatened by new ideas and new tools, will be pitted against a new generation increasingly resentful at attempts to curtail its growth and rights. (1998, p. 12).*

There are many reasons that K–12 student change agents benefit themselves as they help change education and other systems. Robert Epstein's landmark book *Teen 2.0* (2010) identifies why empowering teens often helps troubled teens, and that giving kids responsibilities results in responsible adults.

> *Evidence that even troubled American teens sometimes straightened out overnight when given heavy doses of responsibility and respect.*

> *Teen problems in the United States are caused by two factors related to the artificial extension of childhood: we treat young adults as if they are still children, and we isolate them from adults, trapping them in the media-controlled world of teen culture.*

More recent work in the field of youth infusion can be found on Wendy Lesko and Adam Fletcher's comprehensive website.[4]

Conclusion

Computers have been in US K–12 schools for fifty years. Since Papert and Solomon's 1971 paper, there has been a substantial progression of knowledge technology and Kid Power that Seymour Papert identified as necessary factors in achieving school reform. So why has this not resulted in the new kind of learning Papert espoused throughout his career?

The 1971 paper ends by discussing the cost of expanding the technological infrastructure into all K–12 schools. It is a major shame of the United States that every K–12 student does not have a modern and appropriate computer. The COVID–19 pandemic of 2020–21 with its resulting need for distance learning has laid bare that this universal need has not been met. So funding is still another factor for a new kind of learning.

I will list a few other factors necessary for to achieve Papert and Solomon's new kind of learning without going into detail:

- A willingness to embrace change
- Digital equity
- Ending systemic racism
- Redefining digital literacy
- Cooperating political parties
- Teacher preparation

We know the kind of education we need for our twenty-first century learners. Perhaps the most important factor to change is the willingness and perseverance to do it.

References

Epstein, R. (2010). Teen 2.0: Saving Our Children and Families from the Torment of Adolescence. Quill Driver Books.

Harper, D. O. (1985). Computer Education for Developing Nations. International Society for Technology in Education.

Harper, D. O. (1989). Logo Theory & Practice. Brooks/Cole Publishing.

Papert, S. (1980). Mindstorms: Children, Computers, and Powerful Ideas. Basic Books.

Papert, S. (1990). Computer Criticism vs. Technocentric Thinking (M.I.T. Media Lab Epistemology and Learning Memo No. 1, Issue. papert.org/articles/ComputerCriticismVsTechnocentric.html

Papert, S. (1997). Seymour Papert on Generation YES and Kid Power [Interview]. vimeo.com/9473209

Tapscott, D. (1998). Growing Up Digital: The Rise of the Net Generation. McGraw-Hill

Notes

1 Archive of all International Logo Exchange and Tom Lough's Logo Exchange journals - cmkfutures. com/logoexchange

2 2B1 event - web.media.mit.edu/~nicholas/Wired/WIRED5-06.html

3 Generation YES - yesk12.org

4 Youth Infusion - youthinfusion.org

Education Technology @ Fifty Something: My Personal Perspective

Karen J. Billings

When I recently re-read *Twenty Things to Do with a Computer* by Seymour Papert and Cynthia Solomon, I realized that in 1971 I was already teaching with computers. But I do not recall knowing who they were at that time; I would certainly learn of them soon thereafter and continually learn from them and the other visionaries. Now fifty years later in re-reading their introduction, their very first statement especially resonated with me, "When people talk about computers in education, they do not all have the same image in mind."

For many people, the term "computers in education" conjures up first an image of a hardware device. Sometimes that picture includes a context for its use and perhaps even a user. But my images are those of the people who worked hard over the past fifty years to advance the best uses of technology in education. Some led efforts to develop programming languages while others designed instructional software programs. Some were visionaries who wrote research papers, magazine articles, and books that in turn inspired future leaders. Their philosophies, ideas, and passions provided the impetus for others to develop products or start education companies. A few people, like Seymour Papert, did many of those things, and in so doing, helped create a movement that transformed computer use over these past fifty years.

Looking Back

When I first started teaching with computers in the late sixties, it was before the seminal Papert and Solomon article was published. I was teaching my mathematics students in Iowa to program in Fortran. They would write each statement on mark-sense card that I would then batch and carry to a mainframe computer housed at a nearby university. The next day, I would hand students the computer printouts of the results of their work. They never saw the hardware that produced their results.

A few years later my students in Oregon could use a computer (teletype) terminal connected to a minicomputer housed at our regional education agency. They learned to program in BASIC and inserted punched paper tape to experience the first Oregon Trail simulation.

But during the mid-seventies in Oregon, I attended a conference session in Portland where I watched a large mechanical turtle move around on the floor as it was given instructions by the session leader seated at a computer terminal. The turtle was tethered by a long cable to the terminal which was in turn connected to MIT by a phone line. I had taught several programming languages by that time, but nothing was as interactive or as interesting as what I saw that day.

But then, some years later I watched students program a turtle on an Apple IIe screen using Apple Logo and later, LogoWriter. Soon they could build and program LEGO robots to interact with each other. Today, students think about what they want the computer to do and use new coding skills to create animated objects or to develop interactive games for others.

What Happened during Those Fifty Years?

And how did we get to where we are today?

The hardware changed and software products were developed

The computer hardware got smaller, faster, cheaper, and more mobile. Thus, the technology become more accessible to younger students, those with all abilities and all age levels and in any classroom—not just those in my mathematics classes. The hardware was no longer housed in a remote building. Microcomputers came into schools and were moved around to wherever the user wanted to work.

Each generation of computing hardware brought new programming languages from Fortran to BASIC to Pascal to Logo and HTML. As computers could hold more data, more computer applications were developed, like computer-assisted instruction packages, productivity applications, graphics tools, assessment tools, and student information systems. And software program delivery transitioned from time-shared services and phone lines, to applications delivered by floppy disks, then CDs and DVDs. Now most everything that students, teachers, administrators, and parents want to do with the computer is possible through the internet—the big time-share in the sky.

Leadership grew—from visionaries to classroom educators

At the federal level, National Science Foundation grants provided funding to support research and development efforts. Surprisingly, it was the Department of Defense support of military projects that led to the development of some of our computer-assisted instructional systems, the Logo language, and even the internet. The US Department of Education funding supported initial computer use for special education students as well as school pilots and professional development projects.

Researchers, such as those at BB&N and MIT, continued to work in on the development and use of the Logo language. Classrooms provided fertile ground for doctoral dissertations through the years—from the effectiveness of computer-assisted learning to the efficacy of online learning. One popular dissertation, Thomas Malone's "What Makes Things Fun to Learn" described how instructional computer games could be designed and extended the notion of *drill and practice* at that time (1980).

State and regional education leaders provided school-level support through computer services, consortium buys, curriculum materials, and professional development opportunities. They founded new organizations at the state and national levels to provide guidance to the growing number of teachers who were new to technology. New conferences and journals sprung up for *computer-using educators*. Seymour Papert was a popular speaker at those conferences and inspired many educators.

Different philosophies of computer use emerged

Over the past fifty years, different leaders espoused different philosophical and pedagogical uses for technology. Computer Literacy skills were important for a while. Interest grew in computer games. Productivity tools proliferated once AppleWorks came out. Programming courses became important as the nation needed more skilled technology workers. Laptop schools became a key component of technology implementation plans. Schools created Computer Science departments, budget lines, and new positions like IT Directors and Network Administrators. Some schools used Logo, while others installed Computer Curriculum Corporation labs.

Today, the schools have shifted their focus to helping students learn while online or via hybrid or blended models, and most recently from home.

Robert P. Taylor's 1980 book, *The Computer in the School: Tutor, Tool, Tutee*, brought together essays written by the early pioneers in educational computing. But forty year later, the major ideas from Seymour Papert, as well as from Patrick Suppes, Lud Braun, and Alfred Bork, still represent the way technology can be used and are being used today. In these past few decades, no one philosophy became the primary use of computers. Instead, education leaders understood that it was not an either-or use of computers. Each child today can use the computer however it best fits a need, like finding an online course for a subject not offered in their school, to communicate with students in other countries, or building a computer game to share with friends.

Seymour Papert's 1980 book *Mindstorms: Children, Computer and Powerful Ideas*, showed the potential of technology to change the educational system. His vision then was that children could program the computer to get it to do what they wanted it to do. Forty years later, most students are not using Logo but they are using other languages and coding skills. The programming that kids are doing today exemplify Seymour's vision of computer use. And we see increased participation by young women and students from underrepresented groups, things that Seymour would celebrate. These coding experiences become a part of their education and it reminds us that Seymour's ideas about how computers should be used still resonates with students today.

What Have We Accomplished?

Fifty years of education technology gave us a rich and important history, whether our first computer was a mainframe, desktop, laptop, or a handheld; our first use was a programming language such as Fortran, BASIC, Logo, Pascal, or a new coding language; or our first software use was Oregon Trail, AppleWorks, Reader Rabbit or internet browsers. Over the decades, both visionaries and implementers used computers in ways that aligned their philosophies with student needs and supported the learning process.

When Papert convened a symposium at MIT called *Teaching Children Thinking* in 1971, the idea that children would teach computers was pretty radical. But now, fifty years later, that idea is common practice in so many classrooms.

His presentations to education leaders at conferences provided a vision for so many through these past fifty years. Even so, it was often asked: "What is Logo? And who needs it?" While we may not *need* Logo in 2021 to do those *Twenty Things*, we continue to need the visionary leadership of people like Seymour Papert and Cynthia Solomon.

Where Are We Now?

We know that after fifty years, technology has become much more global and mobile, allowing for more social connection and communication among students of different cultures to learn together and for more collaboration as they work together more effectively on projects. But that effective and transformational use of technology takes a long time and a lot of hard work. Visionaries such as Seymour Papert and Cynthia Solomon provided ideas and inspired others to implement changes within schools—just not as quickly as the technology has changed. Its growth has produced a digital divide and the recent pandemic has taught us how many students could access their courses and teachers easily from home, while many could not.

With the student population more diverse in the US and the jobs they want more competitive, it is important that technology serve all learners, so they can accomplish the things they want to do and help them be ready for college or a career.

Fifty years ago, Papert and Solomon's paper described the various ways computers could be used to "produce some action." While their *Twenty Things* provided key ideas around the computers existing then, those ideas still resonate today. Current technology, with continued leadership, can build on Papert and Solomon's action items so that learners are successful in the twenty-first century.

References

Malone, T. W. (1980). What Makes Things Fun to Learn? Heuristics for Designing Instructional Computer Games. *Proceedings of the 3rd ACM SIGSMALL Symposium and the first SIGPC Symposium on Small Systems*, 162-169.

Papert, S. (1980). *Mindstorms: Children, Computers, and Powerful Ideas*. Basic Books.

Taylor, R. (1980). *The Computer in the School: Tutor, Tool, Tutee*. Teacher's College Press.

To Be or Not to Be ... (a Programmer)

John Stetson

An adolescent boy in a double-wide trailer is playing pong.

The year is 1999—is there an adolescent boy who does not want to play a video game?

You, also an adolescent boy, have just arrived and have been invited to play.

"Would you like to play a video game? Yes? All you have to do is create the game."

Did Seymour say that the essential choice we can make is to decide if we will be the programmer or will we allow ourselves to be programmed?

The boy who has just arrived looks at the game on the computer screen and starts asking questions. And this is where it starts. As the philosopher Mortimer Adler, said, "Wonder is the beginning of all wisdom."

The new boy looks at pictures of projects on the wall above and around each student's computer and work area. The pictures invite the new boy to ask about these projects. Documenting student projects and displaying student work is not a novel idea. This is what good schools do. In a regular high school the drama teacher knows that posters of past shows should be displayed in the school so that students will see that they, too, can participate in the next spring musical.

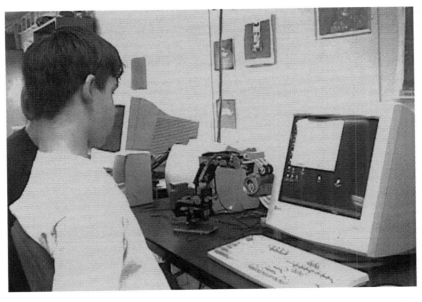

The new boy also sees students on the floor with robots. One vehicle, not much longer than eight inches and not much taller that four inches, appears to be following a ten foot long piece of black tape on the floor that is arranged in an irregular, wavy pattern; another student has a robot bumping into things and redirecting itself so as to keep moving. (If you are thinking about the Roomba, the robotic carpet sweeper, you are on the right track, but the Roomba was not commercially available until 2001.) Another vehicle is climbing an incline.

The new boy also sees boxes filled with LEGO parts: gears, axles, wheels, beams, connectors, and hinges, yellow Mindstorms bricks, etc.

The process of learning something about programming in Logo begins with a boy at a computer showing the newb a line or two of code. `If touching, RD` (reverse direction).

For these students, who are residents of a youth correctional facility, the idea, just the possibility, that they might have some control of something in this world, control of anything, is ecstatically liberating.

Yes, to being a programmer.

Who were the adults on the floor with the students playing with robots? One student came to me with the answer to that question; he said he had it all figured out. Dr. Papert has a full beard, David Cavallo had a trim beard, Gary Stager had a mustache, and I was clean shaven. The student's thought? The more facial hair the smarter the adult. Wiseass.

Don't underestimate the significance of humor in a correctional facility. The facility's special education director addressed the Constructionist Leaning Lab (LEGO Lab) faculty and the facility education faculty, and in her much-too-long speech she said that, "Students here were not ready for humor." I had a strong desire to interrupt her and say that the word "humor" and "human" had the same root. Humor? In the Lab it was a sign that students had a voice. Where there is humor there is a human connection.

One morning in the LEGO Lab students were invited to participate in a theater warm-up exercise that involved bouncing one ball and then several balls between students standing in a circle. The game is designed to start slowly and become chaotic as more balls are introduced. While a student was documenting this exercise with a video camera, another student was captured in a moment of laughter and joy. The photo was placed on the wall near his computer during lunch. When he returned to the classroom, he pulled me aside and said that as much as he appreciated that he had fun playing the game before lunch, he was not ready to see a photo of himself laughing. Further, he said that to navigate living in a juvenile facility he needed to wear a mask of disinterest in order to avoid the attention of others who could potentially harm him.

How Did Being a Programmer Manifest Itself?

Here is how programming and Seymour's LEGO Lab affected several students :

Robbie

Robbie was just fifteen in 1999 in a facility populated with residents who tended to be older. Many were in their late teens, and a few were as old as twenty-one. From what we could gather he had run away from foster care placements and group homes several times and was incarcerated for no other reason than the state could not find a more appropriate placement.

When he came to the LEGO Lab, we were told that he could not read and little more. In the Lab he found some voice recognition software to help him with writing. The irony was that he needed to speak into a microphone so that his voice could be recognized by the software. He quietly read the sample text. Could he read? Yes, he said, "Of course, I can read. I just didn't want my captors to know." I am glad he did not consider the LEGO Lab to be a place he was held captive. That brings to mind an aphorism from the ancient Greek historian, Xenophon, "Nothing forced is beautiful." In the LEGO Lab students selected to be there, and they selected projects that they found to be of interest. For the next several years Robbie loved building robots and being a central figure in the Lab.

One manifestation of Robbie's LEGO Lab experience was that he became a public speaker. In the winter of 2000, a group of adults, teachers from Iowa were in Maine in the LEGO Lab for a day of robotics and programming. At the end of the day Robbie was invited to demonstrate one of his robots. He was reluctant to speak in front of this group of adults. I told him that he could just let his autonomous robot do the talking. He came to the lab, put his robot on the ground in front of the teachers and program didn't work. Robbie started to describe what the robot was designed to do, how he built it, and he showed the teachers what he had put together for the program on his computer. He had the full attention of the teachers who had just been through a day-long introduction to such things. On the way back to his living unit, I asked him how he got the courage to speak to the group. Robbie said that he built the robot, and so he knew everything about it.

A month before his eighteenth birthday, his release from the juvenile system date, he announced that he had one more project he wanted to complete in the LEGO Lab. I must say that my first, naive thought was that he wanted to do more programing or another robotics project. No, Robbie wanted to write his autobiography. He said he wanted state officials and administrators at the juvenile facility to know what kind of childhood he had experienced as a ward of the state. Eighty-eight pages later he was satisfied that he had told his story.

A year later I saw Robbie on the local news. Lewiston, Maine had a new community garden. Who was the spokesperson for the garden who was speaking with the newscaster? Yes, Robbie.

Cary

Cary came to the LEGO Lab and said he wanted to learn "everything about computers." On day one we got into a conversation about writing code and binary numbers. I put the decimal numbers 1–10 on a whiteboard and started the pattern of binary numbers next to the decimal numbers. 0, 1, 10, 11, 100 … and I stopped with a pregnant pause. Cary did not miss a beat. He stepped up to the whiteboard and started writing … 101, 110, 111, 1000, 1001.

So, Cary clearly could see the pattern. He could take an idea and run with it. In his year at the facility he built robots and programmed in Logo. He also took an online class with the Virtual High School, a school started by Bob Tinker, one of Seymour's friends. The class was "Measuring the Earth as Eratosthenes Did 2000 Years Ago." Measuring the earth involved using a gnomon (a stick) on either the vernal or autumnal equinox to determine one's latitude, a calculation of the distance to the equator, and trigonometry.

After using the gnomon to measure the earth, Cary asked about documenting the relationship between the sun and the earth over the course of a year. What is produced? An analemma. This is where we get the mathematical symbol for infinity. (Cary was over 18 years old, and he signed a release for this photo. He also appeared with his analemma in the Portland Press Herald and at the NASA Spaceweather website.)

WINTER SOLSTICE

SUMMER SOLSTICE

One day when we were in the hall marking the gnomon's shadow at a specific time each clear day, a guard said, "Don't you have anything better to do?" My first thought was, "No, this is it."

Upon release from the facility he took computer science classes at the local community college.

Joey

Joey was showing another student how to write with "bubble letters." What are bubble letters used for? Graffiti. Do I understand that people have need to express themselves? Yes. Is spray painting graffiti on a bridge in town the most positive way to express oneself? I asked Joey if he would like to create a portrait of his friend. The following day I gave him access to a camera obscura that would project an image into a dark space in such a way that the image could be traced. Twenty minutes into his first experience with the camera obscura, Joey had his first portrait drawing completed. A week later Seymour made himself available as Joey's model. The pencil drawing was scanned, and color was added to the digitized image.

DRAWING COMPLETED WITH A CAMERA OBSCURA

Joey's stay at the facility included participation in radio production. He interviewed other students, and his story with the irreverent title, "Pee in the Pudding" has been featured locally on the college station, WMPG, and also nationally on *This American Life*.

So, thank you, Seymour, for creating a place where kids who had had few positive educational experiences could construct something meaningful. And thank you Seymour for writing a recommendation for my admission to graduate school. In that letter you did say that my understanding of technology was "idiosyncratic and incomplete." I am working on it.

Programming? Yes.

Change Is Certain, Progress Is Not[1]

Ron Canuel

When I received the invitation from Dr. Stager to write my thoughts about the 1971 article by Dr. Seymour Papert and Dr. Cynthia Solomon, *Twenty Things to Do with a Computer*, I paused and reread the article. The various usages of how computers can be used were fascinating and truly insightful. But as a long-standing educator, now over forty-four years, I again re-read the dire predictions and observations that were made in 1971 and realized how truly little has changed in education. I was first made aware of this article in 2002, after meeting Dr. Papert and Dr. Stager in Orono, Maine, during the initial rollout of the Maine 1:1 laptop state-wide initiative. That article had an important impact on myself and my team who accompanied me during that summer. Why? We decided to be Canada's first 1:1 school district in 2003 and second only in North America. To this day, I don't regret a single decision on our initiative. Could it have been better? Certainly, but our 1:1 laptop initiative was a truly enlightening journey into how the world of education functions and, most importantly, how it perceives innovation and change.

So, in reading this article, the first quote that stood out, "How strange, then, that 'computers in education' should so often be reduced to using bright new gadgets to teach the same old stuff in thinly disguised versions of the same old way" has been particularly relevant during this pandemic. We have witnessed how the massive carpet-bombing of technology into the hands of students and educators to support online learning has been, overall, a major failure. It has even led to a new term in the world of education—*Learning Loss*! It must be remembered that education has persistently and consistently wanted to avoid any technology being introduced into classrooms, hence the existence of the crappy computer labs. These labs still continue to function as visible demonstrations of how education "gets it" regarding technology. Even when I am asked to act, at the invitation of a school or district, to be a critical friend regarding technology, I shudder when I enter these twenty-first century schools (whatever that means) and observe fancy computer labs still in place. So that quote above still haunts me to this day!!

Now I know that readers of this essay will contest my observations and state that their use of technology is way above that of the computer lab reality. It might be, but I am certain that they are in the clear minority and are simply tolerated by their colleagues. The end result is that technology has not dumbed down education, as some have claimed. It is the exact opposite. Education has dumbed down technology for over fifty years now.

When educators state that their use of technology is cutting edge, I immediately think of my favorite comedian, John Pinette, and say "Nay, Nay!" One can only imagine what the world of education would look like today, had technology been accepted and appreciated for creating new dynamic learning and teaching environments decades ago. I am being told stories by parents who are observing their children receiving online instruction during the pandemic and how, overall, they have become opposed to the usage of technology for learning and teaching purposes. To provide further evidence, even today in some school districts and stakeholder websites, wifi is considered a danger to the health of those working in schools and there are those who think it should be banned from all schools. These policies are still in place.

But why did we get where we are now? This brings me to another quote from the Papert-Solomon article. "Why not use them [computers] to produce some action? There is no better reason than the intellectual timidity of the computers-in-education community, which seems remarkable reluctant to use the computers for any purposes that fails to look very much like something that has been taught in schools for the past centuries."

This is not at all surprising. Teachers were never provided with professional development to teach online or with technology; were never prepared to assess what they are teaching; were seriously restrained by the infamous Tech in Education departments policies on *accessing* or *searching* on the internet (remember, control above anything else); were never provided with a curriculum to match the potential of technology in learning; and most faculties of education continue to ignore using technology effectively as a solid pedagogical approach, to name a few challenges.

I believe that there is also another explanation. The structure of education is simply not built to support innovation, plain and simple. It is built to support fundamental societal expectations: *control, compliance,* and *conformity.* To further illustrate my point is when I enter a school district's head office or a school and am introduced to the *Director of Innovation.* Whew, for a second, I thought that every educator should be their own *Director of Innovation,* so this position delegates that responsibility off the shoulders of educators, who can then focus on the real *business of learning.* Being what? Operate the system using key industrial efficiency axioms—produce the best, with the fewest possible resources, and accept that failure is a key indicator of quality control? It is no wonder that we see high attrition rates of teachers leaving the system and burn out now being a critical issue across North America.

This current structure of education supports a failure rate of 15–20%, pivots any new educational approach into an infamous *pilot program,* and then takes the potential of technology and moves it into management systems for schools and districts. (Aside: in my conference presentations over the past couple of years, I show pictures of schools, juvenile detention centers, and warehouses. I ask the delegates to indicate which ones are the schools. To date, nobody has gotten all the right answers. The biggest result is that juvenile detention centers are often confused with schools!)

So for the countless *education change evangelists* out there (I am one of them!), we somehow expected that a rock can change itself into a gardenia. I now realize that that won't happen under the current circumstances and structures. We need to seek viable, pragmatic alternative solutions that appeal to the current stakeholders in education and provide them with some value-added elements. Otherwise, why change?

So, how to correct this situation?

For those who know me, I have always favored the pragmatic aspirations over the lofty aspirations that fly above everybody's head. We also know that once a student exits kindergarten and grades 1–2, we witness a decline of curiosity and inquiry until they leave in the final year of high school.

Education change evangelists need to focus on creating contexts and working environments that will encourage risk-taking, creativity, and innovation. The simplest approach is to have these elements included in the performance appraisals of educators, *at all levels.* Basic human resource management states that employees will work on what they are being evaluated upon. Does the evaluation criteria make specific mention of courage?

I read a recent posting for a senior education position where there is much emphasis placed on leadership. In the over twelve leadership expectations, not once are the words innovative, creative, risk-taking, or courageous mentioned! So the leadership outlined is to ensure a smooth operation, but definitely no change. And guess what? You are correct! The person who will be appointed to that position will not make changes to create any new dynamic learning or teaching contexts. That person will be evaluated on what was outlined in the job posting. I am often quoted for stating that "no courage, no change." That is the truth.

We also need to remind ourselves that education is highly labor intensive, usually over 80%

of a school board's budget is attached to salaries and benefits. As previously mentioned, we can also promote some of the current models of instruction closer to the world that Papert and Solomon envisioned, specifically the kindergarten class. Why not make that model for all levels of learning in elementary and high schools? It is holistic in approach, seeking to develop and strengthen the best of human character, skills, and competencies without any negative repercussions. The greatest lament that we hear from educators and students is that relationships drastically diminish over a period of twelve years. Effective teaching is entirely about relationships built with students. Change is a human resource challenge. Poor, irrelevant curriculum, outdated assessment rubrics including standardized assessments, outdated classroom design, etc. are indicators of *control-conformity-compliance*.

Again, I want to be clear that I have the utmost admiration and respect for educators, and I also recognize that they must work under very challenging contexts and situations. Teaching is truly the greatest profession on this planet. However, when the environments that they work in reflect centuries-old structures, they cannot be miracle workers.

So, now back to 1971 and the great article by Dr. Papert and Dr. Solomon. I bring forth another quote that resonates with me today and illustrates what, I believe, was their underlying message to us:

Life begins at the edge of your comfort zone. — Neale Donald Walsch

Notes

1   "Change is certain, progress is not." E.H. Carr, British historian 1892-1982

Twenty Things and Moving Forward: An Embodied-based Scenario for Kindergarten Children

José Armando Valente

Introduction

The Logo Memo #3 entitled *Twenty Things to Do with a Computer* was a seminal paper, creating a new paradigm in terms of how to use computers in education. To understand its role and its importance it is necessary to know the historical context in which it was produced.

During the 1960s, programmed instruction was a very popular teaching method and several researchers such as Patrick Suppes from Stanford University and computer companies such as IBM were implementing this education method in computers, what was known as Computer-Assisted Instruction (CAI). The basic idea was to convert knowledge from practically all areas into these programs and use them in K–12 and higher education.

The creation of Logo was a proposal in a different direction. The Logo Lab Memo *Twenty Things to Do with a Computer* was an attempt to show that there were other things we could do with computers beside transmit information to students. Papert and Solomon's proposal was that children should be teaching the computer instead of computers teaching children.

Papert and Solomon's paper opened up lots of doors in terms of new ways computers could be used in education. It was also a very interesting and intelligent paper since it was not restricted to these twenty things. The twentieth activity was an invitation for us to come up with other ways to use computers in education. This is what the Logo community all over the world has been doing since 1971. Certainly with the advancement of digital technology it is expected that other possibilities can be proposed. The paper anticipated several ones such as programming, robotics, puppet show, and yardstick-balancer. However, I would like to discuss two fundamental ideas that can be added to the original paper: one is the constructionism theoretical framework which made explicit the reason and importance for using digital technology to create public objects as a way of expressing our mind; and the other is the possibility of constructing a performance with the body, which can be considered a public expression of our mind, as proposed by constructionism.

In this essay, the following section presents the CAI context in which Logo was created. The next two sections discuss the constructionism framework and how it is possible to construct public actions with and through the body. The last section presents a work that I am currently involved—an embodied-based scenario for kindergarten children in which they have, as a group, interacted with a robot to solve a particular task. In this scenario children's interactions can be considered a constructed public performance that can be analyzed in terms of type of actions and knowledge used.

CAI versus Logo

Programmed instruction consists of breaking particular content down into small pieces of information called frames. A frame is presented to the students so they can study it by themselves and at their own speed. After completing this study the students' comprehension is evaluated by answering an examination test. If they master the content of this frame, they can move to the next one. Otherwise, they have to go back to the material and study it again. The computer was the perfect machine to implement these programs, which was known as Computer-Assisted Instruction (CAI).

Patrick Suppes, a professor from Stanford University, was a champion of the development and dissemination of CAI as an education method. In 1963 he developed a CAI system to teach math content, sets, and numbers, to first and fourth grade students, and mathematical logic to sixth-graders (Suppes, 1965). In the beginning of 1970, he designed an instructional system and a curriculum for teaching mathematical logic to undergraduate students at Stanford (Goldberg & Suppes, 1976).

Based on the results from his studies Suppes published several papers showing the advantages of CAI as an educational system. He argued that traditional programmed instruction was not very efficient since a teacher could keep track of about thirty students. A CAI system could manage a much larger number of students. It was very simple to scale this system to different knowledge content areas and levels of teaching. Another advantage was that computers could provide an immediate feedback and correction to the student, and also, based on the student's performance, the teacher could have an immediate evaluation of the student progress. Finally CAI made possible individualized instruction by arranging the sequence of concept frames and adjusting it according to different student's needs and level of previous knowledge (Suppes & Jerman, 1970).

Suppes visited the Logo Laboratory at MIT in the late 1970s and gave a talk in which he presented himself as the most productive professor in the world since his courses served thousands of students. He published about the use of CAI in education until 2014 and his collected work is very organized and presented in his site (Suppes, 2014).

CAI systems were disseminated and produced by companies such as IBM, RCA, and Digital and used mainly at universities. PLATO (Programmed Logic for Automated Teaching Operations) produced by Control Data Corporation and the University of Illinois, was undoubtedly the best known and most successful CAI (PLATO, 2010).

During the 1970s there were several researchers who were in favor of using CAI throughout the education system. This was clear at the Ten-Year Forecast for Computer and Communication: Implications for Education conference held in September 1975 and sponsored by the National Science Foundation (Seidel & Rubin, 1977). The papers presented indicated the existence of a controversy among the authors who defended the use of CAI and those like Papert (1977), Minsky (1977), and Dwyer (1977) who defended the use of computers to facilitate a total reform of the educational system.

Thus the creation of Logo and its dissemination was an attempt to propose a different way computers could be used. The temptation to automate education was enormous! It is interesting that the sixteenth activity in Papert and Solomon's paper is a CAI written in Logo. In 1975, as a professor of Computer Science at the State University of Campinas (UNICAMP), I developed, in collaboration with an undergraduate student Marcelo Martelini, an instruction program written in BASIC to teach BASIC programming to school teachers. When I showed this program to Papert and Marvin Minsky, who were visiting UNICAMP at that time, they mentioned that I should know Logo and invited me to spend some time at the Logo Lab. I was fortunate to be able to go to MIT and to do my master and doctoral studies with Papert. I was rescued from the CAI pathway!

Up to the 1980s, digital technology was very limited and basically confined to the universities. Logo was only running on mainframe computers and on the GTI 3500 microcomputer designed by Minsky. In the 1980s the personal computer became available and started to be implemented in K–12 schools. Although, in the *Mindstorms* book, Papert tried to highlight the important ideas that had informed the Logo project, a more robust theoretical framework was still missing (Papert, 1980, p. 216). This came with the constructionism framework, developed in 1986, which has allowed the expansion of how to use computers in education (Papert, 1986). Since then, this theoretical framework has been used to support the creation of different learning environments and it has developed and expanded as digital technology has evolved. I consider constructionism the key element that has helped not only to expand what we can do with technology but to understand how a technology-based educational environment can foster knowledge construction.

Constructionism

Papert coined the term "constructionism" as part of a proposal that was submitted and financed by the National Science Foundation in 1986. In this proposal he stated that:

> *Learning is particularly effective when it is embedded in an activity the learner experiences as constructing a meaningful product (for example, a work of art, a functioning machine, a research report, or a computer program) (Papert, 1986, p. abstract).*

Later on, Papert (1991) explained what constructioNism (**with N**) adds to Piaget's constructiVism (**with V**). For Piaget, knowledge about the world is not transmitted to children, but actively constructed by them as they interact with the objects and people around them (Piaget, 1985). Constructionism goes one step further. For Papert, knowledge is constructed when children are engaged in making a meaningful product, an external artifact that can be public. However, building this product goes beyond *hands-on*. The fact that "children are working to make something, and especially the fact they are making something they believe in, adds extra dimensions" (Papert, 1986, p. 9). The construction process was not just a hands-on activity but also a head-in activity.

This meaningful product has several roles, as mentioned by Ackermann. First it projects out children's "inner feelings and ideas, making them tangible and shareable so as to help children communicate with other people." Second, the construction of the objects "creates the opportunity for children to 'dive into' the learning situation, rather than observe it from a distance" (Ackermann, 2001).

From the educational point of view, the product has another important role. The analysis of it can indicate the knowledge the learner used in its construction and an educator can help the learner to debug and improve her ideas to achieve higher levels of understating.

Since constructionism was proposed in 1986 it has been used as a theoretical foundation of several major works reported in at least three books: *Constructionism* (Harel & Papert, 1991), *Constructionism in Practice* (Kafai & Resnick, 1996), and *Designing Constructionism Futures* (Holbert et al., 2020). This shows that this concept is in constant reconstruction and elaboration according to the evolution of materials, especially the digital technology used to make things. Clearly it is a concept in construction!

In the *Constructionism* book, Papert explained the difference between constructivism and constructionism and stated that the public entity can be "a sand castle on the beach or a theory of the universe" (Harel & Papert, 1991, p. 1). He elaborates on what the public product can be:

the object constructed does not have to be a concrete, tangible object, but a theory; and the construction process can be done with or without the use of the computer, a sand castle.

In the second book organized by Kafai and Resnick (1996) other dimensions were added to the idea of constructionism: learning through design, learning in communities, and learning about systems. According to the authors, design can be seen as a process to understand objective constraints and subjective meanings. Community is a theme emphasized in several chapters that describe work in classrooms, urban centers, and virtual communities. And the development of computational tools, such as StarLogo and robot-design competition, is very important to understand systems consisting of many interacting parts.

The third book by Holbert, Berland, and Kafai (2020) incorporates the incredible evolution of digital technology that has taken place in the last fifteen years such as Scratch, ubiquitous devices, digital fabrication technologies, and different types of sensors, activators, and controllers. These technological developments have enabled the creation of a series of activities that expand even more what had been created in terms of constructionist learning environments. The book mentions work developed in makerspaces and art studios, and activities exploring storytelling, online writing, and constructing through the body. Also the book explores themes such as how to support large numbers of learners and in diverse contexts as schools, home or virtual spaces; equity so constructionism can be experienced not only by the privileged; sociocultural implications so to understand the social dimension for learning; creativity so learning can be seen as a creative construction process; and finally the future of constructionism, describing several visions for how constructionism can be expanded even further in the future.

A particular chapter called my attention since it is related to *body syntonicity*, a theme that Papert had mentioned early on (1980) and the researchers have taken it a step further, as discussed in the next section.

Constructing with Body Action

The body had a fundamental role for creating learning contexts and was an important resource in Papert's thought. In the spring semester of 1976 he taught a class with other professors from MIT, which was known as the Loud Thinking Course. In it, the participants had to do activities like balancing sticks, juggling, walking on sticks, and one-wheel cycling. As they were performing these tasks, they had to say aloud what they were doing with their body. His intention was to show that in order to understand the learning process you have to catch yourself in the act of learning (Turkle, 2017). This collection of activities was not random. Papert had been thinking about them prior to the course and was a master in doing them all!

The importance of the body in thinking is described in two passages in *Mindstorms*. One is related to the role of gears in Papert's ways of understanding about mathematical ideas; the other one is body syntonicity.

For Papert the gears that he played with in his infancy, besides helping to connect with the formal knowledge of mathematics, also helped to connect with the "body knowledge"—the sensorimotor schemata of a child.

> You can be the gear, you can understand how it turns by projecting yourself into its place and turning with it. It is this double relationship - both abstract and sensory - that gives the gear the power to carry powerful mathematics into the mind (Papert, 1980, p. viii).

As a researcher, Papert's challenging task was how to create objects for children to play with that could do what the gears did for his thinking. His solution was the turtle (first the floor turtle and then the one on the screen) which was a Logo hallmark. The turtle was the object to think about mathematical ideas and a way to connect with body-knowledge.

The Logo commands to move the turtle are very similar to terms we use to move ourselves in space. When a learner has to understand how to command the turtle to do a particular task, one strategy is to *play turtle* and to observe the actions she is doing with her body. Based on what was done, the learner can translate these actions into Logo commands. Papert called this "syntonic learning" to refer to what a person does with the body to reason about ideas that are difficult to grasp. Thus, the turtle was designed so turtle geometry could be body syntonic because it can be related to children's knowledge about their own bodies.

The strategy of putting oneself in the place of the object the person is trying to understand is a powerful idea. Ubiquitous technology and sophisticated digital sensors and activators can provide new ways to explore this idea. They are enabling the body to be part of techno-logical embodied-based environments. In these environments people's actions can be seen as a construction that can be considered a form of public artifact. This is proposed by Danish and Enyedy (2020). Their proposal can be an interesting way of expanding constructionism and is related to the work that I am currently involved, presented in the next section.

In the Danish and Enyedy chapter, "Constructing With and Through the Body," they describe results of several experiments that show how the body supports individual cognition and how it plays a role in social and collaborative activities. For example, students played the role of being water particles and had to move around in space enacting the different water states—they had to move slowly for ice and more quickly for liquid and gas. For gas they had to run and this was analogous to the speed of gas particles. Through this experience they could relate the energy they felt while running and the energy necessary to move particles in a gas. As the students played collectively, live video projected their action overlaid with a simple visualization that indicated the state of the matter the students were currently producing. Even though the students did not understand how they were controlling the visualization, this feedback system helped them to create and recognize different patterns in their motions and the motions of particles, and how this contributed to different states of matter.

The students' collective performance can be considered as a public object they have constructed with their body which can be analyzed and unpacked in terms of expressive power and how it can support reflection and knowledge construction. Our work about development of an embodied-based scenario for children has a similar approach.

An Embodied-Based Scenario for Kindergarten Children

We created an embodied-based scenario that includes a robot system for kindergarten children, ages four to five years old, who have not yet mastered the use of written language. This work is part of a larger research project (Baranauskas, 2015) developed at the State University of Campinas (UNICAMP) related to the development of socioenactive systems.

We use the concept of enactive systems to explore embodied-based scenarios. An enactive system consists of a computational system that dynamically connects people and technological processes using sensor data to allow them to interact via feedback cycles. These cycles permit a person to affect the technology as well be affected by it (Kaipainen et al., 2011). The socioen-active system that we are developing expands the enactive idea to include the social aspect so a group of people can interact with the technology affecting themselves and being affected by it.

The designed activity is based on the *Little Red Riding Hood* narrative adapted to the children's daily lives, addressing playful aspects of interaction and collaboration among the children. Children played the role of rangers (instead of hunters) who had to interact among themselves and coordinate their actions to help a robot (a mBot characterized as a Robot-Wolf) to find the Grandma's laboratory so she could fix its GPS (Caceffo et al., 2018). Children wore boots that were used to interact with the Robot-Wolf. The objective of this study was to understand how children as a group could interact with the robot and to understand social interactions and the concepts they used to solve the task proposed (Caceffo et al., 2019; Valente et al., 2020).

The study was conducted in two similar workshops involving twenty-six children (eleven females, fifteen males) between four and five years old. They were from an educational space that is open to children or legal dependents of UNICAMP's employees and students between the ages of six months to fourteen years old. The scenario created for Workshop 1 is shown in Figure 1. The children's activities were videotaped and analyzed using the Grounded Theory methodology.

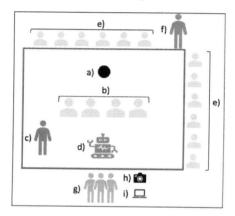

Figure 1: Workshop 1 Scenario a) Grandma's lab; b) group of children acting as rangers; c) facilitator; d) Robot-Wolf; e) children acting as forest trees; f) teacher; g) researchers; h) camera; i) computer system. The space of action representing the enchanted forest is delimited and contains elements a), b) c) and d). Source: (Valente et al., 2020)

Figure 2a shows the Robot-Wolf, Figure 2b a child interacting with the Robot-Wolf through his boot, and Figure 2c illustrates a moment in which a child places his boot in the Robot-Wolf's path, forcing it to change its direction, thus reorienting its heading. Meanwhile, the other children in the rangers' group shout instructions to each other. The children outside the scene cheer for the rangers, also trying to help by positioning their boots and shouting out tips.

Figure 2a, the Robot-Wolf is at the Grandma's lab (left); Figure 2b, a child interacting with the Robot-Wolf

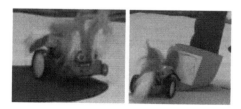

through his ranger's boot (middle); Figure 2c, a group of children are guiding the Robot-Wolf to Grandma's lab (right) Source: (Valente et al., 2020)

A total of three hours of video were produced during the two workshop sessions with two groups of children. The video was analyzed and children's actions were categorized as follows:

- Coordinated action – sequence of actions in which children interact with each other and with the robot in a coordinated way towards a common objective
- Leadership – situations where a group member takes the lead
- Anticipation – when a child (or group) anticipates a successful or unsuccessful situation

- Body expressiveness – when a child expresses his/her feelings according to a given situation

The analysis also showed that children's body expressions indicated that they were passionately engaged in the activity. For example, gesturing towards the robot to show something to a colleague; putting their hands on their head in an expression of apprehension; expressing euphoria by clapping their hands and jumping. Also they were able to coordinate their actions to successfully accomplish the mission to guide the robot to Grandma's Lab.

These results reveal that the proposed embodied-based scenario was successfully used by these kindergarten children and was adequate for them. In this scenario the activities were a product of children's own body. What they performed can be interpreted as an external product in which it is possible to observe that children used concepts such as direction, orientation regarding a reference point, distance estimation, and timing, among others, revealed especially in their anticipation of the robot's behavior. The next step is to understand whether the scenario can help these children to construct and improve their knowledge about these concepts.

Final Considerations

Papert and Solomon started with twenty things to do with the computer. As identified in just the books mentioned in this essay, we may have today more than a hundred things. The constructionism theoretical framework has opened up many doors for the development of these activities and certainly much more can be added.

Among the activities described so far, construction with the body has only recently been proposed. The embodied-based scenario presented here is a contribution in this direction. Also this study can contribute to expand our comprehension about constructionism and body syntonicity. What is constructed does not have to be a product of hands-on and head-in, but it can be a construction involving the whole body. In addition, the body can be used to not only reason about ideas, but can be an integrated part of the product being constructed.

Thus the development of socioenactive systems can be an interesting research topic in the direction of implementing learning scenarios that afford spontaneous involvement of social interaction of people's bodies. The scenario presented here constituted the first attempt to understand how kindergarten children could use the scenario proposed. However, it cannot be considered yet a socioenactive system since it does not include the feedback cycle. This is what is currently being studied as part of the project's next phase.

Acknowledgments

I gratefully acknowledge the supporters of this research: São Paulo Research Foundation (FAPESP), grants #2015/24300-9, #2015/16528-0, #2014/07502-4 and #2018/06416-8; and the National Council of Technological and Scientific Development (CNPq) grants #310854/2019-9 and the State University of Campinas (UNICAMP). I thank all the researcher colleagues who participated in the development of the embodied-based scenario. Also in this study, all parents signed a Term of Consent, allowing their children to participate in the study, and all children expressed their consent as well and I thank them. The research was approved by the State University of Campinas' Research Ethics Committee on October 2017, under number CAAE: 72413817.3.0000.5404. I do not wish to declare any conflict of interest.

References

Ackermann, E. (2001). Piaget's Constructivism, Papert's Constructionism: What's the Difference? *Future of Learning Group Publication*, 5(3), 438. learning.media.mit.edu/content/publications/EA.Piaget%20_%20Papert.pdf

Baranauskas, M. C. C. (2015). Socio-enactive Systems: Investigating New Dimensions in the Design of Interaction Mediated by Information and Communication Technologies. *FAPESP Thematic Research*

Project #2015/16528-0.

Caceffo, R., Abreu, J., Gonçalves, F., Takinami, O., Romani, R., & Baranauskas, M. C. C. (2018). Socio-enactive Systems: The Educational Scenario. *Technical Report, 18-01*(Institute of Computing, University of Campinas, SP, Brasil).

Caceffo, R., Moreira, E., Bonacin, R., Reis, J., Carbajal, M., D'Abreu, J., Brennand, C., Lombello, L., Valente, J. A., & Baranauskas, M. C. C. (2019). Collaborative Meaning Construction in Socioenactive Systems: Study with the mBot. In: P. Zaphiris P. & A. Ioannou (Eds.). *2019. Lecture Notes in Computer Science*, vol 11590. doi.org/10.1007/978-3-030-21814-0_18

Danish, J. A., & Enyedy, N. (2020). Constructing With and Through the Body In N. Holberg, M. Berland, & Y. B. Kafai (Eds.), *Designing Constructionism Futures: the art, theory, and practice of learning designs.* MIT Press.

Dwyer, T. A. (1977). An Extensible Model for Using Technology in Education. In R. J. Seidel & M. L. Rubin (Eds.), *Computers and Communications: implications for education.* Academic Press.

Goldberg, A., & Suppes, P. (1976). Computer-assisted Instruction in Elementary Logic at the University Level. *Educational Studies in Mathematics, 6*(4), 447-474. jstor.org/stable/3481883

Harel, I., & Papert, S. (Eds.). (1991). *Constructionism.* Ablex Publishing Corporation.

Holbert, N., Berland, M., & Kafai, Y. B. (2020). *Designing Constructionism Futures: the Art, Theory, and Practice of Learning Designs.* MIT Press.

Kafai, Y. B., & Resnick, M. (1996). *Constructionism in Practice: Designing, Thinking, and Learning in a Digital World.* Lawrence Erlbaum Associates.

Kaipainen, M., Ravaja, N., Tikka, P., Vuori, R., Pugliese, R., Rapino, M., & Takala, T. (2011). Enactive Systems and Enactive Media: Embodied Human-machine Coupling Beyond Interfaces. *Leonardo, 44*(5), 433-438. dx.doi.org/10.1162/LEON_a_00244

Minsky, M. (1977). Applying Artificial Intelligence to Education. In R. J. Seidel & M. L. Rubin (Eds.), *Computers and Communications: implications for education.* Academic Press.

Papert, S. (1977). A Learning Environment for Children. In R. J. Seidel & M. L. Rubin (Eds.), *Computers and Communications: implications for education.* Academic Press.

Papert, S. (1980). *Mindstorms: Children, Computers, and Powerful Ideas.* Basic Books.

Papert, S. (1986). *Constructionism: A New Opportunity for Elementary Science Education. A Proposal to the National Science Foundation.* Massachusetts Institute of Technology, Media Laboratory, Epistemology and Learning Group.

Papert, S. (1991). Situating Constructionism. In I. Harel & S. Papert (Eds.), *Constructionism* (pp. 1-11). Ablex. papert.org/articles/SituatingConstructionism.html

Piaget, J. (1985). *Equilibration of Cognitive Structures.* University of Chicago Press.

PLATO. (2010). *Plato-Computer History Museum.* distributedmuseum.illinois.edu/exhibit/plato/

Seidel, R. J., & Rubin, M. L. (Eds.). (1977). *Computers and Communications: Implications for Education.* Academic Press.

Suppes, P. (1965). Computer-based Mathematics Instruction. *Bulletin of the International Study Group for Mathematics Learning, 3,* 7-22. suppes-corpus.stanford.edu/bibliography?page=18

Suppes, P. (2014). *Collected Works of Patrick Suppes.* Bibliography. suppes-corpus.stanford.edu/bibliography?page=18

Suppes, P., & Jerman, M. (1970). Computer-assisted Instruction. *Bulletin of the National Association of Secondary School Principals, 54*(343), 27-40. suppes-corpus.stanford.edu/sites/g/files/sbiybj7316/f/computer-assisted_instruction_105-1.pdf

Turkle, S. (2017). Remembering Seymour Papert. *London Review of Books.* lrb.co.uk/blog/2017/february/remembering-seymour-papert.

Valente, J. A., Caceffo, R., Moreira, E. A., Bonacin, R., Dos Reis, J. C., Carbajal, M. L., D'abreu, J. V. V., Gonçalves, F. M., Brennand, C. V. L. T., & Baranauskas, M. C. C. (2020). A Robot-based Activity for Kindergarten Children: An Embodied Exercise. *Proceedings of Constructionism Conference 2020, Dublin,* 137-146.

Math Classes Are Failing the AI Age Workforce

Conrad Wolfram

In *Twenty Things to Do with a Computer*, Seymour Papert and Cynthia Solomon proposed ways that computers could support deeper understanding of mathematics. Why did they feel this was needed? It's the same reason today, fifty years later. School math doesn't match real-world math. It's not the fault of the teachers or the administrators, or the students or even the parents. It's the subject's fault.

And the problem's getting worse—much worse. The difference is simple to state. At school, almost all the calculating is done by humans; in the real world, it's almost all done by computers. This changes everything: where math applies, what toolset you use, how hard a problem you solve and how you go about it. The root of the problem is that no math curriculum in the world was built assuming computers exist. They were conceived before that reality—making perhaps 80% of the subject matter suboptimal.

Most of us don't directly use most of the math we were taught above primary education. When was the last time you solved a formal long division problem by hand? Probably never—except to help your children with their homework! To be clear, long division problems still come up in real life, but if you needed more than a good estimate, you'd reach for some kind of computer, e.g. a laptop, smartphone, or Siri. I have yet to see a mainstream math curriculum support the increasingly complex interplay between human and machine that the AI age requires. I can see the extent and harm of this divergence from so many perspectives: user, maker, employer, supplier and innovator of computational technology. We need to do better.

So, what does a math curriculum that assumes computers exist look like?

Firstly, it's full of context, front and center. Start with a question like "Can I spot a cheat?" or "How happy are people in my country?" Normally, school math starts abstract (e.g. solve $x^2 + 2x + 1 = 0$), and weeks later, if they're lucky, after all the calculating, students might try and apply what they learned to a real problem that has something to do with their life.

Except mostly they can't. The current contexts are simplistic, the problems unreal—restricted by what can be calculated by hand. That's a tiny fraction of today's techniques. There were some contexts that worked well pre-computer, such as parts of physics, accounting, and economics.

Conversely, the likes of biology, modeling of complex systems or what we now call data science, did not. Math or computation is applied so widely outside education because computers made this possible—they liberated math from hand calculating. It's only since the dawn of computers, and often recent gains in their power, that math really helps us with many of today's hard, fuzzy questions.

Secondly, the tools of the computation trade one learns are very different: machine learning for primary schools; applying calculus for 10-year-olds; and 3D geometry, not just 2D. There is much more to problem solving than calculating: complex problems need more definition, better abstraction, and more sophisticated interpretation and verification.

It is important to note that the computer-based math I describe is not dumbed down math, it is every bit as intellectual or conceptual as today's math education. Nor does it remove mental agility or thinking. Rather than mindlessly following procedures for hand calculating, students will learn to interpret and verify what the machine has told them at a higher level. It's often more amenable to students from a wider range of backgrounds. Context relevant to their lives may help them get engaged where abstraction first did not.

Calculating is only one of four steps of the math process: define the problem, abstract it to a language so it can be calculated, calculate it, then interpret the answer in relation to the question you originally asked, verifying it makes sense. The third step—calculating or computing by hand—is what school math is spending most of its time on. But that's what computers do so much better, almost always. It's the other steps that remain much more human. Don't have students compete with what computers do best and lose.

Repercussions of this educational failure are twofold: (1) virtually no societal inoculation against computational misinformation and (2) poor distribution of the power of computation (prosperity and jobs) through society. These problems will grow as we enter the AI age, increasingly disenfranchising large sections of the population. To avoid a data science dictatorship, we need a computational thinking revolution, and it starts with fixing math education.

The End of Knowing – and a New Way to Learn

Sugata Mitra

A dream came true in the summer of 2010— I met Professor Seymour Papert, whose work with children and computers in the 1970s had rocked the world of education. I was in Maine, USA, speaking at a conference and Prof. Papert, who lived there, wanted to meet me! I explained my work with children and the internet as briefly as I could. Then he beckoned to a student of his and said, "get him here." That is all he said.

Seymour Papert and I – Maine, USA, 2010

In 2011, Professor Nicholas Negroponte invited me to a visiting professorship at the MIT Media Lab. It was a year that changed my life in many ways.

In 2012, I spoke at the Media Lab.[1] The lecture was called *The Future of Learning* and it was in a largish lecture hall that was quite full. People wanted to hear the story of the Hole in the Wall,[2] no matter how hard I tried to steer them towards what I knew was going to come next. But that day was different. Nicholas Negroponte was sitting in the first row. A bit nervously, I built up the story of the history of education from the Greeks through to now. The story of Professor Aristotle's student, Alexander, who conquered the world but whose general was eventually pushed back out of India by Professor Chanakya's student, Chandragupta. Both students created empires—we don't know if their professors approved. I moved on from the battle of professors to the story of empires, ending with the British and the education system they left behind all over the world. A system where the teacher was called the Master.

People don't like calling other people Master and young people have always resisted such hierarchies. My lecture began to get a little bonkers at this point. I even had an awful slide that I am truly ashamed of, but reproduce here for the sake of academic integrity. Gulp.

Young people don't like authority, while traditional education is based on the authority of the teacher

Mercifully, I moved on to the Hole in the Wall and that the Master need not be human at all, just a big enough network will do.

The MIT audience began to lean forward, and I warmed up to my theme. "With continuous and invisible access to Google, can a person pretend to be educated? Is that really pretending?" I raised some questions before closing:

- How do we examine a connected student?
- Is it necessary to learn new languages?
- Is arithmetic obsolete?
- Is vocational training meaningless?
- Is the absence of a teacher a pedagogic tool?
- Can cheating improve learning?

There were a few giggles, some mutterings about senility. But I knew I was getting there. "Is education obsolete?" was my last slide. As that slide came up, Negroponte spoke, "Knowing is obsolete," he said. "Yes," I responded with relief, "It is the *end of knowing*."

Learning and Knowing

This essay is about learning and knowing, so obviously, we need to understand what knowing and learning are. If you try looking those words up, you will realize that their definitions in dictionaries are often circular—learning, knowing, and knowledge are all mixed up. Knowing means having knowledge. Knowledge is something that you get by learning. Learning is something that you do to get knowledge. And so on. For example, a particularly nutty example of a definition of learning is, "Acquiring knowledge and skills and having them readily available from memory so you can make sense of future problems and opportunities" (Brown, 2014).

In general, *learning* is something that you do in the past so that you *know* something inside your brain just in case you ever need it in the future. It is assumed that the problems you will face in the future will be like the ones you solved while learning about them, in the past.

First Experiments

The Hole in the Wall was an experiment, leading to many other experiments with children and the internet.[3] I had conducted the first of these in a slum in New Delhi in 1999. The experiment was simple—an internet connected computer was embedded in a wall of the slum at a child-friendly height. It was turned on but there was no supervision or, indeed, any adult in the vicinity. The children of the slum of that time had not seen a computer or heard of the internet, nor did they know any English. They flocked around and figured out how to make the computer do things. In a week, they began downloading games, in nine months they were just about as good as an average office secretary. Groups of children clustered around the internet can learn anything by themselves. The story exploded across media worldwide. I ended up with funding to repeat the results in other places to see if children would behave similarly elsewhere. They did.

The first day of the Hole in the Wall experiment in January 1999

I began to get curious about the conditions under which the Hole in the Wall worked. There must not be any supervision, the children must be in groups and, of course, the location should be safe and public. Under those conditions, and only under those conditions, *learning* and *knowing* would happen by themselves—spontaneously. The children were not learning just in case they would ever need the knowledge; they were learning just in time to have some fun. You must let it happen.

Schools, on the other hand, are in closed, private, supervised spaces where children are seldom in groups. Here learning and knowing are supervised exercises to prepare children for all that they may face in the future, just in case. Schools make it happen.

The difference between schools and the hole in the wall is a bit like the difference between architecture and gardening. Architects make buildings and bridges and so on. Gardeners make gardens and landscapes. Architects create and make things happen, gardeners can only let creation unfold.

It took twenty years to figure out the main principles of letting learning happen. In those twenty years, billions connected themselves into the world wide web, converting what was just a network to start with into an entity called *the cloud*. Computers evolved into pocket-sized devices that have replaced almost everything from ages gone by. Telephones, telex, fax, television, radio, gramophones, recorders, cameras, letters, newspapers, books, tapes, discs, film, maps, clocks, torches, mirrors… ahh, you can have some fun completing this list, if you are more than sixteen years old. If you are not, you may not have heard of many of these. So, what would *the cloud* do to learning and knowing?

Signs of Change

Between 1999 and 2020, the Hole in the Wall had become a product that has been installed in hundreds of places in India and elsewhere. The last estimate I have from the NIIT foundation that builds and installs these is that over 2.5 million children have used these facilities over the last ten years. Meanwhile, the idea of the Hole in the Wall converted itself into Self Organized Learning Environments (SOLEs). In England, I introduced the idea of SOLEs into schools in Gateshead in the northeast of the country. SOLEs are unsupervised learning environments like the Hole in the Wall, but they are created inside classrooms. The idea spread across from the UK to every continent within a few years. Today, thousands of teachers use SOLEs and many have written about them in the social media.

Do children *really learn* in a SOLE? Do they *really understand*? Do they *really know*? Many critics think not and I hesitate to argue because the meaning of *really learn, understand,* or *know* is not very obvious to me. What I have seen and reported is that groups of unsupervised children, clustered around the internet can answer questions—usually quite accurately. They don't get to erroneous answers or get taken in by fake information. Groups have a way to get to the right answer. Groups can search for, understand, and communicate complex ideas better than any single individual in the group can. Just as a single bee cannot build a hive but all of them together can. But is the ability to answer questions or solve problems a necessary and sufficient proof of *knowing*? I don't think this question will be answered until we have a definition of *knowing*.

There are taxi drivers in India who can use a smartphone with Google Maps to get from one place to another in the best possible time and cost. Many would not be able to read a paper map, indeed, may not have seen one. Do they know how to use maps, or is that ability no longer needed? Geography "masters" of the nineteenth century would shudder at the thought.

You can learn to cook with a connected tablet, learn a new language, play a musical instrument. But do you get to *know* these things? I decided to check for myself.

First, I must find something useful to learn. I chose programming.

New Ways to Learn

A long time ago, I used to be a good programmer. I was working on a PhD in physics and all my computing work was done on an ICL1909 mainframe computer at the Indian Institute of Technology in Delhi. I never got to see the computer, it was in a big building all on its own. I could only go up to the reception, take my shoes off, and hand over a stack of punched cards. Each punched card was a line of code and the whole stack was my program. If I needed to change a card, there was an attached room with rows of card punching machines that looked like oversized typewriters. After handing my program over, I would have to come back the next day and collect my output—a printed page. All output had to be on paper. The ICL1909 was about ten thousand times slower than my current smartphone. It was 1977 after all.

I used to write programs in a language called Fortran IV. My PhD supervisor had asked me to learn Fortran IV. He showed me the printout of a long program about molecular orbital calculations and said that it had some errors in it that needed to be corrected. The printout looked like a poem from a distance. When I asked what it was and how I would learn it, he said, "Get a book, there is a cheap one by Rajaraman." That is how I learned Fortran IV.

```
0081            SUBROUTINE GROUP
0082            DIMENSION LIM(12)
0083            COMMON/BLK/CH(3),IBD(5000),NLN
0084          1 (566),PR(120)
0085            DO 1 I=1,12
0086            NSS(I)=0
0087          1 LTOT(I)=0
0088            DO 2 I=1,N
0089            IF(IBD(I).LT.LIM(2))GO TO 3
0090            DO 4 J=3,12
0091            IF(IBD(I)-LIM(J))0,4,4
0092            K=J-1
0093            NSS(K)=NSS(K)+1
0094            LTOT(K)=LTOT(K)+NLN(I)
```

A bit of code in Fortran IV, from 1977

I knew everything about Fortran IV and once I had the logic worked out in my head could write code almost as fast as I could write English. In the three years or so that it took to complete my PhD I wrote more than 100,000 lines of code.

Later, in the 1980s I learned BASIC on PCs, and after Windows came along I learned Visual Basic. I just learned them by trial and error and by looking at other people's programs. I realized that I could learn programming by correcting errors in other people's programs and even wrote a paper about it for a San Diego conference (Mitra & Pawar, 1982). Nobody paid the slightest attention.

Because I was a good programmer, I was made a manager and then into a senior vice president, so I would not write programs again. Between 1995 and 2019 when I retired, I wrote no programs.

I now wanted to write an app. So I looked for a book, like back in 1977. There were none that were of the slightest use, they were all out of date by the time they were printed. I looked for teachers and there were none that were any good. App developers would have to be out of their minds to become teachers. In any case, they would be constantly out of date if they did. But this time, I knew another way to learn from the street children of Delhi and the eight-year-olds of Gateshead. I knew I needed a self-organized learning environment.

Visual Basic was still around, I discovered, but you could not write code on pieces of paper with a pencil anymore. You need a studio. A studio is an application that you load into your computer off the web and it helps you to write programs. By the way, you don't *write programs* anymore, you *develop systems*. I installed Visual Studio on my laptop and stared at it, but it just stared back. I thought of the children at the hole in the wall, and started clicking at random on the menus. Very quickly, bits of code started to appear in the Studio. It did not look like the Basic I used to know at all. It had hideously long and frightening words. I copied *sender As Object, e As EventArgs* into Google, just like those children who knew nothing would do when they encountered the unknown. And like Alice through the looking glass, things began to happen. A place called StackOverflow appeared where there were many people wondering about the same words as I was. "Groups of unsupervised children clustered around the internet…" the professor part of my mind said, much to my annoyance. In minutes, I knew that "EventArgs **e** is a parameter called **e** that contains the event data." Did I *really* understand? Of course not.

In less than half an hour, I had written a program (sorry, I cannot bear to say *developed a system*) that showed a button on the screen with the words **Click Me** on it. When clicked, the words **You are really stupid** appeared on the screen. I felt really smart.

Several years ago, I had worked on simulating cellular automata that can sense their own future. I had published that work, but there was work left to do about what exactly happens when this rather odd retrocausality happens. Working six hours a day, it took less than two months to simulate a discrete dynamical system that could look at its own future and reproduce images present there. In Visual Basic. I am not writing this to prop up my flagging confidence, but to demonstrate the power of self-organizing systems. The hive-like groups of developers on the internet, videos of people explaining ideas, automatic studios to correct mistakes and type things ahead of your fingers, all together makes up this new kind of learning. Did I *really* understand what I was doing? Of course I did! The professor part of my mind was quiet and thoughtful—the old geezer was watching.

There is a logic game called *Bulls and Cows* that we used to play in our university days. Two players choose a secret four-digit number with non-repeating digits. For example, one player may choose 0724 (a leading zero is allowed). The other player tries to guess the number, each guess being scored as having a number of *bulls*, correct digits in the correct positions and number of *cows*, correct digits in the wrong position. For example, a guess of 5702 for a chosen number 0724 would get one bull for the 7 in the correct place and two cows for 0 and 2 in the wrong places. Using these scores as the clues, one of the two players will get to the number chosen by the other, and win.

With my newly relearned Visual Basic, I wrote a version of this game, where you can play against the computer. It worked fine and I made a Windows installable for it. Now I wanted to make this program into an app for smartphones.

After a bit of searching, I discovered that Visual Basic programs are not really considered suitable for converting into apps. Windows does not run on most mobile phones, the most popular OS being Android. The cool way to make Android apps is to write the code in Java. I did not know Java.

"How do I learn Java?" I asked Google and it produced free courses in a jiffy, of which I selected the first. A helpful man from South Africa, Johan Jurrius, has produced video lessons on Java that I found highly effective. I don't think Johan knows all that much about instructional design, nor is he a trained teacher. He just shows you how to do things and lets you experiment. About a day is all it took to get the basic idea of how to write programs in Java. Like human languages, computer programming languages have similar linguistic structures, only spellings and grammars are a bit different. It is these outer trappings that take up all the time while learning a new language. But then, like Visual Basic, you are not supposed to write Java with paper and pencil. Instead there is IntelliJ IDEA, Johan and Google told me. This is an editor that fixes the spelling and the grammar of Java for you. And then there is an Android Studio that works along with IntelliJ if you want to use your Java code to make Android apps. You do not need to know Java in order to use it to make working programs, I realized. You just need to know where to look and you need to be friends with the folks in the neighborhood like StackOverflow and other such places. "The end of knowing…" the professor part of my mind started to say but I shut him up.

It took about a month of work with Java to get the *Bulls and Cows* program working for smartphones. After the first ten days or so I left Johan's course—I did not need it anymore. Instead, I would turn to my unsupervised groups of friends and they would always point me to the right examples. Sometimes, I would find someone else's question about some part of Java and realize that I could answer it. It was a great feeling, posting those answers and getting an

"OMG what a dummy I was!" in return. That is how hives work.

Now that I had working versions of my game for Windows and Android, I realized that people who do not use Windows or Android, like the people who use Apple computers and phones would get left out. Not only that, you cannot run the Windows version on smartphones and the Android app on a Windows or Apple computer. Is there no way to build software that will run on everything, without having different versions? The groups on the internet said yes there was a way. If my game could run on a browser, then it would work on any device that uses that browser. A browser is like a library assistant whom you follow around to find the books you want. The world wide web is too big to navigate without an assistant and the browser is that assistant. Luckily, the same browser can work on all kinds of devices. For example, the browser called Chrome can work on Windows and Apple computers as well as on just about all smartphones. So, anything the browser can do, will work on all devices. "Hooray" said I, "Hey Google, how do I write a program that runs on a browser?"

It turned out that browsers use a language called HTML to show things on the screen or play sounds and so on. But then HTML cannot make your device do things, like move objects on the screen for example. For that, you need to put in a *doer* inside HTML—a language that can make devices do things and that can sit inside HTML and it would not mind. A bit like how our bodies allow bacteria to live inside and do the dirty work inside our intestines. There is a language that can live inside HTML. It is called JavaScript. I thought JavaScript was a form of Java, but it turned out to be a new language. A strange and quite likeable language.

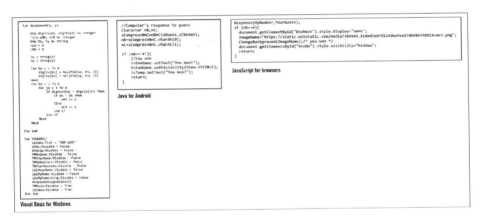

Bits of code to do similar things in Visual Basic, Java, and JavaScript

JavaScript is colloquial. You can make all kinds of mistakes in spelling and grammar and it will be accepted. Of course, what comes out when you run such a program may be quite odd and not at all what you wanted, but that is the price we all pay for not using formal language. The advantage is that you get to do what you want quite quickly. It's a bit like if you wanted to find out the price of a bottle of instant coffee powder in a shop. You could take the bottle to the shop counter and say, "How much is that?" The person behind the counter might reply, "Oh, about 200 grams I think." So, you would say, "No no, I mean how much does it cost?" and so on. Instead, you could have gone up to the counter and said, "Excuse me, could you tell me what the price of this bottle of coffee powder is?" and got the right answer by talking less. That is somewhat like the difference between JavaScript and Java. Nevertheless, we all use colloquial language most of the time, don't we?

I found a JavaScript tutorial on the internet and did a few exercises. It took less than an hour. After that I discontinued the tutorial and started to write my game in JavaScript. I would write a bit and test if it was working. If there was a problem, I would go to a self-organizing group and ask or look for examples. The program got done in a couple of days. Now, my game would run on all kinds of computers, smartphones, and any device that can run a standard browser.

I don't *know* JavaScript and I don't think I need to know it. I know how to use it and get it to do what I want. You can play the game I made in any browser.[4]

That was the end of my experiment with learning programming. The educational conclusion I could draw from it is, rather obviously, *Do not teach learners what they can learn by themselves.*

But, can the results of this experiment be extended to cover other subjects?

Limits to Self-Organized Learning?

In 2007, in a village called Kalikuppam in Southern India, I had put in two hole in the wall computers. The local children were Tamil speakers with a faint smattering of English. Their school had been washed away in the Indian Ocean tsunami of 2004 and was still not quite rebuilt.

Hole in the Wall computers in village Kalikuppam in Southern India

I had downloaded material on biotechnology and genetics into the computers. It was university level text in English. The children complained that they could not understand anything. I told them I did not expect them to understand and I did not understand much of it either! "There is no chance you will understand any of this stuff. Pity, because it's so interesting and important," I said and left the village for three months. When I returned, the children were talking about DNA replication, twisting their hands together to show what a helix was. They had not understood the material like university students, of course. They had understood it like children. I published the results (Mitra & Dangwal, 2010).

A series of experiments followed, carried out all over the world from Gateshead, England to Montevideo, Uruguay.[5] Each time, the children showed the same surprising results. To plan such experiments is not easy and I had to make many compromises. My sample sizes were small and getting control groups was nearly impossible. It is not easy to tell some children not to do what others were doing. I tried many different ways—sometimes dividing a group into two halves and having each half act as control to the other. There was criticism and it was depressing. "Control groups are immoral," Nicholas Negroponte had once said and that kept me going. Then, teachers from every continent started to post similar results, but then school teachers don't publish peer reviewed papers. I guess if we totaled up all the children in all those experiments, we would get a really large international sample with lots of controls, but I don't know how to do that or if it is even allowed. Instead, I wanted to see where internet-based SOLEs would stop working.

What if a question was incomprehensible—in a script and languages learners did not know?

To find some indications of what the answer to this might be, I turn to an experiment conducted in 2016, using FaceBook.

The post showed an image of a piece of text.[6]

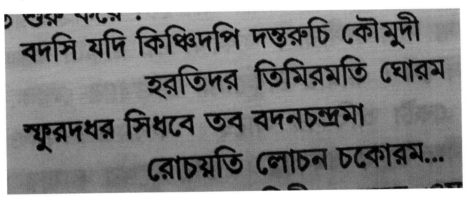

Image of a script in, to most readers, an unknown language

The instructions were:

Can you tell me what the following lines mean? If you can read and understand it, you are not eligible for the experiment, please. Use the Internet. All methods are allowed.

What followed on that Sunday can only be described as *linguistic archaeology*. People from England to New Zealand, from Japan to the USA, joined the investigation. Since the text was given as an image, it could not be pasted into Google, so it took several hours for people to realize that it is Bengali script. Someone used a camera-based translator, another tried drawing the script into a translator. It was hilariously enjoyable for all concerned. They concluded that the content was some archaic form of Bengali. It was not. It took some more time before someone discovered that the text was Sanskrit written in Bengali script. After that, it took an hour or so before a teacher from England translated the text. She did not know either Bengali or Sanskrit. In the next few minutes the full reference to a thirteenth century Sanskrit poem came from Japan. The whole process took five hours. However, comments on the post did not end. To my surprise, teachers started to write about how this was not learning, that it would have gone so much better with a trained Sanskrit teacher. I tried to give neutral responses, not always very successfully. Then someone said I was a teacher-hating neo-liberal. I had no idea what that meant, but, fortunately for me other teachers responded vigorously to defend SOLEs. I thought they had glimpsed the end of knowing.

What would it take to understand a page from a research paper in theoretical physics?

The photon's momentum is,

$$\Delta p = \frac{\hbar}{r} \qquad (7)$$

Therefore, if we want to the change the particle's momentum during a time interval of **dt**, a following equation is valid:

$$\frac{dp}{dt} = \frac{dN}{dt} \times \frac{\hbar}{r} \qquad (8)$$

where **dN** is the count of absorbed photons during **dt**.

There is a strong reason to see the photon "ticks" as information units. Therefore the $\frac{dN}{dt}$ can be called "information per time unit", signed as $\frac{dI}{dt}$.

On the other hand, $\frac{dp}{dt}$ is the Coulomb force, which is,

$$F = \frac{k_e \times q_1 \times q_2}{r^2} \qquad (9)$$

Combining Eqs. (8) and (9) gives

$$\frac{dI}{dt} = \frac{k_e \times q_1 \times q_2}{\hbar \times r} \qquad (10)$$

Considering the potential energy:

$$U = \frac{k_e \times q_1 \times q_2}{r} \qquad (11)$$

With (10) we get:

30

Page from a paper about photons and information

Is it true that it would take twelve years of schooling and several years at an university to understand this page of physics? Is it *that* different from reading Sanskrit poetry in Bengali script, understanding genetics in university language, or programming in JavaScript? I haven't done this experiment with physics yet, but I suspect that given sufficient motivation, a group of unsupervised people on the internet will figure out the meaning of that page in a few hours.

The End of Knowing

What are all these experiments and experiences telling us? To put my thoughts together, I turned to the world of street-smart people. In 2009, a film called *Slumdog Millionaire* had won many Oscar awards. It was about street-smart children and it had been inspired by the Hole in the Wall, I was told.

Street-smart people do not have a formal education, they learn as they go. If formal education is an attempt to equip a mind with things *just in case* they are ever needed, then the world of street-smart people is about learning *just in time* to negotiate life's hurdles. People with formal education look down on street-smart people and, surprisingly, the feeling is often mutual. It is as though two systems of education are at odds with one another. They do not need to be.

The formal education system that we have is from ages gone by, a time when continuity was an important requirement for development. The future had to be like the past, so knowledge from the past could be used to negotiate the future. This resulted in an education system that was almost entirely about the past. Think of what you learned in school—it was all about what we, humanity, had learned in the past. The future is never taught in school because no one knows what it may contain. We can only hope that the future will be like the past. In 2020, a virus changed all that.

Knowledge is valuable. It consists of things that are known. Knowledge is stored in books and all kinds of other media, many of which are now digital and resides on servers on the internet. No one actually *knows* all of it, but it is generally believed that the more of all the knowledge you *know* inside your head, the better and, of course, the more knowledgeable you are. We get overly impressed by people in quiz shows who can pull out esoteric and, usually utterly unimportant knowledge out of their heads. If a person uses Google to answer a quiz question, we are not impressed at all. We value *knowing*.

On the other hand, there are people who know extraordinarily little. Just a tiny subset of everything there is to know, just enough to live by. They pick up bits of knowledge as they live, from the environment, from media, from each other, from experiences and, increasingly, from the internet. When they grow old, they are called worldly-wise, because their brains synthesize all the random knowledge into a sort of distillate that enables them to work out shortcuts and strategies to solve problems that seem intractable to others. They are street-smart people. We do not like them much but use them when we are in real trouble and in situations where education does not help much.

Knowing was valuable in a world where information and knowledge were hard, or even impossible, to access when we needed them. Such was the case throughout human history until the internet was developed. Our education systems are based on the premise that knowing is the most efficient way to access knowledge. In many instances, this premise is no longer valid. You do not need to know how to get to places, the ingredients in a recipe, how to solve an equation, or even learn a new language. In a world where knowing is no longer essential, or even desirable perhaps, education needs to be redesigned from scratch. "I don't need to know everything, I just need to know where to find it when I need it" in Einstein's words. Perhaps this will be the basis for the new design of education.

Stored knowledge improves our chances of survival. This is probably the reason why memory evolved in the first place. However, we still do not know what our brains store and why. We know that some of the stored material is kept for quick retrieval, some for longer term use, and the rest is strangely transformed and stored inside what we call the subconscious. For millennia, human beings have attempted to create artificial storage systems—painting, writing, and building being the earliest ones. All of these have access times that are too slow as a replacement for human memory. It is only in the last fifty years or so that we have created artificial storage and retrieval mechanisms that are fast enough for instant action. Like nature, our artificial storage systems have evolved into arrangements for instant retrieval, for slow retrieval of massive amounts of information, and increasingly, coded sections that are inaccessible consciously, but are crucial for survival. These artificial memory and access devices have shrunk in size so that they can be with us and available instantly when needed. Indeed, they may become small enough to be implanted in our bodies. You can see the beginnings of these devices at projects such as MIT's AlterEgo.[7]

Single brains are limited in their ability to solve problems. Evolution attempted to network us using our sense organs—photons for sight, phonons for sound, small molecules for smell, and larger ones for taste and touch. These networks are geographically limited to a radius of a few meters, but interacting small networks have created massive societies and civilizations.

Networks of artificial memories and processors interact through electromagnetic fields. The internet spans the earth and beyond. A brilliant strategy by nature—to evolve an organism that can control its own evolution.

The results are beginning to emerge. The first of them is the *End of Knowing*.

References

Brown, P. C. (2014). *Make It Stick*. Harvard University Press.

Mitra, S., & Dangwal, R. (2010). Limits to Self-Organising Systems of Learning—the Kalikuppam Experiment. *British Journal of Educational Technology, 41*(5), 672-688.

Mitra, S., & Pawar, R. (1982). Diagnostic Computer-Assisted-Instruction, a Methodology for the Teaching of Computer Languages. *Sixth Western Educational Computing Conf. Nov. 1982, San Diego, USA.*

Notes

1 MIT Media Lab event video - media.mit.edu/events/media-lab-conversations-series-sugata-mitra/

2 See, for example, us.corwin.com/en-us/nam/the-school-in-the-cloud/book257918

3 Check my website cevesm.com for references

4 Play Bulls and Cows - cevesm.com/bullsandcows

5 Many examples listed in the publications section of my website - cevesm.com/publications

6 Investigating unknown language SOLE - facebook.com/photo?fbid=10153954609873338& set=a.10150744422628338

7 AlterEgo - media.mit.edu/projects/alterego/overview/

The Evolution of Logo Connections to the Physical World, From 1971 to Today

David D. Thornburg

I was introduced to Seymour Papert in the early 1970's by Alan Kay when I was at the Xerox Palo Alto Research Center (PARC). Alan had met Seymour before, and was impressed with the idea that children might someday explore topics like mathematics with software like Logo. Alan felt that kids would use their own computers, and his work was focused on both the hardware and the software. While Alan's software focus resulted in the Smalltalk language, it was implemented with the inspiration of Logo developed from LISP by Wally Feurzeig, Seymour Papert, and Cynthia Solomon in 1967.

In 1971, the year I joined PARC, Seymour and Cynthia wrote a paper, *Twenty Things to Do with a Computer* that took a pioneering look at how computers could be used by students as vehicles of exploration in several fields. It is important to note that, at this time, graphic displays for computers were rare, and home-based personal computers were still years away from development. The Alto computer developed at PARC was fairly unique in that the entire display was graphic and text consisted of bit-mapped images on the screen that could be displayed in various typefaces.

The rarity of graphic computer displays in the early 1970s led to the use of a physical robot (called the turtle) that could be programmed to draw images on large paper sheets, instead of drawing them on a computer screen. This turtle was connected to the computer with a cable through which signals could be sent.

While anyone familiar with Logo and its derivatives will see, the bulk of ideas expressed in this paper continue to be explored by students today. But, because of the connection to a physical robotic turtle, this paper had some truly groundbreaking ideas—ideas that extend into a domain that is only being fully addressed recently—the connection of student projects to the physical world. The paper describes things that can be done by connecting the physical robotic turtle to various sensors, actuators, and lights. Communication with these external elements came from sending text characters to the devices through a cable connected between the computer and the various devices.

Once personal computers came into existence in the late 1970s, many of these computers had parallel ports that made it easier to attach special products that could control external motors, lights, and sensors. Some of the early products in this category were the Canadian Chameleon, the HyperBot in the US and the Super Robby developed by ARS Consult in Brazil in the 1990s. Through Super Robby use, students were oriented to develop projects that involved the use of a programming language, such as LogoWriter, or Megalogo, and the construction of models that "come to life," either in terms of lighting or movement, controlled through the computer by a program developed by students themselves.

Most models were built with scrap material, resulting in extremely low cost, considering that it involved only the inexpensive electronic components used, such as lamps, LEDs, motors, sounders, and light, sound, touch, or heat sensors.

The use of recycled scrap has a special flavor. It allows the students to focus, when looking at an object considered disposable, on how to use it in new ways. The student starts to "see," for example, in a box of eggs, the shell of a turtle; in a can of soda, the seat of a Ferris wheel; in a carton of milk, the body of a truck.

Since then, new standalone microcontroller boards have been developed, such as the Arduino, and BBC micro:bit, both developed in the early 2000s. While these devices can be programmed to operate on their own, they can also be connected to computers running derivatives of Logo like Snap4Arduino.

The challenge with these controllers is making them easy to use, and this is aided through the use of special add-on boards like the HyperDuino and the MakerBit, both made by Roger Wagner's 1010 Technologies. These add-on boards not only add new capabilities (e.g., true touch sensors) to the controllers, they eliminate the need for special breadboards containing, for example, resistors needed for each LED and some sensors. This ease-of-use capability, pioneered years before, is designed to let students get on with their larger projects, rather than focus on the minutiae of hardware assembly.

In this regard, this is similar to block-based programming languages like Snap4Arduino, Scratch, and others, in that the assembly of programs eliminates the need for specialized punctuation marks associated with text-based versions of Logo. Consider this Snap! version of a program that draws geometric shapes like squarish spirals (called squirals):

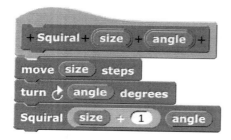

Note that this definition contains the squiral itself, only with a slightly larger size. This is an example of a programming technique called recursion, one of the cornerstones of "first class" languages. The resulting image uses a starting size of 1, and an angle of 91°:

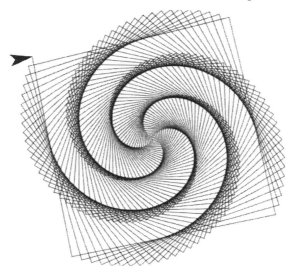

The text version of the relevant code (using the Lynx version of Logo) looks like this:

```
to squiral :size :angle
fd :size
rt :angle
squiral (:size+1) :angle
end
```

The colon before the variable name signifies that we want the value of the variable, not the variable name itself.

While it is obvious that Snap's blocks are easier to use when building programs, Logo started out as a text-based language, so why not continue that tradition. Snap! started out as a language called BYOB (Build Your Own Blocks) by University of California professor Brian Harvey. From there it evolved into Snap!, the language that forms the basis of a college-level programming class, The Beauty and Joy of Computing.

As for why Professor Harvey chose blocks instead of pure text, he says:

I get it. You're a teenager, it's the first day of what was billed as a serious computer science course, and you're confronted with drag-and-drop blocks in primary colors. You've seen this before, back when your age had only one digit, and you played around with Scratch. Been there, done that. But Snap! (Build Your Own Blocks) isn't Scratch. It's a very serious programming language, in disguise.

The reason for the disguise is that most programming courses spend most of their time and effort on the details of the notation used by whatever programming language they choose. Here's the classic example: In your "grownup" programming language you write some

```
stuff;
some more stuff;
and yet more stuff;
```

These are three instructions to the computer, with semicolons in between. Now, what about that semicolon at the end? If the language is Java, C, or C++, that semicolon is required. If it's Perl, Pascal, or PL/I, that semicolon is forbidden.

Not exactly easy to learn. But if, instead, the code looks like a stacked assembly of blocks then there's no need to remember punctuation rules. The visual layout of the code is the notation. (Harvey, 2019)

The most common block-based language influenced by Logo is Scratch—designed for younger users. But there is no limit to making powerful languages block-based.

Programming languages like Snap4Arduino allow both the HyperDuino and MakerBit to be controlled by almost any computer you have, whether it is a Macintosh, Windows, or Linux-based as well as working with Chromebooks.

For example, a couple of years ago, I made a small HyperDuino-based CubeSat that was designed to be carried aloft by weather balloons instead of being launched into space.[1] This was made using a case made on my 3D printer and included sensors for light and temperature.

The following Snap4Arduino program plots data from both sensors.

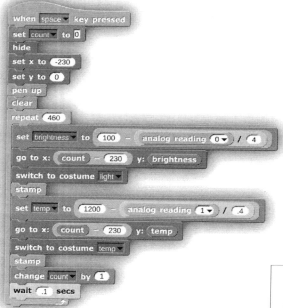

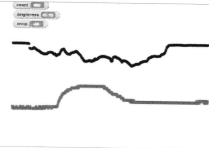

Instead of plotting the data, we made two dot-shaped costumes and stamped them on the screen to make lines. The upper line represents light, and the lower one signifies temperature.

Projects like this are natural offsprings from the 1971 paper by Papert and Solomon, and we can scarcely imagine the breadth of other projects that can be done today. For example, the MIT language Scratch now works with the BBC micro:bit, expanding the base of potential users even more.

But there is a problem.

While a large number of young schoolkids may be using Logo-ish block languages like Scratch, even this modest effort has not become mainstream in schools.

While Scratch has over 64 million users, according to MIT it is only taught in about 800 schools worldwide. This paltry penetration into schools is amazingly poor. In the early days of personal computing, programming was taught in many schools, but in a world filled with commercial apps for myriad applications, it appears that the bulk of today's students don't have the actual useful ability to create something new based on what they were taught.

Why is this important?

Let me start by making the point that the goal is not to turn all kids into software developers. That said, the discipline of learning to code is quite valuable, no matter what topic is being explored. For example, it is common for programs not to work the way you intended the first time they are run. The process of correcting errors is called debugging, and its necessary skills of critical thinking and persistence applies to many disciplines.

The process of learning to program builds resilience and supports creativity. It can also foster collegiality as sophisticated projects may involve several students working on different aspects of a program at the same time. The idea of sharing is an important part of the process, and programming affords many opportunities to tinker and improve programs already written.

When the decline in numbers and skills of students applying for Computer Science became a concern for a team that included Eben Upton, Rob Mullins, Jack Lang, and Alan Mycroft at the University of Cambridge's Computer Laboratory in 2006, the need for a tiny and affordable computer came to their minds. The resulting Raspberry Pi computer is quite cheap, requiring only access to a keyboard, mouse, and display to make a full-blown computer. Recently, a special version was created, the Raspberry Pi 400, that includes a keyboard and other essentials. In the US this configuration retails for only $100.

While millions of Raspberry Pis have been sold, it is unclear if it has reached the desired goal of encouraging young people learning how to write their own programs. I visited a school once that had kids using Raspberry Pis to play Microsoft's Minecraft game—hardly the goal envisioned by the creators of this inexpensive Linux-based computer. Yes, I know that Minecraft can be played using player-based programming commands to build objects in the game, but that is not like the set of skills needed to teach the true scope and capabilities of a computer language.

There have been some attempts to correct the problem, including the Hour of Code launched through Code.org launched in January 2013 by Iranian-American brothers Hadi Partovi and Ali Partovi, as a non-profit focused on making computer programming more accessible. The initial focus was on creating a database of all computer science classrooms in the United States. At the time, Hadi Partovi stated that about ninety percent of US schools do not teach programming, despite it now being considered a foundational field.

The first step in the organization's efforts as regards the curriculum of schools was to work with US school districts to add computer programming as a class. Most US schools did not have a course for computer sciences, in order for schools to be able to offer coding as a class. After this, the next step was to create free online teaching and learning materials for schools to use if instituting computer science classes. By 2014, Code.org had launched computer courses in thirty US school districts to reach about 5% of all the students in US public schools (about two million students). By 2015, Code.org had trained about 15,000 teachers to teach computer sciences, able to reach about 600,000 new students previously unable to learn computer coding, with large percentages of those being either female or minorities. To date, Code.org has prepared over a million educators world-wide to teach computer science.

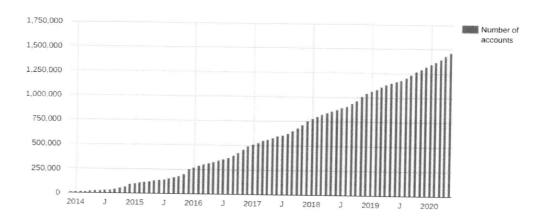

In 2015, Code.org partnered with about seventy of the largest US school districts (including the seven largest), representing several million students. The company also partnered with other computer businesses and private entities to provide additional computer learning materials and opportunities. As of 2015, six million students had been enrolled in Code.org curriculum classes. In 2018, Code.org celebrated record participation by girls and underrepresented minorities in Advanced Placement computer science classrooms, driven in large part by students in the Code. org Computer Science Principles classrooms.

An effort in Canada, Code to Learn, offers free coding classes in English, French, and indigenous languages like Ojibwe and James Bay Cree. The Code to Learn course app even exists on the Roku, Fire TV, and Apple TV platforms, allowing recorded teaching sessions to be seen at home.

At the time this is being written, the world is dealing with the COVID-19 pandemic and, in the US and Canada, many, if not most, students are learning from home.

Since the majority of Scratch users are logging on from home, this is the perfect time to expand projects that bring coding skills to students. If schools are unwilling or unable to bring coding into the classroom, maybe we should just expand the home-based use of coding tools along with inexpensive controllers like the BBC micro:bit, Arduino, or expanded versions like the HyperDuino or MakerBit. The vision proposed in the 1971 paper by Papert and Solomon remains relevant today.

I've spent five decades trying to get kids involved with languages like Logo or its derivatives, and it is time to finally deliver on the promise.

References

Harvey, B. (2019). *Why Do We Have to Learn This Baby Language?* snap.berkeley.edu/doc/Brian-Harvey_Baby-language.pdf

Notes

1 How to make a HyperDuino-based CubeSat - instructables.com/HyperDuino-based-CubeSat

Learning Togeth

David Cavallo

My Introduction to Computation

The first time I had the chance to program a computer was in school, although not in a regular class. It was an informal opportunity with an incredible teacher, Mr. Bristol, who always proclaimed mathematics needed to be "true, right, and beautiful," and who managed to obtain a dial-up connection to a university computer. It is important to note that the primary idea was to *play* with it, not in the sense of playing games on the computer but in playing with a new entity to see what could result without harm.

Programming was new to everyone. It was appealing to some of us because we liked puzzles, challenges, the unknown, and for me in particular, things that were not compulsory. We did not have lessons. Activity was not pre-planned and pre-ordained. We became peers of a sort with our teacher. He clearly knew more than we did, but we explored together. This relationship and this culture of mutual exploration into the unknown, on problems that we chose to pursue, with colleagues sharing the wonder of the newly possible, was invigorating in ways that, to me, ordinary school was not. Ideas were the currency, not age, authority, or position.

We could think about and work on problems that if we had to approach them by hand, we knew we could not do them (except perhaps with infinite time). While some initial activities were familiar and trivial, sorting a class list in milliseconds for example, the ability to define the mechanism and let the machine do the grunt work was liberating. We were freed to push boundaries. What things that previously appeared impossible, might actually be possible? This sentiment fit with the zeitgeist of the times, challenging ugly elements of life such as racism, unending war and violence, inequality, ecology, and thinking that a different world was not just possible but practical.

Thinking in systems, thinking of mechanisms, thinking about more complex thinking about how to describe the world in a functional way and letting machines do the drudge, mechanical work, and then doing such projects was liberating and empowering. Through a now familiar iterative process of writing, testing, debugging, we could refine our thinking until we were satisfied (or sufficiently frustrated to decide to try again another day).

How I now wish we knew about the work of Seymour Papert, Cynthia Solomon, and the Logo group as the twenty things to do with a computer would have been so helpful to point us towards interesting things to do without telling us exactly how to do them, letting us learn, engage, and explore and not just appreciate what they did but to think in better ways, as well as to come up with our new list of twenty things to do.

Beginning to Program for Real

Because programming was at the time a rare skill, even as a student I was able to work on real projects, including analyzing satellite data to help determine the state of deforestation and beach erosion in New Jersey; designing and implementing a database and applications to eliminate corruption, enable fairness, and speed the process and thereby lower costs for an urban development; searching to see if there are sequences in non-abelian groups of higher order; and others. In each case, the work could not be done quickly or at all without a computational approach. Paper and pencil could not suffice.

Before commencing on the project in group theory, I knew absolutely nothing about the area. With the help of the professor, by programming the project I learned key concepts in group theory in a way that I personally would not have learned in a typical course. I had to make the ideas functional in order to explore a real hypothesis in the field. I did it to help discover something new about the world, not to personally discover what everyone else already knew. Moreover, for me, the process of working to make or discover something new in the world provided the best motivation and environment for learning.

There are many genres of computer programming, but designing and developing applications particularly suited me. There is not space here to go into any meaningful detail about the projects, which included an environment for the better practice, research, and administration of healthcare; training air traffic controllers; administering environmental protection; predicting rainfall for flood prevention; and others.

In every case one primary goal was to design and develop *environments for others to do more things better with computers*, and to provide tools and for them to extend, customize, and make their own for what they want to do. In this way I thought of every environment as a learning environment and developed the idea of emergent design in order to design carefully while remaining open for adaptation and evolution as the world changed, as people learned to do more, and to thoughtfully adjust for unknowns and uncertainties.

When I worked in the AI technology center at Digital Equipment Corporation, a Vice-President of Software once said, "No one wants to buy a computer. They want to do things." Doing things to help people do more things is immensely gratifying. Helping to develop new cultures that can take advantage of new things to do in order to help create more just, equitable, and environmentally friendly worlds is immensely more satisfying, particularly when helping to provide environments for populations that have been excluded.

Excluded populations include children. Papert and Solomon saw early that in the same ways computers would come to facilitate the rapid growth of knowledge in the world, which is by definition learning, so too could creative, expressive, constructive, and collaborative uses of computers could also facilitate children's learning in ways other technologies, including pencil and paper, could not.

Solomon wrote that the impact of their work was not just from a particular programming language, but from "ideas, people, a culture, and a language." All are essential to giving power to doing things with computers. Not having one of this minimum set diminishes potential returns.

Utilizing experience designing and making software and environments for organizations to enable learning, improve collective efficacy, and evolve their practices informed the types of things I would subsequently do with children and communities. My goal was not to try to teach a bit of programming, or mathematics, or electronics/robotics/making, or something else out of the context of use, although learning programming, mathematics, expression, communication, and documentation of ideas was always a major underlying component of activity. The overarching goal was to develop better environments for learning and doing by mindful learning and doing in an integrated fashion on projects of interest. I will highlight one such example.

A Case Study of Professional Learning

Air traffic control (ATC) is highly complex and certainly critically essential to get right. Otherwise people die. To their credit, air traffic controllers understand the magnitude and importance of their everyday work. This is the primary reason burnout in the profession is so high. Therefore, when training people to become air traffic controllers, the authorities know the learning must be correct, complete, deep, and real, not an area where someone can pass the exams but not really know what they are doing.

I was trepidatious coming to the national training center for the first time. I was told that almost all the administrators and trainers were military or ex-military and I was dubious that they would be open to the type of learning that would be fundamental to the system I would design. I fully expected to have a quick trip to Oklahoma City, have meetings, a nice meal, and an early flight home.

To my surprise, the administration and the people in charge of learning and training were among the most progressive educators I have ever met. They knew and understood the importance of real learning and the construction of knowledge. They did not merely acknowledge the relevance of Piaget and Vygotsky, they were insistent upon applying their theories. They did not want a rigid, regimented, mind-numbing, drill-and-kill approach any more than I did. They wanted the best in learning and not the worst of traditional classrooms because of the existential importance of truly learning the complex task.

In retrospect, it should not have been surprising. Of course they require the best in learning. Not learning was not an option. Because the criteria for assessment were objective and because the teachers and evaluators themselves were knowledgeable practitioners, they knew if people learned appropriately or not. As the ATC system was in crisis due to increasing air travel, more and faster planes in the sky, the high cost of traditional training and lack of equipment which was based upon the actual machines and conditions, combined with the need to replace the managers and previous retirees brought back into the system after the government fired controllers in an effort to bust their union, the need to properly train people was critical. People were retiring faster than replacements could be trained. (Learning about the crisis, and especially after a Friday bull session over beer where the expert controllers recounted stories of near disasters made me consider walking back to Boston.)

Creating computer-based simulations was one obvious and essential step. However, learning by working with simulations in an unguided manner where others determined the rules of the simulation that were opaque to the learner was insufficient. Thus, there was a need to put intelligence in the system. What evolved, though, was a system that used its intelligence to help people to better use theirs.

The computational complexity of the domain, with so many unknowns, uncertainties, and possibilities, made it such that it could not be completely automated. The expert air traffic controllers told us that there is no one right way to perform properly. People needed to develop their own styles and capabilities. People needed to make and learn from mistakes during training in order to better understand the problem space and find their best methods to do their work. They knew that to become a good controller was not to memorize and follow rules, to passively try to apply rules without regard to circumstance, but to deeply learn, to assimilate the best ideas, and to accommodate oneself to adapt to how one needs to perform better.

I designed a system that borrowed from ideas of Marvin Minsky about a "society" of mind, with multiple agents with specific but limited expertise offering themselves to help. However, the trainee remained in control and was the integrator, as this was an essential part of what they needed to learn. I also borrowed from interface ideas of Muriel Cooper where the agents presented themselves more strongly or weakly based upon system knowledge and prior learner choices. However, the path through the material remained with the learner so they could focus on what they needed at the moment. Using analytics the system could demonstrate the certain essential ideas and practices that needed improvement or that were being neglected. Trainees would work through the scenarios without fear of being penalized for "mistakes," availing themselves of agents as they thought best, try out their crazy ideas, work through scenarios, and, with computational and personal assistance, explore, experiment, and investigate until they were satisfied with their understanding.

People, experienced and novice, adored the prototype system. However, again what in retrospect should have been obvious but what attracted attention at the time, was that what they all liked best was the scenario generation tool I made for myself and team to expedite making training scenarios. The experienced and novice controllers preferred discussing what would make for good learning scenarios, set up the conditions, and then run them, pausing as desired to debate the options and potential problems. Not surprisingly, they thought that collaboratively constructing their own challenges was better than following someone else's instructional design, and that an environment that fostered collective efficacy was better than one only for individual work.

The training had some advantages over typical school environments. The ratio of teachers to learners was low. The teachers were learning and doing with the students, and not just transmitting information about things. There were people with a mixed range of experience working together, as controllers would return from the field for re-training. They had the advantage of sufficient numbers of computers for all people. Spending was appropriate to enable all to learn. They were learning by doing and reflecting upon what they do. They created an environment that encouraged big thinking and trying out ideas, including crazy ones. They created an environment where each supported the other, not competing with them.

Educational systems do not make such choices. However, they could. There are demonstrably better ways to do and organize learning environments. There does not have to be a world where more is spent on weaponry that on children's education. These are questions of our priorities. Thankfully, people in charge of air traffic control education make choices to improve the safety and functioning of their part of the world. It would be better if we made the same types of choices for and with our children.

Some Principles for Learning Environments

Papert and Edith Ackermann emphasized that preferred activities are "hands-on and heads-in," to differentiate the activities from students being told information about things but not engage in doing them concretely (hands-on), as well as from mindless making, where one might make things but not necessarily learn or engage in the what and how of making (heads in).

Mel King described our collaborative activities as designing and making things supported by caring others while building community and providing opportunities to those typically excluded.

Paulo Freire inspired our work to engage people in conversation with their community. Freire concerned himself with developing critical consciousness, where literacy was an empowering tool. To us, computational literacy in the deepest sense of literacy was another empowering tool. Freire emphasizes the importance of generative themes where all participants would have their own ideas of what to do within the theme.

I co-directed the MIT Media Lab Future of Learning Group with Seymour Papert. We adopted, integrated, and complemented these fundamentals in our work with children. We created cultures of creativity and learning focused on learning, but in the context of making a better world, of social justice, of developing community by making things for one's community. Just as in my early experiences programming, we all learned together through exploration and investigation. Ideas and expertise were valued, not positions. We all learned and taught as partners. We all researched understanding of human learning through our projects, most often in pursuit of improving community, justice, and positive development.

Again, space will not permit a full, detailed accounting of all or any of the projects. We worked in schools and communities across the world, including a project in Thailand to help modernize the educational system and where several villages transformed the socio-economic conditions through a constructionist learning approach using computation to change local conditions; creating an alternative school in the Maine juvenile jail where the youth involved transformed their lives through a different approach to learning with computation; creating a variety of programs for youth at the South End Technology Center of Boston focused on designing and building with computational technologies to improve life in their communities; and more. While all of these projects are in some ways different, for different people in different places, in other ways they are the same by *providing better things to do with computers with others and in learning environments designed to facilitate learning, doing, sharing, and community.*

In each case, while the projects differed and built upon each other, they shared the same underlying principles of learning through programming and making artifacts and models of what the learners deemed important, particularly in order to improve their communities. By doing these projects in the environment we jointly created, they learned how to learn by making and reflecting on their thinking, to problem solve by working through the myriad problems encountered in actualizing their projects, to think critically in order to determine what to do and how it might help community, to develop individual and collective efficacy by making their projects, and positively critiquing projects of their colleagues. The environment was integrated and whole. They were learning not just to follow directions but to imagine, think, create, and debug. We worked together, thereby working in a more egalitarian, democratic way, and thereby learning about democracy and society by doing, not by being told information about the concepts.

In Maine, Boston, Thailand, Senegal, Rwanda, Costa Rica, Brazil, Colombia, and elsewhere, we worked on projects students chose to improve their communities. Many projects were brilliant and, at times, actually put into practice in the real world, not just as school models. I choose just one to demonstrate a way of working.

A Case Study

In Brazil we developed a project called *The City We Want*, supported by the public schools of the municipality of São Paulo, Rodrigo Mesquita, and by the Bradesco Foundation. In a residential school in Bodaquena, in the Pantanal, the world's largest inland wetlands and an unfortunately threatened ecosystem. An important project for the students was to research how to cool their classrooms and dormitories. The climate is intense. On the day we arrived the temperature was 40C (104F) with humidity of 90%. They had fans, but not enough for every student. The rooms had two windows on each of two walls, and a small window at the second level over the door.

How could they cool the room? They assumed that all of us, coming from MIT and having PhDs or being graduate students would just know the answer. Perhaps we should have, but none of us did. The students looked at us like we were frauds. How could we not know? However, when they saw how excited we were about figuring this out, and did not try to hide that we did not know, they began to see intelligence as not already knowing an answer to something, but as the ability to figure something out correctly.

We began to discuss and decide how to solve this problem. The world talks of the importance of learning to learn, particularly now in a rapidly changing world, but exactly how to learn to learn, and not just be told, is under-explored and under-theorized. The teacher is the most experienced learner in the classroom, but schools are engineered to never let the students observe the teacher learn anything. The process of working together to collectively solve the chosen problem, with our greater experience in research, problem solving, and using the technologies at hand was probably the most meaningful aspect of the experience.

The students determined how to set up the experiment, which, naturally, was not correct on the first pass. They only checked the indoor temperature, since they figured that was the primary determining factor for comfort. We pointed out that if they did not know the outside conditions, its temperature, whether it was sunny or cloudy, how windy it was, and perhaps other factors, they would not know enough to arrive at a real solution.

We worked on what were the factors that led to comfort or discomfort. They had to think about why a fan cooled people. They knew comfort was not merely due to temperature and also involved humidity. But what exactly is humidity and how do you measure it?

As we explored, there were many ideas about what to do and how to arrange the fans for maximum comfort for all. Cross ventilation was not possible. Heat rises. Should they point the fans upward to push the air out the top window and cooler air could perhaps enter from the first floor windows? Should they try to blow the air out the windows? Should they try to arrange the fans in a circular pattern?

As they experimented they also began to look at other factors. What was the composition of the roof? Could they make an automatic sprinkler system to cool the roof and would that have more impact? If they placed buckets of water in front of the fans, would that help?

The technologies facilitated running multiple experiments, data collection, graphing, comparisons, and successive refining of ideas. In pursuit of a solution, the underlying mathematics and physics became necessary. They were not studying issues such as heat transfer, conduction, air flow, and the mathematics of measurement in the abstract, to be forgotten after the exam. They needed the ideas to solve their chosen problem.

They eventually arrived at a solution, but even with their graphs, they felt dissatisfied about understanding what was really happening. Because it was a residential school and had a small farm where they kept bees, they used the bee equipment to generate smoke and videotaped its dispersal and flow as the fans operated. This further made concrete what was happening. As they told us later, the downside was that the smoke remained in the classroom for two weeks, which was another illuminating lesson. Perhaps the most important lesson was that they had the agency and capability to work on and solve difficult problems.

Some More Principles

Whether cooling a room in a tropical climate, determining the health of the forest in Thailand, water management almost everywhere, improving quality of life in an arid city in Chile, reducing violence in the periphery of cities—in each case we did not know the best answer beforehand. However, through exploration, investigation, design, prototyping, testing, analyzing, debugging, and re-formulating, collectively we arrived at a satisfactory place with satisfactory technologies and an improved environment. Moreover, we all learned, in context, and with values, and we learned how we learned. We discussed our learning explicitly, taking the same approach to learning about learning, that we did to learning to cool the classroom. We struggled at times as these are complex problems, but by overcoming it, we developed the socio-emotional factors people now recognize as important. We developed them not by being told about them, but by succeeding at hard tasks.

Our way of working with young people was similar to our way of working with adult and organizational clients. We respected them, their thinking, and their values. We would not try to impose a solution on them. Rather, we worked to co-develop solutions. While working we would strive to make connections to the underlying powerful ideas and knowledge. Each participant has particular expertise, and collectively we work towards an agreed upon outcome. Often there are surprises, felicitous and less so, along the way, which can be built upon or negated or worked around.

Our way of working was not to just show kids what to do, or do things. We engaged in their explorations and projects whether we knew what to do or not. Thinking about how to improve one's community, for example, is an essential project. Imagining and creating projects to accomplish this is not only a wonderful learning opportunity, it also can be transformative for the person and even the community. Many times, young people are treated as one of the biggest problems in the community. Beginning to see themselves as powerful agents of change is an incredible and transformative outcome.

We needed to understand how they were thinking and making meaning in order to see better how to interact with them to successfully make their projects and acquire the deep ideas. By making concrete artifacts, whether expressed in code or physical materials, gave concrete insight into what they thought. Through debugging it became possible to think about one's thinking about what they were doing.

I developed the concept of emergent design while working in industry to address the unpredictability of the future, to enable systems to evolve based upon the learning of the participants, and to provide more dimensions for more just, inclusive, and democratic decision making. While working at the micro level with learners as well as working at the macro level to try to facilitate systemic change, emergent design also provided a strong framework to enable more democratic control and better, more just outcomes. Doing things with computers in order to learn in more effective and organic ways functions better when activities are more emergent based upon the people and the situation. We do better and learn better when we can think about and do not in fixed, pre-determined, and externally controlled ways, but when we all can be the protagonists of our own learning, informed by our environments, cultures, and knowledgeable and caring others.

Conclusion

The role of the computer as constructive, creative, and expressive material is essential. Without computational materials most of these projects could not be realized. By using the computer only as a delivery mechanism of text and image, we could gain more information about the issues. But by designing and defining in a formal language on the computer, it becomes a concrete view into our thinking and thereby debuggable and available for reflection on our thinking,

When simplified critiques of what technology cannot do, or how computers in classrooms only look at what classrooms *have* and not what people *do*, we are left with an inaccurate and misleading picture. With the current pandemic, we witnessed that a vaccine could be developed within ONE WEEK from the discovery of the structure of the virus. Neither the vaccine nor the structure of the virus could have been discovered so quickly without the computational technologies available to the scientists. Fortunately, in medicine and public health people do not try to reduce the activity to having technology or not. People do not say that the technology by itself solved the problem. Why would we expect otherwise, either for vaccine development or for learning?

The *Twenty Things* article pointed us towards a recursive list of things to do for learning. However, there are also recursive lists for the other elements in Solomon's formulation. There are many possible cultures, many powerful ideas, and many people with whom to do these things, without a unique one right way to do them.

I describe my trajectory briefly here. Others describe theirs. It is not that only one is the right one, or even that all learners would resonate with the same one. What does matter is to create and evolve better learning environments for all, that bring the possibility of many wonderful, engaging things to do that provide access to powerful ideas and deep learning, many ways to do them, in many different settings, with a diverse set of knowledgeable, caring people, utilizing the best principles for learning, and discovering more along the way, actively and collaboratively constructing and re-constructing the environment and the knowledge.

Section 4 — Recursion Line

20. Recursion Line

Think up twenty more things to do.

—Twenty Things to Do with a Computer (1971)

Thoughts on XX

Tom Lough

Ever since I can remember, I have always been fascinated by Roman numerals, and I enjoy playing around with them. It was about XL years ago that I first heard of Logo. I was fascinated by its simple yet sophisticated structure. In MCMLXXXII I started the *National Logo Exchange*, a newsletter to help teachers who were using Logo in their classrooms.

After a few years, the newsletter grew into a magazine called *Logo Exchange*, of which I was the founding editor. By then, it had attracted a loyal following and a nickname—LX. (At the time, this was not confused with the Roman numeral for sixty, although I'm not sure why.)

What's the Problem?

Those two references give me a convoluted way to arrive at a Roman numeral arithmetic problem I had in mind.

LX – XL = ? At first glance, it looks sort of palindromic. It almost whispers a tag line that we did not recognize all those years ago: With the *Logo Exchange*, you can excel.

But let's look at it as it was intended, an arithmetic activity. What's the answer? XX, of course! A very special number, as we will see shortly.

Reader alert: For the next several paragraphs, you may detect a Roman numeral overload. The best advice is to work through it and just keep going.

Hang Onto Your Xs and Ls

It was about L years ago (in MCMLXXI to be exact) that Seymour Papert and Cynthia Solomon released *Artificial Intelligence Memo Number CCXLVIII*, also known as *Logo Memo Number III*, with the title, *XX Things to Do with a Computer*.

I am happy to join in the celebration of that memo and its far-reaching effects. It has certainly stood the test of time.

One of the most recent realizations of its value for me came during the Logo Foundation TurtleArt webinar of January 23, 2021. *TurtleArt – from Digital to Physical* was organized by Michael Tempel and hosted by Artemis Papert and Brian Silverman. Part of the promotional information said, "For decades, turtle geometry designs have been viewed on computer displays, printed on paper, or drawn by a robot turtle. In recent years new technologies have allowed a wider range of artistic expressions of turtle designs. These include 3D printed and laser cut objects, laser etched designs on wood, embroidered patterns, vinyl cutouts, and ceramic tiles crafted from turtle graphics images. This workshop will… present projects that [engage students] in digital to physical processes."

Artemis and Brian provided many examples of how TurtleArt can be connected to different aspects of the maker movement. Cynthia Solomon supplemented their presentation with brilliant examples of her own recent and past work.

As I participated in the workshop, I also reflected back on the early Logo years when we were celebrating the turtle as a connection between abstract and concrete geometry. Then it occurred to me that the connection between the digital/abstract to physical/concrete was closely connected to the *XX Things* memo. In particular, it reminded me of the first thing in the memo—make a turtle. Both here and in the TurtleArt workshop, digital processes were manifested as physical artifacts. I was hooked!

Did You Get the Memo?

After the workshop, I read the original memo again and realized that we had published articles in the LX related to many of the XX things in the memo. But I wanted to know more!

The Logo Foundation and MIT Media Lab have graciously made the PDF files of all 117 LX issues available online.[1] On impulse, I decided to see how many of the original XX things from the memo we matched in our first year of LX publication. I was astounded!

Let me invite you, dear reader, to pick one of the other XVII publication years and see for yourself how many LX articles you can find that are matched to the XX things in the memo. If you do this, you can experience the astonishment and delight I felt as I made these cross-connections with our Logo heritage.

Meanwhile, let me share with you my own findings from Volume I of the LX in the listing that follows. [Disclaimer: These findings are not exhaustive or complete. I am confident that you, dear reader, will be able to develop an even more comprehensive set of Volume I articles, if you so choose. But I hope that you will select another publication year and develop your own listing—and enjoy the process as well.]

The things from the memo are listed below with their corresponding Roman numerals. Here we go!

Thing I, Thing II

I. Make a Turtle. Linda Razzano's article, "Children and the Turtle Down on the Farm," on page 1 of the May 1983 issue gives details of her kindergarten and first grade students with a Tasman floor turtle. How many of you remember that beast? el.media.mit.edu/logo-foundation/resources/nlx/v1/Vol1No9.pdf

II. Program the Turtle to Draw a Man. In his *Tipps for Teachers* column, "From Turtling to Programming," on page 3 of the January 1983 issue, Steve Tipps takes his readers through the transition from "turtling around" to writing procedures and subprocedures that can be used to draw a stop sign, a zigzag, a star, and even a human figure if desired. el.media.mit.edu/logo-foundation/resources/nlx/v1/Vol1No5.pdf

III. Turtle Biology. This thing focused on the use of floor turtle sensors, but the idea behind that process is for Logo to test a setting continuously and react when that setting changes to a specified value or to within a specified range of values. This idea showed up in "Hawaiian Students Love Logo Overlays," a page 1 article in the November 1982 issue. With a procedure named CONTROL, students could direct the movements of a screen turtle with single key presses. el.media.mit.edu/logo-foundation/resources/nlx/v1/Vol1No3.pdf

Note: The CONTROL procedure was extended in a small item on page 8 of the December 1982 issue.

IV. Make a Display Turtle. Sprite Graphics were all the rage in the early 1980s and their ability to carry shapes meant that students could design their own screen turtles. In his page 1 article, "How to Make Your Own Sprite Graphics," in the March 1985 issue, Jim Fry gives examples of how to do this. el.media.mit.edu/logo-foundation/resources/nlx/v1/Vol1No7.pdf

V. Play Spacewar. Back in the day, the Apple II computer had a set of paddles that could provide program input for two players; this would have enabled them to play games such as Spacewar. Alas, there were no articles about Logo and paddles in the first year of LX Publication. However, Steve Tipps mentions a less combative game than Spacewar in the inaugural piece for his *Tipps for Teachers* column. On page 3 of the September 1982 issue, he gives details of the *Hit My Finger* game for two players. el.media.mit.edu/logo-foundation/resources/nlx/v1/Vol1No1.pdf

238

VI. Differential Geometry. Throughout its first year, the LX published many articles illustrating the differential nature of turtle geometry, mainly through the use of procedures with variables. We published one of the first reviews of Abelson and diSessa's comprehensive book, *Turtle Geometry*, on page 1 of the October 1982 issue, and continued with a differential geometry example in "Fractal Fun with Logo" on page 7. el.media.mit.edu/logo-foundation/resources/nlx/v1/Vol1No2.pdf

VII. Draw Spirals. As far as I could tell, this thing focused on the concept of tail recursion. "Logo Your Boat," an article on page 7 of the September 1982 issue, made use of this idea in its CROSS procedure. el.media.mit.edu/logo-foundation/resources/nlx/v1/Vol1No1.pdf

Note: A more fully developed article was published in the November 1982 issue of *The Computing Teacher*. learntechlib.org/p/169394/

VIII. Have a Heart (and Learn to Debug). What better way to learn debugging skills than to debug? Jay Sugarman's page 1 article, "Brookline Students Hunt Logo Bugs," in the December 1982 issue tells how he worked with his students to develop both a debugging attitude and effective debugging skills. el.media.mit.edu/logo-foundation/resources/nlx/v1/Vol1No4.pdf

IX. Growflowers. "Logo Quilting Party," a page 7 article in the December 1982 issue shows how to incorporate procedures and subprocedures with variables of scale in developing complex graphics with repeating patterns. el.media.mit.edu/logo-foundation/resources/nlx/v1/Vol1No4.pdf

X. Make a Movie. Frame by frame animation was included in Glen Bull's *Microworlds* column piece, "Introducing the Text Screens," starting on page 5 of the February 1983 issue. He shows how to achieve screen animation by drawing an object, erasing it, and redrawing it slightly changed. In this case, he demonstrates how to animate text objects. el.media.mit.edu/logo-foundation/resources/nlx/v1/Vol1No6.pdf

XI. Make A Music Box and Program A Tune. On page 3 of the October 1982 issue, Steve Tipps develops a strategy for using Logo to program a pattern of actions and of sounds, a process similar to that used by composers of tunes. el.media.mit.edu/logo-foundation/resources/nlx/v1/Vol1No9.pdf

XII. Play with Semi-Random Musical Effects and then Try Serious Composing. Starting on page 3 of the March 1983 issue, in his *Tipps for Teachers* article, "Random Thoughts," Steve Tipps introduces several concepts for applying random processes within Logo procedures. Although he does not reference music directly, the ideas are similar to those in this thing. el.media.mit.edu/logo-foundation/resources/nlx/v1/Vol1No7.pdf

XIII. Computerize an Erector Set Crane and Build a Tower of Blocks. Glen Bull's *Microworlds* article "Teaching Grammar to a Computer II," starting on page 5 of the May 1983 issue, contains many of the same strategies required to build a tower of blocks—except in this case, the blocks are words. el.media.mit.edu/logo-foundation/resources/nlx/v1/Vol1No9.pdf

XIV. Make a Super Light Show. The marquee described on page 6 of Glen Bull's *Microworlds* column piece, "Introducing the Text Screens," in the February 1983 issue is similar to the ideas in this thing. el.media.mit.edu/logo-foundation/resources/nlx/v1/Vol1No6.pdf

XV. Write Concrete Poetry. "The Other Side of Logo," in Steve Tipps' *Tipps for Teachers*, starting on page 3 of the February 1983 issue, contains details for composing and printing text-based projects, including poetry. el.media.mit.edu/logo-foundation/resources/nlx/v1/Vol1No6.pdf

XVI. Try C.A.I. and Psychology. In his "Random Thoughts" article starting on page 3 of the March 1983 issue, in his *Tipps for Teachers* column, Steve Tipps includes strategies for designing computer assisted instructional procedures and allowing for user input. el.media.mit.edu/logo-foundation/resources/nlx/v1/Vol1No7.pdf

XVII. Physics in the Finger-Tips. The balancing activity described by Steve Tipps in "Logo for All," the article in his May 1983 *Tipps for Teachers* column, corresponds to some of the ideas of this thing. el.media.mit.edu/logo-foundation/resources/nlx/v1/Vol1No9.pdf

XVIII. Explain Yourself. Sandy Towberman's page 1 article, "A Parent Looks at Logo," in the October 1982 issue makes the case that Logo enables a child to boost both creativity and the ability of self-expression. el.media.mit.edu/logo-foundation/resources/nlx/v1/Vol1No2.pdf

XIX. Puppets. This thing is related closely to the ideas of external control by a computer, something akin to the first thing about the robot turtle, with the puppet strings corresponding to the controlling procedures. Linda Razzano's previously referenced article, "Children and the Turtle Down on the Farm," on page 1 of the May 1983 issue chronicles how her students developed an understanding of how to control the floor turtle as a sort of puppet. el.media.mit.edu/logo-foundation/resources/nlx/v1/Vol1No9.pdf

XX. Recursion Line. For this thing, I am unexpectedly leaping out of the first year of LX publication and into the September 1985 issue. In my opinion, Molly Watt's page 1 article, "Twenty Powerful Ideas," makes the needed connection with this thing's recursive nature. el.media.mit.edu/logo-foundation/resources/nlx/v4/Vol4No1.pdf

Is That All?

And there you have it. A surprising XX-thing connection to the first year of LX publication, realized only in hindsight.

But let's not lose sight of the original motivation—the connection of Logo computing to the outside world. Many of the things in the MIT memo focus on this idea, but it took several years before they were realized (e.g., LEGO TC Logo in the late 1980s, compared with the Mindstorms robotic systems of today). It is no surprise that Logo through TurtleArt has connected strongly with the maker movement,[2] and that it continues to enable creators of all ages and abilities to transfer their ideas from an abstract computer screen to a concrete piece of material.

For me, this reinforces the relationship between atoms and bits that Nicholas Negroponte and others have used as the basis for so many wonderful projects and programs.

Ever FD indeed!

Notes

1 Archive of *Logo Exchange* - el.media.mit.edu/logo-foundation/resources/nlx/index.html
2 See *Invent to Learn: Making, Tinkering, and Engineering in the Classroom* - inventtolearn.com

Reflections on Papert and Solomon from the History and Civics Classroom

Heather Allen Pang

The one big thing we can do with computers is empower children. That was true when Papert and Solomon wrote *Twenty Things to Do with a Computer* and it is true now. Empowering children, however, looks a little different today. The power children need is to control the information that flows out of the computer at them at an alarming rate, and harness it for their own creativity and needs. If they can't take control of that information, then, as Papert and Solomon feared, the computer will program them. There are so many ways to empower students, and significantly more than twenty come to mind, but I want to focus on something that has been on the mind of history and social science teachers: civics. The computer and the information we get through it have become essential tools through which civic engagement happens. Mastery over these systems can promote the intellectual habits needed for active engaged citizens. Or at the very least that mastery might help people stop believing the lies fed to them through mismanagement of information systems by those with anti-democratic agendas.

There have been editorials, calls for legislation, and a certain amount of outcry recently over the need for better civics education in the wake of the 2016 election, the COVID–19 pandemic, almost everything the Trump administration did, and the January 6, 2021 assault on the US Capitol. I think even the most casual observer would agree that doing a better job of combating misinformation would lead to a better-informed citizenry which is a precondition for a functioning civil society. Most of the calls to restore civics education are well-intended, but in most cases limited in imagination. Historians of all people should know better than to call for a return to any supposed golden age of anything, but nevertheless there have been editorials from politicians and educators bemoaning the move to STEM because in our rush to teach science, technology, engineering, and math, we have neglected history.[1] Some pretty smart people, like Sam Wineburg, leader of the Stanford History Education Group (SHEG), have put time and research into curriculum initiatives that show better ways to teach the skills everyone needs to navigate the world of online civics. As the SHEG authors rather dramatically put it in the release of *Students' Civic Online Reasoning: A National Portrait* in 2019, "If we don't act with urgency, our students' ability to engage in civic life will be the casualty." To be fair, Wineburg and his group have some pretty smart ideas about how some of this education should be focused on fact checking (lateral reading is the key) and historical reasoning (historical thinking is a skill, it has nothing to do with memorizing anything).[2] I think that is only half the story, and perhaps ideas from fifty years ago might help us with the other half.

So how does thinking about an article about the possibilities presented by computers in the classroom a half a century ago help us empower citizens today? Before we look further, I want to state what should be obvious. We need to get rid of the idea that students' minds are a limited zero-sum commodity. Time may be limited, it is probably the biggest limitation in learning, but otherwise, this is not pie. We don't need to stop teaching STEAM subjects so that we can teach civics. I don't think students can learn to be good citizens, no matter how you define good citizenship, if they are not learning math and science and art! Civics and history teach students tools to think about and understand their world, just like other subjects. In the twenty-first century, showing them how to use those tools must be one of the things that we do with computers in the classroom. Papert and Solomon were right, we need to make sure the computer is not programming the child, the child must be programming (and otherwise controlling) the computer. Civics education and STEM cannot be seen as a zero-sum game despite the fact that all subjects compete for time; that especially these days, students need to know some science to make sense of policy arguments etc., and need some civic education to have a vision for how powerful technologies should be used. Arguably the Americans who de Tocqueville wrote about would have understood technologies that reduced civic engagement, or promoted epistemological nihilism, as a real problem.

Papert and Solomon can help us understand what an active, involved, engaged civics education might look like if we let them! They wrote, "Only inertia and prejudice, not economics or the lack of good educational ideas, stand in the way of providing every child in the world with the kind of experience of which we have tried to give you some glimpses." The devices are in the hands of many students, and I hope that the pandemic has shown us that we need another push to make them universally accessible. If all we do is use these devices to replicate textbooks and worksheets over distance, we have failed. Students should demand better of us, and the computer itself might be one tool they could use to do just that.

If I were to make an update to Papert and Solomon's list, it would be to stress the need for students to experience their own power over information, not just mathematics, linguistics, music, or physics. While Papert and Solomon rightly focused on the Turtle and drawing possibilities of the computer, they also brought up many computer tasks that students today may take for granted because they can do them with a basic phone. One seems most relevant to civics education—movie making. I appreciate the effort going into the Turtle coding to create the frames of a movie showing a flower grow in #10, I think the civics lessons in the abilities of a child with a camera and basic editing software are what we need in the classroom today. As a fundamental tool of communication, video, and video editing and manipulation are as essential to student skills as handwriting has been in the past. Students should learn from their own experiences how they have the power to create powerful, emotional, and dare I say it, viral video content. The power to talk to the rest of the world, or just to their classmates, to influence friends and strangers on topics they care about through their ability to write, shoot, and edit video will not only provide the power of a tool they can use themselves, but it can also expose the manipulation tricks that others use when they make the video content students (and adults) consume by the hour on a wide variety of platforms. What better way to learn how not to be fooled than to learn the techniques for influencing others? Deepfakes and other kinds of digital manipulation are the tools of communication, just as important as public speaking or convincing writing. Students will also have the opportunity to discuss the ethics of such video techniques.

It seems appropriate to link the empowerment of students through their control of computers and information to another thinker on the subject of civics education. When John Dewey (1937) argued that we had lost our way with regard to education and democracy, he probably could not have imagined the firehose of information we drink from on the internet. But he saw a related problem. "The trouble, at least one great trouble, is that we have taken democracy for granted; we have thought and acted as if our forefathers had founded it once for all. We have forgotten that it has to be enacted anew in every generation, in every year and day, in the living relations of person to person, in all social forms and institutions. Forgetting this, we have allowed our economic and hence our political institutions to drift away from democracy; we have been negligent even in creating a school that should be the constant nurse of democracy."

Today, we have allowed social media and corporations to create a system of information dissemination that is not the democratic utopia that some predicted as the internet took off.

In 1996, Bill Gates wrote, "The Internet is the first medium that will make it easy for citizens to explore and participate in the issues of the day, as much or as little as they like. This will put the citizen in a fundamentally more powerful position than ever before." Classrooms might be the one place to put these two ideas together, and return to students the power that they have in their hands when they control a computer. The price we are paying today for letting that power slip through our hands is too high to contemplate. Which is not to say that I want to argue that Bill Gates is right. But if we listen to Papert and Solomon, and don't forget Dewey, he might be right in this one case. Otherwise, we will just continue to let the computer program us.

History and civics instruction must empower kids to see that they, as citizens of the nation and the world, have the power to program the computer and the world they live in, and also challenge any information that comes to them via that same computer. If students experience learning as creators, and in that process see democracy as not a passive but an active proposition, that will not only help them, but it will help everyone. Learning by controlling computers can, as many computer science educators will tell you, promote better habits of logic and perhaps rationality; I argue that when students see how they can use computers for civic engagement, and fight those who wish to undermine that engagement in democracy, then we are really doing something with computers in the classroom. We might even activate a more alive civic sensibility that could animate better deployment and use of technology too. It would be a start.

References

Breakstone, J., Smith, M., Wineburg, S., Rapaport, A., Carle, J., Garland, M., & Saavedra, A. (2019). Students' Civic Online Reasoning: A National Portrait. *Stanford History Education Group & Gibson Consulting.* purl.stanford.edu/gf151tb4868

Dewey, J. (1937). Education and Social Change. *Bulletin of the American Association of University Professors (1915-1955), 23*(6), 473-474. doi.org/10.2307/40219908

Gates, B. (1996, July 21). Internet Will Improve Democracy. *Deseret News.* deseret.com/1996/7/21/19255319/internet-will-improve-democracy

Notes

1 I think most historians are capable of putting the blame elsewhere. Standardized testing would be first on my list of culprits, and the generally abysmal state of funding for all education comes in for significant blame. See for example, "Opinion: Our democracy is ailing. Civics education has to be part of the cure. (Washington Post, 2 March, 2021) washingtonpost.com/opinions/2021/03/02/our-democracy-is-ailing-civics-education-has-be-part-cure/

2 The Stanford History Education Group runs several relevant websites: Civic Online Thinking and Reading Like a Historian heg.stanford.edu/

A Language for Making Physical Things

Leo McElroy

"Where do you think we should cut that board?" This may have been one of the best questions I ever asked, at least from a pedagogical perspective.

I was living in the Himalayas in Northern India working at an alternative school. Out of necessity due to its remote location and a desire to instill in its students a sense of responsible environmental stewardship the entire school was self-sufficient and off-grid. A passive solar heating system which consisted of a large collection of mirrors pointed at a single spot was used for cooking and boiling water. Shortly before I arrived, the school had acquired a large Fresnel lens which could suitably take the role of the mirrors. In order to do so however we had to construct some sort of frame which would allow us to point the lens at the sun as it moved throughout the sky during the day and year. This leads us to the circumstances of our question.

A German fellow, Victor, and I volunteered to take on the task of designing and constructing the frame with the help of some students. The students delighted in the task and would frequently make up excuses to skip their regular classes and come work outside in the open-air woodshop. Materials were somewhat scarce because we were constructing the entire frame out of wood which we found in the small waste heaps of the school.

One morning while working on the project I noticed two of the students hovering over one of our few good boards, saws in hand, engaged in a lively discussion. I joined in asking, "Where do you think we should cut that board?" Evidently it was a question that had already emerged for the students in order to continue with their work. But it appeared their resolution was closer to settling on a guess rather than really convincing each other that there was a compelling rationalization to approach a solution.

As I considered the question myself, I realized there was in fact quite some significance embedded within it. The board would be one of the main support struts which would determine both the height and angle of the lens in its resting position. Due to the large size of the lens the focal point sat about two meters behind the frame, so the lens needed to sit sufficiently high up that its focal point would be accessible and not beneath the ground. Additionally, the frame had to be angled properly to have a range of motion which would allow it to point directly at the sun throughout the day all year long. To know where to cut our board we would have to consider all these things and associated concepts. Suddenly, in order to determine our best course of action we would have to foray into optics, Snell's Law, trigonometry, geometry, and astronomy. Curiously, many of these topics were being covered in the classroom next door, which the students had fled to come cut wood. Suddenly it had all become interesting!

What Was Different about Our Woodshop Question?

Our question in the shop was discovered by the students on their way to a goal they already had. Hypotenuses, opposites, adjacents, and angles may all seem to have arbitrary rules associated with their relationships. But when the students held the frame in their hands while trying to get the lens to point towards the sky these concepts became real things. These relationships were not arbitrary but something of consequence, something that would determine whether our contraption worked, or didn't. When the time came for students to put names to these concepts they didn't have to section off a little portion of their mind for "things I learned in school which I'll soon forget." Instead, they were able to place the concepts among their experiences with the frame. In the classroom, they would have been told this is what sines and cosines are and asked questions which exist for the sole purpose of exercising the answers. This is inverted. While cutting wood the students understood why the concepts were worth inventing, by experiencing the asking of the question in the first place. And their interest arose naturally from the concepts having meaningful bearing on the work they were doing.

Our question was actionable. The question came from the students' desire to do something. That desire to do formed the foundation for the student's desire to understand something. The question was actionable because it was oriented around the frame and the board—concrete things. When we formulate questions around the physical world it becomes natural to cast these questions in forms of what we will do and what sort of actions we will take. Additionally, because of the familiarity of the physical world, the students were well-equipped to conceptualize the question. They didn't have to learn something new to understand the question.

Our question was embedded with other questions. The story about constructing the lens frame is actually incomplete. What was left out, is how I knew what meaningful questions were embedded within trying to determine where to cut the board. I had discovered these questions the weeks prior when Victor and I designed the frame in a computer-aided design (CAD) program on my computer. We actually had designed the frame wrong at least seven times before we finally picked the design we would try to fabricate. Once, the lens was too far out and would be blown over by the wind. Another time the focal point fell upon the contraption which would burst our wooden frame into flames. Then the range of motion was insufficient for our latitude, but after adjusting that the base became imbalanced. With each iteration I had to debug. And with each iteration I discovered a new question which I didn't know to ask before. In a sense debugging was the process of uncovering the questions I didn't know to ask. What I lamented, was that I was the one doing the debugging. As part of the workshops I ran at the school I tried to teach some CAD tools. The students enjoyed the tools when the tools worked, but more often than not they were hampered by outdated hardware, slow internet, and complex interfaces. The biggest challenge however, was that it was difficult for students to see past the particulars of a tool to the powerful ideas underneath. What we needed was a tool which was approachable and which would support a conversation between the student and the computer about making a physical thing.

If the students building the solar tracking frame had simply cut boards until one was the right length, they could have succeeded in completing the frame (although they probably would have run out of wood first) but they would have lost the chance to learn something meaningful. They would have fallen into the trap of making things without making sense. The students' excitement around building the frame demonstrates the benefits of orienting learning around physical stuff, but in order to derive meaning from the experience we need tools which allow students to represent their own thinking and to reflect on those representations. Making things provides an opportunity. But without the proper support to dive deeper into questions, it's an opportunity wasted.

Gram – A Language to Make Things We Want

I've long since left the school in the Himalayas but still often think about the powerful promise of making sense while making things, and what was missing from the tools the students had to support them in this process. Let's review the lessons from the lens frame which formed the foundational design principles for the tool I'll propose, a language called Gram (gramlanguage. com).

The learner should be able to learn the tool in service of something they already want to do. In our case, in service of making something!

The learner shouldn't have to learn a complicated new language or tool in order to begin playing with possible solutions. Part of the beauty in building our conversation around physical stuff is that people already have terms for describing patterns in these things. People don't have to learn a new language to begin to talk about symmetry or repetition in objects they interact with every day. Describing something physical allows the learner to focus less on learning something new and more on thinking about how they organize what they already know.

The learner needs to be able to reflect on and debug their thinking. This means our tool needs to represent the learner's thinking explicitly and to provide feedback, so the learner can verify their thoughts.

Gram is designed to be accessible to anyone, even if you have no experience programming. It is technically a programming language but instead of making applications, Gram is for making designs for fabrication. More importantly though, Gram is designed to help practice thinking clearly while delighting in fabrication. Let's explore these ideas in a conversation with the computer by reducing our construction of the lens frame to a simple assembly of pieces. We'll talk to the computer about building this simple construction set in Gram.

We'll start with some turtle geometry to make a square.

```
1  for 4:
2      forward 10
3      right 90
4
5
6
7
8
9
10
```

Using turtle geometry allows us to capture the side lengths and angles of our shape. It provides us with the ability to *dimension*. This sort of dimensioning is highly useful when describing physical stuff. But even more importantly turtle geometry allows us to describe shapes in terms of the *relationships between the elements*.

Now we want to create the joints by cutting a rectangle out of our base shape. We could do this by modifying our original instructions to the turtle like so.

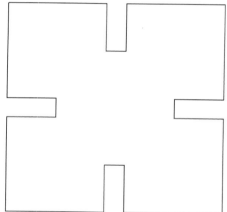

```
1  for 4:
2      forward 10
3      right 90
4      forward 5
5      left 90
6      forward 2
7      left 90
8      forward 5
9      right 90
10     forward 10
11     right 90
12
13
14
```

This general shape is right, but our side length is completely different from before because now each side consists of five lines instead of the one we started with. It would be nice if our language would allow us to talk about transforming a shape we already have. Additionally, when thinking about patterns it's often just as meaningful to describe what's not there as well as what is. With these ideas integrated into our drawing model we could describe our joints in terms of cutouts.

The base shape of our cutout is another rectangle. Because we are starting a new shape let's put each piece of the drawing on a layer of its own.

```
1  layer:
2    for 4:
3      forward 10
4      right 90
5
6  layer:
7    for 2:
8      forward 1
9      right 90
10     forward 3
11     right 90
12
13
```

Modifications we make on one layer affect only that layer and will not affect other layers. Now we want to move the center top of our cutout rectangle to the center top of the original base shape. If we give each layer a name, we can then reference those layers in a **move** command. In our move command **this** refers to the current layer.

```
1  base = layer:
2    for 4:
3      forward 10
4      right 90
5
6  cutout = layer:
7    for 2:
8      forward 1
9      right 90
10     forward 3
11     right 90
12   move this.ct base.ct
13
```

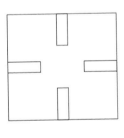

By adding the notion of layers to our drawing model we can start to think about *components* of what we're making. These components may end up forming separate pieces of something we make, but they can also be pieces of a pattern as is the case with our cutouts. Components become powerful when paired with tools to *compose* them into new patterns, like we do when we reference the base layer in our move statement. If we were to modify our original square (let's say by making it bigger) then our shape still retains its essential patterns.

Returning to our construction kit piece we now want to describe a repetitive pattern with some sort of modification to each iteration. In keeping with our idea of composing components we already have, let's describe the operation as a transformation on our cutout rectangle. Let's copy and paste (**copypaste**) the cutout rectangle three times and for each iteration **rotate** around the center of the base shape 90 degrees.

```
1  base = layer:
2    for 4:
3      forward 10
4      right 90
5
6  cutout = layer:
7    for 2:
8      forward 1
9      right 90
10     forward 3
11     right 90
12   move this.ct base.ct
13
14   copypaste 3:
15     rotate base.cc 90
16
```

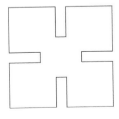

Now we just need to actually cut out our cutout rectangles. We'll use the **difference** command to subtract the cutout rectangles from the base shape.

```
1  base = layer:
2    for 4:
3      forward 10
4      right 90
5
6  cutout = layer:
7    for 2:
8      forward 1
9      right 90
10     forward 3
11     right 90
12   move this.ct base.ct
13
14   copypaste 3:
15     rotate base.cc 90
16
17 difference
18
```

249

We've now got a piece for our construction kit which we can easily modify to accommodate materials of different thicknesses.

```
1  base = layer:
2    for 4:
3      forward 10
4      right 90
5
6  cutout = layer:
7    for 2:
8      forward 2
9      right 90
10     forward 3
11     right 90
12   move this.ct base.ct
13
14   copypaste 3:
15     rotate base.cc 90
16
17 difference
```

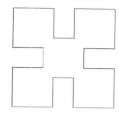

Or if we decide our corners are too sharp, we can round them by modifying our base shape.

```
1  base = layer:
2    for 4:
3      forward 10
4      right 90
5    roundcorners 2
6
7  cutout = layer:
8    for 2:
9      forward 1
10     right 90
11     forward 3
12     right 90
13   move this.ct base.ct
14
15   copypaste 3:
16     rotate base.cc 90
17
18 difference
```

We could also change our base shape altogether.

```
1  base = layer:
2    circle 5
3
4  cutout = layer:
5    for 2:
6      forward 1
7      right 90
8      forward 3
9      right 90
10   move this.ct base.ct
11
12   copypaste 3:
13     rotate base.cc 90
14
15 difference
```

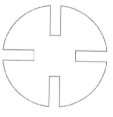

Here are two versions with different depths of cutouts made out of wood.

Let's explore turning our shape into another pattern using the same radial array technique we used to make our cutouts.

```
1  base = layer:
2    for 4:
3      forward 10
4      right 90
5    roundcorners 2
6
7  cutout = layer:
8    for 2:
9      forward 1
10     right 90
11     forward 2
12     right 90
13   move this.ct base.ct
14
15   copypaste 3:
16     rotate base.cc 90
17
18 difference
19
20 n = 3
21 copypaste n-1:
22   rotate this.cc 360/n
23
```

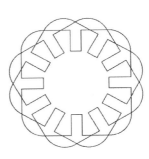

This is pretty but if we were to actually cut out the pattern we would end up with a mess of pieces. How might we go about turning this into a fabricable shape? One approach may be to take the **outline** of the shape.

```
1  base = layer:
2    for 4:
3      forward 10
4      right 90
5    roundcorners 2
6
7  cutout = layer:
8    for 2:
9      forward 1
10     right 90
11     forward 2
12     right 90
13   move this.ct base.ct
14
15   copypaste 3:
16     rotate base.cc 90
17
18 difference
19
20 n = 3
21 copypaste n-1:
22   rotate this.cc 360/n
23
24 outline
```

This will come out as one piece, but it's lost a lot of the detail which made our pattern interesting.

What we would like to do is **thicken** our lines so that the shape remains in one piece when cut.

```
1  base = layer:
2    for 4:
3      forward 10
4      right 90
5    roundcorners 2
6
7  cutout = layer:
8    for 2:
9      forward 1
10     right 90
11     forward 2
12     right 90
13   move this.ct base.ct
14
15   copypaste 3:
16     rotate base.cc 90
17
18 difference
19
20 n = 3
21 copypaste n-1:
22   rotate this.cc 360/n
23
24 thicken 0.3
25 outline
```

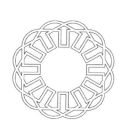

Playing with just one number we can discover some other interesting shapes which we may want to make.

```
1  base = layer:
2    for 4:
3      forward 10
4      right 90
5    roundcorners 2
6
7  cutout = layer:
8    for 2:
9      forward 8
10     right 90
11     forward 2
12     right 90
13   move this.ct base.ct
14
15   copypaste 3:
16     rotate base.cc 90
17
18 difference
19
20 n = 3
21 copypaste n-1:
22   rotate this.cc 360/n
23
24 thicken 0.3
25 outline
```

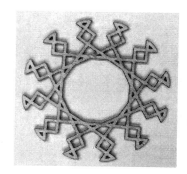

Making Sense While Making Things

Gram provides means for describing geometries which are both functional and aesthetically pleasing. It builds on turtle geometry as a way of thinking about relative relationships of elements and dimensioning. The language introduces layers as a way of isolating components. It provides techniques for composing these components by referencing key points on them or using them as tools to alter other layers. It also offers techniques for forming fabricable shapes from lines. The objective of the Gram language is to offer learners a tool to clarify their thinking. It does this by providing the learner with a means of expressing themselves clearly with feedback from a computer, in pursuit of questions most readily accessible to them: questions about the physical world.

What the experience with the lens frame taught me is that making things provides an inspiring *opportunity* for learning, but it doesn't *guarantee* it. In order to benefit from making, learners have to reflect on thinking. As Seymour and Cynthia pointed out fifty years ago in *Twenty Things to Do with a Computer,* the computer is one of the most powerful tools ever created for reflecting on thinking. We should build computational tools which support this sort of reflection while serving the learner's desire to make something physical. The Gram language is my attempt at such a tool.

Things to Do with a Computer in an English/Language Arts Classroom (Besides Word Processing)

Kate Tabor

Beyond the essay, writing a story, or answering a question on a test, computers can bring the world of the English/Language Arts classroom to life. Here are a dozen things you can do with a computer beyond word processing.

Analog Publishing

I know. Yes, it starts with word processing, but what is interesting is what you *do* with the word processing. When students write for real audiences, those real audiences can access their work through electronic and traditional paper publishing. Electronic publishing in blogs and on-line journals is great, but don't forget: **Paper is Good**. Each year for the last decade we have published a paperback book—an anthology of the collected and connected short stories written by the seventh grade. Using Adobe InDesign, I lay out the book, sharing a galley proof of each story with its author. The PDF galleys are carefully proofread by their authors and returned. We use an on-demand printer who takes

The printed volumes of collected short stories make a big impact on student writers.

the final PDFs (cover and text) and prints and perfect-binds the books. There is magic in the day that the books are distributed. When students see what they have made together and they read their words in a book, they are amazed, excited, and anxious to read all the stories.

Turn the movie in your head into visuals

Students can create book trailers, film scenes from books, create character documentaries, make stop motion animations, or illustrate a character from a book or a story. Making text visible allows students to share their thinking in a way that brings it alive for other students. For the past few years, I have asked students to create ads for books that they think need some *book love* and a wider readership. Our ads, or book trailers, run in the library on the big video screens. They are silent, so the emphasis is on visual storytelling. The work is public—not just created for the teacher—so students want them to be great and for people to read books that they recommend.

Create a resource for a public domain text

Use a book like Jean Toomer's *Cane*, Fitzgerald's *The Great Gatsby*, E.M. Forster's *A Passage to India*, or *The Box-Car Children* by Gertrude Chandler Warner. Begin with a public domain electronic text, and give your students free rein to annotate, illustrate, make connections to history, and expand the text to become a living document and resource. I can imagine an

American Studies focused deep-dive on a text like *Cane*, looking at the all of the social and political forces at play in each piece. The project could include archival photos, contemporaneous news and criticism, music, art, and history. There is also the wonderful structure of that novel to explore—a collection of prose, poetry, and vignettes that connect through theme and context. A new text could be chosen every year to annotate as new work enters the public domain.

Remix

Thinking more about public domain, imagine what could be done with silent films like Harold Lloyd's *Hot Water* or *The Thief of Bagdad* starring Douglas Fairbanks. New scripts, new soundtracks, new title cards, or films mixed together. There are so many challenging and thought-provoking films now available to dissect and blend and interrogate. Consider D. W. Griffith's *America*, a silent film depicting a romance during the Revolutionary War. One of the critiques of the film when it was released was that the narrative structure was confusing. Looking at it as an artifact of history would be one approach. Recutting it, changing up the order of scenes, thinking about visual vs. written exposition, and considering the film's audience and purpose are others. There is a lot we can do with resources that are just becoming available.

Collaborate

We collaborate with students, with other teachers, and with writers and thinkers not in our school. Students in my classes are working together to create a collection of stories that all connect through character and location. Their collaboration is facilitated by the Google suite of tools, sharing character documentaries (made with Adobe Spark), histories, and a character census. My own collaboration with each student-thinker is facilitated by shared documents where I can make suggestions as well as provide the writers with the perspective of the reader.

Interact with your physical spaces

Physical spaces, both indoor and out, are overlooked sources of story. Every artifact in the halls–every mural, quilt, painting, trophy, statue–has a story. Let the artifacts tell that story. I asked students to look, really look, at the entire school to find and capture images of art and artifacts around the building that had become wallpaper to them, to see them for the first time. Students used research from previous seventh grades and brought the artifacts' stories to life. Using digital tools, they created Buzzfeed style quizzes, gifs, maps, stories, games, stop motion films, art, augmented reality, and immersive video to interact with and to share their stories with the school community. As there were so many projects and so much technology in use, there could be no one expert in the room, so students' problems were solved through their own

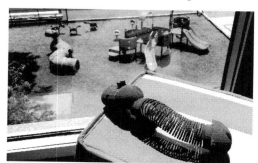

Using Tinkercad, a student created a slinky model of one of Dennis Pearson's Beasties, a favorite sculpture on campus.

3D printed slinky-style Beastie looks out at their inspiration.

exploration. They turned to each other as experts or were excited to share with others as they created their projects.

Expand

Students can expand their worldview and the reach of their ideas through reading and writing blogs, and listening to and creating podcasts. Knowing that there is a real audience for their writing and their ideas and research transforms work from an assignment for the teacher into a passion project for students. Now that we are publishing on a public platform, our high school newspaper has become more aware of its journalistic responsibilities. This awareness has translated into better journalism and greater engagement with the entire school community.

Build a virtual world

Using Scratch or CoSpaces, create virtual narratives and worlds that can be filled with magic. Students might follow a classic story structure in a Choose-Your-Own-Adventure style narrative with multiple pathways to resolution. They might create a world where dragons are real and apt to arrive in unexpected ways. Perhaps student stories link through shared spaces or characters. If you are fortunate enough to have Oculus headsets to view a CoSpaces story, the "reader" becomes immersed in the adventure. Sharing and interacting with each other's stories allows students to physically see where revision would improve their work to create a stronger narrative. This is an editing and revision process that feels organic. Students seem less put off debugging a virtual story than revising a written one.

Connect the disciplines

The lines of history, mathematics, science, art, and English classes blur into each other with projects that ask students to solve problems—make a claim, provide evidence, and explain your reasoning. This is the basis of a lot of problem solving, and it can be the source of an essay or an experiment. It can also be the start of a major building project that starts with a question. We have a fall fair every year, and each grade level creates an activity for the rest of the school. The seventh grade asked the question: who in our JK–12th grade school is not being served by activities at our County Fair? Students fielded research and determined that we needed less food and more fun, and the idea of the obstacle course was born. Students designed and built a course that became the centerpiece of the fair, and each year since the initial design, they have used continuing research and user experience to redesign and rebuild the course from PVC pipe, lumber, tarps, zip ties, pool noodles, and inspiration. The amount of qualitative and quantitative data, the experience with physics, the design, and the connection to community are tangible. Computers allowed students to collect and analyze data, create CAD models, prototype, and record their experiences for the next grade to take on the challenge. In English class students worked to carefully create research questions that would get them the data that they needed and not the data they thought they would get. They closely read answers to open ended questions and analyzed that information to spot trends and find insight into the user experience. Language mattered because the language mattered.

Insult

Well actually, randomly generate phrases and sentences, like insults. My first year at the CMK Summer Institute, I used MicroWorldsEX to create a random Shakespearean insult generator. I had never tried to program anything, though I have used computers since 1986 when you typed DOS command strings at the C: drive to execute programs. It took some time, but I finally got my turtle to insult another turtle who in turn either replied with a witty riposte or with a slow "duh." I have been thinking about how this could be applicable to a number of texts. Perhaps a Homeric epithet generator while reading *The Odyssey* or a Russian name generator as students wrestle with Chekov. I know that they exist already on the internet, but having students develop the list and then program the random generator is an act of critical reasoning and analysis. Plus, it's serious fun.

Think syntax

Working with MicroWorlds and TurtleArt, I learned from coding, both in a word-based project and in a more mathematical challenge of tessellating a form across a field, the importance of clear syntax. I could get the sections (the sentences) to run, but getting the sentences to flow one to the next (creating paragraphs) was not always successful.

Seeing the very concrete connection between coding, and punctuation and syntax in English helps understand how sentences and paragraphs fail to convey their intended meaning. As middle school students are both more concrete than their upper school counterparts and developing more complex language skills, this is a great opportunity to use one type of writing to inform another.

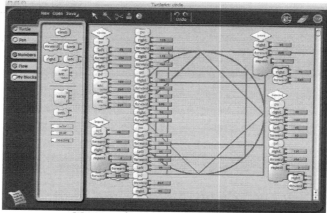

Writing code is like writing paragraphs.
Sometimes the program does what you tell it to do, not what you want it to do.

Listen

Computers allow us many ways to listen. We can use or create audio books. We can record and save/share the voices of our community. As we are living through interesting times, a StoryCorp style project could archive community memories. We can listen to our students tell us what they think. We can find ways for students to use audio and video to record their responses to projects and to give feedback. We can mine archives and listen to voices that are gone. The oral histories in the Library of Congress are available through a simple search, and open up the stories of the Depression, Appalachia, and Indigenous people—to name just a small slice of the folklife that is available.

Find joy

Nothing is better than hearing the joy of creating, feeling the energy of shared inquiry, and laughing with students as they try, revise, and accomplish something. The joy is infectious, and when you smile all day, it doesn't matter that you have seventy-two separate projects spinning around you.

Twenty Things to Make with Biology

Yasmin B. Kafai & Justice T. Walker

Introduction

In "Twenty Things to Make with Biology" we are extending the constructionist vision of engaging learners to converse, interact and design with living materials in new ways. While computers in the 1970s introduced computation with zeros and ones, today's world of biology as design uses As, Ts, Cs, and Gs as their building blocks. In bioengineering, designers can make their own DNA—gene by gene—and then grow their designs into real applications by inserting them into living things such as microorganisms (Endy, 2005). In the following sections, we describe twenty things to make with biology. More than half of our suggestions have already been implemented with middle and high school students in schools and community labs (Kafai et al., 2020). Some of these activities make use of everyday materials such as yeast, kombucha, soil, sand, and tea found in people's homes and pantries while others use mycelium (i.e., mushroom roots) or Escherichia coli bacteria which can be ordered online. In some instances, they require lab setups such as petri dishes, plastic droppers, and incubators while others use home kitchen materials such as pots of warm water or baking sheets. Most importantly, readers need not think about how cells will actually make the things but more about how they can use general biology and practical knowledge to design new applications. In the last section of this paper, we share some of our observations about how making things with biology is either the same or distinct from doing things with a computer.

Twenty Things to Make with Biology

1. Create a Smell

In Eau that Smell learners can genetically modify bacteria (e.g., Escherichia coli) to selectively emit a banana scent at different stages of cell growth (Kuldell, 2015). Smell functions like an indicator and showcases how genetic perturbations can be introduced and programmed very precisely. It also illustrates how synthetic aromatics or flavor food additives can be sustainably produced.

2. Grow a Brick

The company Biomason (2019) grows bricks by the thousands by combining sand and bacteria in a cast. By feeding the bacteria with a liquid cocktail that generates a binding substance and letting them dry for a few weeks, the bricks are formed. This approach uses far less energy than existing methods that require stone/mineral extractions, transport, and a kiln for curing.

3. Bake Enriched Food

Take a plasmid, a pre-coded segment of DNA, and insert it into yeast (Saccharomyces cerevisiae), to reprogram the cells to produce beta carotene, also known as vitamin A (Kuldell, 2015). Growing more yeast with vitamin A this way can be used to bake a cake, or bioCakes (Walker et al., 2018), which is enriched with important nutrients.

Figure 1. Making with Biology: Color (A), Sensor (B), and Food (C) (Source: Walker & Kafai, 2021).

A. BioLogo design using bacterial pigment to make colors:
(left) 'Painting' with bacteria; (right) A completed logo design.

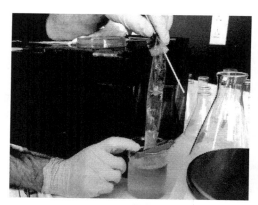

B. BioSensor construction using bacteria as detector:
(left) Putting the transformed bacteria into the dialysis bag; (right) The completed sensor contraption.

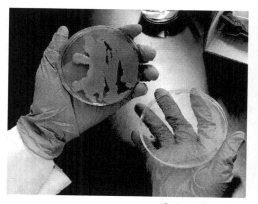
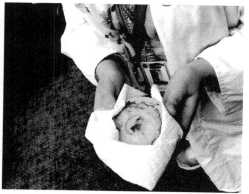

C. BioCake using yeast with vitamin A:
(left) Petri dish with mixed colonies of yeast cells; (right) Student holding her freshly baked enriched cake.

4. Build a GMO Detector

To find out whether food contains Genetically Modified Organisms (GMOs), collect DNA from uncooked fruits or vegetables and add a mix of DNA strands that react with known GMO elements. If your food contains a GMO, the DNA strands are designed to fluoresce in the presence of UV light (GMO Detective, 2019).

5. Feed a Battery Light

To make a battery, collect a soil sample from your garden. Place the soil in a container that has conductive chicken mesh at the bottom, attach this chicken mesh to an insulated wire made of zinc, and connect a LED at the top. Take a second mesh/chicken wire—this time attached to an insulated copper wire—and place it at the surface of the soil. Provide water for the microbes in the soil. After two days, the bacteria residing in the lower part of the container where there is much less air will produce enough electricity to turn on the LED light (Magical Microbes, 2019).

6. Grow Insulin

The Open Insulin Project (2019) has reprogrammed yeast to produce human insulin at large scales. The yeast needs to be grown in standard nutrient broth to produce purified insulin hormone molecules. This makes insulin very compatible with humans and more affordable.

7. Spin Fibers for Fabric

Spider silk is not only light weight, but also incredibly strong which makes a very durable and versatile fabric. To grow silk with similar features, bacteria are genetically reprogrammed to produce the strong and elastic collagen proteins found in spider silk. This is protein is then purified, dried, and spun into thread to weave fabric. Adidas (Franklin-Wallis, 2017) and The North Face (Forbes, 2019) already used this approach for making shoes and jackets.

8. Dynamic Colors

Make a canvas covered with colorful yeast nutrients that change colors over time as the yeast consume, grow, and age (Yeast Art Project, 2019). Yeast cells are very good at producing beta carotene that can be scrambled up by adding a hormone to produce various pinks, violets, blues, and even black.

9. Power Gears

Rod-shaped bacteria known as Bacillus subtilis can be assembled to rotate microscopic gears and control machines. Tiny gears and screws can be assembled and placed in a liquid environment to keep the bacteria alive and mobile. When enough bacteria are present and move in a common direction—this is called a swarm—they can collectively force the gears to move in predictable directions. Photosensitive bacterial swarms can also be directed by using light (Sokolov et al., 2010).

10. Biodegradable Home Goods

Grow biodegradable home goods and accessories like pots, pencil holders, lamp shades, picture frames and other accent pieces (Ecovative Design, 2019) using mushroom roots, also called mycelium. Once mycelium are fed flour and water, they become active after a few days. To make a shape, fill a container with active mycelium and mix in small wood chips, saw dust, or other materials. After a week, the shape is ready and can baked at low heat to stop the mycelium from working.

11. BioSensors

Bacterial cells can be genetically modified and grown to function as sensors and start to glow in the presence of a contaminating substance. Students can build their own sensor with dialysis tubing (see figure 1b) wherein they put the bacteria and place in a cup filled with water that may or may not have the contaminating substance (in this case a sugar called arabinose). If the cup contains arabinose, then the cells in their biosensor tubes will glow under ultraviolet light (Kafai et al., 2017).

12. Kombucha Plastic

Make a bioplastic using a blend of yeast (Saccharomyces cerevisiae), kombucha bacteria (Gluconacetobacter kombuchae), and lukewarm black tea in a pan. These two organisms work together to produce a biofilm or bioplastic in the presence of nitrogen-rich substances like tea (Shade et al., 2011). After waiting for about 2–4 weeks, a 1–2 inch layer will form in your pan which can be dried and then shaped in many ways.

13. Make an RGB Device

Bacteria such as Escherichia coli can be reprogrammed to glow in red, green, and blue (RGB colors) when exposed to ultraviolet light (Tsien, 2010). These glowing bacteria can be put together in different combinations to create new colors and designs. As long as the bacteria are fed, they will continuously produce these fluorescent colors.

14. Play a Game Under the Microscope

Single-celled amoeba-like organisms called Euglena gracilis are mobile and respond to specific light colors (Lee et al., 2015). It is possible to control their direction. This means that with the right configuration, two players could race to direct their organism across a finish line or compete to trap (or guide) them in a maze. The only thing needed here is a microscope to visualize the race.

15. Make Vegetables Savory

The Impossible Burger is made out of plants but tastes like a burger made of beef (Burger King, 2019). This is made possible by adding the DNA for a protein found in red blood cells, called heme, in plants. Then plant-based produce like tomatoes are not only more savory, but also contain more protein content.

16. Dye Fabric

Manufacturing fabric colors like indigo with petrochemicals is harmful to the environment. The bacteria Streptomyces coelicolor can produce a large amount of rich, long-lasting, and environmentally friendly indigo pigments to dye thread and whole fabrics (Faber Futures, 2019).

17. Make a Photocell

Phylum algae are very effective at producing electricity using sunlight. These cyanobacteria use photosynthesis to generate this energy. They can be collected and placed in printer cartridges to print on conductive paper. By adding a transistor to a printed circuit arrangement, they can be powered and create a sustainable and recyclable household energy source (Zyga, 2017).

18. Grow Construction Kits

Many construction kits are made of plastic that is non-degradable. By using mushroom roots (i.e., mycelium) and fermented kombucha, students can grow biodegradable materials to make a biodegradable toys such as a kaleidoscope, doll clothing made with kombucha bioplastic, or LEGO compatible 3D printed wings covered in kombucha bioplastic (GIY Bio Buddies, 2019).

19. Engage in Critical Discussions

Making things with biology can raise a whole host of thorny issues related to transparency, and impact on environment and humans. Those include, evaluating the risks, impact, safety, and moral acceptability of designs such as perils of plastic waste in the toy industry, and the value of sustainable manufacturing. There are a number of topics to discuss around these issues including those related to food security, environmental sustainability, agriculture, and climate change to name a few.

20. Recursion Line

Think up twenty more things to make with biology!

Discussion

We described a wide variety of things that learners of all ages can make with biology using living materials. One attraction of many digital or physical constructionist activities—such as designing games, printing in 3D, building robots, or crafting electronic textiles—is that students are generating, re-making, or augmenting artifacts with physical and digital tools that are already present in their environment. While biomaking also involves materials and tools that are present in students' homes and science classes, the actual fabrication processes and outcomes are distinct in ways that confront core tenets of constructionist theory. Making things with biology differs in sometimes significant ways in terms of tinkerability, perceptibility, expressivity, and usability (Lui et al., 2019). In the following sections, we discuss these distinctions but also similarities in more detail and what insights provide for constructionist learning designs and tools in making with biology.

How making with biology is different

Constructionism has always valued tinkering (Resnick & Rosenbaum, 2013), a playful, experimental iterative style of engagement wherein makers are continually reassessing their goals, exploring new paths and imagining new possibilities, and having "a conversation with the material" (Schön, 1983). However, tinkering with biology is much more difficult since microbiological processes involve liquids and require a full run of the entire lab procedure before one can see any result. In biology, processes often occur in a holistic fashion and thus fixing a "mistake" frequently means doing a lab procedure all over again and waiting for the result, whereas tinkering in engineering and coding involves discrete processes such as iterating on a gear mechanism or developing a specially defined procedure. The specificity of lab procedures and limitations of materials make it somewhat difficult to engage with on-the-spot messing around so popular in maker activities on and off the screen (Lui et al., 2018).

Another valued aspect in constructionist activities is that computer or physical designs can yield immediate feedback either on the progress or results of making. For instance, a coder can see the result of a bug they fixed in a program whereas in biomaking this process occurs more slowly. While microorganisms grow quite rapidly, it often takes hours or more for any genetic transformation to yield an outcome. More importantly, due to scale and colorlessness of the microorganisms, learners often cannot immediately see the outcomes of their designs or changes. In making with biology, it is also much more difficult—but not impossible—for learners to personalize artifacts or designs. Whereas consumer-grade electronics kits have created opportunities for lay people to create personalized computational designs, people with limited biological knowledge and background are not yet as able to produce biodesigns that fulfill their individual goals and purposes. Instead, learners must often (but not always) depend on existing protocols and materials developed by experts.

Finally, constructionist activities foster designs that learners or others can immediately use such as playing a game made in Scratch (Resnick et al., 2009), making music on a banana piano made with Makey Makey (Silver et al., 2012) or a turn-signal hoodie made with the LilyPad Arduino can be worn while biking and signal directions with flashing LEDs (Buechley, 2006). In biomaking, usability comes with its own set of constraints. Some living designs can perish at some point, so careful consideration must be taken to, when necessary, keep the organism alive, such as supplying them with enough nutrients and at appropriate temperature. From this perspective, making with computers affords numerous ready-made situations for usability while biomaking has not yet reached this point of development in its short history.

What making with biology shares with things to do with a computer

We also saw similarities and connections to constructionist learning. While making with biology activities are limited in tinkering with regard to the scripted steps of the lab procedures needed to create the right conditions for, as an example, bacteria to flourish and produce a desired result, the actual hands-on construction and crafting of applications provides considerable degrees of freedom. For instance, students engage with crafting while: "painting with bacteria" by using hot glue guns to mold shapes for their petri dish logos (Kafai et al., 2017), making kombucha plastic and leather clothes for their paper dolls (GIY Bio Buddies, 2019), or even coloring fabric.

We also noticed that in many of the suggested applications, bacteria were chosen that would reveal a visible change, thus promoting the "perceptibility" dimension prominent in constructionist activities. For instance, in Eau that Smell (Kuldell, 2015) bacteria signal change by emitting a banana smell, in Faber Futures (2019) and the Yeast Art Project (2019) microorganisms signal change when they produce pigments, or—in another case luminescence (Tsien, 2010)—to make outcomes more "visible" to students. While not all biomaking activities provide the expected feedback, it was sometimes precisely the lack of feedback (beakers that did not glow and "stinky" bacteria) that provided contexts for conversations around the science of the process.

Finally, in terms of usability making with biology involved product designs that reached beyond the personal. For instance, in BioLogo, it involved a company focused on sustainable product design, while BioSensors involved researching contexts in which sensing pollution would be of importance, and BioCakes involved thinking about food products that could benefit from nutritional enrichment. It is here where we saw the imagination of students flourish as they recognized the usability—both personal and societal—of their designs. Other examples include Ecovative (2019) and GIY Biobuddies (2019) that both leverage mycelium properties to build a whole swath of products including furniture, home accessories, toys, and constructions kits. Or Biomason (2019) and the North Face (Forbes, 2019), who use bacteria to construct building material and clothing. These examples illustrate new frontiers in biology wherein products are not only usable, but they also provide a space for student discourse around manufacturing, sustainability, material life cycles, and their collective impact on the planet.

How to make things happen

The development of programming languages and construction kits that let learners do things with computers both have been a driving force in promoting constructionist learning. Previous constructionist efforts focused on making digital designs by controlling a turtle on the computer screen or on the floor. The design of portable and programmable bricks (Resnick et al., 1996) allowed learners to move designs into the physical world and build autonomous creatures no longer tethered to terminals.

Recent developments of simple to use portable lab tools make it possible for K-12 students to genetically alter a wide range of cells for designing a variety of applications. For instance, the biomakerlab (Kafai et al., 2017) is a low-cost portable wetlab device that makes it possible to easily genetically modify and grow bacteria cells. Another even simpler example is BioBits (Stark et al., 2018) which eliminates cells altogether and provides freeze-dried pellets made of cellular parts that, when hydrated, assembled, and incubated, express unique gene designs, such as a full palette of colors that fluoresce in the presence of ultraviolet light. Other examples include Bento Labs (2019) which provides a portable wet lab device that enables users to construct, isolate, enrich, and analyze genetic parts that can later be introduced into living cells. Amino Labs (2019) is yet another example that enables young students to transform (i.e., genetically modify), grow and analyze newly engineered organisms.

Some work is even targeting younger students—namely elementary grades. CRISPEE (Verish et al., 2018) is an example of such an effort as researchers developed a low-cost block-based simulation device that allows young learners to mix and match wooden blocks in a device that illuminates a simulated firefly bulb with a color that is representative of the block combinations created by the user. This activity is meant to help young learners understand what synthetic-based genetic modifications are as a concept and the various ways it impacts living things and their traits. When learners introduce their own genetic perturbations (represented by different block combinations), they gain a sense of how to manipulate and—to an extent—control the design of living things.

Our examples of making with biology provided a glimpse into the foreseeable future in which we engage students with making or growing their designs in petri dishes—just like several decades ago students were first invited to making or coding their designs on computers. Realizing making with biology in K–12 education will require significant efforts but learners themselves have already taken charge. In 2019, for the first time, two teams of high school students participated in the BioDesignChallenge which brings together international teams of college students who compete in developing biodesign applications that solve global challenges related to the environment and manufacturing sustainability. To everyone's great surprise, one high school team of three girls took home the first runner up by creating a biodesign toy kit for other K–12 students. The kit provided microbial-based and mushroom-based packaging for new toy designs to address the perils of plastic waste in the toy industry with more sustainable manufacturing. Indeed, making with biology can introduce learners to twenty-first century ways of doing and thinking just like computers did in the era before.

Acknowledgments

This paper (Kafai & Walker, 2020) was originally published as part of Constructionism 2020 proceedings. It has been slightly modified for publication in this edition. The work was supported by a grant from the National Science Foundation to Yasmin Kafai, Orkan Telhan, and Karen Hogan (#1840933). We want to thank Orkan Telhan and Karen Hogan for many inspiring discussions. Any opinions, findings, and conclusions or recommendations expressed in this paper are those of the authors and do not necessarily reflect the views of NSF or the University of Pennsylvania.

References

Amino Labs. (2019). amino.bio/
Bento Labs. (2019). bento.bio/
Biomason. (2019). biomason.com/

Buechley, L. (2006). A Construction Kit for Electronic Textiles. *Proceedings of 10th IEEE International Symposium on Wearable Computers*, 83-90.

Burger King. (2019). *Impossible Whopper*. bk.com/menu-item/impossible-whopper

Ecovative Design. (2019). ecovativedesign.com/

Endy, D. (2005). Foundations for Engineering Biology. *Nature*, 438(7067), 449.

Faber Futures. (2019). *Colour Coded Forbes Pigment Collection 2018*. faberfutures.com/

Forbes. (2019). *New This Ski Season a Jacket Brewed from Spider Silk*. forbes.com/sites/johncumbers/2019/08/28/new-this-ski-season-a-jacket-brewed-from-spider-silk/#49b5cd94561e

Franklin-Wallis, O. (2017). These lightweight adidas shoes are made from spider silk grown in a lab. *Wired*. wired.co.uk/article/adidas-futurecraft-biofabric-shoes

GIY Bio Buddies. (2019). giybiobuddies.weebly.com/

GMO Detective. (2019). gmodetective.com/about-2/

Kafai, Y., Telhan, O., Hogan, K., Lui, D., Anderson, E., Walker, J. T., & Hanna, S. (2017). Growing Designs with biomakerlab in High School Classrooms. In *Proceedings of the 2017 Conference on Interaction Design and Children (IDC '17)* (pp. 503-508). ACM. doi.org/10.1145/3078072.3084316

Kafai, Y. B., Telhan, O., Hogan, K., & Walker, J. T. (2020). *Learn.design.bio. A NSF workshop report*. learn.design.bio

Kafai, Y. B., & Walker, J. T. (2020). Twenty Things to Make with Biology. In *Proceedings of the 2020 Constructionism Conference* (pp. 598-606).

Kuldell, N. (2015). *Biobuilder*. O'Reilly.

Lee, S. A., Bumbacher, E., Chung, A. M., Cira, N., Walker, B., Park, J. Y., & Riedel-Kruse, I. H. (2015). Trap it!: A Playful Human-Biology Interaction for a Museum Installation. In *CHI '15: Proceedings of the 33rd Annual ACM Conference on Human Factors in Computing Systems* (pp. 2593-2602). ACM.

Lui, D., Anderson, E., & Kafai, Y. B. (2018). Is Making all about Tinkering? A Case Study of High School Students' Activities in Biomaker Workshops. In J. H. Kalir (Ed.), *2018 Connected Learning Summit* (pp. 158-167). ETC Press. connectedlearningsummit.org/cls2018/proceedings/

Lui, D., Kafai, Y. B., Walker, J. T., Hanna. S, Hogan, K., & Telhan, O. (2019). A Revaluation of How We Think about Making: Examining Assembly Practices and Artifact Imagination in Biomaking. In *Proceedings from FabLearn '19 The 8th Annual Conference on Creativity and Fabrication in Education*. ACM. doi.org/10.1145/3311890.3311895

Magical Microbes. (2019). magicalmicrobes.com/products/mudwatt-clean-energy-from-mud?_pos=3&_sid=415d70d49&_ss=r

Open Insulin Project. (2019). openinsulin.org

Papert, S. (1980). *Mindstorms: Children, Computers, and Powerful Ideas*. Basic Books.

Resnick, M., Maloney, J., Monroy-Hernández, A., Rusk, N., Eastmond, E., Brennan, K., Millner, A., & Kafai, Y. B. (2009). Scratch: programming for all. *Communications of the ACM*, 52(11), 60-67.

Resnick, M., Martin, F., Sargent, R., & Silverman, B. (1996). Programmable Bricks: Toys to Think With. *IBM Systems journal*, 35(3.4), 443-452.

Resnick, M., & Rosenbaum, E. (2013). Designing for Tinkerability. In M. Honey & D. Kanter (Eds.), *Design, Make, Play: Growing the Next Generation of STEM Innovators* (pp. 163-181). Routledge.

Schön, D. (1983). *The Reflective Practitioner: How Professionals Think in Action*. Basic Books.

Shade, A., Buckley, D. H., & Zinder, S. H. (2011). *The kombucha biofilm: a model system for microbial ecology. Final report on research conducted during the Microbial Diversity course*. Marine Biological Laboratories.

Silver, J., Rosenbaum, E., & Shaw, D. (2012). Makey Makey: Improvising Tangible and Nature-based User Interfaces. In *Proceedings of the sixth international conference on tangible, embedded and embodied interaction* (pp. 367-370). ACM.

Sokolov, A., Apodaca, M. M., Grzybowski, B. A., & Aranson, I. S. (2010). Swimming Bacteria Power Microscopic Gears. *Proceedings of the National Academy of Sciences*, 107(3), 969-974.

Stark, J. C., Huang, A., Nguyen, P. Q., Dubner, R. S., Hsu, K. J., Ferrante, T. C., Anderson, M., Kanapskyte, A., Mucha, Q., Packett, J. S., Patel, P., Patel, R., Qaq, D., Zondor, T., Burke, J., Martinez, T., Miller-Berry, A., Puppala, A., Reichert, K., Schmid, M., Brand, L., Hill, L. R., Chellaswamy, J. F., Faheem, N.,

Fetherling, S., Gong, E., Gonzalzles, E. M., Granito, T., Koritsaris, J., Nguyen, B., Ottman, S., Palffy, C., Patel, A., Skweres, S., Slaton, A., Woods, T., Donghia, N., Pardee, K., Collins, J. J., & Jewett, M. C. (2018). BioBits™ Bright: A fluorescent synthetic biology education kit. *Science Advances*, *4*(8). advances.sciencemag.org/content/4/8/eaat5107

Tsien, R. Y. (2010). Nobel lecture: constructing and exploiting the fluorescent protein paintbox. *Integrative Biology*, *2*(2-3), 77-93.

Verish, C., Strawhacker, A., Bers, M., & Shaer, O. (2018). CRISPEE: A Tangible Gene Editing Platform for Early Childhood. In *Proceedings of the Twelfth International Conference on Tangible, Embedded, and Embodied Interaction* (pp. 101-107). ACM.

Walker, J. T., & Kafai, Y. B. (2021). The Biodesign Studio: Constructions and Reflections of High School Youth on Making with Living Media. *British Journal of Educational Technology*, *00*, 1-14. doi.org/doi.org/10.1111/bjet.13081

Walker, J. T., Shaw, M., Kafai, Y., & Lui, D. (2018). Biohacking Food: A Case Study of Science Inquiry and Design Reflections about a Synthetic Biology High School Workshop. In J. a. L. Kay, R. (Ed.), *Rethinking Learning in the Digital Age: Making the Learning Sciences Count, In Proceedings of the 13th International Conference of the Learning Sciences (ICLS) 2018* (Vol. 3). International Society of the Learning Sciences. repository.isls.org//handle/1/733

Yeast Art Project. (2019). yeastart.org/

Zyga, L. (2017). Digitally printed cyanobacteria can power small electronic devices. *Phys.org*. phys.org/news/2017-11-digitally-cyanobacteria-power-small-electronic.html

For Real: Some Modern Things to Do with a Computer

Martin Levins

"Twenty things to do with a computer" sounds like an ad you hear on late night television: "It shreds! It slices! It dices…"

I don't mean to dishonor the work of Papert & Solomon—in fact I want to celebrate it, but the context of their 1971 paper is that of the dawn of newfangled educational technology and kitchen gadgets. The seventies were the age of the mainframe and beyond the horizon of the average classroom aside from a few hobbyists. In 1971, I was programming using punch cards that I would carefully carry to the computing center (they were not numbered, so dropping them was a nightmare) and wait 2–3 weeks for them to be returned with the inevitable "there was an error."

In the late seventies, we saw the beginnings of the preparing-students-for-the-workplace road, which has continued today. It was "Everyone will need to know how to use computers" which turned into "Everyone will need to know Microsoft Word" in the late eighties. Of course, no one really used a word processor, they just used a computer as an electronic typewriter—concepts such as outlining, tabulation, and styles were as mysterious and unused then, as they are now. (I still receive documents with page breaks generated by several presses of the Enter key and centering of titles using the space bar.) Does this remind you of the "Everyone can code" mantra that we see today?

After dalliances with the digital, including an annoying Sinclair ZX80 and an Australian designed 6502 processor machine, I was involved in the school rollout of BBC computers in South Australia in the early eighties. The manufacturers had clearly read Papert and Solomon as these machines had:

- Color output
- Serial and parallel ports
- Second processor communication
- Analog and digital interfaces (they were called expansion ports then)

You could do marvelous things with that computer. For example, using that machine in 1988, by connecting a thermocouple to one of the ports, sixteen-year-olds were able to display a cooling curve for solidifying metals using the built-in (and excellent) BASIC language.

Now, we can do the same thing with the micro:bit (curiously also brought to life by the BBC) with six-year-olds, although I doubt you'll see this in a school near you today (this has nothing to do with the subject matter).

Our school connected the BBCs to one of the world's first physical turtles—the Tasman turtle, made by Denning Branch International in Hobart, Tasmania (that's that little triangular bit that everyone leaves off a map of Australia).[1] They released their first robot product, the Tasman Turtle, in 1979. This Logo-based educational robot featured speech recognition, speech synthesis, an electronic compass, touch sensors, a drawing pen, stepper motor motion control, and later, an infrared RS232 interface and expansions ports. Costly, though, with prices in excess of $2,000 AUD (nearly $10,000 USD in 2021).

We borrowed one from a university and with elementary school children, we drew, learned geometry, algorithmic thinking and (gosh) recursion. Of course, that was "outside" of school hours so was considered a quirk, not really a learning tool, despite being told that kids that age couldn't do that sort of math. (That wouldn't happen today, would it?)

Where are we today?

Like a lot of things digital, we have cheaper, smaller, USB, WiFi and Bluetooth connected, gadgets. The turtle has morphed into the BeeBot, or the BlueBot, or the Sphero (albeit nowhere near as powerful).

And we have STEM. STEM continues the "we need workers" trope we've seen before with "everyone must know Office." "Everyone can code" is the mantra, as if decomposition of problems, specification, data collection, pattern recognition, algorithm abstraction, and modeling and simulation were not important in developing solutions. It also projects the merging of disciplines as a new subject, or as a club that meets after school or at lunch.

It's confused: STEM becomes STEAM becomes STREAM… (add your own acronym here). Wikipedia lists twenty-three acronyms for various mixtures of traditional disciplines.[2] Education seems to have a fascination with acronyms that would rival the output of the most avid of social media influencers.[3]

As much as I disparage the bandwagon that is STEM (or whatever it's called this week), the practice of looking at things through different lenses, of seeing the need for and relationship between different disciplines, and of noticing the blur between them is extremely valuable. The difficulty is that it is often put into a separately labeled room implying that it occurs there only.

So, what would a modern *Twenty Things to Do with a Computer* look like? I can suggest a few.

In Elementary School, We Can...

Ask students to teach a younger student something by writing a story in Scratch Jr or Scratch

Improving their own literacy in the process, they must also think empathetically, putting themselves in the shoes of the younger child, reflecting on the process of learning as a result. Aboriginal people (including students) in the Northern Territory of Australia are using this approach to teach both their culture and written language, as well as English.

Explore math concepts using Scratch

I was asked to "do some coding" by a Grade 4 classroom teacher. After showing students how to access Scratch and then leaving the room, I came back ten days later and asked: "What have you done?"

They had learned the Cartesian coordinate system (because they had to, so they could move a sprite to where they wanted), how to create their own sprites (because they had to—they didn't want the ones in the library), and learnt the power of variables (because they had to for scoring a game). When asked, they couldn't remember how they learned these things, or who told them (it wasn't the teacher). Their pronunciation of variables came out as "var-eye-abels" indicating to me that they'd only seen it written somewhere.

It doesn't need to be Scratch, of course, but this is accessible to almost all, in terms of language as well as being able to get it on a computer. I do miss Logo though. I miss the simple "to xxx" where I explain to the machine what I want it to do. I need clarity of purpose and clarity of language to do that.

Keep your garden growing using microcontrollers

When asked if there was a problem that bothered them, students in a multi-age small school in western New South Wales told me that they spent ages making a kitchen garden only to have it die during the six weeks of summer holidays over Christmas.

"Why does it die?" I asked. "Because everyone forgets to water it."

Could we fix that by making it automatic? Eighteen months later, after learning how to measure light levels, soil moisture, how to turn on a tap electrically, and how solar panels can charge batteries, then studying water availability, root systems, soil moisture retention, and when it was best to water plants, a system emerged that followed this algorithm:

```
The water checker should run all the time
If the soil is dry, AND it's dark
    Wait 4 hours
    then water the garden
    Water for an hour and see how things are then
Otherwise turn off the tap
```

We also discovered that the primary cause of plant death in Australia, a very dry continent, was over-watering! You can see an overview of the project at youtu.be/IRdM-zO1igY.

Make more efficient blades for wind turbines

In our region, wind power is big. Grade 3/4 asked: "How do they work?" So we looked for answers and saw pictures. We built our own models of wind turbines using popsicle sticks and the inners of paper towel rolls, connected to a hobby motor that would be spun by the blades. We held our models one meter from a fan, connected the hobby motor to a micro:bit, and displayed the number that corresponded to the voltage produced by the motor.

I'm summarizing here, as there was significantly more work done to learn about the history of windmills and how they work, how micro:bits work, and looking closely at the design of the turbine blades. We looked at the earliest windmills (no, they're not in the Netherlands—look it up) and how the work of David Unaipon, an aboriginal man, theorized about using twin boomerangs as the blades of a helicopter.[4]

Now we could ask, "What if I changed the shape of my blades?" and predict whether it would produce a larger or smaller number on the micro:bit.

Maintain personal space using a proximity sensor

Grades 5/6 calibrated ultrasonic sensors to measure when someone came within 1.5 meters as a COVID-19 physical distancing checker, then theorized about using it as a way of protecting personal space and how big a distance that should be.

Communicate without words using a gesture sensor

After fiddling with gesture sensors, a class was given the task: "You have nine gestures, what are the most important things you might need to say?" and built a sensor/micro:bit system that "spoke" the important things by displaying rolling words or icons on the display.

The tech was easy, but it sponsored a lively (and wonderful) discussion about what the nine things should be.

Build an earthquake proof building using an accelerometer

The same group, later in the year, were studying earthquakes, so we used the accelerometer in a micro:bit and shaking a table to produce a chart onscreen showing movement in the X direction, then the Y, then the Z, exporting results to a spreadsheet to examine what modifications they could make to their model building to make it most resistant to particular types of earthquake.

In Middle School, We Can...

Investigate data

Let's deal with collecting, cleaning, analyzing, and visualizing data. (I can hear the moans from here.) Or we could ask: "Where in the world can I buy the cheapest Big Mac?" Intrigued? I thought so. Have a look at this video youtu.be/QyfOC3RK2q0 .

Investigate our classroom environment

Using micro:bits (for block, Python, or JavaScript coding) or simple sketches in the Arduino development environment, we can use cheap components such as a Light Dependent Resistor, the DHT11 temperature and humidity sensor, and a simple microcontroller with built-in WiFi, such as the member of the ESP family, to broadcast environmental measurements to the cloud. (You don't need an Arduino board to do this, the ESP family of controllers will do it all themselves.)

We can measure whether our classrooms are too hot, too humid, too dry, too cold, or too dark for effective learning.

We can ask the question: "Are we being set up to fail?"

Investigate our world

Our computing environment is vastly different to that used by Papert & Solomon—we have one in our pocket. Forget complex probes and drivers and leads and other distractions. (Where does this plug go?)

Measure and record motion, sound, light, barometric pressure, gravitational and magnetic fields, simple harmonic motion, the Doppler effect, and the audio spectrum using your phone. If your school hasn't banned mobile phones yet (sigh) have your students download PhyPhox (you should too!) and start investigating.

What Are We Learning?

The kids who do these sorts of investigations are working with issues that they have identified or are interested in. (Motivation, check. Individualization, check.) But they are also learning how their world works. Like Douglas Adams' character Arthur Dent in *The Hitchhiker's Guide to the Galaxy*, we don't always appreciate how our world is full of wonderful stuff, and, also like Arthur, we often don't understand it. Arthur C Clarke's "any sufficiently advanced technology is indistinguishable from magic" is apposite here.

After a teacher professional learning session where we were investigating what we could do with microcontrollers, and looking at the soil moisture garden project, I asked for feedback. One of the participants said, "I can see how my automatic windscreen wipers work now."

Wonderful.

Kids who are exposed to the sorts of investigations discussed in this essay can also see how they can change things.

Powerful.

The ideas, the observations, the theorizing of Papert and Solomon remain just as relevant today as they were fifty years ago. Educators who have read *Twenty Things*, or perhaps those reading this will see the power that the computer contributes to learning.

Yet this use of computers, and the creativity and deep learning which ensues, still is uncommon, still has to be explained, still needs support, and still needs advocacy.

We have just begun to sell.

Notes
1 The history of the Tasman Turtle southcom.com.au/~robot/history.html
2 Variations of STEM en.wikipedia.org/wiki/Science,_technology,_engineering,_and_mathematics
3 Secret Teacher: WALT, WILF, EBI – we're awash with useless acronyms theguardian.com/teacher-network/2015/dec/26/secret-teacher-awash-with-useless-acronyms
4 David Unaipon en.wikipedia.org/wiki/David_Unaipon

Twenty Ways to Facilitate Twenty Things to Do with a Computer

Carmelo Presicce, Giulio Bonanome, & Angela Sofia Lombardo

Introduction

Reading *Twenty Things to Do with a Computer*, we were fascinated by the range of possibilities envisioned by the authors so long ago. Seymour Papert and Cynthia Solomon were imagining new possibilities for the future while they were facilitating experiences with children around many of those activities. In fact, some of the activities they describe in their visionary and inspiring paper emerged by working side-by-side with children.

Today the range of possibilities for kids to do things with the computer is richer than ever. And still, not every activity or technology offers kids a playful, creative, engaging, meaningful experience like the twenty described by Papert and Solomon. We started wondering: "What did those activities look like in practice"? We loved the range of activities (the *what*), but we were curious about *how* to facilitate those experiences.

We are particularly interested in facilitation because of our work as organizers and volunteer mentors in CoderDojo, an international network of free coding clubs for children, and also as designers and facilitators of many teacher development programs in Italy and globally. Our backgrounds are different (technical, psychologic, humanistic), and we strive to bring these views together as we continue to learn how to be good facilitators in the field.

In this essay we draw from our direct experience as educators of creative computational workshops for children and adults, both in and out of school. In our workshops, we typically use Scratch, the popular programming language and online community developed at MIT Media Lab. Inspired by the pragmatism of the *Twenty Things* paper, we list twenty concrete strategies, organizing them in three parts that roughly correspond to what happens before, during, and after our workshops.

Part 1 – Prepare

We recently had the opportunity to speak to Cynthia Solomon about this subject: "What would you suggest to educators who want to help children make the twenty things today—and hundreds more?" Cynthia replied with her typical sharp and frank tone, like it was the most obvious thing: "Teachers need to be prepared!" This prompted us to ask: "How do *we* get prepared? How can *we* help others to prepare?" Here are some ideas born out of that conversation.

Wear the learner's hat

A good facilitator is, first and foremost, a good learner. No matter how familiar you are with computational tools and ideas, or how experienced you are in the art of facilitation, it is important to be reminded of what it feels like to participate in an activity as a learner.

Today there are many hands-on learning experiences for educators, in person or online. One of our favorite examples of Scratch activities for educators is Getting Unstuck, organized by the Creative Computing group at Harvard, where educators are invited to create and share a Scratch project every single day for a few weeks. We love to participate in this experience because it fully engages us as learners. We find ourselves staying up late to work on our Scratch projects, we experience the joy and frustrations of the creative process, and we always learn something new by reflecting on our own experience and seeing other people's projects. Plus, by observing how organizers design and facilitate the experience, we discover interesting activity prompts, design principles, and facilitation strategies that we can remix and apply with our students.

Make time for pizza

In our CoderDojo clubs we welcome volunteer facilitators from a wide variety of backgrounds, from school teachers (often intimidated by technology) to software developers (often intimidated by children). Working with people with a diverse range of skills and perspectives is extremely important, but learning from each other doesn't come automatically by being in the same room—it requires building strong relationships and trust.

We can't overstate how important it has been for our group of facilitators to meet outside of work. The most interesting discussions and bonding among facilitators happen in front of a pizza, right after the workshop or at the end of a planning meeting. Teachers can build and consolidate trust relationships outside of school and learn from each other in informal settings. For example, Scratch Educator Meetups are informal groups of educators who meet on Saturdays to experiment and share ideas, activities, practices... and food!

When hanging out is not possible (like in the middle of a pandemic), there are online communities you can join. We know it's not as tasty as eating a pizza in Italy, but if necessary, a virtual tea over Zoom can do the job.

Choose a theme, or pick a card

Some coding activities consist of puzzles where students need to find the correct answer, like finding the only correct way out of a maze. While this can be interesting for some students, it is not enough to help students gain computational fluency (Resnick & Rusk, 2020). In our experience, open-ended activities engage a wider range of students and provide more opportunities for learning. When they are working on a project, students naturally encounter problems and are more motivated to solve them. Still, coming up with a compelling and generative theme for projects might be difficult. If you need inspiration for creative prompts, pick a Scratch card!

The activities in the Scratch Cards propose generative themes that can lead to a variety of outcomes, while providing detailed guidance and support. Example activities include—animate the letters of your name, create a chasing videogame, or invent a story. Even if you don't use Scratch with your students, the Scratch Cards are a great example of how to design generative prompts and provide open-ended scaffolding. Then, design your own activity cards and try them out with your students.

Prepare good examples

When designing open-ended activities, it is crucial to inspire students by showing them a wide range of possibilities. One common mistake is to show them only one example of a very complex project made by an expert. In one of our first CoderDojo workshops, one of the mentors proudly showed off a cool spaceship videogame, featuring hundreds of blocks and making use of advanced computational ideas. While the kids (and the adults) in the room were very impressed, the example wasn't very generative—students wanted to play the game, but weren't inspired to make their own. Plus, showing only one example pushed students to imitate it, resulting in a very narrow range of projects.

Rather than showing off our skills as experienced developers, we instead try to prepare a wide variety of sample projects, at least three or four, to give a sense of the possibilities and to show different interpretations of the prompt. We show advanced examples, but we also make sure to show projects that are simple, unfinished, or that don't work perfectly—yet. Some students feel excited because they know that they can do better, others feel reassured that everyone can work at their own pace and make mistakes. By providing examples, we also try to *set* an example.

Set up the space

Setting up the space is one of the most overlooked elements of the design of a learning experience, especially when it has to do with computers. The typical layout of a computer lab where students sit in rows at fixed workstations is far from the ideal place for a hands-on workshop. Students can't look at each other's faces and screens, let alone collaborate, inspire, or help each other. Even for facilitators it is often hard to move around and support students in those spaces, as they are designed around a model where the teacher is supposed to stay at the front of the room.

We aren't always able to choose or set up the space, but when we can, we fully leverage the opportunity. As soon we enter a room, we start moving tables and chairs around. When possible, we like to have students sitting around tables in small pods using laptop computers. It doesn't matter if people aren't facing the projector screen, it's more important that students can easily move and interact with each other.

Similar considerations apply to online spaces. When we moved our workshops online because of the pandemic, we chose video conferencing tools that support students working and interacting in small groups in breakout rooms, and multiple screen sharing so that they can see what others are doing at any moment and get inspiration and support. Whether you work in a physical or online environment, think about ways to support students' interactions—even small changes can make a huge difference.

Part 2 – Practice

No matter how much you prepare, it never feels like enough because you can't anticipate what you'll need to know as you facilitate. As we discussed with Cynthia Solomon, to be prepared also means to be prepared to improvise and take detours from what you had originally planned. We often reassure teachers that they don't need to be computer scientists to introduce Scratch to their students, and we encourage them to "jump in the water" even though they might not know how to swim—yet. Of course, it's important to learn some rudiments and bring resources that can act as swimming floats, but nothing can replace practice in the art of facilitation—the more you facilitate, the more you learn. Here are some ideas about how we facilitate computational activities.

Set the tone

Helping students feel comfortable is important in any learning experience, but it is particularly important for computational activities. Some people are intimidated by technology and might see computers as unfriendly and cold. That's why from the very beginning, we try to create a warm and friendly environment for everyone.

Setting an informal tone works very well even when we work with adults, such as university students, or in our teacher professional development workshops. We love experimenting with ice-breaker activities that make people connect, relax and laugh, or we invent silly ways to take attendance. Even just asking: "What did you have for breakfast, today?" helps people connect and relax.

Of course, different warm-up strategies might be appropriate in different environments and each facilitator has different preferences and their personal style. In any case, reducing the distance between students and teachers and creating a relaxed and playful environment is not only more effective, but also more fun!

Get hands-on as soon as possible

When introducing a computational activity or a new tool to a group of students, it can be hard to resist the temptation to dump a lot of information upfront. Although it is important to provide students with enough context before diving in, sometimes educators indulge in talking for a long time before students can even see what they are talking about and this quickly brings their engagement down.

In our workshops, whether they are for children or for educators, we always try to minimize the time between the session begins and when participants can start experimenting. We typically keep the introduction less than 15 minutes. Once students are engaged in their work, questions will naturally arise and it will be possible to share information when it's most relevant.

Speak "drinkable"

One of the goals of computational activities is to help students acquire a vocabulary to express computational ideas, but sometimes technical language is a barrier to learning. Keeping this in mind, we always try to speak in a simple and understandable way and we gradually introduce technical terms only after we notice that students have developed enough familiarity with the concept. In Italian, the colloquial expression *"parla potabile"* literally means: speak in such a way that others can "drink" what you say.

For example, when we introduce Scratch we don't need kids to learn a formal definition of *sprite* or *script*—it's more important that they create their own understanding by using them. Once they are familiar with the idea of what a character is and what you can do with it, it's much easier for them to realize that it's the same thing that we sometimes call *sprite*.

Let trucks fly

In one of our workshops for children, we were showing how to use the *glide* block in Scratch to make characters move around the screen, showed a couple of examples, and invited kids to make their own characters move. We noticed a parent sitting next to their son telling him something like: "This is wrong, that's not what you are supposed to do." One of the facilitators went closer to check—the kid had created a funny story where a truck was lifting off, but his mum kept insisting that "trucks don't fly." This was an opportunity for us to kindly reassure his worried mum, in Scratch trucks *could* fly, and she was happy to realize that her son was doing a great job using both programming blocks and his fervid imagination.

When facilitating we always try to support children's ideas, even when they look crazy (actually, we love crazy ideas)! Sometimes children take different paths to explore the ideas we want to highlight, like in the flying truck example. Other times they go in a totally different direction and they encounter ideas and problems we weren't expecting. We love to see children taking the initiative and the courage to explore uncharted territories, and every time they ask, "Can I do this?" we do our best to say "Yes!"

Ask: How is it going?

One of the best things a facilitator can do is to listen and to observe students, constantly trying to guess what they are thinking and how they are feeling. Looking at screens and faces (in person or in a video call) can give us a sense of how everyone is doing, but of course it's hard to know it unless they tell us. A simple and genuine: "How is it going?" goes a long way.

In our experience, we noticed that students of all ages are often reluctant to acknowledge a struggle or to ask a question unless we check in with them individually.

Check in often, but not too often! While it's important for a facilitator to have a sense of how students are doing, it's also important to give them time and space to struggle productively with problems and experiment on their own.

Ask: What have you tried?

When a student asks for help, we always feel the temptation to give them a solution right away. Of course, for trivial issues (for example, related to the user interface) there is no need to hide the answer, but many problems encountered while coding are an opportunity for the student to explore and discover. Even when a facilitator guides a student toward a solution, there is the risk of guiding them toward the solution that is in the facilitator's head. That's why it's always useful to ask: "What have you tried?"

When students describe a problem, they often suddenly realize how to solve it. Even when this doesn't happen, learning about their previous attempts can help you understand what they know and what they think—"crawl into their heads", as Cynthia Solomon once put it. Being open to students' ideas, experimenting, and testing hypotheses together is a rich learning experience for a facilitator as well. The goal is not to find the best idea, but supporting the "having of wonderful ideas" (Duckworth, 1972).

Help students help each other

While coding, oftentimes a student might ask a question that some other student might know how to answer. When possible and appropriate, we act as connectors and encourage students to help each other. This can be a precious opportunity for students to get to learn from each and to get to know each other better.

We love to see peer learning happening, but we are also aware of the risks, especially those related to power dynamics among children. Through experience, we have learned to avoid situations in which some kids are invested by adults in formal roles of facilitators. We instead prefer to create situations in which children help each other in more authentic and informal ways, for example by chatting with their neighbors as peers.

Work together fairly

What happens when students, instead of working individually, engage in a four-handed or six-handed creative coding activity? In the software industry, pair programming is very common among developers because working in pairs and comparing ideas improves the quality of the code. In an educational context, working in pairs or small groups is also a valuable opportunity to build social skills.

Working in pairs or in small groups can be fun and exciting, but it can also be frustrating as it requires continuous negotiation of ideas and watching carefully for unbalanced power dynamics. As a facilitator, there are several things you can do to help make collaboration a rich learning opportunity. Sometimes roles naturally emerge, other times it's better to assign them. A classic strategy is to have students switch frequently between the role of the driver (who controls keyboard and mouse) and the navigator (who observes and comments).

It is also important to experiment with the composition of the groups—observe how people work together, notice the power dynamics, intervene when necessary, and provide opportunities for students to work with others in a healthy way.

Noise is nice (most times)

When a learning experience involves exploration, construction, and collaboration, it's completely normal to expect some movement and, above all, some noise. That noise is often a good sign—it is a sign of life. Try to recognize the joyful cheers when something suddenly works, the intense chatting of a group confronting different ideas, and the voice of a child helping another to debug.

Of course, noise is not always enjoyable or productive, and some people need a quiet space to focus. Rather than imposing silence, try to understand what type of noise you are hearing and strive for the right balance between lively and respectful.

Use the shark fin

It's great to see engaged children working on their projects, but sometimes it's also important to take a break from time to time. When we are in front of a screen, it's easy to forget that in addition to a head, we also have a body that needs to move, eat, and breathe fresh air. Also, taking a break can help us get unstuck or get new ideas.

Halfway through our workshops we always schedule a break so that kids can have a snack together and socialize. If you have trouble getting children (or adults) to move their hands away from the keyboard, you can invite people to do the *shark fin*—everyone puts their hands on their head mimicking a shark fin, and kids and adults move together towards food as a shoal of sharks.

Share and care

Even when students engage in individual projects, they can learn from each other by sharing their work. For example, we often encourage students to have a look at what others are working on to get ideas and inspiration. Children and teachers are often surprised because this is usually forbidden in schools. Instead of creating a competitive environment, we try to promote a culture of cooperation in which students are happy to see their ideas being appreciated and remixed by others.

We also make time for students to show their projects at the end of a workshop, or in the last session of a series. We leave it optional for children to present in the final show and tell, but we also try to make it less intimidating. For example, we make it a point to celebrate all projects, no matter their complexity, and reassure everyone that sharing a work-in-progress is always welcome and that a project is never really ready. We also collect Scratch projects in a shared online studio so that everyone can check them out later, see the code, and leave some comments.

As facilitators we try to provide personalized and constructive feedback (not just a generic "like"), and we encourage our students to do the same. Giving good feedback is never easy, as it requires empathy and practice. We try to set a good example by using structures such as, "What I liked about your project is …" or "I wonder what it will be if …"—doing our best to be more thoughtful and less judgmental.

Part 3 – Reflect

There is no learning without reflection, and it's important to make time to do it. Whether it happens in the heat of the moment or after some time with a cooler head, reflecting is a habit that can be cultivated in several ways, alone or with others. The challenge is to shift the attention away from the mere evaluation of a tangible product, and focus instead on the underlying creative process that made it possible. For us, the goal is to create a context where children develop the habit to reflect on their own practice and facilitators get used to debugging their own practice.

Ask about their process

The final show-and-tell or the project gallery walk can be valuable opportunities to help students of all ages reflect on their creative process. As facilitators we usually ask questions that allow them to share their experiences and notice significant aspects. For example: What was challenging? What is the part of your project you are particularly proud of? What would you do if you had more time?

If you have observed each student working, you can also ask about aspects of their experience that are worth highlighting. For example: "I noticed your game keeps the score, how did you do that?" or "I saw you drew your own character, how did you get the idea?" These questions have no right or wrong answers, and help students recognize and give value to aspects of their creative process that they didn't think they were worth mentioning. The goal is not to evaluate, but to consolidate a reflective practice that will transfer to other projects in the future.

Debrief

As soon as the session is over, when memories are still fresh, find the time to reflect with others about what just happened and how it went. Sometimes we organize observations using three colors: Green: What went well? Red: What do we need to change next time? Yellow: What questions do we have?

In our debriefs, we noticed a tendency to focus more on the logistical and technical aspects of the experience, and less on the pedagogical aspects of our personal experience as facilitators. Of course, it's easier to talk about technical issues rather than questioning our own interactions with the children or giving constructive feedback to other facilitators without hurting their feelings. But getting feedback from another facilitator is the only way we can see our blind spots, and we try to use debriefs to promote honest and constructive exchange and growth.

Even when you don't have other facilitators to debrief with, it's always worth taking the time to reflect on your experience. What did you notice about your interactions? What were the moments in which you weren't sure what to do? What will you try next time?

Take notes

Taking notes is a simple but powerful habit. Whether you use a pencil or your smartphone, the important thing is that you observe carefully (and discretely). What are you noticing in the environment? What is something surprising or unexpected a child said or made? We know it's very hard to document while facilitating, but it's something worth practicing. Taking photos can also be very helpful to capture an artifact or to document an interaction.

If you can only take mental notes, try to write something down as soon as possible, right after the session. The act of writing down your impressions when they are still vivid in your mind is an incredible way to increase your awareness as a facilitator—at the very least you can notice what you are noticing, seek to understand what was important and valuable for you about the experience, and how it changes as you grow as a facilitator.

Your notes and reflections can also be very helpful for others, more often than you think. If you work in a team or with a colleague, notes can be a great starting point for a discussion. Share more broadly if you can—for us, writing a blog post from time to time (or a long essay like the one you are reading) has been worth the effort.

Reflection line

Think up your twenty and more ways to facilitate.

Epilogue: How To Make These Things Happen

The list of facilitation tips we shared is inevitably incomplete, and it's something we keep reflecting and iterating on. Even though this is far from being an exhaustive checklist, the collaborative process we went through as we wrote it has been a rich learning experience. We faced the dilemma of choosing which aspects of our facilitation practice were worth sharing, the issue of bringing concrete examples that could be relevant in other contexts, and the huge challenge of trying to synthesize big ideas without trivializing them. Our hope is that readers will be able to see the underlying pedagogical values that connect all those points, and will be able—as we say in Italian—to look at the moon and not at the finger.

What does this have to do with computing? We believe that the future of computing education has to do less with computing and more with education. In the fifty years that separates us from Papert and Solomon's essay, technology has spread widely around the world, but constructionist ideas and practices have not. This is not so surprising, culture takes a longer time to shift. As technology becomes more pervasive than ever, we still run the risk of falling into technocentrism—the tendency of centering the attention on the computers rather than focusing on the most important components of educational situations—people and cultures (Papert, 1987). As Mitchel Resnick and Natalie Rusk (2020) note, we are at a crossroad, and avoiding technocentrism requires a deliberate choice from each of the millions of educators, designers, and policymakers around the world.

Each of us can contribute by creating the conditions for children to create and express themselves with computers, help each other, share their work, exchange constructive feedback, and reflect on their learning process. Every move you make in that direction can get us a step closer to the vision that Papert and Solomon inspired us to imagine. We know it is hard, we hope it's hard fun!

References

Duckworth, E. (1972). The Having of Wonderful Ideas. *Harvard Educational Review, 42*(2), 217-231. llk. media.mit.edu/courses/readings/duckworth-chap1.pdf

Papert, S. (1987). Information Technology and Education: Computer Criticism vs. Technocentric Thinking. *Educational Researcher, 16*(1), 22-30. learning.media.mit.edu/courses/mas713/readings/Papert,%20technocentric%20thinking.pdf

Resnick, M., & Rusk, N. (2020). Coding at a Crossroads. *Communications of the ACM, 63*(11), 120-127. web.media.mit.edu/~mres/papers/CACM-Coding-At-Crossroads.pdf

A Place for Experimentation: The Library

Carolyn Foote

Fifty years ago, Seymour Papert and Cynthia Solomon published *Twenty Things to Do with a Computer*, asking "Why not use them to produce some action?" Fifty years later, schools, for the most part, have been unable to break out of the confines of presenting material to students, fully formed, rather than using computing to "produce action." There are of course many exceptions—project-based learning, programming challenges, Montessori schools, etc. But even computer science courses, especially those with Advanced Placement (AP) curriculum, are primarily scripted. So even if students are "producing action" in AP Computer Science, much of it is formulaic. What Papert and Solomon wrote, sadly still holds true in too many places: "There is no better reason than the intellectual timidity of the computers-in-education community, which seems remarkably reluctant to use the computers for any purpose that fails to look very much like something that has been taught in schools for the past centuries."

Although there are a plethora of new audio or video tools for student response to assignments, we need to remember that these mostly are just different ways to deliver responses. They aren't specifically designed to ask students to tinker or create something new, or to engage in the "action" that Papert and Solomon wrote about.

But one place in traditional schools that their vision can and does come to life are school libraries. Librarians across the US and around the world have embraced a makerspace mentality, including making in their portfolio of student activities and using components involving robotics and computer science. They have embraced tinkering, experimenting and play for the sake of play, understanding that play equals learning. The early components Solomon and Papert write about, the Logo language and the robotic turtle, have been mostly supplanted by LEGO Mindstorms, and newer items like Sphero, Little Bits, Makey Makey, etc., all of which can now be found in many school libraries (elementary especially), and vary in affordability. Bird Brain Technologies and Trashbots are also found in some schools and allow common objects like cardboard scraps to be utilized in robot building. Students can use apps along with these devices to use the basics of block coding to "produce action," to invent solutions to problems or challenges, and to construct meaning by doing. Some libraries have started coding clubs or joined organizations like Girls Who Code which carry coding beyond simpler applications. But in all these cases, the library serves as a gateway to engage students with coding. The librarian can be a guide, even with limited expertise, because student groups can use the tools to develop their own actions. Librarians can provide spaces, build prompts, and find examples, books, and resources that inexperienced students might need to get started.

A former student of mine, Sidharth Srinivasan, co-founded a company called Trashbots with his brother Rohit, a few years ago. (Trashbots are components that can be used with a tablet app that the brothers created so children can design and code inexpensive cardboard robots.) Sidharth says that when he was younger, he thought libraries were all about books, but as he got to middle school, he experienced libraries as more of a community center for schools. "That is what my view on libraries transformed into—they can make value offerings in the community. Not just literacy with writing and reading, but STEM literacy, technology literacy—that's now all a library's job." He now considers libraries "a community bastion for literacy."

The library's ability to foster and support play, a goal which the rest of a school curriculum isn't truly focused around, is important to the use of coding and robotics exploration. Sidharth comments, "A lot of education is very rote, and basically regurgitation. Not really using any creativity….The role of play is very very important because it almost masks the fact that they are learning." In a real-life coding situation, he explains, if someone is told to go code something, "You have to use your creativity around what functions do I need to be coding, what architecture do I need to be thinking of. All of that involves a lot of creativity skills." Providing spaces and the mindset to support student creativity is paramount for libraries, as Sidharth notes.

Trashbots grew out of visits the brothers made to Indian orphanages. They quickly realized the lack of supplies and access made it challenging to get students there started in coding. That access is another key libraries provide—they are a space accessible to all the students in a school or community, and provide access to materials that students might not be able to afford otherwise.

Part of supporting this creativity is finding ways to make space in a traditional school's library physical space. Whether it's creating a permanent space or finding mobile storage, librarians excel at carving out opportunities for students. One of the cleverest public spaces I've seen is at the Smithsonian National Museum of American History in their Draper Spark!Lab. They have a series of stations with invitational books, supplies for students to investigate/create with, and a rolling cabinet with shelves, tabletop, and drawers for storage—a design which schools could easily replicate.

For libraries that don't have dedicated space, it is possible to use a rolling table or cabinet that can not only store items but also be used to engage with the items. There are a myriad of examples online for storage. It's important to keep an eye on the real purpose, rather than get caught up in clever storage—but it's a challenge that librarians are eager to address.

Draper Spark!Lab

More importantly what's needed to support Solomon and Papert's vision is administrative vision, and a larger understanding of libraries as idea spaces where students interact with ideas. Similarly, administrators need an understanding (especially emerging from a year of COVID-19) of the digital resources that librarians can gather to help students create and code at home. Librarians and other professionals can help administrators see the real value of providing space and time for students to engage in creative problem solving in libraries.

Libraries have always been places where people construct meaning—by interacting with printed texts, electronic texts, other people, librarians, and now with crafts and robotics. The sense of discovery is intrinsic in a space that isn't bound as much by curriculum, achievement test scores, or expectations. Libraries are centered around inquiry, a fact which many people forget because they think they are centered around books. But what are books but collections of people's questions and musings, meant to make sense of the world through story?

Libraries are the heart of inquiry, the place that centers around supporting student curiosity. It is that very philosophy that makes experimentation with robotics in library settings a good fit.

Computer Modeling, Data Collection, and Programming in Middle School Science

Donna Collins

In the summer of 1971, while Seymour Papert and Cynthia Solomon first published *Twenty Things to Do with a Computer*, I was just finishing up the third grade. My days were filled with things that occupy the nine-year-old mind, the joy of a whole summer away from school, spending time outside all day, exploring the woods, building forts, reading new books, and of course Saturday morning cartoons.

One of my favorite Saturday morning cartoons, *The Jetsons*, was already in reruns. I would watch and wonder when we would have some of the futuristic things that Elroy had, robots, teachers, doctors via computer screens, and especially flying cars.

Where Papert and Solomon focused their paper on things to do with a computer, my curiosity from a young age has been in the area of how things work. What would happen if I twist the bars of my playpen? (Yes, playpens had bars back in the early 1960s.) Why does the spring of my crib bounce? (To the cringe of my sisters who slept in the same room and had to listen to me testing the spring.) How do hinges work? Why did the wheel on my trike fall off? Why is pulling my wagon full of my rock treasures so much harder than pulling it alone? Just a few of many things that I explored as a child with the simple rules of our family and neighborhood to be home when Mom called, stay off the main road, and most of all to stay out of the pond where there was quicksand. My parents encouraged us to learn things of our own interest and in our own way.

In their paper, Papert and Solomon explain ways to teach both children and adults programming as a means for greater understanding of all educational content areas. Unfortunately, for many of us who were children at the time that this paper was written, we were being educated as Papert and Solomon describe, "the same old way." Schools in the small New Hampshire city where we lived did not invest in computers for the classroom at the elementary level nor when I was in high school. It wasn't until I was in college that I had my first experiences with computers, where I eventually minored in computer science, with a focus on programming.

Fast forward to 2021, a long and interesting fifty years after Papert and Solomon published their paper, and finally, due to COVID–19 and remote schooling, one of Seymour Papert's dreams of computers in the classroom, one computer per child has finally happened for the first time. This might not be true in all schools or school districts, but in my school we were able to make it happen this year. In previous years computer use in the classroom was scheduled with specific lessons and planning around the needs of other teachers in our building. This year we have had the opportunity to use the computers at any time to meet student needs for things such as completing calculations for an acceleration lab on a spreadsheet instead of by hand with a calculator and paper, playing math games, sharing stories in language arts and creating unique Spanish culture slideshows.

Personally, I have several things that I do with computers with middle schoolers—sixth, seventh and eighth graders. Some are fun programming activities, or using modeling software to understand science concepts, and even using different ArcGIS apps to gather data and to create interesting connections between where we live and the Earth as a biosphere. Today we can even use our phones as tools for science with data collection applications that we can program and by the simple task of taking photos of landscapes or through a microscope.

In most respects I use the same modeling software with middle schoolers that is often used in high school and in some cases college to study and understand climate change and how earth systems work together in our everchanging world.

I find it interesting that modeling or data collection are not among of the twenty things mentioned in the paper, even though that was probably what most computers were used for by scientists at the time. Perhaps it was just a given that eventually students would do this too, yet it is still rare in middle and even high school science.

Modeling especially gives students a new perspective on their surroundings, and it is a worthwhile exploration for middle school. As students learn about the history of Earth, we begin to work with how scientists know about the age of sediment, fossils, and the evolution of different organisms. Carbon dating is one way that scientists can analyze and determine the age of once living organisms preserved in sediments or in ice. Being able to analyze real data provides the students with insight and computational tools that will serve them well in the data-filled future they will live in.

Modeling Earth Systems - Radiometric Dating

The isee Exchange website[1] is a student version of the Stella modeling software from isee systems. The student software has all of the system building materials that the main but limits the use to two stock blocks to keep the usage free for educational purposes.

When discussing how carbon-14 changes over 5,370 year periods of half-lives into nitrogen-14 students begin to question what a half-life means and how that helps us know how old something is. There is often confusion over what is happening to the isotopes each half-life and where the changed isotope goes.

Using this a system model with some mathematical equations, students are able to see how the number of isotopes that they remove from the carbon-14 stock can be added to the nitrogen-14 stock, resulting in a crossover graph of decreasing and increasing numbers of isotopes for each half-life. Quickly students realize that regardless of the number of starting isotopes, there can only be nine possible half-lives of any radiocarbon or radioactive isotope dating and it is just a matter of applying the number of years of the half-life to the ratios of isotopes to determine the estimated age of an object.

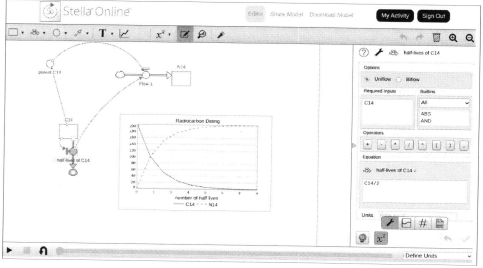

Here is an analysis of the system graph by a sixth grader:

Below is a graph of the results of this model over nine carbon-14 half-lives.

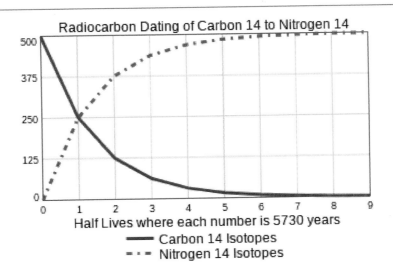

This graph above, shows the progress and time that it takes for the carbon-14 to change into nitrogen-14 as a living thing dies. In this graph you can see that in each half-life the carbon-14 is decreasing, which is the solid line, by half. Then, in each half-life the dashed line, which is nitrogen-14, rises by half.

When looking at my graph I can see that before the first half-life there are more carbon-14 isotopes and less nitrogen-14 isotopes. At the first half life there are an equal number of both types of isotopes, I know this because the lines for carbon-14 and nitrogen-14 both meet at 250 isotopes. Between half-lives 1-5 the isotopes in carbon-14 and nitrogen-14 change at a similar rate, but the amount they change decreases and becomes smaller. Then with each change the angle of each line is not as steep because there are fewer and fewer parent carbon-14 isotopes.

Finally, when I look at my graph between half-life 5 and 9 I notice that the lines don't have as much change because there are less carbon-14 isotopes.[2]

With any modeling software used by children, there will be those kids who get it right away and need little instruction and others who need a bit more time and guidance. I find this software allows students to break a complex idea down into its parts and to gain a better understanding of how radiocarbon dating works.

Another way to use this software is by working with populations. A group of seventh graders used the isee systems modeling software to simulate the results that they had from a game that modeled a wolf pack survival over a fifteen-year period. The survival of the wolf pack depended on a variety of limiting factors and students used the ratios of their game results to create a system model on their computers.

Below is a student analysis of their progress on building the system model:

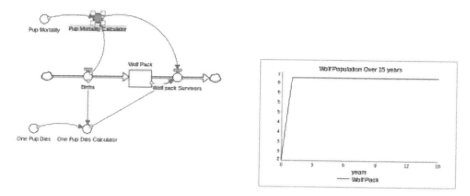

*In the graph above showing pup mortality and one pup dies I used this calculation (Births -1) * One_Pup_Dies of 10%.*

In this graph I factored in another death, which is one pup dies. The graph barely changed at all from the previous graph.

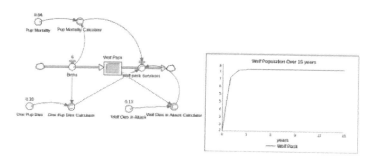

*In the graph above showing pup mortality, one pup dies, and wolf dies in attack I used this calculation (Wolf_Pack -1) * Wolf_Dies_in_Attack of 13%.*

In this graph I added a third death, which is wolf dies in attack. This of course means one pup dies. The graph changed from the previous one, by where this one curves a little more."[3]

The isee systems exchange allows for much more use of creating system models and gives students the opportunity to compare models with what they are observing in the world around them as well as concepts related to science phenomenon and mathematics.

Modeling Global Climate Systems

When faced with the different aspects of learning about climate change, middle school students often have misconceptions related to what they read on the internet, hear at home, and a general lack of experience in understanding complex and long-term climate systems.

A few months before we went into remote learning last spring (March 2020), my seventh and eighth grade science classes were using the EzGCM (Easy Global Climate Modeling) software to visualize climate change over the past fifty years in comparison to fifty-year climate models during the last ice ages.

The EzGCM is a version of the EdGCM software that is set up for high school students with twelve different simulations of climate change from the distant past and projected into the future. The simulations for this modeling system are preset so that students do not have to wait the four to eight hours or longer of processing time that they would using the EdGCM software, and the price is more affordable for my budget. My plan was to use this modeling system again in the spring as we prepared for two field trips to the local seacoast, but unfortunately that did not happen.

To use the EzGCM modeling software there is some instruction needed, mostly on how to set up the models and the content of what we were trying to map such as comparing sea surface temperatures to surface air temperatures over the past fifty years, and creating anomaly maps to show areas of the world that where temperatures are changing faster.

I found that students really enjoyed making their own anomaly maps and quickly figured out that they could show the data in several different ways to support a claim for or against their personal view on climate change. This was especially true of the eighth grade class that I had at the time who were very fond of debating their personal opinions in class and went to great lengths to find information to support their theories.

When I worked with the seventh grade in modeling anomaly maps, their goal was to compare sea surface temperatures with surface air temperatures over a thirty-five year period that connected to the same years when data was collected by undergraduates of the organisms that live on the rocky shore of Appledore Island, Maine. The question that students were asked was "Is the surface air temperature or the surface sea temperature warming faster?" With a follow up question of "If so where?"

Below is an example of comparative anomaly maps showing sea surface temperatures over a five year period, the map on the left 1983 to 1987 and the map on the right 2013 to 2017.

The seventh grade classes divided themselves up into seven groups each which created two anomaly maps for a specific five-year period, one for sea surface temperatures and one for air surface temperatures. Then they presented their results by setting up their computers in a darkened room with each computer set to a different time period.

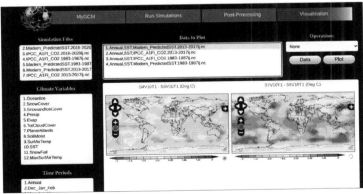

The photos that were taken during this activity are pretty dark and don't show the "Oh wow, look how different that one is!!" exclamations that the kids had during their analysis sessions. This group of seventh graders quickly figured out that they could make some interesting climate models, share them with each other, and extrapolate personal meaning from the models.

Since I was using this software for free during the 2019–2020 school year, the person who connected me to the system asked me to write up my lesson plans and send them to him at the end of the year. A link to my document is referenced below.[4]

Although this software is set up for high school students to use, usually in Advanced Placement classes, I have found that twelve- to thirteen-year-old students are just as capable of using it and seem to understand how the anomalies work much better than even some adults who still argue about whether climate change is real or not.

GPS, Cameras, and Data Gathering

"How much trash is in your neighborhood?" is a question that I ask my sixth graders each fall, and most say "a lot" to which I respond: "Define a lot and give three examples." With this, students usually come up with a good list of all kinds of things that they see on the side of the road near their homes, in parking lots, and even outside our school building and playground.

During September of the 2020–21 school year, our sixth grade class was introduced to some new data collection technology to help us figure out just how much trash there really is around us. Students were quick to identify the different types of trash that they see, but wanted to know which was the highest percentage of trash overall.

We started with a prediction based on a list of ten items that we slimmed down from an extensive list of possible trash.

- Plastic
- Paper
- Glass
- Smoking debris
- Appliances
- Metal
- Clothing
- Food
- Electronics
- Construction debris
- Other

Students predicted that plastic would have the highest amount of trash and construction debris the lowest based on what they had seen in their neighborhoods recently.

Working together, students built a QuickCapture app on the school ArcGIS site and launched it for use. This app was set up to record the item name on the button and the geolocation of the item based on where the collector is when the button is pressed. From our research while learning how to set up the app properly, students learned that this app is used for things such as documenting disasters like hurricanes and can even be used by planes as they fly over disaster areas to locate people that need rescue, etc.

Students made their application with one page of buttons that would be easy to use with a phone or tablet that could be taken on a walk around their neighborhood. To the right is a photo of the button page that we made.

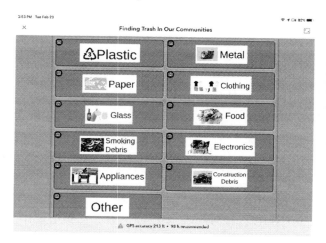

Within the first week of use, students started to troubleshoot some of the problems that they had set up in their application, such as requiring a photo for each entry and the color of the background being difficult to see in direct sunlight.

Going back into the application setup page, students reset the app to allow the photos but not require them, and changed the appearance to a blue background with orange buttons for better visibility outdoors.

Data was collected over a two-week period by a variety of students, some more enthusiastic trash searchers than others, but all contributed some data to the project. The challenge was to see if we could find over 500 pieces of trash in our area just by walking around our neighborhoods and we were successful at that.

Once the survey was started, students went on to build their own dashboards to chart the data that was being collected with the goal of finding out which type of trash had the highest percentage of occurrence. Below is one of the sixth grade dashboards showing a pie chart, a running quantity meter, and a map of locations for the various items.

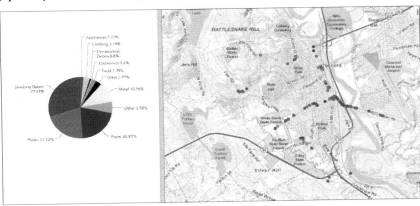

One thing that this student did was to match the pie chart slice colors to the colors of the identified QuickCapture items in the legend for the map which helps in identifying where specific items are.

By clicking the individual dots on the graph you can see a pop up that identifies the type of trash and if a photo was added, shows the photo. The next image shows a pop-up with the photo of the trash item collected by the QuickCapture app that the class made.

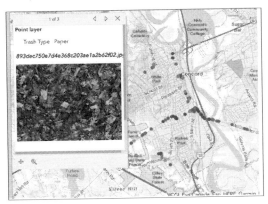

Students came to the conclusion within just two weeks that smoking debris was the highest category of items collected. They quickly realized that the tiny items added up fast to the amount of trash in the area and went on to ask questions about what happens to the smoking debris as it sits on the ground over the winter and beyond. That became another project using our smartphones and Google documents, but not included in this essay.

Since sixth graders work on earth science for a full year at my school, we tend to go back to our ArcGIS software often to find other information such as depth of oceans, plate tectonics, meandering rivers, and other interesting geospatial features. As in the different models discussed above, this software is often used with older students, but I feel that any student of any age can use many of the features of the ArcGIS software, including a drone application that would be easy to use for any student who has a drone of their own.

As we approach spring this year, 2021, students have asked if they could do some projects using QuickCapture or Survey123 to record the changes in the environment as we transition from winter to spring. One group plans to use the apps to record migrations of birds back to the area and another the emergence of leaves and flowers. We have a nice group of emerging citizen scientists in our middle school this and every year.

Scratch Coloring Pages and Fun Programing

Finally, something that Papert and Solomon would be familiar with—programmed art by students. To introduce my sixth graders to coding I use the Scratch programming language since it has some complex features that can be programed relatively easily by just about anyone.

We annually make a programmed coloring page booklet as a buddy gift for Catholic Schools Week in January. Prior to beginning the coding process we discuss how many angles make a square, triangle, and the constant angle change of making a circle. Students then draw a simple design on paper using just three geometric shapes to make a scene, then think about the process of how they moved their pencil or pen to draw those shapes.

Logging into Scratch, students are given a fifteen minute introduction to how to find the pen extension, set the pen to black, then put the pen down and pick the pen up blocks, and then the motion blocks for angles and movement. After letting the students explore and draw for a while they eventually start asking questions such as:

"The cat went off the edge, how do I get it back?"

"How can I make the square stay in the same spot each time I run my program?"

"Is there a way to make a circle bigger or smaller?"

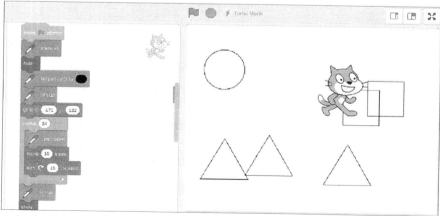

An example of a sixth-grade first-time programmer who programmed Scratch to draw three geometric shapes.

With questions, I am usually able to ask, "Does anyone know how?" but this year, 2020–21, none of the kids had been to a summer technology camp due to COVID–19 restrictions and shutdowns, so I helped them out a bit by showing them how the (x,y) coordinates worked with the go to block. At the end of a forty-minute class period, most of the kids had something drawn on their screens, saved, and placed in the class studio so that we all could see and share ideas.

Over a few days, working together and sharing ideas, students begin to develop skills in spatial reference within the stage that Scratch allows for drawing or graphics. The next step was to give students time to draw a scene that a younger child would want to color. This year the 6th grade class really took this to heart and by working together created a nice coloring book of winter scenes.

In the scene below, the student who made this program wanted the mountains to look like more than just triangles and tried the glide block, eventually building a nice flow of lines that looked like the mountains that they envisioned in their pre planning drawing.

Another sixth grader went as far as to program several different short subroutines using the

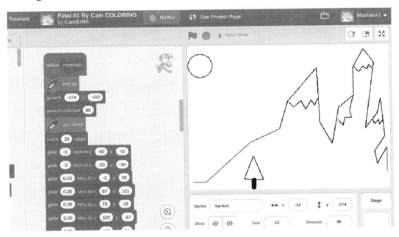

My Blocks function to make their own block. Here the student wrote a short or long program section that could be used in different locations repeatedly to draw the coloring page. This

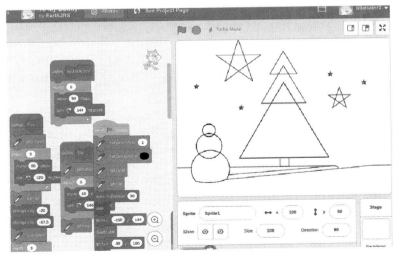

student showed their creativity by including some shadowing near the snowman, and provided some perspective to the scene.

One final Scratch program shows that abstract art is fine too. In this program the student also used subroutines to draw multiple placements of the same shape, and to create a separate routine the nesting circles.

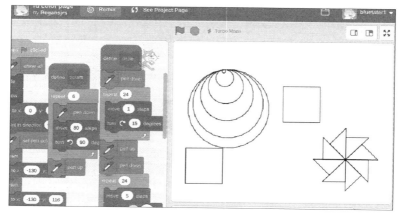

A screenshot was taken of each coloring page and placed into a shared Google document with each student adding their name to their respective work. Then the document was printed and folded into a book format with each student creating a special cover for their preK or third grade buddies. This year due to COVID–19 we were not allowed to visit the buddies in their classrooms so instead made large envelopes and placed the coloring books inside, then delivered the envelopes to the teachers outside in the school parking lot. The coloring books were well received by all of the younger students who sent thank you notes to the sixth graders.

Final Thoughts

Computers and how we use them have come a long way in the past fifty years. Above are just a few examples of things that we do with computers at my school.[5] In the past year we have changed quite a bit of how we have done things due to remote schooling with COVID–19 restrictions. In some ways the predictions of my favorite cartoon, *The Jetsons*, actually happened as I spent many hours teaching via computer screen this year.

Finally, of all the things that can be done with a computer, during remote learning in the spring of 2020, students and teachers in our middle school were able to stay connected in a fun way by sharing photos taken by our smartphones, tablets, or digital cameras. This photo sharing was initiated by a student one morning who posted, "We had bears in our yard this morning!!" in their Google classroom stream. Not long after, other students asked if they had taken a photo of the bear and soon the sharing started.

This eventually morphed into a daily *11:00 Nature Break* where we all dropped our video meetings or other online classwork and went outside to take a photo of something in nature in our own yards. We had an amazing amount of participation from students in all three grade levels. Though not programming a moving turtle as Papert and Solomon described, we did indeed see students initiate use of their handheld computers to interact with each other over the distances in meaningful ways, which did include a turtle photo at one point along with a variety of spring flora and fauna.

In one additional connection to *The Jetsons*, the state of New Hampshire, USA, where I live, legalized flying cars in 2020.[6] Now I just need to get my students to invent one for me.

Notes

1 Stella computational model repository - exchange.iseesystems.com

2 Copy of 6th grader Radiocarbon Dating. docs.google.com/
   document/d/1to87QFCF0PyYZCJdcRnUhyvsasXjwpis7PpthKjD004/edit?usp=sharing

3 7th grader Population Over 15 Years. docs.google.com/
   document/d/1kZ1cq1_YRTdBvCVCX_qyZj0BT_kCTOgO8rwuySCUSnQ/edit?usp=sharing

4 Fall 2019 Modeling Climate using EzGCM. docs.google.com/
   document/d/15GnEE8S19AumuG7Fby9PR-drc_DCc6b7xIBXmJxEatw/edit?usp=sharing

5 Donna Collins website - sites.google.com/stjohnregional.org/mrscollins-science-classes/home

6 New Hampshire Becomes the First State to Legalize Flying Cars. robbreport.com/motors/aviation/
   new-hampshire-legalizes-flying-cars-2944135/

Theo's Rockets

Gary Stager

Seymour Papert loved sharing children's learning stories as a way of illuminating powerful ideas. His stories recounted the learning adventures of kids in classrooms, in popular culture, and even observations of his own grandchildren at play. Aside from evidence of his storytelling prowess, Papert's parables resulted from his careful observation of children's thinking and personal insights. Please indulge me as I attempt to extend this tradition.

The Real World

School leaders and politicians often justify education policies, curriculum, and pedagogical practices by claiming that they are "preparing students for the real world." Upon hearing this magic incantation, I brace myself for their depiction of the "real world." Typically, they err in two ways.

1. The real world is deeply unpleasant

An example might be, "Fifth grade needs to be miserable because you will not believe how awful sixth grade is." Alfie Kohn calls this BGUTI, the Better Get Used to It curriculum. (Kohn, 2006)

2. The person speaking has no idea whatsoever happens in the real world

At best, this is rooted in nostalgia for a world that no longer exists. I get the sense that the speaker lives in a fantasy world where Mom and Dad wake up at 6 AM. Mom cooks breakfast. Dad dresses in a suit, tie, and fedora, kisses his wife on the forehead and grabs the lunch pail she prepared for him to eat at the office. This nostalgia manifests itself in teachers saying things like, "Your geometry notebook must be handwritten neatly because college professors do not allow laptops and penmanship matters" or, "You must wear a uniform that makes you look like an extra in a Dickens film because when you get that job on Wall Street…"[1]

> *"Education is not preparation for life; education is life itself. Education, therefore, is a process of living and not a preparation for future living"(Dewey, 1897).*

The calls for real world preparation tend to diminish learning in several important ways:
- Vocational preparation is prized over the value of learning for its own sake.
- The curriculum is narrowed to teach primarily that which is tested on standardized tests.
- Extrinsic motivation is favored.
- Children are too often expected to solve intractable problems perplexing adult experts, such as climate change or hunger.
- Learning is equated with labor and viewed as unnatural.
- The calls for real world learning disrespect the wonder and whimsy of childhood.

Generations of teachers and parents see merit in seven-year-olds building dinosaurs out of cereal boxes. The creativity, design, fantasy play, and language development involved in such a project is consistent with timeless ideals of childhood. First graders don't need to be cleaning the local stream in order engage in real world learning. When you are seven, that cardboard dinosaur play *is* the real world.

Twenty Things teaches us that if we value cardboard dinosaurs, but today's children have access to technology that allows children to program the dinosaur to sing, dance, or send a text message to Grandma, that experience is enriched and wholly consistent with being a child in the real world of today.

Blast Off!

Theo is my five-year-old grandson. He lives in China which limits our time together especially over the past two years of the COVID-19 pandemic. As Theo completed preschool, he decided that he would like to give a gift to each of his twenty-six classmates. That was a lovely sentiment demonstrating his generosity and empathy. Theo could have asked his parents to buy something for each of the kids, but he had a better idea.

Young Theo opened Tinkercad on his iPad and proceeded to design three-dimensional rockets. Then he downloaded his design plans to the low-cost 3D printer his other grandfather sent him. After a bit of prototyping and tinkering, Theo manufactured dozens of original plastic rockets of his own design to give as gifts.

The kids loved getting one of Theo's rockets even though they look like rockets invented by a preschooler. Perhaps the kids appreciated the rocket more than a polished store-bought toy because their peer made it for them. It was an authentic gift—personal, modern, fun.

A decade ago, very few adults would have had the engineering expertise or access to the technological hardware required to make a class set of rockets, regardless of their aesthetics. Several years ago, schools may have purchased a 3D printer and taught kids much older than five how to use it. Even in those pioneering schools, many kids just 3D print roughly identical Yoda keychains from a file they found on the Internet.

Today, my grandson has his own 3D printer at home. He can design objects of his imagination in CAD software on his iPad. Theo is an engineer, designer, and inventor of 3D toys all before he can read, write, or be taught arithmetic. He can ask one of a half dozen devices in his home, "How do giraffes sleep?" and they will respond, just as Papert predicted in 1993 (Papert, 1993). One must wonder if educators realize what is about to hit them?

My fear is that when tiny DaVincis like Theo enter school, they will suffer the fate described by Papert during a late 1980s conversation with Paulo Freire.

> *I think it's an exaggeration, but that there's a lot of truth in saying that when you go to school, the trauma is that you must stop learning and you must now accept being taught (TV PUC São Paulo, 1980s).*

When children arrive at school with specific expertise, interests, curiosity, talents, and other gifts, it is incumbent upon educators to build upon those blessings and help them develop well beyond what a child might have achieved on her own. More importantly, school has an obligation to introduce children to things they don't yet know they love. Democratizing access to experience, expertise, and materials is school's highest calling. In an age of engineering and fabricating your own toys at five, kids enter school with a different relationship to knowledge construction and sense of themselves as learners than in previous eras. Schools that fail to acknowledge the world of children and adjust accordingly, do so at considerable peril.

My daughter, Theo's aunt, is a prime example of the real world in 2021. She has been fully employed with a salary, health insurance, and an apartment since the day she graduated college with a degree in art. Even Barack Obama used to take cheap shots at the expense of those pursuing art degrees. It's the low-hanging fruit for those who view education in transactional terms. After eight years or so in the workplace, my daughter moved to a new state and earned an MFA in Textiles from the School of the Art Institute of Chicago. She can draw, animate, weave, sew, crochet, knit, edit video, code, write, speak, teach, cook, support herself, and design a dress that walked New York Fashion Week. She recently got a new job. The job allows her to live anywhere and has no office to report to—ever. Her new position comes with unlimited vacation time. Let that roll around in your head for a moment. Unlimited vacation time for a career entirely based on remote work.

If schools were sincere in preparing Theo for the real world, how would the educational process be designed to reflect the world of his aunt and a growing number of others in careers their guidance counselors never could have imagined—solving problems their teachers never taught them to solve?

References

Dewey, J. (1897). *My pedagogic creed*. EL Kellogg & Company.

Kohn, A. (2006). *The homework myth: Why our kids get too much of a bad thing*. Da Capo Lifelong Books.

Nguyen, L., & Jeng, M. (2021). A Wall Street Dressing Down: Always. Be. Casual. *The New York Times*. nytimes.com/2021/08/02/business/wall-street-casual.html

Papert, S. (1993). Obsolete skill set: the 3Rs; literacy and letteracy in the media ages. *Wired*, 1.2(May/June), 52. wired.com/wired/archive/1.02/1.2_papert.html

TV PUC São Paulo. (1980s). *Freire and Papert*. vimeo.com/20497106

Note

1   The New York Times recently published a report (Nguyen & Jeng, 2021) on how the sartorially conservative Wall Street industries of finance and investment have dropped their dress codes quite virtually overnight. "As workers return to the financial district, longstanding dress codes have been relaxed. Right now, almost anything goes. Even jeans."

Ten Things to Do with the Internet

Tom Lauwers

This snowy February morning, stuck in the doldrums of the pandemic, I watch my children learn remotely and am reminded of Papert and Solomon's opening paragraph in *Twenty Things to Do with a Computer*. They write "Some think of using the computer to program the kid; others think of using the kid to program the computer." Replace *computer* with *internet* and you have instantly updated this statement for 2021. Far too much of the online content my children, and millions of others, are receiving is just a retooling of the same lessons that have been used to program kids since formal schooling began. As Mark Twain is purported to have said: "History doesn't repeat itself, but it often rhymes."

That said, and to remix another turn of phrase from Papert and Solomon, my purpose here is not to complain of what other people have not done, but to tell of some exciting things you can do with the internet you are connected to now. Each of these sections describes a way of using connectivity for playful creation. They intentionally rhyme with many of the original twenty things.

1. Make a Turtle or Other Robot Work Remotely

A remote robot is a robot that is connected to and programmable via the internet. The robot can be on another floor in your house, or on another continent. Remote robots have been around for a few decades (Nourbakhsh et al., 2007), and some have even gone to Mars.[1] Remote robots are a specific kind of Internet of Things (IoT) device.

Fortunately, you no longer need to work at NASA's Jet Propulsion Lab to create your own remote robot. I have been working on ways to make my company's products, the Finch Robot and the Hummingbird Robotics Kit, into remote robots for the last year.[2] To make a Finch Robot or Hummingbird Robotics Kit remote, all you need is a Windows or Mac laptop, a robot, and a camera to stream the robot. It takes under an hour, and no text programming experience, to set one up.

Kids can program the robots from any device, in a blocks-based environment that is not so dissimilar from the Logo language developed by Papert and Solomon.

2. Program the Remote Turtle to Draw a Person

Like many educational robots made in the last half century, the Finch Robot is modeled on the turtle robot design laid out in Papert and Solomon's paper. As such, programming a remote Finch to draw a person is entirely possible.

To try this, make your Finch Robot remote, then send the sample project link to someone that you want to program your robot.[3] I recommend a top-down video stream so that they can watch the robot make its drawing.

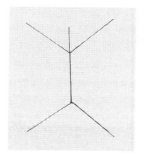

3. Remote Robot Biology

Papert and Solomon emphasized the importance of sensors to make robot behavior more lifelike, and I likewise emphasize to kids that a robot isn't a robot unless it can sense and react. Fortunately, remote robots are capable of reacting to their sensors. Even with a program running from another continent, the speed of messages over the internet is such that a robot will respond within two seconds of a sensor value changing. This is certainly much slower than the microsecond reaction times of modern robots, but it is fast enough for a wall follower of the kind Papert and Solomon describe.[4]

4. Make Multiplayer Spacewar

Papert and Solomon described the joy of fifth graders, in 1971, recreating the first video game, Spacewar. Thanks to Logo and Scratch, this game-making joy has been shared by millions of kids. Most of us enjoy video games even more when we play with and against other humans. Fortunately, there are now platforms that allow kids to design games using blocks programming that include a multiplayer mode.

One such platform is NetsBlox, which was developed to add networking capabilities to a kid-friendly blocks programming environment. NetsBlox is the environment that powers the remote robots examples of the last three sections. NetsBlox is based on Snap! which is based on Scratch 1.3, which is itself based on Logo.

With NetsBlox, a single designer can create multiple roles and then send those roles to different users. For example, in this Pong game,[5] one user can control the left paddle and the other the right paddle. NetsBlox also has a collaboration mode, allowing multiple kids to collaborate on a single project in real time. It doesn't look like anyone has made multiplayer Spacewar and published it to the NetsBlox site yet—perhaps you and your friends can be the first!

5. Make an App, Share it With Grandma

Papert and Solomon created a wonderful project, Growflowers, and then showed how kids could use it to make a movie animation. Millions of kids now program movies and animations and share them widely. With modern tools kids can create not just movies, but self-contained, interactive apps. BitsBox is one platform that has made this process kid-friendly, allowing kids to deploy their programs as web apps that are optimized for phones and tablets, and then share those apps with Grandma (or anyone else).

6. Make a Puppet, Then Invite the World to Program It!

One of my favorite remote robots is a diorama of the nineteenth century Emperor and Empress of Austria, *Sisi und Franzl - ein programmierbares Figurenspiel.*[6] They are in a discotheque, and you can program them to dance, while also programming an accompanying light and sound experience.

Photo Credit: Vienna University Children's Office

What I find exciting about this project, beyond the joy of playing with it, is that I learned something about Austrian culture by programming the robot. Kids can now create projects that represent their location or culture, and then kids from other areas of the world can program those projects, facilitating an exchange of cultures and creative experiences at the same time.

7. Make a Twitter Poetry Bot

Here's a simple prompt—create a Twitter Bot that posts a randomly generated poem once per day. This project idea is a mashup of Papert and Solomon's Concrete Poetry project and the Accidental Haiku Twitter Bot,[7] which searches for tweets with seventeen syllables and then reformats them as haikus, often with hilarious results.

Making Twitter Bots is very well documented online,[8] and many can be created with no coding at all, though I suspect that a poetry bot might require a few lines of code.

8. Collect Real Data, Visualize It!

Every day, billions of sensors collect thousands of readings per day, and these readings are available in real time in publicly accessible databases. The reason that data science is such a hot field is because our capacity to create data far outstrips our capacity to visualize, analyze, and use that data to make good decisions.

Kids can tap into this ever-growing pile of data using blocks coding. NetsBlox, in particular, includes blocks that access dozens of databases. For example, you can: 1) access air quality or climate data by latitude and longitude, 2) scrape Twitter for keywords, or 3) access street view images. You can even create and publish your own data stream for others to access. There are many example projects made with these data service blocks on the NetsBlox site; one example is a project that displays the air quality of the area you click on.[9]

9. Collect Real Data, Explain It!

It's one thing to visualize data, but the real challenge of data science is analyzing and explaining the data. Even analysis is becoming an increasingly low floor, high ceiling activity. Blocks-based environments like Snap! and NetsBlox already include powerful libraries for doing things like making bar charts, creating databases, and doing matrix operations or frequency distribution analysis. It is absolutely true that some of these libraries may be incomprehensible until kids learn the appropriate computer science or statistics concepts, but what better way to motivate such learning than to tell kids they're going to make something that uses actual data to better understand and explain a real-world phenomenon.

10. Crowdsource Line

I've made a Google Doc where you can suggest your own creative uses of the internet.[10] Please add your ideas to the growing list!

References

Nourbakhsh, I., Hamner, E., Lauwers, T., DiSalvo, C., & Bernstein, D. (2007). TeRK: A Flexible Tool for Science and Technology Education. *Proceedings of AAAI Spring Symposium on Robots and Robot Venues: Resources for AI Education*, 118 - 123. aaai.org/Papers/Symposia/Spring/2007/SS-07-09/SS07-09-027.pdf

Notes

1 Mars rover. en.wikipedia.org/wiki/Mars_rover
2 Control Remote Robots. birdbraintechnologies.com/remote-robots/
3 RemoteFinchDrawPerson. editor.netsblox.org/?action=present&Username=captainled&ProjectName=RemoteFinchDrawPerson&editMode=true&NoRun
4 RemoteFinchWallFollower. editor.netsblox.org/?action=present&Username=captainled&ProjectName=RemoteFinchWallFollower&editMode=true&NoRun
5 Pong. editor.netsblox.org/?action=example&ProjectName=Pong&editMode=true
6 Sisi und Franzl - ein Programmierbares figurenspiel. digikidscampus.at/sisi-und-franzl-ein-programmierbares-puppenspiel/
7 Accidental Haiku. twitter.com/accidental575?lang=en
8 How to make a twitter bot: The definitive guide. botwiki.org/resource/tutorial/how-to-make-a-twitter-bot-the-definitive-guide/
9 AirQuality Project. editor.netsblox.org/?action=example&ProjectName=AirQuality&editMode=true
10 Many things to do with the internet Google Doc. docs.google.com/document/d/1tBSA4EZhkgBktgp4FvnnALM2pscpD06hFyP_ll-iB_c/edit

Three European Robotics Projects Inspired by Twenty Things

Michele Moro & Dimitri Alimisis

In 1995 I (Michele) was asked by a junior secondary school in Venice, Italy to help set up a computer lab. I found some old PCs cast off by a company, and with very limited resources I searched for an educational environment runnable on such machines and suitable for students around the ages of eleven to thirteen. That was my initiation to Logo. Even though I had been interested in programming languages for years for research purposes, I was exposed only to languages for industrial applications. Surprisingly, I had no knowledge of Logo at that time though it was known and used in Italy in the school system. For me it was a revelation, a flash of inspiration—I started to understand what an important role education with computers could mean. After a period of only reading about it, I started to attend the Eurologo (now Constructionism) conferences. In 2005, during the conference in Warsaw, I met Dimitris Alimisis, at that time professor at the High School of Pedagogical and Technological Education in Patras, Greece, who was looking for partners for a European project about Educational Robotics. I thought it was a good opportunity to be much more involved in the subject. Our collaboration started there and has lasted for more than fifteen years.

It is extraordinarily exciting to observe how many things you can do with a computer after more than fifty years. From an educational point of view, terms like computational thinking, project-based learning, and learning-by-doing would have much less meaning or none at all without the use of today's personal computers. However, educational robotics dictates the use of computers as Papert taught us to appreciate since his early turtles—to create tangible objects to think with.

Over the years, many of the projects we were involved with embodied different facets of the *Twenty Things* proposed by Papert and Solomon. Three of these projects are shared here.

Teacher Education on Robotics-Enhanced Constructivist Pedagogical Methods (TERECoP) Project 2006-2009

At the beginning of this pioneering project (terecop.eu), which involved eight partners from six different countries, the use of robots for educational purposes had been pioneered by only a few. The LEGO company, after its DACTA initiative started in 1989, had introduced the RCX robot in 1998 and the new Mindstorms NXT in 2006. It was clear to us that we faced two main challenges. The first was how to prepare effective robotic-enhanced curricula, based on a proper methodology and easily implementable in class. In our second challenge, we were deeply aware the only way to promote the development of educational

robots was, and still is, teacher training. The pedagogical framework adopted was a constructivist/constructionist and learner-centered learning approach suitable for the use of educational robots such as LEGO NXT.

RoboESL Project 2015-2017

The TERECoP project was in use for years by our partners and collaborators to organize teacher training courses and effective robotic activities at school. One of the risks we were aware of was that these activities could become only exclusive to only a few students. When robotic labs are extra-curricular, they are often more easily accessible to already motivated pupils. This conviction led us to design a new project, RoboESL (roboesl.eu), to give special attention to less privileged members of the school population, students not motivated and stimulated, or at risk of dropping out of school. For this RoboESL project, we developed ten curriculum units for the new 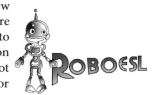 and more powerful LEGO EV3 robot, maintaining the constructivist approach but focusing on developing stimulating scenarios and strong relationships with real-life situations to better motivate our target group.

eCraft2Learn Project 2017-2018

With the advent of the maker movement, educational robotics has assumed a broader meaning including digital fabrication and making technologies for creating computer-supported artifacts. The eCraft2Learn project (project.ecraft2learn.eu) used a combination of a suitable programming environment (an adapted version of Snap!) and affordable hardware (Arduino) to once again reaffirm Papert and Solomon's vision found in *Twenty Things to Do with a Computer.*

A Robot Petting Zoo

John Umekubo

In 1971, the year Papert and Solomon published *Twenty Things to Do with a Computer*, I had no concept of a computer. I was six years old and wouldn't get to use one until the late nineteen eighties, in college. And that was primarily for word processing. Yet, in reading this work and the concepts it covers, make a slight adjustment to the tools' names, and we could be talking as if it were happening today.

With the introduction of low-cost microcontrollers a little over a decade ago and the development of block-based coding languages, the process of physical computing (real-world systems controlled by code) has become accessible to the masses, including students of all ages.

The fact that Scratch (a block-based coding language developed at MIT) is free, accessible to anyone with a computer, and connects to external devices like a microcontroller, makes the connection between coding and the physical world a reality for just about anyone with the ability to read.

Today, for under $100 and with access to a computer, anyone can write a program that controls lights, motors, audio, and can read data from sensors to trigger events in the real world.

The New Turtle

How much has changed in coding and physical computing since 1971? The truth is that much has remained the same while the rest has transformed our world. Coding concepts such as loops, variables, and conditions remain essential to coders looking to read data from a sensor that then triggers a reaction. Electronic components like LEDs, servo motors, and sensors (light, sound, distance) have changed little over the years.

What has changed, however, is the increased availability of low-cost, powerful microcontrollers that handle the code and execute the commands. Their proliferation has created a colorful marketplace where makers and educators can find specific hardware for particular purposes, all while addressing the varying needs of diverse learners. Alongside the advances in hardware, there have been changes on the software side that have lowered the floor to entry for even the youngest coders. The ease with which one can assemble coding blocks into logical sequences makes coding fun, inventive, and exploratory.

Take a look at the following set of blocks. Can you tell what is happening here?

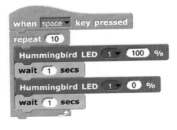

Turning the above set of code blocks into a regular sentence might look something like this.

When I press the SPACE bar on the keyboard, turn the LED connected to Port 1 on for one second, then turn it off for one second. Repeat this procedure ten times, then stop.

Let's look at a similar set of code blocks, this time to introduce the reading of a sensor and reacting to the values it sends back:

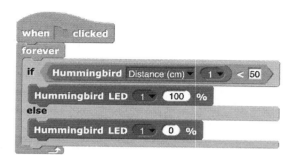

In plain English, it says:

When the program starts (green flag clicked), activate a forever loop with the following instructions. Read the distance sensor on Port 1. If, at any time, the sensor value goes below 50 (i.e., if an object has come closer than 50mm), set the LED on Port 1 to ON. If the sensor value is 50 or greater, set the LED on Port 1 to OFF.

Without an ounce of coding in their background, upper elementary school students can visualize what is going on in the above scenario. The blocks and their arrangement follow a logical sequence of events. Papert might have described this kind of tool as having a low floor (easy entry) and high ceiling (potential for increasingly complex explorations over time) (Resnick, 2008).

One of the biggest challenges to text-based coding for young learners is following exact syntax when writing code. Additionally, different coding languages often follow different syntax rules, so the learning curve can be high. Block-based coding eliminates the need to follow strict syntax rules. Assembling blocks that can only fit within specific shape parameters guides coders into the correct syntax. Debugging is mostly a matter of moving blocks around until something works.

Couple this basic knowledge with the building of a physical object, a creature, a vehicle, a robot, and you are now interacting with the real, physical world. Use code to bring something to life, to work from inanimate to animate. Give your creature eyes, or ears, or a sense of touch. Make the creature react to its surroundings through a growl, a howl, a dance, or a song.

From Turtles to a Zoo

An engaging approach for propagating these concepts into the classroom is for students to share their newfound knowledge and coding/design skills through a Robot Petting Zoo. Born out of the minds at Tech Hive at UC Berkeley, the Robot Petting Zoo can take several forms, but here is the basic idea:

- Students work to design and build a robotic creature that contains motors, lights, and sensors that can interact with its surroundings. Reactions might occur due to changes in ambient light, the proximity of objects in front of the creature, or the pressing of a sequence of keys on the keyboard. The robotic creature might have LEDs embedded in the eyes, a tail controlled by a servo motor, a distance sensor for a nose.
- Students share their final projects through an exhibition, with each robotic creature demonstrating interactive behaviors with zoo visitors.

While a Robot Petting Zoo can work with many different coding and hardware platforms, we will use the Hummingbird Bit board, a micro:bit, and Snap! coding for demonstration purposes. The micro:bit will be our connection to the code written on the computer, and the Hummingbird Bit board will execute the majority of the various functions, such as sensing, lighting up, performing movements, and emitting sounds. This hardware setup provides a simple solution for connecting the LEDs, servo motors, and sensors for these actions to take place.

Engineer, Coder, Maker

There are three essential functions for putting this project together—engineer, coder, and maker. For students working in groups, each team member could take the leadership role for each of these functions. For students working alone, they would perform all of these functions, shifting between them at different times, depending on the task at hand.

The **Engineer** is responsible for the assemblage and troubleshooting of all robotics equipment. The engineer understands how all of the components work and how to connect them to the boards.

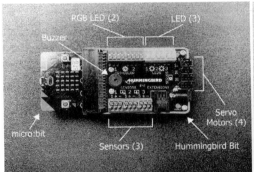

Diagram of Hummingbird Bit with labels and a sample setup with electronic components connected

The **Coder** handles all of the coding development and changes. The coder also understands how each of the electronic components works and knows how to call them into action using the correct combination of code blocks. The coder can troubleshoot the programming when something doesn't appear to work as planned.

In the example below, a student has attached wheels to rotation servos on ports 3 and 4. The intention is that when the ambient light in the room surpasses a certain level, the motors move the robot forward. However, instead of moving forward, the robot turns in circles. What happened?

307

It turned out that the student attached the rotation motors to either side of the robot—but in opposite directions. This results in the motors *also* turning in opposite directions, making the robot go in circles. To resolve this issue, the code must be adjusted by changing the rotation servo value to a negative number. Now, both motors will move the robot in the same direction.

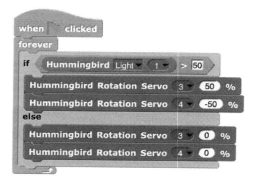

The **Maker** handles the design and building of the actual creature using established materials. The maker uses the cutting tools and fasteners, understands how to include support brackets and possible hinges and linkages, and knows the electronic components' appropriate location within the final work.

The material makeup of the robotic creature is limited only by one's imagination. Cardboard scraps first come to mind but don't stop there. Foam packing, pipe cleaners, popsicle sticks, and bottle caps bring whimsy to the design. Vary the textures, the shapes, and the colors of building elements. Peruse the junk drawer at home and the recycle bin at school. Visit the next neighborhood yard sale.

There might also exist a fourth role, that of the **Storyteller**. Discovering the story behind each robotic creature is an enjoyable extension of this project. How did this creature come to be? What adventure is it on? If you study ecology and environmental science, was there something that caused a mutation to make this creature into what it is? For a specific take on this concept of storytelling, see the Legends of the Trash Creatures project from Westside Neighborhood School[1].

In practice, the build-up to the final creature exhibition can take several days. You might focus the initial learning experiences on the robotics and coding side and leave the design to the latter half of the lessons. Conversely, you may choose to approach design first and let that serve as the foundation for coding and engineering. You may decide to have some ready-made robots that simply need the coding. It is up to you and the learning goals for your classroom.

Exhibition Day

The code has been written, tested, debugged, adjusted, and proven to work. All electrical and robotic components are connected correctly, and the creature design is complete and stable. It is exhibition day, and the Robot Petting Zoo is here. It is time to celebrate the culmination of all the focused effort, inventiveness, and creativity that produced the robotic creatures on display.

In truth, the day is likely much more chaotic and unpredictable. "Code that was working just yesterday has decided not to run today." "That arm fell off!" "The wiring disconnected, and I can't reach back into that tight spot to reconnect it." This iterative process is an essential part of learning, and while we hope to work through most of the hiccups before exhibition day, a flawless performance is rare. It is vital to embrace learning at all moments in the process.

Variations and Extensions

The Hummingbird and micro:bit approach is just one of several opportunities for creating a Robot Petting Zoo. While the examples shown here use the Snap! coding language, one might choose to program in another block-based language such as Scratch or MakeCode or dive into text-based coding using Python or the Arduino IDE. You can tailor the coding experience to the level of the learner.

The project can work with other hardware devices as well. For the younger set, LittleBits is a solution with a lower floor for entry. Using magnets to connect components, these simple yet powerful tools can adapt to the same concepts of sensing the environment and reacting to it through light, sound, and motion. A Circuit Playground Express and Crickit motor controller using Python might be a proper fit for middle school and high school students. An Arduino with a motor shield using the Arduino IDE could serve the next level up.

The Robot Petting Zoo, as described above, doesn't currently have any specific curricular integration. We use the zoo to demonstrate knowledge of coding and physical computing, share our learning, be creative, and have fun.

You might see the relevance of a project such as this to the topic of environmental sustainability. You may see a relationship of the design and coding methodology with principles of mathematics or physics. And there is the potential for integration with literature and storytelling. How might you approach the Robot Petting Zoo differently? How might you make it more relevant to what you already do in the classroom? How might the age level and experience of the students you teach change the software and hardware tools you select?

Are You Ready?

I've created a site with video tutorials, coding samples, resources for further learning, and ideas to get you started on your own Robot Petting Zoo[2]. I recommend you start as the learner, taking on each of the roles above and creating your very own robot pet. Share your new creation with the students to jump-start the Robot Petting Zoo.

Whether you teach a class, are in school yourself, or are a lifelong learner, there is no better time to explore the world of coding and physical computing. The technology is affordable, the coding languages are freely accessible, and recycled materials make your best building blocks.

References

Resnick, M. (2008, March 25). *Mindstorms Over Time: Reflections on Seymour Papert's Contributions to Education Research* Special Session of the 2008 American Educational Research Association Annual Meeting, web.media.mit.edu/~mres/papers/AERA-seymour-final.pdf

Notes

1 Legends of the Trash Creatures, Westside Neighborhood School - bit.ly/LTCproject
2 Make your own Robot Petting Zoo - bit.ly/rpz21

Collaboration Rules! Twenty Insights About Online Collaborative Learning

Yvonne Marie Andres

Twenty Things to Do with a Computer (authored in 1971 by Seymour Papert and Cynthia Solomon) began with the claim, "When people talk about computers in education they do not all have the same image in mind."

Today the same claim can be made about online collaborative learning. Everyone says that they want to collaborate, but the concept of collaboration often means different things to different people. The idea of collaboration seems simple enough. Collaboration is when two or more people make contributions towards a shared goal, task, or project. However, in reality it can be challenging.

Applying the rules of collaboration is an effective way to engage learners and deepen their knowledge. Through teamwork, discussion groups, and action learning groups, learners can apply their problem-solving skills as well as learn how to actively listen to diverse opinions and receive constructive feedback—skills that are critical for success in the workplace, across all industries—and life in general. So, my aim is to convince you that **collaboration rules**!

Twenty Things goes on to tell educators about twenty exciting things their students could do with a computer while using the turtle-based Logo programming language. They could engage in problem-solving activities like making a movie, programing a tune, playing a game, writing concrete poetry, and computerizing a crane to build a tower of blocks.

Yet, I couldn't help noticing that teamwork and collaboration were not mentioned at all, even though I know from my own personal experience that students often did work in teams. In 1971 the relationship was mostly between the student and the computer, or as stated in *Twenty Things*, "the transaction between the computer and the kid will be some kind of conversation."

That all changed in 1983 when my colleague, Al Rogers, created a word processing program called FrEdWriter (Free Educational Writer) that ran on Apple II computers and was offered free to all schools. This application became the first in a suite of tools that Rogers created to support effective writing instruction. FrEdWriter introduced the concept of "prompted writing" and enabled teachers to focus on the development of effective writing instruction. Because FrEdWriter was free, schools were able to design a writing program without concerns about software budget limitations, making it the de facto standard for years.

Next came the FrEdMail (Free Educational eMail) Network, because a good writing program also requires an audience beyond the teacher. FrEdMail proved to be an effective

```
**********************************
*×        FrEdWriter             *
*                                *
*     V 4.1  JUNE 2, 1985        *
*                                *
*     MAIN  PROGRAM  MENU        *
**********************************

      DATE: <NO DATE>

      TIME: <NO TIME>

   1. Read This First
   2. Start FrEdWriter
   3. Set Date and Time
   4. Format a New Disk
   5. Copy a Disk
   6. View, Delete or Copy Document
   7. Credits

 TYPE YOUR CHOICE:×
```

way to encourage students to write and participate in collaborative learning activities. The FrEdMail Network grew to 12,000 participating schools across the globe. In 1993 the non-profit FrEdMail Foundation changed its name to Global SchoolNet Foundation (GSN) and created an educational website that focused on collaboration called "Global Schoolhouse." Global Schoolhouse's vision was to provide a living curriculum that made the world a laboratory, promoted the quest for lifelong learning, and established a global collaborative learning community that would benefit all sectors: education, health care, government, business, music, the arts, and the home.

I conducted my first Online Collaborative Learning (OCL) project in 1984 as a middle school teacher with very low-achieving 6th graders, via the original FrEdMail Network. Since then, I have facilitated many thousands of collaborative projects with millions of students of all ages, from 115 countries, allowing me to identify time-proven principles and guidelines for successful OCL that blends offline and online learning. OCL incorporates many features of traditional project-based learning (PBL). But OCL also includes participation of people outside the traditional classroom. OCL projects create opportunities for all students to learn, practice and apply knowledge, skills, and complex learning strategies—across geographically dispersed and culturally diverse environments. The power of OCL comes from connecting learners with a real audience in meaningful ways and receiving peer feedback.

The COVID-19 pandemic has had a profound and wide-reaching effect on youth, from the quality of instruction they receive to their social, emotional, and physical well-being. Transitioning from in-class learning to online learning has become an essential public health measure for primary and secondary schools. Yet, students can become distracted while learning online, with many reporting burnout, general fatigue, and isolation from limited opportunities to socialize.

In contrast, approaches that balance hands-on activities, fieldwork, and online collaboration can keep students motivated and engaged. This pandemic presents a unique opportunity to put authentic learning at the center of education and reimagine engaged learning. Using OCL, students can learn with the world, not just about it.

Ten Basic Elements of Online Collaborative Learning

For online collaborative learning to be beneficial for all, outcomes must be discussed and all collaborators must agree on certain basic elements. However, each collaborator should also establish their own individual goals and implementation plan. The structure of OCL projects will vary depending on the purpose or task, the participants, the timeline, and how the collaboration will be evaluated.

Basic elements that should always be discussed and agreed upon include:

1. What is the purpose, task, or activity?
2. What type of partners are you seeking and why? How will collaboration add extra value to the learning experience?
3. Who are the key beneficiaries or stakeholders (e.g. students, teachers, parents, school, local community)?
4. Which collaboration tools will be used?
5. Which project elements will be shared and why? Sharing everything is not recommended.
6. How and where will the project elements be shared? Who is the audience (e.g. project participants, the school, local community, the general public)?
7. Who will facilitate or moderate the project? What are their responsibilities?
8. What is the timeline? Take into consideration different time zones, testing schedules, and vacation and holiday breaks.

9. What risks could affect the collaboration (e.g. weather conditions, technology issues, varied time zones, unexpected illness)?
10. How will the collaboration be evaluated, for example by individual collaborators and/or by the group?

Ten Examples of Online Collaborative Learning

Many learning experiences benefit from including online collaboration. The ability to work well with others to collaborate on ideas and solve problems is an important skill. Below are some examples of different types of OCL.

1. **Group Publishing:** Students contribute original writing, research, interviews, art, music, photos, and videos to create an online magazine, newspaper, or virtual gallery.
2. **Electronic Appearance or Q & A:** Students interact with a special guest (e.g. an expert, author, explorer, elected official). Exchanges can be conducted real-time during a video conference, or asynchronously via email or electronic forum over a period of several days or, sometimes, weeks.
3. **Global Classroom or Intercultural Exchange:** Classes exchange and discuss information about their own cultures. Students write and share about work, leisure, daily school and community life, sports, music, art, food, religion, customs, life-passage celebrations, languages, local landmarks, and other topics of interest.
4. **Information Exchange:** Students collect, exchange, and discuss information about a specific topic or theme (e.g. animals, insects, rocks and geology, water quality, plants and forests, weather, astronomy, local music, art, environmental issues, etc.).
5. **Live Expedition:** Students monitor or observe an actual field trip, excursion, or expedition conducted by another classroom, an expert, or a global adventurer. Interaction takes place in real-time during the period of the excursion. Students can read timely reports from the field, listen to real-time audio, participate in video conferences, ask questions and sometimes pose research questions for the expedition members.
6. **Mentoring:** Telementoring enables professionals and experts to interact electronically with students on an on-going basis to enhance their research, knowledge and understanding of a subject or career. These can be conducted one-on-one or with a small group of students and participants develop a more in-depth relationship than they do with an electronic appearance.
7. **Parallel Problem Solving:** Students in two or more locations study a common problem and then share and compare, contrast, and discuss their varying conclusions or solutions.
8. **Pooled Data Analysis:** Students collect data at two or more locations which is then combined and organized for further analysis and interpretation.
9. **Sequential Creation:** Classes create something sequentially (e.g. poem, story, picture, song, video) by passing the creation from one class to the next. Each class adds or modifies the creation and then passes it along to the next. After a number of passes, everybody shares the finished product.
10. **Social Action:** These are action-oriented, multicultural, humanitarian projects that seek to address concerns or issues (e.g. bullying, digital divide, endangered species, environmental awareness, gender equality, human welfare, poverty, racial equality, social justice).

Basic Online Collaboration Tools

When organizing OCL activities it is essential that all the collaborators have access to the agreed upon tools. The good news is that over the decades, the tools for online collaborative learning have become increasingly better and more widely available. More importantly, there are a variety of no-cost versions, so everyone can have access to the same tools.

It is very important for collaborators to discuss how time will be divided between synchronous and asynchronous activities, before choosing the collaboration tools for your project. For example, it doesn't make sense to meet synchronously over video conferencing while someone reads something that could have been shared asynchronously.

Make sure the agreed upon tools work on all the different devices that will be used (e.g. tablets, computers, smartphones) by all the collaborators and build in adequate time for everyone to become familiar with the tools.

New technology tools come and go quite quickly. So, rather than name specific tools that are available in this moment in time, I recommend that collaborators select the type of basic tools that will best serve particular needs of their project or activity.

OCL Projects You Can Join

If you are new to OCL, it's always best to join an existing project. Below are three of my favorite well-established, well-supported OCL projects (offered by Global SchoolNet) that you are invited to join.

International CyberFair (*Ages 8-19*) GlobalSchoolNet.org/gsncf
2022 will be the 27th anniversary of International CyberFair. Launched in 1996, the focus of CyberFair is collaboration—first at the local level and then on an international level. Youth conduct research and publish their findings using digital media. The purpose of CyberFair is for youth, their schools, and their local communities to use digital media to share resources, establish partnerships, and work together to accomplish common goals. The annual competition/exhibition has involved more than 6 million students from 50,000 schools across 115 countries—and is considered the longest running international online event of its kind.

Global Forest Link (*Ages 11-19*) Facebook.com/GlobalForestLink
Global Forest Link is an award-winning S.T.E.A.M. (Science, Technology, Engineering, Arts, Math) education program that engages high school and middle school students in the collaborative analysis of local forest health and helps them explore the impact of environmental change factors. Students share results online via photographs and digital stories with peers in other cities and countries, giving them a local and global perspective. Students learn about forest health from satellite images and self-paced tutorials; participate in webinars; consult with industry experts, collect their own images and videos to validate satellite observations; and interpret data using innovative visual analysis tools.

OUR PRIDE Education *(Ages 11-19)* OurPride.org
OUR PRIDE is a collaborative blended-learning educational program for youth to create and share digital
stories about significant LGBTQ+ people, places, and
events through video and social media in a variety of
genres, incorporating original music, poetry and other

creative content. Participants learn collaboration, evidence-based journalism, creative writing,
music, arts, and digital media production skills while researching, studying, and sharing stories
that address a wide range of subjects related to LGBTQ+ heritage, lives, and community. Through
research, collaboration and production, the program is designed to create a new awareness and
understanding of history, culture, and issues, while directly connecting youth with mentors and
elders in a cross-generation learning and personal growth experience.

Benefits and Challenges of Online Collaborative Learning

An understanding of both the benefits and challenges associated with OCL is useful to teachers,
school administrators, teacher preparation institutions, policy makers, and instructional
designers who want to integrate effective instructional methodologies that enhance student
learning, support higher levels of achievement, and prepare students to be literate and responsible global citizens.

In 2004, for my doctoral dissertation, I conducted a study to identify the predominant
benefits and challenges of online collaborative learning for K–12 students and teachers. Using
a modified Delphi technique, I explored the perceptions held by teacher experts who had
included online collaborative learning activities as part of their students' curriculum for at least
five or more years.

Analysis of the data indicated a strong consensus among participants that the benefits
of OCL significantly outweighed the challenges and obstacles. My research found that OCL
provided many more unique opportunities for authentic learning, student achievement, and
professional growth than traditional classroom-based instruction. As example, OCL enabled
students to follow the expeditions of real-world explorers, help scientists around the globe
collect data, or provide their views and concerns to business and political leaders. In addition,
students were more motivated to produce high quality content when they knew they would be
sharing their research findings with partner classrooms.

There was strong agreement that one of the greatest benefits of OCL was evidence of
improved reading, writing, and communications skills in students. Teachers believed that
students involved in OCL projects read more, wrote more, and communicated better than
students who received traditional classroom instruction. My research found that teachers,
themselves, benefited from OCL because professional development and growth opportunities
increased through interactions with their colleagues.

My study also confirmed that online collaborative learning presents unique challenges,
limitations, and obstacles, which must be understood in order to be dealt with effectively.
The challenges that were cited most frequently were that OCL activities require an extra time
investment; high stakes testing and exam-oriented courses do not encourage innovative teaching
methods; and that not enough funding is made available to implement online learning projects.

Because the evidence indicated the benefits of online collaborative learning far out-weigh
the challenges, the lack of implementation of OCL is unfortunate—especially since 2020 has
shown there is a growing need for people to function effectively in both online collaborative
learning environments and online collaborative *work* environments.

So, that's why I believe that **collaboration rules**!

Make a Turtle!

Miles Berry

The first thing on Papert and Solomon's list of twenty things is *make a turtle*. Over the intervening fifty years the programmable turtle has featured as many young people's first introduction to programming, both on the floor and on the screen. It still has much to commend it. It is simple enough for children to grasp the basic idea of the robot's operation—it moves forwards or backwards; it turns to the left or to the right; and it can draw, or not draw, as it moves. The hardware itself is simple enough too. Motors for each of the main wheels, able to turn independently; and a pen that can be raised or lowered that fits right in the middle of these wheels. As a "notional machine" (du Boulay et al., 1981), it seems much easier for a child to grasp conceptually than a smartphone, a tablet, or a distant website. It is also a friendly sort of thing. It is neither too big, nor too small; it often develops some sort of character, at least in the child's eyes; and, crucially, the child can put herself in the turtle's place. The humble turtle is capable of great things, and many realize they can move on from drawing regular polygons or simple pictures to stunning, complex geometric figures.

Turtles All the Way Down

Often a child's first experience of programming, even if it's not called that at the time, is with some sort of floor robot, such as Bee-Bot. While it is not a true Logo turtle, the Bee-Bot can be given a sequence of move and turn instructions, and even very young children quickly figure out for themselves what it can and cannot do. More sophisticated floor turtles are available, such as Pro-Bot and InO-Bot, both of which are proper turtles in the sense of being able to draw. The former can be programmed using buttons on the device in a crude version of Logo, the latter on screen using a building-block language inspired by Scratch. These devices seem less popular than Bee-Bot itself, perhaps because of additional expense or because teachers think that when a pupil is ready to move on from the Bee-Bot, they are ready to move on to Scratch.

Scratch takes Logo turtles as a starting point. Sprites in Scratch can move and turn just as turtles do. They can also say things, play sounds, change their appearance, interact with other sprites, respond to external events, and do lots of things that floor turtles can't. However, in the current version of Scratch they can only draw using an additional library of **pen** commands, and they are confined to the world of the screen.

Sooner, or hopefully later, the young programmer moves on from block-based programming in Scratch or a similar environment, to text-based programming, perhaps using a Logo interpreter here to help bridge this gap, or perhaps jumping straight in to Python programming. Even here a good teacher might scaffold the transition to the additional cognitive load of text-based programming through working in the familiar territory of turtle graphics by importing the necessary methods from Python's turtle module. This is a sophisticated toolkit, and there are some lovely examples available such as a playable, but unbeatable version of Nim, arguably the first computer game (Flesch, 1951).

However, in all these instances, from toy robots through to programming in Python, the child never *builds* a turtle; they just use one, either on the floor or on screen, built by the experts. Back in 1971, I think Papert and Solomon had in mind something a little more visceral. How might we replicate this today?

Physical Computing

As well as the on-screen programming, many have argued for some sort of physical computing to go with this—providing some introduction to input and output beyond mouse, keyboard, and screen . LEGO Mindstorms, named after Papert's (1980) book (Bumgardner, 2007), offers one possibility here. While the step-by-step build instructions for a floor turtle are not included in the standard materials, a master builder would be able to figure these out for herself. For others, books (e.g. Astolfo et al., 2007) can provide an outline of what's needed.

Another approach might be to make use of a BBC micro:bit as the brains for a floor turtle, using the edge connector to link this to a powered control board for motors. There are kits readily available to make something like this using a micro:bit, and this approach comes close to Papert and Solomon's idea of building one's own turtle.

Processing

Another approach to making a turtle would be to reinterpret this as making a *virtual* rather than physical turtle—adding at least some of the turtle graphics commands to a language which doesn't have these already, such as Processing.

The Processing language project was initiated back in 2001, thirty years on from Papert and Solomon's paper. It took some inspiration from Logo as a visually expressive language, and one suitable as a first programming language. Processing offers a way of using code to create beautiful visual and interactive media, as well as modeling applications. Originally developed in Java, it can usefully be seen as an introduction to programming in that language, doing lots of the heavy lifting needed to get something interesting up on screen whilst still scaffolding the syntax and approaches. There's also a Python syntax version, but much of the most recent development work has happened in the native JavaScript version, p5.js. For those working in schools this has the huge advantage of not needing anything installed locally—there is an editor right there in the browser, as well as the storage and persistent URLs needed for folks to share their programs (*sketches* in the Processing jargon) with a global audience.

One reason that Processing, particularly in its p5.js incarnation, works well as an introductory text-based language is that it provides some immediate motivation for moving on from Scratch. It is hard to persuade pupils who've created games, animations, and music in Scratch of the value to be found in searching through or sorting arbitrary lists in Python, but much easier to convince them that it is worth learning the syntax to create an amazing generative animation in p5.js.

While Processing is designed with graphics in mind, out of the box it has no implementation of Logo's turtle, but rather adopts an entirely Cartesian model of the canvas. *If you want to program a turtle in Processing, you have to make one.*

Turtles as Objects

To me, the most natural way to make a turtle in Processing is as an object. The turtle has **properties** (its position on the screen, its heading, whether the pen is up or down, and perhaps the color and thickness of the line drawn), and **methods** (moving forward, backward, turning left or right, picking the pen up, putting the pen down, heading home, and perhaps even reporting where it is and where it's headed).

The turtle becomes not merely an object to think with for geometry, but an introduction to object-oriented programming, and a reference object for thinking about some of these, often quite subtle, ideas.

Here is one attempt at defining a class of turtles and constructing a new object in the class, right at the center of the canvas:

```
class Turtle {

    constructor(x_ = width / 2,
                y_ = height / 2,
                direction_ = -90,
                penDown_ = true,
                penColor_ = color(0)) {
        this.x = x_;
        this.y = y_;
        this.direction = direction_;
        this.penDown = penDown_;
        this.penColor = penColor_;
    }
//...
}
```

We might then go ahead and start adding some methods, starting with moving forward. As we are converting from the turtle-centric polar frame to the canvas's Cartesian frame, the math here is high school level, but then so is object-oriented, text-based programming.

```
forward(d) {
        let oldX = this.x;
        let oldY = this.y;
        this.x += d * cos(this.direction);
        this.y += d * sin(this.direction);
        if (this.penDown) {
            stroke(this.penColor);
            line(oldX, oldY, this.x, this.y);
        }
    }
```

Turning right and left though are just changes in the turtle's direction:

```
right(a) {
        this.direction += a;
    }

left(a) {
        this.direction -= a;
    }
```

319

Similarly, pen up and pen down instructions simply change the value of the turtle's penDown parameter:

```
pendown() {
        this.penDown = True;
}

penup() {
        this.penDown = False;
}
```

Once all the necessary methods have been written, it's time to put this to the test. The code here, run once as part of p5.js's setup procedure, draws a regular pentagon as expected. You can see the code borrowed from Logo and that which is native JavaScript:

```
function setup() {
    createCanvas(windowWidth, windowHeight);
    angleMode(DEGREES);
    background(220);
    ted = new Turtle();
    var i;
    for (i = 0; i < 5; i++) {
      ted.forward(200);
      ted.right(72);
    }
}
```

More interesting examples might be experiments with Papert's notion of the *squiral* (Papert, 1980, p. 73):

```
function setup() {
    createCanvas(windowWidth, windowHeight);
    angleMode(DEGREES);
    background(220);
    ted = new Turtle();
    var i;
    for (i = 0; i < 50; i++) {
      ted.forward(10*i);
      ted.right(74);
    }
}
```

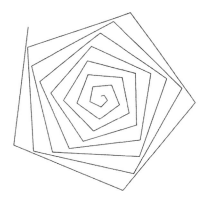

Which produces the pentagonal squiral shown here:

Petagonal squiral

Or, we can go further still, and implement recursion to create a fractal, such as the Koch snowflake (Koch, 1904).

```
function setup() {
    createCanvas(windowWidth, windowHeight);
    angleMode(DEGREES);
    background(220);
    ted = new Turtle();
    for (i=0; i<3; i++) {
      edge(400);
      ted.right(120);
    }
}

function edge(size) {
  if (size < 1) {
    ted.forward(size);
  } else {
    edge(size / 3);
    ted.left(60);
    edge(size / 3);
    ted.right(120);
    edge(size / 3);
    ted.left(60);
    edge(size / 3);
  }
}
```

Koch snowflake

There is, of course, plenty more that can be done in turtle graphics, and Processing itself. I have shared my turtle class and an example sketch online for the reader to extend further. (editor.p5js. org/mberry/sketches/XE-TOpv2)

Papert and Solomon's old idea of *making a turtle* can be a way to understand some far deeper ideas than just learning about exterior angles of polygons or making pretty patterns on screen. *Making a turtle* crosses an abstraction boundary into hardware, or at the very least, objects, properties, and methods, all the while staying within reach of the familiar home ground of the turtle itself.

References

Astolfo, D., Ferrari, M., & Ferrari, G. (2007). *Building Robots with LEGO Mindstorms NXT*. Syngress Publishing, Inc.

Bumgardner, J. (2007). The Origins of Mindstorms. *Wired*. wired.com/2007/03/the-origins-of-/

du Boulay, B., O'Shea, T., & Monk, J. (1981). The Black Box inside the Glass Box: Presenting Computing Concepts to Novices. *International Journal of man-machine studies*, 14(3: 237-249).

Flesch, R. (1951). *The Art of Clear Thinking*. Harper.

Koch, H. (1904). Sur une courbe continue sans tangente, obtenue par une construction géométrique élémentaire. *Arkiv for Matematik, Astronomi och Fysik*, 1: 681-704.

Papert, S. (1980). *Mindstorms: Children, Computers, and Powerful Ideas*. Basic Books.

#11: Make a Music Box and Program a Tune

Walter Bender & Devin Ulibarri

All musicians are subconsciously mathematicians.
—*Thelonious Monk, jazz pianist and composer*

Why Music?

Enumerated by Seymour Papert and Cynthia Solomon as "thing to do" #11, music is used as an entry point for engaging in computational thinking. Computation and music share important concepts. And music, like computation, requires a person to think on an abstract level. Moreover, music has some benefits that the traditional computing pedagogy does not, including the potential to improve social-emotional skills. See Table 1 for some examples of shared concepts between music and programming.

Music composition and performance require practitioners to follow basic control flow such as: sequences; conditionals and loops; data abstractions such as changes in timbre, tone, and meter; functions and operators such as transpositions, inversions, and retrograde; and debugging—making corrections to a composition, perfecting a transcription, or working through a section of music on an instrument—that leads to a deeper understanding of music theory.

The social aspect of musical performance also parallels the perspective that computing is both collaborative and creative (Brennan & Resnick, 2012). An analog can be built between the way programmers work together, building communities around sharing and remixing code, and the way in which musicians build communities of interest through performance, sharing, and debating best practices. Programmers review code and musicians critique performances. Both musicians and programmers modify, improvise, and derive inspiration from the work of peers and mentors.[1]

According to the National Endowment for the Arts: "Childhood arts education provides important gateway and formative experiences in the arts... School-based arts education is of particular importance because schools are the only institutions that reach vast numbers of children, particularly low-income children, who are unlikely to receive arts education any other way... [A] body of solid research and innovative practice continues to grow and show that arts education has serious benefits to students as students, and that arts learning is strongly associated with higher levels of achievement, positive social and emotional development, and successful transitions into adulthood" (Bawa et al., 2010).

In another study, "an analysis of longitudinal data on 25,000 students showed that those with higher levels of involvement with the arts did better across a wide range of outcome variables than those with lower arts involvement, and that low-income students benefited from their involvement in the arts more significantly than did higher-income students" (Catterall et al., 1999).

Students demonstrably benefit from an engaging music education. Demand today is in science, technology, engineering, and mathematics (STEM) and EdTech. Why not give people and institutions the option to learn both STEM and music?

Programming concept	Musical counterpart
Sequences	A series of notes (or phrases), in order
Loops	Repeating phrases, drum loops
Conditionals	Using conditionals for 1st and 2nd endings
Data structures	Note structure (note length, pitch name, and pitch octave) and phrase structure
Modularity and abstraction	Actions, transpositions, intervals, ornamentation, inversions, etc.
Debugging	Using one's ear, e.g., does the result sound correct? Understanding of music theory, e.g., where is the meaningful musical structure?

Table 1: Shared concepts: programming and music

Computation, Not Coding

As recently as 2006, during the launch of *One Laptop per Child* (Bender et al., 2012), there was pushback from educators and pundits regarding children using computers. But fifteen years and one global pandemic later, few argue against children having access to computing. The role of computation in learning, however, remains open to debate. In an article in the *New York Times* (Singer, 2017), Tim Cook, CEO of Apple, Inc., representing the point of view of Silicon Valley, said "Coding should be a requirement in every public school." But to what end? To ensure a "skilled workforce"? Beyond the false promise that by learning Java you will get a job at Google, we take the position that *learning to code* is not the same as becoming literate in *computational thinking*. Computational thinking, rather, is "solving problems using techniques from computing" (Sharples et al., 2015) and it has ramifications far beyond job training; it is about expression of ideas, problem solving, and creativity, all important life skills.

Acknowledging that computational thinking is about more than learning to program leads to a number of questions: How should we go about leveraging the latent capacity to learn? How can we transform a consumer-oriented culture into a learning-oriented culture? And is it possible to design a learning platform that respects the diversity of educational context found across a diversity of learning populations?

Music Is "Hard Fun"

In a 2008 memo "Questioning General Education," Marvin Minsky proposed that we "re-aim our schools towards encouraging children to pursue more focused hobbies and specialties—to provide them with more time for (and earlier experience with) developing more powerful sets of mental skills, which they later can extend to more academic activities." Minsky goes on to argue that the organization of our cognitive resources into towers with different levels of processes is what "enables our minds to generate so many new kinds of things and ideas." These levels span agencies, each of which specializes in areas such as gaining knowledge from experience, planning and causal attribution, the construction of models, and identifying values and ideals. A focus on achieving meaningful goals, not just the accumulation of simple knowledge objects, exercises all of the levels in a cognitive tower, helping a child "develop proficiencies that can be used in other domains" (Minsky, 2019).

A focus on achieving meaningful goals, not just the accumulation of trivial knowledge, helps a child "develop proficiencies that can be used in other domains." A focus on hobbies, where interest is authentic and sustained, as opposed to curricula organized around the sequential achievement of fragmented goals, has the potential for deep engagement across multiple levels. Albert Einstein summed up the focus on hobbies succinctly when he said, "Love is a better master than duty." It was in this spirit that Minsky's Music Box spawned the music ideas in the *Twenty Things* memo (Solomon et al., 2020).[2] Music was and is a vehicle for deep engagement.

Note the emphasis on "deep" engagement. There is a strong temptation to make things as simple as possible so as to reach the broadest possible audience. However some things (e.g., music and computation) are inherently complex. The hard part of "hard fun" of learning is in reaching towards complexity. Using an app is easy. Writing an app is harder. Listening to music is easy.[3] Performing and composing music is harder. Children should not miss out on the learning that takes place when engaging with complexity.

Musical Microworlds

Papert used the term *microworld* to describe the world of geometry explored when children used Logo. A microworld is a "subset of reality or a constructed reality whose structure matches that of a given cognitive mechanism so as to provide an environment where the latter can operate effectively. The concept leads to the project of inventing microworlds so structured as to allow a human learner to exercise particular powerful ideas or intellectual skills." (Papert, 1980)

In a microworld, an individual is able to use a technological tool for thinking and cognitive exploration that would not be possible without the technology. But not just any technology. "The use of the microworld provides a model of a learning theory in which active learning consists of exploration by the learner of a microworld sufficiently bounded and transparent for constructive exploration and yet sufficiently rich for significant discovery" (Papert, 1980).

In a microworld of music, a student might start by exploring pitch and rhythm while using affordances for repetition, transposition, etc. The tools are more than an interface to a synthesizer and more than a transcription/engraving tool (e.g., Finale, Sibelius, Musescore, etc.)—they are scalable and modular collections of essential building blocks that are at the crux of all powerful ideas in music.

The microworld is designed to introduce a specific concept with parallels in both music and computer science. For example, a workshop on rhythm utilizes a rhythm making tool that introduces the concept of loops, which are used for drum machines implemented by *while* loops.

Music Blocks

"Music is a hidden arithmetic exercise of the soul, which does not know that it is counting." — Leibniz

Music Blocks[4] (musicblocks.sugarlabs.org) is a visual programming language and collection of manipulative tools for exploring musical and mathematical concepts in an integrative and fun way. Music Blocks is a fork of Turtle Blocks,[5] an activity with a Logo-inspired graphical turtle that draws colorful art based on snap-together visual programming elements. Its *low floor* provides an easy entry point for beginners. It also has *high ceiling* programming, graphics, mathematics, and computer science features that will challenge the more adventurous student.

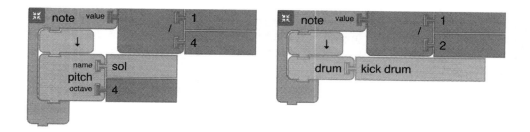

Figures 1 and 2: Note-value representation as visual programming in Music Blocks. Note value is a quanta of time expressed as a ratio; ¼ is the same as a quarter note in music. Whatever is contained within the note value clamp will be done over the length of time of a quarter note. The example on the left will perform G (in the 4th octave) for the length of a quarter note; the example on the right will perform a kick drum sound for the length of a quarter note.

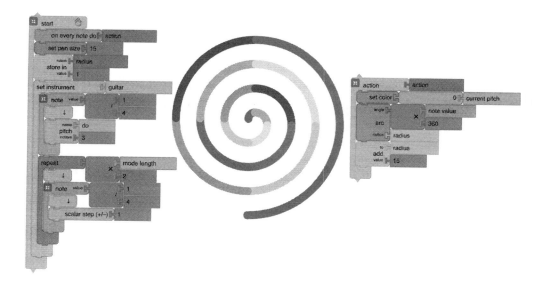

Figure 3: In this example, two octaves are played during which a portion of a spiral is drawn with each note. The angular distance traversed is determined by the note's value. The line color is determined by the note's pitch. The resulting spiral serves as an example of an alternative notation system created by a student using Music Blocks.

Music is not an add-on to the Music Blocks language; the *note* is a core datatype in the language (See Figures 1–3). The note expresses a quanta of time as a ratio, because the relative length of a note and their relationship to other notes is the fundamental basis of rhythm.[6] From there, Music Blocks has various ways to express pitch: solfege (e.g., do, re, mi), musical alphabet (e.g., C, D, E), and Hertz (e.g., 440Hz for A in an equal temperament tuning system), which are pedagogically important expressions of pitch for making music.[7]

Music, like computer science, offers a rich environment for exploration and problem solving, of which the intersection of their shared concepts allow for integrative learning. Music Blocks is designed to leverage the tools of the trade by using well-established scaffolding in music instruction and building analogous tools (or widgets) to help shape the introduction of powerful ideas, such as polyphonic rhythms, key and mode, intervals, tuning, and temperament. The software widgets are also tied to concepts in computer science. In other words, the widgets don't just produce music, they output code that is descriptive of concepts found in music, such as generating rhythms, changing tempo, and using samples.

The configuration of each widget is programmable (using blocks) and every widget can be used to write and export code (as blocks). Along with the activities defined by the widgets, students also: identifying and differentiate patterns; explore proportions, ratios, and relationships expressed through chords and intervals; read and represent musical ideas with a graph; use conditionals to express a melodic sequence; and program canons to explore concurrency.

The activities in which the students engage are constructive rather than instructive. Music Blocks provides scaffolding without over specifying the end results. Consequently, there are also numerous mechanisms to support *debugging* of both the music and the code.[8] In the spirit of Papert and Solomon, some things to do with Music Blocks are listed in Table 2.

1. Animate polyrhythms	13. Explore beat and rhythm	28. Program strange loops (recursion)
2. Broadcast conductor instructions	14. Explore chance	29. Build a record player
3. Program a canon	15. "Face the Music"	30. Explore musical symmetry
4. Explore circles of fifths	16. Use dictionaries to control ornamentation	31. Explore synesthesia
5. Program a circular rhythm maker	17. Design a notation system	32. Use the heap to explore variations on a theme
6. Use conditionals in music	18. Explore intervals	33. Build a xylophone
7. Explore representations	19. Make a piano	34. Make a musical valentine
8. Musical cookie hunt	20. Build a better mousetrap	35. Program *Musical Racko*
9. Design a crazy keyboard	21. Make a music video	36. Program a version of Set, where the dimensions are musical
10. Debug a composition	22. Program *Music Deducto*	
11. Design theme music for heroes and monsters for a video game	23. Make music paint	37. Build a metronome
	24. Use an oscilloscope	38. Build a one-string guitar
	25. Hunt for hidden music	39. Explore harmonics
12. Use events for interactivity	26. Explore quiet and loud	40. Invent 40 more ideas
	27. Incorporate sensors for interactivity	

Table 2: Some things to do with Music Blocks

Beyond Music Blocks

A musical microworld is not a destination. Rather, it is a waypoint along a road to achieving fluency in both musical comprehension and computational thinking. We want the students to dive deeper into musical representations and programming constructs than they could do in a single session. Therefore we provide mechanisms to go beyond tools such as Music Blocks to give the learner both the ability to communicate with the mainstream worlds of music and computer science and access to a rich set of tools that they may use to further augment their explorations. Our workshops, by design, do not confine a user to its tools—rather it is a tool to propel the ambitious learner to other rich and authentic discoveries (Bender et al., 2016).

```
\version "2.18.2"
mouse = {
\meter
\tempo 4 = 75
 \time 4/4
<e' c'>2 <f' a>4 <f' a>4 <e' c'>2 <d' g>4 r4
<e' c'>2 <g' g>4 <g' g>4 <g' c'>2 <a' f>4 g'4
<e' c'>2 <f' a>4 <f' a>4 <e' c'>2 <d' g>4 r4
<e' c'>2 <g' g>4 <g' g>4 <g' c'>2 <a' f>4 g'4
}
\score {
<<
\new Staff = "treble" {
\clef "treble"
\set Staff.instrumentName = #"mouse" \mouse
}
>>
\layout { }
}
```

Made with LilyPond and Music Blocks (http://musicblocks.sugarlabs.org/)

Teddy Composition

Teddy Dildine

Figure 4: Lilypond is a music engraving program. The Save as Lilypond option in Music Blocks exports a Music Blocks composition into sheet music, thus connecting traditional musical notation with the block language. (Shown is part of a composition by then seven-year-old T. Dildine.)

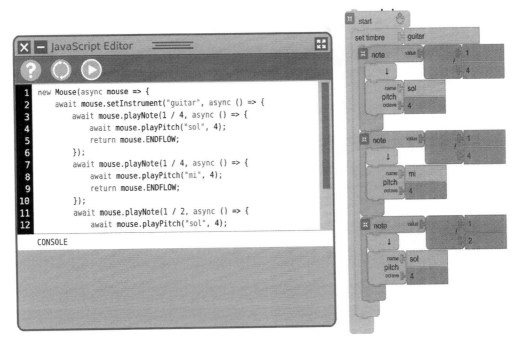

Figure 5: There are practical limits to the size and complexity of Music Blocks programs. At some point we expect Music Blocks programmers to move on to text-based programming languages. To facilitate this transition, there is a JavaScript widget that will convert a Music Blocks program into JavaScript. (This feature was added to Music Blocks by Anindya Kundu for Google Summer of Code.)

Music Blocks and Assessment

It is unrealistic to propose an intervention in education without acknowledging the current emphasis on measurement and evaluation. With Music Blocks, the goal is to ensure that any interventions have some positive socio-economic impact on children, so an evaluation is used that looks more broadly than those data that are captured by standardized tests. Evaluation occurs at different levels (Urrea & Bender, 2012): micro (at the level of individual students, teachers, and parents); mezzo (at the level of a classroom or school); and macro (national and global indicators). These mechanisms, briefly reviewed below, are orthogonal to the typical standardized-testing regimes; the two approaches—one serving administrators, the other serving learners—coexist.

At the micro level, Music Blocks maintains a digital portfolio to support reflection that can help students (as well as teachers and parents) become aware of their own learning, and do so by documenting their work and thinking over time. Digital portfolios are part of a "comprehensive system that combines formal, informal, and classroom assessment, including portfolios, to inform the state, the district, the school, and the teacher" (Stefanakis, 2002). Without a way to make visible what students do and what teachers teach, it is difficult to make changes to improve those dynamics. Both music and coding produce artifacts that are readily captured in a digital portfolio—for example, musical compositions, code, and geometric art. As with a source-code management system, each *commit* is accompanied by a *commit message*, where the learner is asked to document their work.

At a mezzo level, Music Blocks has tools that help teachers understand the impact and evolution of the program in a larger context—at the level of the classroom or the school. The goal is to navigate and visualize data automatically derived from the learning activities in which the learners are engaged. These data help teachers, administrators, and other stakeholders understand the impact of a program and make adjustments to it. Music Blocks has a built-in set of rubrics (Bender & Urrea, 2015) that can be used to visualize and track student progress.

At a macro level, Music Blocks supports strategies for understanding the use of computation in learning at a much larger scale. These strategies involve the design and implementation of a repository of objects or artifacts designed by children from different programs. There are a number of similar repositories with artifacts from an individual already in existence, for example, the Scratch website and the Music Blocks Planet (server with student published projects, accessible world-wide). Such collections make possible the analysis and understanding of impact at a large scale, and the learning that emerges, not only at the individual, but also at the collective level. In the respect that these sites allow users to *remix*, they bear a close resemblance to popular tools used in computer engineering, such as GitHub and GitLab.

Music+Code Teaching Artists

Around the time that he invented the Music Box, Minsky served as the AI consultant on Stanley Kubrick's movie adaptation of Arthur C. Clark's *2001: A Space Odyssey*. Both the HAL 9000 computer and the notion that children would be programming music were considered science fiction in 1971. Fifty years later, Siri et al. can "open the pod-bay doors" and play a competitive game of chess; any child with access to a web browser can program music with Music Blocks. But who will mentor these children? Who will guide them in their exploration of a musical microworld? Who will introduce them to the powerful ideas inherent in both music and computation?

STEM education is in high demand. Policy makers are mandating schools teach computer programming in their classrooms, which creates a demand for teachers trained in computation. Primary education, however, is not seen as a competitive or desirable career for many who have computer programming skills. So who will teach these skills?

Music education, with its rich blend of theory and practice, has proven benefits to early education and yet, because of financial and time pressures, it is largely sidelined in public education. Is there a way we can capture the benefits of music education that has been pushed aside in order to advance STEM education?

Musicians graduate from conservatories and colleges with few career prospects other than part time teaching jobs and freelance performance gigs. Professionals who specialize in music and who teach music both inside and outside of traditional settings are called "Teaching Artists" (Booth, 2009). Teaching Artists, even those working at the world's most prestigious institutions, typically work multiple part-time jobs in order to scrape by financially (National Endowment for the Arts, 2011b).

The many skilled Teaching Artists who are graduating at a steady rate from music schools can introduce young learners to programming and programming can be used as a vehicle to surface the powerful mathematical structure inherent in music. Teaching Artists can play a central role in primary STEM education, while simultaneously providing the proven cognitive and social-emotional benefits of a quality music education (Gaser & Schlaug, 2003; Hutchinson et al., 2003; Lee et al., 2003; Schlaug, 2001; Skoe & Kraus, 2012). Engaging and employing Teaching Artists into the booming economy of EdTech provides rich exposure to computational thinking, while not compromising music's proven benefits to a child's cognitive development and overall well-being.

While music is not typically associated with computer science, there is a depth of literature (Brindle, 1987; Garland & Kahn, 1995; Nierhaus, 2009) drawing parallels between music and mathematics. By focusing on the parallels between music and computation, and the knowledge and insights gained through designing and critiquing their musical and programmatic constructs, Teaching Artists offer novel perspectives of both music and computer science to learners, educators, and the public.

Music is a universal language. Leveraging music and music teachers has the potential to reach a global audience. Under-employed musicians, who are statistically proven to be highly educated and demographically diverse (National Endowment for the Arts, 2011a), are a global phenomenon, one that we leverage both in terms of mining latent skills and also filling a need for more diverse and engaging mentorship in computational thinking. Teaching Artists using Music Blocks will foster basic computer science skills and broaden public engagement in computer science in a large, diverse population that has been underserved by existing efforts for broadening participation in computer science and engage and enable a talented but underemployed group—music teachers—in fulfilling both pedagogical and societal needs.[9]

References

Bawa, S., Williams, K., & Dong, W. (2010). *Audience 2.0: How Technology Influences Arts Participation*. National Endowment for the Arts.

Bender, W., Kane, C., Cornish, J., & Donahue, N. (2012). *Learning to Change the World: The Social Impact of One Laptop Per Child*. St. Martin's Publishing Group.

Bender, W., Ulibarri, D., & Khandelwal, Y. (2016). Music Blocks: A Musical Microworld. *Constructionism 2016, Constructionism in Action*.

Bender, W., & Urrea, C. (2015). Visualizing Learning in Open-Ended Problem Solving in the Arts. *RED-Revista de Educación a Distancia, 46*(2). doi.org/10.6018/red/46/2

Booth, E. (2009). *The Music Teaching Artist's Bible*. Oxford Univ. Press.

Brennan, K., & Resnick, M. (2012). New Frameworks for Studying and Assessing the Development of Computational Thinking. *Proceedings of the 2012 annual meeting of the American Educational Research Association (AERA), 1*, 25.

Brindle, R. S. (1987). *The New Music: The Avant-garde Since 1945*. Oxford Univ. Press.

Catterall, J., Chapleau, R., & et al. (1999). Involvement in the Arts and Human Development: General Involvement and Intensive Involvement in Music and Theatre Arts. In E. Fiske (Ed.), *Champions of Change: The Impact of the Arts on Learning* (pp. 1-18.11). Washington DC: Arts Education Partnership and President's Committee on the Arts and Humanities.

Garland, T. H., & Kahn, C. V. (1995). *Math and Music: Harmonious Connections*. Seymour (Dale) Publications.

Gaser, C., & Schlaug, G. (2003). Brain Structures Differ between Musicians and Non-Musicians. *Journal of Neuroscience, 23*(27), 9240-9245. doi.org/10.1523/JNEUROSCI.23-27-09240.2003

Hutchinson, S., Lee, L. H., Gaab, N., & Schlaug, G. (2003). Cerebellar Volume of Musicians *Cerebral Cortex, 13*(9), 943-949. doi.org/10.1093/cercor/13.9.943

Lee, D., Chen, Y., & Schlaug, G. (2003). Corpus Callosum: Musician and Gender Effects. *Neuroreport, 14*(2), 205-209. doi.org/10.1097/00001756-200302100-00009

Minsky, M. (2019). Questioning General Education. In C. Solomon & X. Xiao (Eds.), *Inventive Minds: Marvin Minsky on Education*. MIT Press.

National Endowment for the Arts. (2011a). Artists and Arts Workers in the United States. *NEA Research Note #105*.

National Endowment for the Arts. (2011b). Findings from the American Community Survey (2005-2009) and the Quarterly Census of Employment and Wages (2010). *NEA Research Note #105*.

Nierhaus, G. (2009). *Algorithmic Composition: Paradigms of Automated Music Generation*. Springer.

Papert, S. (1980). *Mindstorms: Children, Computers, and Powerful Ideas*. Basic Books.

Schlaug, G. (2001). The Brain of Musicians: A Model for Functional and Structural Adaptation. *Annals of the New York Academy of Sciences, 930*, 281-299. doi.org/10.1111/j.1749-6632.2001.tb05739.x

Sharples, M., Adams, A., Alozie, N., & Ferguson, R. (2015). *Innovating Pedagogy 2015* (Report No: 4).

Singer, N. (2017, June 17). How Silicon Valley Pushed Coding Into American Classrooms. *New York Times*

Skoe, E., & Kraus, N. (2012). A Little Goes a Long Way: How the Adult Brain Is Shaped by Musical Training in Childhood. *The Journal of Neuroscience, 32*(34), 11507-11510. doi.org/10.1523/JNEURO-SCI.1949-12.2012

Solomon, C., Harvey, B., Kahn, K., Lieberman, H., Miller, M., Minsky, M., Papert, A., Silverman, B., & Shepard, T. (2020). History of Logo. *Proceedings of the ACM on Programming Languages, 4*(HOPL). doi.org/10.1145/3386329

Stefanakis, E. H. (2002). *Multiple Intelligences and Portfolios: A Window into the Learner's Mind*. Heinemann.

Urrea, C., & Bender, W. (2012). Making Learning Visible. *Mind, Brain, and Education, 6*(4), 227-241.

Notes

1 With both Music and Free/Libre Software, there is complete transparency—nothing is hidden from the student, giving them the opportunity to both debug and remix.

2 It is worth noting that Wally Feurzeig—one of the co-inventors of Logo—was both a mathematician and a pianist (Solomon et al. 2020).

3 Our intention is not to demean the demands of serious listening, but popular culture so often invites people to be passive consumers of music.

4 Music Blocks is available under the GNU Affero General Public License (AGPL) v3.0, a free, copyleft license.

5 Turtle Blocks is a fork of Brian Silverman's Turtle Art.

6 Other languages such as MAX, Scratch, or SuperCollider require the user to specify quantas of time from seconds and create their own functions in order to express time in this manner—perhaps this is why musicians do not universally find those languages useful for teaching concepts from music.

7 Music Blocks also allows the student to explore concepts such as mode, key, timbre, and temperament (See github.com/sugarlabs/musicblocks/blob/master/guide/README.md).

8 See github.com/sugarlabs/musicblocks/blob/master/Debugging.md

9 Some Music Blocks lesson plans are available at mapflc.com/lesson-plans/

The Future is Computational

Gary Stager

In celebrating Papert and Solomon's work over the past half century, I wish to assert that the future is computational. Logo was originally intended to help children be mathematicians, rather than being taught math. Yet, even at the beginning children used Logo to play with language and make music. Mathematical thinking encompassed more than the school math curriculum. Yet in order to *do* the things suggested in *Twenty Things,* computer programming is required. Programming is perfectly suited to match a young person's capacity for intensity and can be quite satisfying.

Educational technology must be more than getting kids computers or using them in class-rooms. Our efforts need to be directed towards empowering kids to control their world and explore new intellectual terrain.

I have admired Thomas Edison since first visiting his laboratory in New Jersey on a third-grade field trip. Edison posted signs containing a quote by Sir Joshua Reynolds throughout his R&D complex. The signs read, *"There is no expedient to which a man will not resort to avoid the real labor of thinking."* When I think about the use of computers in schools, I cannot help but conclude, *"There is no expedient to which educators will not resort to justify not teaching children to program computers."* Consider the decades of wasted time and tortured rhetoric used to rationalize denying students access to such powerful experiences. It's a sin.

Such oppositional behavior may be blamed on anti-intellectualism, mathphobia, or an inability to add one more thing to a morbidly obese curriculum. It could be that adults are afraid of knowing less about something than children, but that has long been the case. Just consider dinosaurs, Harry Potter, song lyrics, or nearly any hobby children engage in. Papert suggested that what's different about kids learning to program computers is that the knowledge and skills such children possess is perhaps for the first time coveted and valued by adult society. That creates a power imbalance for insecure adults. We delight in the tales of the thirteen-year-old coder who made a million dollars programming an app, but do we really want her in our class?

There are many reasons to learn to program computers. You can:
- Make things
- Make things work
- Express yourself
- Develop habits of mind
- Solve problems
- Concretize abstractions
- Contextualize mathematics
- Develop debugging strategies
- Do it by yourself or with others
- Programming mirrors the writing process and various design cycles
- Programming is "hard fun"
- New jobs and careers are made possible by knowing how to program

The vocational argument is perhaps the least compelling of all. The best reason to teach programming is that it is a new liberal art. Programming gives children agency over an increasingly complex and technologically sophisticated world. At a time of rising authoritarianism, accusations of fake news, science denialism, and "alternative facts"—systems thinking, especially when you are in command of the system, is critical experience for navigating a world in which you will be required to solve problems your teachers never imagined.

During one school visit, the principal introduced me to a group of five or six fifth-grade girls who had just won a statewide competition to design the best app. After demonstrating their app, which was fine, I asked a couple of questions. "What else have you programmed?" They looked blankly at me and didn't offer a response. So, I asked another question. "What would you like to program next?" In unison, the students turned to their teacher awaiting a hint.

This brief encounter concerned me deeply. The reason to teach students anything is so they may appropriate that knowledge—make it their own—and use it to learn other things. One great thing about computer programming is that is generative in nature. You test a hypothesis or try something new and based on the feedback you receive. You engage in debugging or are inspired to test a larger hypothesis, embellish, decorate, or improve upon your creation. An ingredient of fluency is a desire to create something else. Programming is like singing, dancing, writing, cooking, or painting. The more you do it, the more you want to do it. You should have ideas for what to do next, even if your dreams exceed your talent. The lack of motivation displayed by the contest winners is an all too familiar school phenomenon. Realizing the aspiration of lifelong learning requires a great deal more empowerment, voice, and agency.

We should be capable of holding two thoughts simultaneously.

1. All kids should learn to program across the curriculum.

2. Some children will select computer science as their project.

School systems should offer a range of computer science courses for some children to pursue, but we also need to democratize programming so that it is part of every child's bag of tricks, across the curriculum. Rather than democratize computing and make meaningful programming experiences available to all children, many schools and school systems choose the illusion of progress over real action. Hour of Code, an advocacy event, has become the thing schools do for an hour or two annually to wink at modernity. Students solve a few puzzles and schools are off the hook for another year.

More ambitious systems with digital technology mandates spread a pile of vocabulary words—binary, byte, algorithm, compression—over eight to twelve years and often absent any actual experience using the concepts. Even when the curriculum includes some programming this incremental scope and sequence approach leads to teaching *IF* in 2nd grade and *THEN* in 3rd. Again, there seems to be little urgency for children to develop computing fluency. I would be quite wealthy if I had a nickel for every educator who told me, "We do a little Scratch!" I would be a lot more impressed by classrooms in which kids did a *lot* of Scratch and whose projects revealed powerful thinking and creativity.

My second variation on the Sir Joshua Reynolds quote is, *"There is no expedient to which a school will resort to create fake experiences for children when real ones are readily available."* When schools even lack the interest to create an illusion that they teach students how to do something like program computers, a new discipline is invented as a form of obfuscation. Computational thinking is used to justify self-parodies such as Computer Science Unplugged or similar Potemkin curricula that pretend to teach computer science without all those pesky computers. Even if this is an earnest objective, why is it necessary? Have all the personal computers suddenly vanished? We can teach cooking without food and utensils or dance while sitting behind desks, but why bother?

Computer science author, lecturer, and Snap! designer Brian Harvey said that "Computational thinking without programming is just math." Since school math is shambolic, turning computing into math is a mistake. I am concerned that in the hands of those Papert called

"Schoolers," computation has been denatured and fossilized. That said, there are smart people thinking a lot about computational thinking, not as a course of study, but as an intellectual habit.

Academics have spent decades arguing over semantics and seeking to prove or disprove claims that using computers, or even programming them, transfers to other domains (Lodi & Martini, 2021).[1] If they wish to dedicate their time and life's work to such skirmishes, bless their hearts. The movement initiated by Seymour Papert and Cynthia Solomon, set forth in documents such as *Twenty Things*, share simpler and simultaneously more profound objectives. We seek to create the conditions in which children can form relationships with powerful ideas and love learning. Computers are not going anywhere. Digital technology is at the center of our lives. Kids tend not to be intimidated by it. Therefore, wouldn't it be grand if children could control that technology and use it as an intellectual laboratory and vehicle for self-expression?

It seems cynical and myopic to turn such humane goals into a game of gotcha, intent on "proving" that one intervention or another failed to elevate test scores. Such "scientism" (Papert, 1990) distracts us from taking obvious steps to make the world a better place for kids. The quest for empirical proof in education is another form of inaction. Brian Harvey explores this conflict between traditional educational research and progressive goals:

> If you're making a revolution, you don't have to prove that you achieve the goals of the ancien régime. Papert was impatient, as am I, with the apparatus of Group A and Group B, pre-tests and post-tests, "p < 0.05." In one famous or notorious proposal for funding, he suggested that the funding agency agree to support his project for five years, without oversight or progress reports, and at the end of that time, "if any observer is tempted to apply statistical methods, declare the experiment a failure." (I'm quoting from memory so I'm not sure those are his exact words, but they're close.) That proposal wasn't funded, and Papert learned to use less inflammatory rhetoric, at least when talking to funding agencies. But the principle remains intact; Logo was not meant to do a slightly better job of teaching curriculum, whether traditional or innovative (Harvey, 2014).

I choose to live in a world in which children wake up in the middle of the night counting down the minutes until they can return to class to continue working on a project and their teachers wake up every morning to ask themselves, "How do I make this the best seven hours of a kid's life?" My friend and hero, the great civil rights activist Jonathan Kozol, reminds us that a child is only seven years old once. We must embrace a greater sense of urgency. *Twenty Things* is fifty years old. Microcomputers have been widely available for more than four decades. We cannot afford to dither while depriving a third generation of experiences compatible with their potential and consistent with this moment.

It's Time for Action!

Schools use computers in many ways, but I wish to make one more attempt to advocate that mathematics, computation, and programming offers the most fertile ground for educational progress today and in the future. There are at least six reasons to justify this assertion.

Reason #1: New ways of knowing and new things to know

I choose to say "programming," rather than "coding." Too often coding implies breaking a code or solving a puzzle. The code you write is an artifact of your thinking and debugging. Educators should deal in verbs, not nouns. Programming is the process one engages in as a way of concretizing abstractions to make a computer work for you. I use the term, computing, to describe a broad range of activities in which a user creates with a computer. I must confess to sloppiness while writing about mathematical thinking, computing, and computation. Fortunately, Stephen

Wolfram, arguably one of the world's most accomplished mathematicians and computer scientists offers clear and satisfying definitions.

Let's try to define what we mean by "computational thinking." As far as I'm concerned, its intellectual core is about formulating things with enough clarity, and in a systematic enough way, that one can tell a computer how to do them. Mathematical thinking is about formulating things so that one can handle them mathematically, when that's possible. Computational thinking is a much bigger and broader story, because there are just a lot more things that can be handled computationally (Wolfram, 2016).

Wolfram and his colleagues have developed Wolfram Language, a programming language that allows users to engage in more natural language than traditional programming languages. Wolfram Language powers Mathematica, the software used for serious mathematics and science, as well as the knowledge engine, Wolfram Alpha. Wolfram Language affords users, even children, mind-boggling opportunities to solve problems, explore new intellectual domains, and supercharge project-based learning.

The Wolfram Language is knowledge based: it knows about things in the world—like cities, or species, or songs, or photos we take—and it knows how to compute with them. And as soon as we have an idea that we can formulate computationally, the point is that the language lets us express it, and then—thanks to 30 years of technology development—lets us as automatically as possible actually execute the idea.

The Wolfram Language is a programming language. So when you write in it, you're doing programming. But it's a new kind of programming. It's programming in which one's as directly as possible expressing computational thinking—rather than just telling the computer step-by-step what low-level operations it should do. It's programming where humans— including kids—provide the ideas, then it's up to the computer and the Wolfram Language to handle the details of how they get executed.

Programming—and programming education—have traditionally been about telling a computer at a low level what to do. But thanks to all the technology we've built in the Wolfram Language, one doesn't have to do that anymore. One can express things at a much higher level—so one can concentrate on computational thinking, not mere programming (Wolfram, 2016).

Note that Wolfram does not substitute computational thinking for learning to program. He views programming as part of computational thinking that now has even greater affordances.

Watching Stephen Wolfram demonstrate Wolfram Language is like watching a wizard engage in alchemy. The power afforded by this programming environment borders on the mystical; the seemingly impossible becomes possible, right on your screen. There is no doubt that computational environments, like Wolfram Language and its likely descendants, will be used by anyone engaged in serious intellectual or creative pursuits. Such technological progress is wholly consistent with the vision of *Twenty Things*.

Now you might not think that the work of kids is intellectual. If you don't think that, that's why we're in such trouble, it is and ought to be and so they want to have this instrument and having said that we turn to the longer answer, including why is it that anybody would resist this? Why would it occur to anybody to deprive them of this intellectual tool since many of the people who are to deprive them of the intellectual tool themselves would protest vehemently if we tried to deprive them of their computers (Papert, 2000).

If teachers were to embrace such opportunities, their students would not only be better prepared for careers, but for life itself.

> *Doctors, lawyers, teachers, farmers, whatever. The future of all these professions will be full of computational thinking. Whether it's sensor-based medicine, computational contracts, education analytics or computational agriculture—success is going to rely on being able to do computational thinking well.*
>
> *I've noticed an interesting trend. Pick any field X, from archeology to zoology. There either is now a "computational X" or there soon will be. And it's widely viewed as the future of the field (Wolfram, 2016).*

Stated in more crass terms, the future of any field is also likely to be its most lucrative branch. Enabling children to develop computational fluency may help them do good and do well.

Reason #2: Harm mitigation

The current approach to math instruction is doing great harm. Regardless of your political ideology or pedagogical perspective, there appears to be unanimity in concluding that school math is a disaster. Mathphobia is rampant. Democracy is threatened by innumeracy. Parents are frustrated. Kids hate math class and educational opportunities are stymied by students' inability to climb an artificial, yet intractable, curricular ladder of required coursework (Moses & Cobb, 2001; Richardson, 2009).

By nearly every measure, even standardized testing, the continuous attempts at improving math instruction demonstrate the catastrophic failure of instructionism. There may be no other school subject that embraces instructionism so thoroughly. Math class is predicated on one person teaching and the smaller people learning. This pedagogical myth has endured for centuries. David Thornburg likes to show audiences a painting of a medieval math class, hardly distinguishable from a contemporary depiction of math class.

We have simply run out of new ways to teach the same content absent meaningful experiences or contexts for learning. The stance of Papert and Solomon, as found in *Twenty Things*, offers a constructionist course correction. Through the end of his life, Seymour Papert argued that a new diet of mathematics was required. *Twenty Things* embodies his ethos that our efforts should be invested in developing a mathematics children can love rather than inventing tricks to teach them a mathematics they hate.

> *What I try to do is to find ways of offering kids and everybody opportunities to get a taste of what real mathematical thinking is like so that if they love it, they have a chance of falling in love with it. I believe they can get a lot of pleasure out of it, and I believe that having more mathematicians in the world will lead to a lot of advances in other ways that would be valuable for society (Papert, 2002).*

Reason #3: What we're teaching isn't mathematics

There may be no other instance where the gap between the discipline and the teaching of that discipline are as wide as the distance between mathematics and the stuff taught in schools called math. Mathematics is a great jewel of human intellect and empowerment. Math classes are a sorting mechanism in which a few children win, and most others lose.

> *Certain notions of mathematics are not sufficiently embedded in the culture for children to learn in their natural way, so they come to school to learn them. Once children are in school, we try to impose mathematics on them in much the same way it was imposed on us: we*

begin by making them work at unimportant and uninteresting problems on little squares of paper. If before we ever allowed children to dance, we insisted that they spend hundreds of hours drawing dance steps on square papers, and only when they could pass a test on the ability to draw dance steps on paper would we let them actually get up and dance, many children would find dancing impossibly difficult. Those gifted in dance would give up. And I think this is exactly what we do with mathematics. We teach it to the children in a way quite analogous to drawing dance steps on paper, and only those who can survive twelve years of that ever get to use it, to dance with it (Papert, 1984).

While the pace of change in math education remains glacial, mathematics continues to evolve with great alacrity.

In 1989 the National Council of Teachers of Mathematics Standards reported, "50% of all mathematics has been invented since World War II" (Romberg, 1989). This is the result of two factors: the social science's increasing demand for number and the increasing ubiquity of computing. We live in an age in which we are awash in data to make sense of and our way of life benefits from increasing computing power.

New branches of mathematics are beautiful, useful, playful, visual, wondrous, and experimental. Computing makes some of these domains accessible to even young children, and yet you are unlikely to find the likes number theory, chaos, cellular automata, fractal geometry, topology etc., in a K–12 math curriculum. Such new branches of mathematics should not be viewed as post-graduate dessert one earns after consuming twelve or sixteen years of asparagus. Computational environments make messing about with these domains possible and provide a context for learning some of the other math schools have long sought to deliver children.[2]

Access to new intellectual domains is exciting, but traditional math instruction is also terribly inefficient. Conrad Wolfram estimates that schools spend 106 human lifetimes each day and 20,000 student lifetimes per year engaged in mechanical (pencil and worksheet) calculations (Wolfram, 2010, 2020). Expressed another way, such wasteful instruction is the equivalent of spending twelve years educating kids to be a poor facsimile of a $2 calculator. Forty years after the advent of cheap portable calculators, we are *still* debating whether children should be allowed to use one.

Actually, I am against the use of calculators in math class, but not for the usual reactionary reasons. It strikes me as peculiar that billions of dollars have been spent on graphing calculators for school use. For forty years high school students have been required to purchase them. Why was this such an easy sale? Why aren't there calls to justify graphing calculator use by the folks who argue that math scores have flatlined (or worse)? I suggest that the popularity of graphing calculators is fueled by a recognition that they made it possible to teach the same old math curriculum in a virtually unchanged fashion, while adding a patina of modernity to the classroom. Fear and loathing of high school math generally leaves critics to shame teachers and students without making specific recommendations for improvement. There is nothing per se wrong with digital calculation, that functionality is built into the computer every child should own and use in school.

We are allowing education policy and curriculum to be shaped by the mathematical superstitions of a lunatic fringe. The folks who attend school board meetings because they have not been taught to decipher their daughter's math worksheet, and pound their fists while shouting, "2 + 2 always equals 4," are unqualified to set education policy. Educators need to take mathematics back and let textbook publishers keep what they call math.

Reason #4: A threat to the viability of schooling

I was with Seymour Papert in 2004, and while I cannot remember the specific context, he was on a tear about the need to revolutionize math education with all the urgency our society can muster. I teased Seymour about fetishizing math education because he was a mathematician and he exclaimed, "No! No! No!" before rattling off at least a dozen reasons why fixing math education was a priority. I wish I had been recording the conversation, but one of his arguments stuck with me.

Papert believed that no pedagogical innovation of the past century had any tangible impact on math education. If that were not disconcerting enough, it ultimately meant that in practice, no matter how progressive or learner-centered a school aspired to be, there would come a time in the school day when coercion was reintroduced into the system. Math class is when kids feel badly about themselves and are being taught irrelevant tricks they *might* need one day.

Papert argued that such coercion was ultimately corrosive to any other constructive efforts undertaken by a school, eventually undermining efforts like project-based learning, authentic assessment, student led inquiry, and other aspects of constructivist teaching.

Fundamentally, there is no way to make a noxious math curriculum more palatable and that alone undermines all other progressive efforts in a school. Ask any of the great progressive school educators of the past half century about the weak point or greatest challenge in their school, and they will confess it is math.

Reason #5: Greatest room for improvement

The vast majority of schooling is concerned with language arts and vocabulary acquisition. Add computers to the mix and it's nearly the whole ball game.

The phrase, "technology and education" usually means inventing new gadgets to teach the same old stuff in a thinly disguised version of the same old way. Moreover, if the gadgets are computers, the same old teaching becomes incredibly more expensive and biased towards its dumbest parts, namely the kind of rote learning in which measurable results can be obtained by treating the children like pigeons in a skinner box (Papert, 1970).

Sadly, this is not a new phenomenon. Perhaps the greatest return on investment for computers in education is to use them for more than language arts and in a non-instructionist fashion. When computers are employed in math or science contexts, they are used to drill kids, test existing knowledge, or simulate passive phenomena much better suited to hands-on experiences. It would be sensational if students were using word processing, multimedia creation, and collaboration software to challenge expectations or create work they can be proud of. Even if that were reality, computation offers a portal to a more expansive universe of possibilities.

If our goals are no more ambitious than children learning the current math curriculum to perform better on standardized tests, we would be teaching computing. Far too much of the existing curriculum lacks any meaningful application or relevance in a paper and pencil world. That changes with the availability of computation. If mathematics is a way of making sense of the world, computing or computation is a way of making mathematics.

I once observed a sixth-grade math lesson on absolute value. After the breathless thirty-seven-minute lecture, I asked the teacher, "What would you use absolute value for?" She thought hard for a moment, shrugged, and replied, "I don't know. I suppose seventh-grade." That is a familiar variation on to the question, "Why do I need to learn this?" "Because" seems inadequate, but if you are teaching absolute value because of a faith-based relationship with the textbook, that may be the only truthful response. However, absolute value becomes really handy if you are trying to get your spaceship to land near a target in the videogame you are programming or when teaching a robot to navigate unfamiliar refrain. I would never trade children developing geometric relationships via the Logo turtle with the store-bought angle posters adorning so many fifth-grade classroom walls. Who do you think is reading those posters and why have powerful ideas been reduced to vocabulary words?

Absent a computational context, much of the extant math curriculum *is* irrelevant and difficult to learn. When simple tasks are made easy, complexity becomes possible. When children can solve a problem they encounter, when they need to solve it, they are motivated to tackle larger challenges.

Teachers who embrace a pedagogical stance similar to *Twenty Things,* frequently encounter the joy of children exclaiming things like, "Oh, I know what's wrong! It's not greater than, it's less than!" while programming or designing a cybernetic creature. Their conversation with computational materials leads children to construct knowledge in a natural way, at times with much greater efficiency than through traditional instruction.[3] This book is filled with ideas for authentic learning adventures in mathematics, science, and computation.

Reason #6: Fertile ground on which to rethink teaching and learning
When you want a teaching faculty to think differently or think about thinking, a good strategy is to create a level playing field that is a bit alien to all involved. Computing in the spirit discussed in this book creates such a productive context for professional learning.

My colleagues and I have enjoyed great success promoting progressive practices, such as project-based learning and teacher-as-researcher, through open-ended computing and engineering prompts using Logo-like software, found materials, and microcontrollers. Asking a room full of teachers to "Make a bird—singing and dancing is encouraged," "Design a wacky miniature golf hole," or "program Turtle Art to design a painting for above my couch," allows teachers to suspend their disbelief, exit their subject area silos, become reacquainted with their own creativity, think about thinking, and hopefully recognize that their teaching practices need not remain static.

Since mathphobia and math anxiety that impacts student learning are high among elementary school teachers, and likely other educators as well (Beilock et al., 2010; Gresham, 2007; Gunderson et al., 2013), it seems reasonable to suggest that enjoying playful, complex, and creative computational/mathematical/cybernetic experiences, particularly with colleagues, may benefit their students. An improved personal relationship with computation should boost confidence in educators and make powerful ideas more lovable for the children they serve.

Computation brings together multiple disciplines, ways of knowing, modernity, and prospects for making thinking visible. It is an excellent way to introduce or sustain progressive education ideals in a school or district.

We Can Do This!
We need to provide opportunities for young people to enjoy a greater diversity of non-superficial computing activities. This book features a host of examples and barely scratches the surface of what is and will be possible for children to achieve via computation. In the spirit of the recursion line in *Twenty Things,* I would like to share two recent epiphanies that I will continue to explore.

Who's the boss?
While teaching a computing and mathematics class to fourth graders, I wanted to introduce coordinate geometry, along with variables, constants, scale, and various computer science concepts simultaneously through a playful project. Sight unseen, I ordered $60 worth of dot-to-dot coordinate books for teachers. I hoped the books would feature a list of coordinates

that when connected on graph paper would reveal a surprise line drawing. Much to my chagrin, most of the examples were simply excuses for coloring and were not composed of a single stream of connected points. The few examples that did generate the sort of figures I craved suffered another shortcoming—all of the coordinates were in the positive|positive quadrant of the X|Y axis. Why bother teaching coordinate geometry if negative numbers are not used? Right, we are making pictures in order to color them in. Ugh!

Since I wanted kids to gain experience with the X|Y axis and negative numbers, I needed to shift the coordinates across the origin of the axis. I did this by writing a program in Logo that took a list of coordinates I entered and subtracted a constant value from each number in the coordinate pairs. Voila! Now, I could give those coordinates to the students to graph. Of course, they would produce their graph with the Logo turtle on a computer screen, not graph paper.

Once the students pounded in a procedure with a long list of *setpos [number number]* *makeadot* commands and debugged any typographical errors, the turtle drew a tiny little chicken on the screen. I anticipated that squinting at the result would lead to the inevitable question of how to make the picture larger. Since there was no knob for doing so, computation was necessary. The kids did a bit of brainstorming and arrived at the idea of multiplying each number in the list of coordinates by another number. The first person to speak up suggested 5.

Concerned that we would soon run out of class time and the teachable moment would be lost, I became cheerleader for a sprint in which the kids performed the necessary mental multiplication verbally together and changed all of the coordinates in their program. More than one child announced their multiplication-induced exhaustion with a great big grin. Unless there was an easily fixable bug in their program, the turtle would now draw a chicken five times larger than the original. The scale changed while the figure stayed the same.

I was pleased when a student asked me how I knew how to do this and I retold the story of purchasing the terrible workbooks and writing a procedure to slide the coordinates over, but then I ran out of time. Time is the scarcest resource of all in schools and teachers need to move mountains for reclaim it in order for constructionism, project-based learning, or *Twenty Things* to flourish.

Had there been more time, I would have taught the students how to modify their program so that a user could enter a list of points and a number representing a level of modification so that the computer would perform the calculations and produce the images at a specific scale. That of course would lead to list processing, stop rules, and recursion—all possible and within the fourth graders' zone of proximal development. Writing "smarter" programs would not only increase efficiency, but likely lead to other discoveries as well.

What if we want the drawing to be somewhere between the size produced by a scale of 2 and 3? Oh, there are numbers between numbers? What if we change the scale to a negative number? Can we write a program to take a list of coordinates and automatically draws the largest image that fits on a screen? Can my program draw a graphical representation of large data sets I find online?

Learning to program becomes programming to learn. The four types of geometric transformations: translation, reflection, rotation, and enlargement, become something students can play with and understand—years before these topics appear in the curriculum. Experience writing a program that can eat through a list of data and manipulate it is a programming paradigm useful in countless contexts.

Working with the nine-year-olds led to me to realize that much of what we teach kids to do with computers, even when the spirit of *Twenty Things*, falls short of what's possible. For most children, computation is a way of causing you to think. That is the genius of Logo programming. Your thinking is manifest in the actions of the turtle. **However, the real power of computation is when the computer begins working for you. Few children ever get to experience the other side of that tipping point.**

With the addition of computation, what could have been a rainy-day math activity of connect-the-dots, became a microworld in which a dozen or so mathematical ideas were employed in the service of doing something children enjoy, drawing a picture, and introduced a number of powerful computer science concepts all while pointing to a larger goal of the computer working for us.[4]

The many faces of computation

Computation and computational thinking may take many forms. Just as Wolfram suggested it will impact every future vocation, computation today allows for many more things to be created with a computer. New Logo descendants, like Beetle Blocks, TurtleStitch, and App Inventor allow children to turn their ideas into 3D objects, textiles, and phone apps. Robotics and engineering no longer need to be gendered or focused on designing trucks that can kill another school's truck. An animated Marie Antoinette wig or coin-operated carnival fortune teller (Stager, 2020) achieves the same technical objectives within a more diverse world of epistemological pluralism (Turkle & Papert, 1990).

Even the most enduring invention of Papert and Solomon, turtle geometry can take on new forms. At one of our recent institutes, an atelier was established for exploring art, design, and textiles. Participating educators used Turtle Art and TurtleStitch programming to create art that took the form of temporary tattoos, wearable embroidery, vinyl cut stickers, and iron-on t-shirt transfers. Many of the same computational ideas were realized in different forms, including a wall quilt comprised of blocks created with turtle graphics and a digital vinyl cutter and a fabric quilt assembled after the workshop that incorporated all of the teachers' designs. Some of the fabric-based art could easily had interactive electronics embedded. Had there been a 3D printer or laser cutter available, a greater range of expression would have been possible. The Logo turtle lives on in many forms.

Fabric quilt of teacher programs by Janine Maletsky

Teacher-made vinyl-cut quilt "patches"

Much More Work to be Done

We need *Twenty Things* now more than ever. It is imperative that there are viable means for smart people to create computationally-rich software environments for children that democratize computing with a low threshold, high ceiling, and wide walls (Resnick, 2017). It would be fantastic if a Swiss-Army-knife piece of software emerged that allowed users to do all of the things described in this book, but that might be too much to ask for. I truly fear that the most popular construction environments available to children are decreasingly computational in their functionality and power. This should come as no surprise in an increasingly anti-intellectual world that fears anything looking like mathematics, but readers of this book know better.

Tod Machover shared a Papert quote I love. Seymour said, "Everyone needs a prosthetic." We must develop software and hardware materials that start from the child and provide an infinitely complex galaxy of opportunities to make, learn, and do what we cannot yet imagine. Our mission must be to empower children and their teachers. We may not believe that kids are competent if we behave as if their teachers are incompetent.

Cynthia Solomon and Seymour Papert have failed to earn the respect they deserve as giants in the pantheon of progressive education history. They are the father & mother of educational technology, yet their contributions are rarely acknowledged. This may be due to ignorance, amnesia, or as punishment for committing four sins.

1. Exposing the education community's idea aversion
2. Messing with the commercialization of schooling
3. Loving children enough to empower them
4. Trusting teachers

Suggesting teachers are competent and can do better challenges those who wish to standardize, mechanize, and deprofessionalize education. Suggesting that children can build, program, and maintain their own computers is an obstacle to the commercial interests dependent on an educational industry more concerned with shopping than powerful ideas. Believing in the inherent good, agency, and intellectual power of children scares a good many adults with a vested interest in control and compliance.

Please attempt some of the ideas in this book yourself and with children, talk with your neighbors about a different intellectual diet for children, get involved, explore the other resources shared in these pages, dream, build, create, play, think, and even program. We need the provocative inspiration of *Twenty Things to Do with a Computer* now more than ever.

FORWARD 50!

References

Beilock, S. L., Gunderson, E. A., Ramirez, G., & Levine, S. C. (2010). Female teachers' math anxiety affects girls' math achievement. *Proceedings of the National Academy of Sciences, 107*(5), 1860-1863.

Gresham, G. (2007). A Study of Mathematics Anxiety in Pre-service Teachers. *Early Childhood Education Journal, 35*(2), 181-188.

Gunderson, E. A., Ramirez, G., Beilock, S. L., & Levine, S. C. (2013). Teachers' Spatial Anxiety Relates to 1st-and 2nd-Graders' Spatial Learning. *Mind, Brain, and Education, 7*(3), 196-199.

Harvey, B. (2014). *Whatever Happened To The Revolution, Part 2: In Which I Get Seduced By The Lure Of A National Curriculum.* Constructionism 2014, Vienna, Austria.

Lodi, M., & Martini, S. (2021). Computational Thinking, Between Papert and Wing. *Science & Education, 30*(4), 883-908. doi.org/10.1007/s11191-021-00202-5

Moses, R. P., & Cobb, C. E. (2001). *Radical Equations: Civil Rights from Mississippi to the Algebra Project.* Beacon Press.

Papert, S. (1970). *Teaching Children Thinking.* World Conference on Computers in Education, Amsterdam.

Papert, S. (1984). Computer as Mudpie. In D. Peterson (Ed.), *Intelligent Schoolhouse: Readings on Computers and Learning.* Reston Publishing Company.

Papert, S. (1990). *A Critique of Technocentrism in Thinking About the School of the Future* (2). (M.I.T. Media Lab Epistemology and Learning Memo. papert.org/articles/ACritiqueofTechnocentrism.html

Papert, S. (2000). *Millennial Lecture at the Muskie Archives.* dailypapert.com/bates

Papert, S. (2002). *Squeakers* [DVD]. dailypapert.com/seymour-papert-2002-interview

Resnick, M. (2017). *Lifelong Kindergarten: Cultivating Creativity Through Projects, Passion, Peers, and Play.* MIT Press.

Richardson, J. (2009). Equity and Mathematics: An Interview with Deborah Ball and Bob Moses. *Phi Delta Kappan, 91*(2), 54-59.

Romberg, T. A. (1989). *Curriculum and Evaluation Standards for School Mathematics.* National Council of Teachers of Mathematics.

Stager, G. (2020). Constructing Modern Knowledge: Crafting the Next Generation of Constructionists. In Y. Kafai, N. Holbert, & M. Berland (Eds.), *Constructionism in Context.* MIT Press.

Turkle, S., & Papert, S. (1990). Epistemological Pluralism: Styles and Voices within the Computer Culture. *Signs: Journal of women in culture and society, 16*(1), 128-157.

Wolfram, C. (2010). *Teaching Kids Real Math with Computers.* TED. ted.com/talks/conrad_wolfram_teaching_kids_real_math_with_computers.html

Wolfram, C. (2020). *The Math (s) fix: An Education Blueprint for the AI Age.* Wolfram Media, Inc.

Wolfram, S. (2016, Sept. 7). How to Teach Computational Thinking. *Stephen Wolfram Writings.* writings.stephenwolfram.com/2016/09/how-to-teach-computational-thinking

Notes

1 The paper, *Computational Thinking, Between Papert and Wing*, does an exceptional job of reviewing the history, semantics, and claims of computational thinking.

2 I make the case for teaching mathematics via computation in *15 Arguments for Teaching Mathematics Through Computer Programming* found online at stager.tv/?p=6098

3 A more detailed collection of related learning stories from actual classrooms may be found in my article, *Real Inequality (not that kind)*, at stager.tv/?p=5985

4 The nuts and bolts of this activity are detailed in the handout found online at inventtolearn.com/wp-content/uploads/2021/08/Graph-a-Mystery-Picture.pdf

Isn't it Time for Us to Grow Up?

Seymour Papert

And as we grow up, we should stop seeing ourselves as specialists of computers in education, because that casts us in the role of a kind of service profession. Accepting the role allows that other people are the ones to decide the big goals of education, what the curriculum is, how learning happens, what's a school. And at our conferences we talk about how their decisions can be served by the computers. Well, fine, up to a point. This certainly allows revolutionary actions as long as we are at the stage of crafting Trojan horses to throw into the system. But at some point we have a responsibility to break out of that marginal role and take on our true vocation, which is not one of service but one of leadership.

— from a speech "Perestroika and Epistemological Politics" at the 1990 World Conference on Computers in Education. Sydney, Australia.

Toolbox

These are just a few resources that support Logo-like learning projects.

Scratch – A block-based programming language for simple storytelling and games. Materials and videos for educators and classrooms. scratch.mit.edu

Snap! – Scratch with first-class objects added to make more complex programming projects possible. snap.berkeley.edu

Turtle Art – A simple yet elegant variation of Logo with an iconic interface intended to create beautiful images. turtleart.org

Lynx – A text-based implementation of Logo in a cloud programming environment supporting project sharing. lynxcoding.club

Turtlestitch – A version of Snap! that outputs files for embroidery machines. turtlestitch.com

Microsoft MakeCode – A block-based programming language for a growing list of microcontrollers. MakeCode runs in the browser with a simulator showing your hardware device. The website has tutorials and project ideas. makecode.com

Beetle Blocks – Visual code block environment for 3D design in the Logo tradition. Runs in the browser. beetleblocks.com

Wolfram Language – A comprehensive programming language with built-in computational intelligence. wolfram.com/language

MIT App Inventor – A block-based language for creating iOS or Android mobile apps. appinventor.mit.edu

Tinkercad – Easy to use, online Computer-Aided-Design (CAD) program for 3D printed objects and circuits. It is a favorite of many schools for its friendly interface and tutorials. tinkercad.com

BBC micro:bit – A non-profit foundation supports the BBC micro:bit, a versatile microcontroller board. Resources for students, teachers, developers, and an online community. microbit.org

Adafruit Circuit Playground Express – A single board microcontroller with onboard sensors and LEDs. Supports multiple coding options including MakeCode, JavaScript, Python, and the Arduino IDE. learn.adafruit.com/adafruit-circuit-playground-express

Hummingbird Robotics Kit – The Hummingbird Robotics Kit by Birdbrain Technologies is designed to enable engineering and robotics activities. It is terrific for making robots, kinetic sculptures, and animatronics built out of a combination of kit parts and crafting materials. It is programmable in dozens of software environments including Scratch and Snap! birdbraintechnologies.com/hummingbirdbit

Raspberry Pi – The Raspberry Pi is a single board computer with many available accessories and add-ons. The Raspberry Pi Foundation website has useful teaching and learning resources. raspberrypi.org

Arduino – Open-source electronics prototyping platform and robotics controller for interactive projects. arduino.cc

LEGO Education – LEGO site for education products and resources. education.lego.com

Contributor Biographies

Dimitris Alimisis, PhD
EDUMOTIVA

Dimitris Alimisis is co-founder & scientific leader at EDUMOTIVA (European Lab for Educational Technology), Greece, activated in EU research & education projects. In the past he has served as professor of educational technology in higher education of Greece. His main interests include: educational robotics and STEAM education with a focus on the integration of constructionism and maker movement in education.

Yvonne Marie Andrés, EdD
GlobalSchoolNet.org

Dr. Yvonne Marie Andrés, an e-learning visionary, founder of (non-profit) Global SchoolNet and creator of the Global Schoolhouse, designs innovative programs that demonstrate the power of collaboration to engage youth in activities that improve their academic performance and help communities, while connecting them globally to benefit humanity. Andrés was named one of 25 most influential people worldwide in education technology, received the Soroptimist International "Making a Difference Award" for advancing the status of women and children, and was inducted into the Internet Hall of Fame.

Eleonora Badilla-Saxe, EdD
Rector at the Universidad Castro Carazo

Eleonora has been committed for more than 35 years to collaborating to improve education in her country of Costa Rica and the Latin American region. She publishes regularly in specialized peer-reviewed journals and in op-ed pages in major newspapers in her country. She is a retired Full Professor and Researcher at the University of Costa Rica (1982-2017), Visiting Researcher at the MIT Media Lab (2001-2004), Advisor to the Minister of Education (1994-1998), and Director of the Computers in Education Program by the Ministry of Public Education and the Omar Dengo Foundation (1989-1994). She holds a master's degree from the University of Hartford and EdD from the University De La Salle in San José. Her research interests are the constructionist use of digital technology in education, innovation in education, learning, and complex thinking.

Walter Bender
Sorcero, Sugar Labs, ReMake Music

Walter Bender is the CTO of Sorcero, Inc., which couples learning by people and machines. He is founder of Sugar Labs, which develops and maintains educational software for children and along with Negroponte and Papert, he co-founded One Laptop per Child. He is also co-founder of ReMake Music, which provides pedagogical support for Music Blocks, a programming language used to explore mathematical and musical concepts. Bender is former executive director of the MIT Media Lab.

Miles Berry
University of Roehampton

Miles is principal lecturer in Computing Education at the University of Roehampton. Prior to joining Roehampton, he spent 18 years in four schools, much of the time as an ICT coordinator and most recently as a head teacher. Over the years he has contributed to a number of computing related projects including England's national curriculum computing programmes of study, Switched on Computing, Barefoot Computing, Project Quantum, Hello World and the National Centre for Computing Education.

Karen J. Billings, EdD
Principal, BillingsConnects

Dr. Karen Billings is Principal at BillingsConnects, a consulting agency that helps companies find potential partners. She serves on boards for education companies and non-profit organizations. Previously, she led SIIA's Education Technology Division, where she drove strategic direction, programs, and initiatives for member companies. In her 50 years of experience within industry and classrooms, she authored books and articles, spoke at many education conferences, and received numerous awards.

Paulo Blikstein, PhD
Associate Professor, Columbia University

Paulo Blikstein is an Associate Professor of Education at Teachers College and an Affiliate Associate Professor of Computer Science at Columbia University, where he directs the Transformative Learning Technologies Lab and the FabLearn Program. A recipient of the National Science Foundation Early Career Award and the AERA Jan Hawkins Early Career Award, Paulo earned his Ph.D. from Northwestern University, following an MSc. from the Media Lab at the Massachusetts Institute of Technology and an M.Eng. and B.Eng. from the University of São Paulo, Brazil. He is a former student of Madalena Freire's lab school in São Paulo.

Giulio Bonanome
Unicorni Team

Giulio is a freelance learning designer and facilitator of STEAM related summer camps, after-schools and workshops for young and adults, both in person and online. He has founded and is a volunteer in a CoderDojo club and is adjunct teacher of "Computational Thinking" course at the University of Bologna. Since 2019 is part of the Unicorni Team collective, committed to spread a playful, creative and experimental approach to learning (and teaching) in Italy.

Ron Canuel
Independent Education Strategist

Ron is an award-winning, innovative Canadian educator, with over 45 years of experience in education. He serves as coach, consultant, guide, and mentor to a wide range of organizations, including extensive work with indigenous populations across North America. Ron is one of the few individuals in education who has "done" it, managed system-wide innovative change (1:1 laptop deployment for all students in 2003, second in North America), and brought about significant improvement in the classroom while closely relating to the issues and challenges that face educators, parents, policy makers, and special interest groups. Ron is proud of the achievements of the people that he has worked with, especially in the context of introducing change in education provincially, nationally, and internationally. He is still very active during these days of the pandemic providing online conferences and sessions to participants across the globe.

David Cavallo, PhD
Director, Centro de Innovación y Diseño Avanzado (Cinnda, Chile) & Researcher at the Inst. of Adv. Studies, USP

Cavallo focuses on learning and computation particularly for improving learning for just, equitable societies. He was Distinguished Visiting Professor at UFSB. He was the Chief Learning Architect and Vice-President for Education of One Laptop Per Child. He was a Research Scientist and co-director with Seymour Papert of the Future of Learning Group at the MIT Media Laboratory, where Papert advised his doctorate. He hates writing bios and addressing himself in the third person.

Angi Chau, PhD
The Nueva School

Angi Chau is an educator, maker, engineer, and creative coder. She loves to infuse play into learning and has particular interest in creative coding, equity-driven design frameworks, and the intersection of technology and justice. Currently, she is the Director of the Innovation Lab program at The Nueva School and teaches required middle school computer science classes. She is a Teaching Fellow at Processing Foundation and on the advisory board for Agency by Design Oakland.

Donna Collins
St. John Regional School, Concord NH and University of New Hampshire

Donna Collins lives in New Hampshire and has been an educator for over 25 years, most recently as a middle school science teacher where she incorporates her own curiosity for learning into all that she presents to her students. Donna earned an Associate of Applied Science in Forest Technology from the University of New Hampshire. She also holds a Bachelor of Science degree in Computer Programming from Southern New Hampshire University and a Master's Degree in Education from the University of New Hampshire. Donna has been nominated twice for the New Hampshire Catholic Schools Teacher of the Year. When not teaching, Donna enjoys hiking and traveling with her husband and two greyhound dogs.

Dale Dougherty
Make: Community

Dale Dougherty is the leading advocate of the Maker Movement. He founded Make: Magazine in 2005, which first used the term "makers" to describe people who enjoyed "hands-on" work and play. He started Maker Faire in the San Francisco Bay Area in 2006, and this event has spread to nearly 200 locations in 40 countries, with over 1.5M attendees annually up until COVID-19 hit. He is President of Make: Community, which seeks to nurture and grow the worldwide community of makers through publications, events and online resources. Dougherty is the author of *Free to Make: How the Maker Movement Is Changing our Jobs, Schools and Minds* with Adriane Conrad.

Carolyn Foote
Library Consultant and free range librarian

Carolyn Foote is a former district librarian in Austin, Texas, and now a consultant on library design, advocacy, technology, and research. A White House Champion of Change in 2013 and AASL Library Collaboration Award winner and Lilead Fellow, she is focused on the intersection between students, technology, and libraries. She mentors new librarians in the Project RUSL grant at Wayne State, and blogs at www.futura.edublogs.org.

Nettrice Gaskins, PhD
Lesley University

Dr. Gaskins earned a BFA in Computer Graphics from Pratt Institute in 1992 and an MFA in Art and Technology from the School of the Art Institute of Chicago in 1994. She received a doctorate in Digital Media from Georgia Tech in 2014. She is the assistant director of the Lesley STEAM Learning Lab at Lesley University. Her first full-length book, Techno-Vernacular Creativity and Innovation through MIT Press will be available in 2021.

Geraldine (Gerry) Kozberg
Deputy Superintendent, St. Paul, Minnesota Public Schools; Director, Logo Foundation

Gerry Kozberg was a leader in the Logo community and the founder of the Saint Paul Logo Project. For 18 years the Saint Paul Logo Project provided teacher education in Logo practice and philosophy to teachers in Saint Paul schools and beyond. She worked in Saint Paul public schools as a teacher and administrator from 1962-1996 with the exception of a leave of absence (1974-1979) to work in Boston with a court-ordered team of educators charged with the desegregation of South Boston High School. She was a life-long activist for social justice who also worked in Cambodian refugee camps. Following her retirement she was a docent at the Minneapolis Institute of Arts.

Dennis O. Harper, PhD
CEO of Generation YES Corporation

Dennis O. Harper has been an educator for 53 years. He began integrating technology into high schools starting in 1973. He received his Ph.D. in Education from the University of California in 1983 followed by faculty positions at UCSB, the National University of Malaysia, Singapore's Institute of Education, Helsinki University in Finland, and the University of the Virgin Islands. Along the way he pioneered distance learning and influenced educational technology in many nations. His books included Logo Theory and Practice. In 1996 Dr. Harper received a $3.8 million Technology Innovation Challenge Grant to research and develop strategies and curriculum to infuse K-12 students as key allies with educators to transform schools. This grant resulted in the Generation YES model that, to date, has been implemented in more than 2,300 K-12 schools. Dr. Harper is recognized as one of education technology's founding fathers.

Stephen Heppell
Professor, The Felipe Segovia Chair of Learning Innovation at Universidad Camilo José Cela, Madrid

Stephen's "eyes on the horizon, feet on the ground" approach, coupled with a vast portfolio of effective large scale projects over three decades, have established him internationally as a widely and fondly recognized leader in the fields of learning, new media and technology. A school teacher for more than a decade, and a professor since 1989, Stephen has worked, and is working, with learner led projects, with governments around the world, with international agencies, with schools and communities, and with many influential trusts and organizations.

Cathy Hunt
Teacher, Author, International Speaker, and Creative Educational Design Specialist

Cathy Hunt is a prominent advocate for the creative integration of technology in education, best known as the founder of iPadArtRoom.com. She is the author of the bestselling e-books iPad Art: Lessons, apps and ideas for the iPad in Visual Art and More iPad Art. She has spent her career developing ground-breaking programs for students around the world that combine hands-on, tactile, and collaborative ways of working with mobile devices. As an award-winning educational consultant, presenter, author and experienced Visual & Media Art, STEAM, Design & Digital Technologies teacher on Australia's Gold Coast, Cathy has worked with thousands of educators globally to connect creative technology and cutting-edge pedagogical approaches with diverse learners.

Yasmin B. Kafai, EdD
University of Pennsylvania

Yasmin Kafai is Lori and Michael Milken President's Distinguished Professor at the University of Pennsylvania. She is a learning designer and researcher of online tools, activities and communities to promote computational making, crafting, and creativity. She worked with a team of biologists, designers, and engineers to develop 'biomakerlab', a portable grow and design tool for classrooms. Kafai earned a doctorate from Harvard University while working with Seymour Papert at the MIT Media Lab.

Ken Kahn, PhD
University of Oxford

Ken joined the MIT AI Lab as a graduate student in 1973. While studying AI, he joined the LOGO Group focussing on new programming programming languages for children and introducing them to AI. After more than a decade of research and teaching in AI and computer science, his interest in programming tools for children was rekindled. He designed and implemented ToonTalk, a programming by demonstration system with the look and feel of a video game.

Bill Kerr, EdD
St. Philips College, Alice Springs

My formative interests were chess and political activism arising from the anti-Vietnam war protests. I've been a classroom teacher in a variety of Australian schools, on and off, since 1983. Seymour Papert interested me for two reasons (1) He made mathematics more interesting and accessible for those who had missed out (2) The epistemological politics of school reform. His writings transformed the way I perceived the computer.

Susan Klimczak, EdD
Learn 2 Teach, Teach 2 Learn, Mel King Fab Lab, Madison Park Technical Vocational High School

For 20+ years, Susan has been the education organizer for a year-round Boston out-of-school time program that brings out the best in youth of color from families living with low incomes. Learn 2 Teach, Teach 2 Learn focuses on #MakingLiberation with art, engineering, coding and design. Teen youth teachers reach 400+ children each summer by offering free summer STEAM camps at community organizations located in neighborhoods most in need of education enrichment.

Tom Lauwers, PhD
BirdBrain Technologies LLC
Tom founded BirdBrain Technologies in 2010 after receiving his doctorate in robotics from Carnegie Mellon University. His research was founded on engaging all students, regardless of background, in robotics and engineering. Tom seeks to design educational tools that catalyze positive making, coding, and engineering learning experiences in the classroom. Tom resides in Pittsburgh's Squirrel Hill neighborhood with his wife, two kids, cat, and a small army of robots.

Martin Levins
Lecturer, University of New England, Australia
Martin has designed, taught, and evaluated courses in Digital Technologies, ICT, Computing, Science, Mathematics, and Design & Technology to ages 5 and up in schools, universities and technical colleges and has helped author the Australian Curriculum in Digital Technologies. He is a tinkerer and a thinkerer and sees play as essential to learning – at least that's his excuse.

David Loader OAM
Hon Assoc Professor, University of Melbourne
David Loader is a passionate advocate of innovative education in Australia: the first worldwide to introduce laptop computers at MLC school and creator of residential settings for learning. His ongoing commitment is to stimulate the education of the whole person. He was a school principal for 32 years and member of a University Board for 9 years. He has written two books and co-authored another. He received the Order of Australia for services to education.

Angela Sofia Lombardo
Unicorni Team
Angela Sofia Lombardo is a freelance learning experience designer and one of the 2016 FabLearn Fellows. She is an adjunct professor of I.T. and Learning Technologies laboratory at the University of Bologna, Graduate School of Education. Since 2013 she has been organizing CoderDojo Bologna coding club. She is part of the Unicorni Team collective, committed to spread a playful, creative and experimental approach to learning (and teaching) in Italy.

Tom Lough, PhD
Logo Exchange Founder
Tom Lough is the founder of Logo Exchange. He has taught science and mathematics at the high school and community college levels, as well as science methods and instructional technology at the university level. In 2004, he received the National Science Teachers Association award for Distinguished Science Teaching. He was a product developer for LEGO Education and is active in the maker movement. He is available for consultation on a variety of educational/technological topics.

Leo McElroy
Independent
Leo McElroy is a technologist who builds physical tools, digital applications, and social organizations to help people turn their thoughts into things. He has created and managed multiple makerspaces, developed open-source digital fabrication machines, invented programming languages for parametric design, travelled the world on a Watson Fellowship visiting makerspaces, and works at Hack Club where he directs a global network of creative technology/coding clubs by and for high schoolers.

Fred Martin, PhD
University of Massachusetts Lowell
Fred Martin is professor of computer science and associate dean for teaching, learning, and undergraduate studies in the Kennedy College of Sciences at the University of Massachusetts Lowell. He leads the Engaging Computing Group, which develops and studies innovative computational systems for young learners. Martin is an avid learner himself and deeply enjoys helping others be successful with their own endeavors.

Sugata Mitra, PhD
Retired Professor, Newcastle University, UK
A PhD in theoretical physics, Sugata Mitra retired in 2019 as Professor of Educational Technology at Newcastle University in England, after 13 years there including a year in 2012 as Visiting Professor at MIT MediaLab in Cambridge, Massachusetts, USA. He is Professor Emeritus at NIIT University, Rajasthan, India. His work on children's education include the 'hole in the wall' experiment where children access the internet in unsupervised groups, the idea of Self Organised Learning Environments (SOLEs) in schools, the role of experienced educators over the internet in a 'Granny Cloud' and the School in the Cloud where children take charge of their learning—anywhere. He received, among many global awards, the million-dollar TED Prize in 2013. Website: www.cevesm.com

Michele Moro
Dipartimento di Ingegneria dell'Informazione, University of Padua, Italy
Michele is an assistant professor in Computer Science Engineering, with teaching experiences in Computer science and related subjects. His research area includes real time control systems, concurrent and object-oriented programming languages and architectures. More recently he has been interested in new ICT-enhanced constructionist education, and more specifically in Educational Robotics. He was local responsible for the TERECoP (Teacher Education on Robotics-enhanced Constructivist Pedagogical Methods) European project (2006-2009) and chair of Workshops on Educational Robotics (2008-2020).

Jennifer Orr
Fort Belvoir Upper School, Fairfax County Public Schools
Jennifer Orr is a long-time elementary school teacher, having taught students from kindergarten through fifth grade. She is a National Board Certified Teacher and the 2012 winner of ISTE's Kay L. Bitter Award. In addition to teaching elementary students, she has taught literacy courses for undergraduate and graduate students.

Heather Allen Pang, PhD
Castilleja School

Heather Allen Pang teaches 8th grade US history at her alma mater, Castilleja School in Palo Alto, CA. When Castilleja built the Bourn Idea Lab in 2011, Heather was one of the early adopters, bringing history classes to the lab to build telegraph machines, cut silhouettes on the laser cutter, 3D print models of 18th century buildings, and prototype monuments to American women. She is part of the 2014 FabLearn Fellows cohort.

Artemis Papert
Independent artist

Artemis is an artist, botanist, nematologist, and shiatsu therapist. She is fascinated by the connection between body and psyche. Her enthusiasm for fairy tales and dream interpretation inspired her to become a Jungian analyst. Artemis' art spans the analog and the digital. She uses acrylic, pastel, and code. Her favorite coding environment is TurtleArt, a programming environment based on turtle geometry and the Logo language Not only an enthusiastic learner, Artemis is also an enthusiastic teacher. She has led TurtleArt workshops for a wide variety of groups in many countries.

Carmelo Presicce
Lifelong Kindergarten - MIT Media Lab

Carmelo is a PhD student in the Lifelong Kindergarten group at MIT Media Lab. His work focuses on the design and facilitation of creative learning experiences for children and educators, in person and online. Recent projects include the Learning Creative Learning (LCL) online course/community and the WeScratch online workshops for educators. Previously, he has been working as a software developer, organizing Coderdojo coding clubs for children, and teaching creative computing at University of Bologna.

Peter Rawitsch

Peter taught in public schools in New Hampshire and upstate New York for 42 years. He was a 1st grade teacher for 38 of those years. He is a National Board Certified Teacher (NBCT) in Early Childhood. Peter is now a public school activist working on educational justice and racial justice in Wilmington, NC. He is currently organizing the community to end school suspensions for 4, 5, 6, and 7-year-old children.

Marian B Rosen
Retired: St Louis City & Ladue Public Schools

In 1968, Marian Rosen left a PhD program in European History to become a first grade teacher; 15 years later discovered Logo; became a technology coordinator. Hooray!

Bryan P. Sanders, EdD
Loyola Marymount University

Bryan P. Sanders is a Doctor of Education and career classroom teacher working in Los Angeles who blends critical theory, social justice, technology, and constructivism. With 25 years of teaching experience, he is actively working on new projects with students to continue and expand the constructionist work of Dr. Seymour Papert. He is active in research, classrooms, discussion groups, publishing, inventing, and also on Twitter.

Evgenia (Jenny) Sendova, PhD
Institute of Mathematics and Informatics at the Bulgarian Academy of Sciences

Evgenia (Jenny) Sendova is a researcher in mathematics and informatics education. Her research includes the development of computer microworlds and models for integrating learning and creative processes. Jenny's main professional interest is in using informatics and information technology for teaching mathematics, languages, music, science, and arts, especially in the context of gifted education. She loves music, jokes and backgammon. She collects aphorisms and turtles, and can usually beat her gifted students in ping-pong.

Cynthia Solomon, EdD
Co-author, *Twenty Things to Do with a Computer*

Cynthia's focus has been on creating enjoyable, personally expressive, and aesthetically pleasing learning environments for children. She collaborated with Seymour Papert on developing Logo, the first programming language designed for children. She has continued creating and advocating for computer-based projects and ways for young people to design their own projects.. Recently, she edited a book, *Inventive Minds: Marvin Minsky on Education* that collects and contextualizes Minsky's essays on computers and children. Currently she is exploring Logo's turtle geometry through TurtleStitch and computerized embroidery machines. In 2016 she was awarded both the National Center for Women & Information Technology Pioneer Award and the Constructionism Lifetime Achievement Award. She is also the recipient of the 2019 FabLearn Lifetime Achievement Award.

Gary Stager, PhD
CEO, Constructing Modern Knowledge

Gary Stager is a recognized pioneer in 1:1 computing, online learning, and computer programming for all students. Since 1982, he has taught learners from preschool through the doctoral level and has helped teachers around the world embrace technology as way of amplifying the potential of each student. Stager collaborated with Seymour Papert on his last institutional research project, creating the Constructionist Learning Laboratory inside a troubled prison for teens. Gary is a popular keynote speaker respected internationally for his fearless advocacy on behalf of teachers, children, and progressive education. He is the founder of the Constructing Modern Knowledge institute for educators, co-author of *Invent to Learn: Making, Tinkering, and Engineering in the Classroom*, and maintains the Seymour Papert archives at The Daily Papert (dailypapert.com). Learn more at professorgarystager.com.

John Stetson
Southern Maine Community College

John Stetson has taught high school math, English, computer science (programming and robotics), college photography, and maintained a solar observatory available for at-risk youth in Southern Maine. After a complete 11 year solar cycle he left juvenile detention and started teaching at an alternative-education high school and at the local community college.

Carol Sperry Sużiedėlis, EdD
Millersville University of Pennsylvania

Carol Sperry was frustrated with traditional teaching when, in 1981, she took a two-week Logo Workshop with Seymour Papert and had her progressive ideas validated and energetically expanded. A subsequent consultancy with the Epistemology and Learning Group at M.I.T.'s Media Lab enabled her to create and facilitate Logo and learning workshops In NYC's District 3 and then throughout the United States. She also designed and led workshops in Lithuania, Moscow, the Czech Republic, and Thailand. Sperry collaborated on the launching of the NYC Computer School and was co-director for two years. As director of Project Mindstorm for the Technology Center of Silicon Valley, Sperry created and led a two-year series of diverse learning workshops. She enjoyed ten years as Educational Foundations professor at Pennsylvania's Millersville University.

Kate Tabor
Francis W. Parker School, Chicago

Kate is a classroom teacher, former English Department Co-Chair and 7th-Grade Team Leader. She is committed to interdisciplinary and student-centered learning and attends Constructing Modern Knowledge as often as possible. Kate considers herself a reading evangelist.

David D. Thornburg, PhD
Thornburg Center

David started his friendship with Professor Papert in the early 1970's and over the years conducted many presentations and workshops on Logo. He has also written several books on Logo and continues his quest in support of constructionist education.

John Umekubo
Educator, Maker, Founder LumenSparQ

John is the Director of Social Entrepreneurship at Westside Neighborhood School in Los Angeles, California. He works with students and teachers on topics involving design, coding, and making with a focus on interdisciplinary capstone projects at the middle school. John is also an education consultant to schools across the country, and is the founder of LumenSparQ Inc., a nonprofit whose mission is to spotlight and support local heroes in education.

José Armando Valente, PhD
State University of Campinas - UNICAMP

José Armando Valente. He is PhD from the Department of Mechanical Engineering and Division for Study and Research in Education at the Massachusetts Institute of Technology (MIT). Full Professor (retired) at the Department of Multimedia, Arts Institute, and Collaborating Researcher at the Nucleus of Informatics Applied to Education (NIED), at State University of Campinas - UNICAMP. Research topics include creating learning situations using digital information and communication technologies. Currently focused on the study of maker education.

Justice Toshiba Walker, PhD
The University of Texas at El Paso College of Education

Justice Toshiba Walker is an Assistant Professor of STEM Education who studies emerging technologies in biology and their use in pre-college education. Dr. Walker uses synthetic biology to explore how cells can be designed and genetically reprogrammed to behave usefully. His recent work involved developing a culturally relevant pre-college curriculum to examine educator argumentation practices around socioscientific issues involving synthetic biology. Dr. Walker holds a doctorate from the University of Pennsylvania Graduate School of Education.

Dan Lynn Watt, PhD
Harvard Institute for Learning in Retirement & Cambridge Co-housing

Dan Lynn Watt was a Senior Scientist at Education Development Center in Massachusetts. He was a teacher, researcher, and curriculum developer from elementary through graduate school, primarily in mathematics, science and technology education. During 1976–1981 he worked with the MIT Logo Group. He and Molly Lynn Watt created The Logo Institute, and the Logo Action Research Collaborative. His many publications include *Learning With Logo* (1983), 100,000+ copies, *Teaching With Logo* (1986) (with Molly) and *History Lessons: A Memoir of Growing Up in an American Communist Family* (2017).

Molly Lynn Watt
Harvard Institute for Learning in Retirement & Cambridge Co-housing

Molly Lynn Watt, educator of students from six months to graduate school, consults internationally to school systems in educational uses of computers for inquiry project-based learning of science, mathematics, language arts and authentic assessment. She works with participant leadership teams to make changes they identify using action research approaches. She was an early adaptor of the Logo Computer language and Banks Street Writer, a contributor to major educational magazines and anthologized in dozens of books. She retired to do literary writing: *Shadow People, On Wings of Song, Consider This* (forthcoming), and *George and Ruth: Songs and Letters of the Spanish Civil War*.

Audrey Watters
Hack Education

Audrey Watters is a writer and historian of education technology. Although she was two chapters into her Comparative Literature dissertation, she decided to abandon academia, and she now happily fulfills the one job recommended to her by a junior high aptitude test: freelance writer. She is the author of the *Teaching Machines* (MIT Press) and the *Monsters of Education Technology* series of books, but is probably best known for her website Hack Education.

Conrad Wolfram
Wolfram Research Europe

Conrad Wolfram is the CEO and cofounder of Wolfram Research Europe, the cofounder of ComputerBasedMath.org and the author of *The Math(s) Fix: An Education Blueprint for the AI Age*.

MASSACHUSETTS INSTITUTE OF TECHNOLOGY
A.I. LABORATORY

June 1971

Artificial Intelligence
Memo No. 248

LOGO
Memo No. 3

TWENTY THINGS TO DO WITH A COMPUTER[1]

Seymour Papert

and

Cynthia Solomon

This report describes research done at the Artificial Intelligence Laboratory of the Massachusetts Institute of Technology. Support for the laboratory's education research is provided in part by the National Science Foundation under grant GJ-1049.

[1]To be published in Educational Technology Magazine (Englewood Cliffs, N.J.: 1972).

TWENTY THINGS TO DO WITH A COMPUTER

by Seymour Papert and Cynthia Solomon

When people talk about computers in education they do not
all have the same image in mind. Some think of using the computer to
program the kid; others think of using the kid to program the computer.
But most of them have at least this in common: the transaction between
the computer and the kid will be some kind of "conversation" or
"questions and answers" in words or numbers.

In the real world computers are used in many different ways.
Some are programmed to fly airplanes; not to <u>tell</u> a human pilot what
to do, but to pull the levers with their own electro-mechanical effectors
and to read the altitudes, airspeeds and what-not with their own electronic sensing devices. Computers are programmed to generate music or
to condition dogs by ringing bells and delivering meat powder while
the modern day Pavlov is happily asleep. Some computers are programmed
to control lathes and milling machines in industrial plants; others
generate pictures for animated film cartoons.

Why then should computers in schools be confined to computing
the sum of the squares of the first twenty odd numbers and similar
so-called "problem-solving" uses? Why not use them to produce some
action? There is no better reason than the intellectual timidity of
the computers-in-education community, which seems remarkably reluctant
to use the computers for any purpose that fails to look very much like
something that has been taught in schools for the past centuries. This
is all the more remarkable since the computerists are custodians of
a momentous intellectual and technological revolution. Concepts from
the sciences of computation -- "cybernetics", "information theory",
"artificial intelligence" and all its other names -- have deeply
affected thinking in biology, psychology and even the philosophy of

-2-

mathematics. Machines from its engineering branches are changing our way of life. How strange, then, that "computers in education" should so often reduce to "using bright new gadgets to teach the same old stuff in thinly disguised versions of the same old way."

But our purpose here is not to complain of what other people have not done, but to tell of some exciting things you can do with the computer you have now or with the one you will be incited to get by the pages that follow. More than half the suggestions we are about to make have been implemented and tested in our elementary school teaching program. This does not imply that they are not of equal or greater value at other levels of education; on the contrary, we are convinced that they give a glimpse of the proper way to introduce <u>everyone</u> of whatever age and whatever level of academic performance, to programming, to more general knowledge of computation and indeed (we say courageously steeling ourselves for the onslaught) to mathematics, to physics and to all formal subjects including linguistics and music.

Each section of this paper describes something one can do with a computer. Most of these things-to-do assume that your computer can spin motors, activate electromagnets, switch lights, read the state of light sensitive cells and so on. The amazing fact is that it is very easy to make your computer do all these things! The last section of this paper says something about how to make it do so if it doesn't already. But while reading the paper you need not (and should not, it is a distraction) think about how the commands we describe will produce their effects. As you read on you will be learning a computer language called LOGO. In order to use a computer language you do not need to know how the computer works -- no more than you need to know how a human brain works in order to give a person instructions. In both cases you need only know how to describe what you want in an appropriate language.

-3-

1. <u>Make a Turtle</u>

      The picture shows one of our turtles . . . so-called in honor
of a famous species of cybernetic animal made by Grey Walter, an English
neurophysiologist. Grey Walter's turtles had life-like behavior patterns
built into its wiring diagram. Ours have no behavior except the ability
to obey a few simple commands from a computer to which they are attached
by a wire that plugs into a control-box that connects to a telephone
line that speaks to the computer, which thinks it is talking to a
teletype so that no special system programming is necessary to make
the computer talk to the turtle. (If you'd like to make a fancier
turtle you might use a radio link. But we'd like turtles to be cheap
enough for every kid to play with one.)

      The turtle can send signals back to the computer. These
signals appear to the computer just like the signals from a teletype -- so,
again, no special system programming is necessary to make a turtle talk
to a computer. Where do the signals come from? They are generated by
sense organs attached to the turtle. Our turtles do not have a fixed
set of sense organs. Rather, they have inlets into which one can plug
wires to attach any sense organs one is clever enough to make. Touch

-4-

sensors, light sensitive cells and sound detectors are obvious examples that require very little cleverness. Accelerometers and tilt detectors lead to more sophisticated fun.

Turtles can have effector organs as well. The activities described here use only a simple one -- a pen located at the turtle's center, which can be lowered to leave a trace of the turtle's path, thus turning it into a remarkable geometric instrument.

-5-

<u>2</u>. <u>Program the Turtle to Draw a Man</u>

A bad way to use a turtle is to know just which character symbols will cause the turtle's motors to move. A better way is to design a good language. This means deciding on a set of intelligible commands and building these into the computer language. For example, we can type LEFT 90 on the console keyboard and thereby cause the turtle to rotate 90° about its central axis in the left (i.e., counter-clockwise) direction. Obviously this is better than having to figure, every time one wants to use the turtle, the number of steps of the stepping motors one needs to produce the desired movement and writing a complicated instruction to send out control characters to produce these steps.

The following diagram explains the main commands in our turtle language.

<u>TURTLE LANGUAGE</u>

At any time the turtle is at a particular <u>place</u> and facing in a particular <u>direction</u>. The place and direction together are the turtle's geometric <u>state</u>. The picture shows the turtle in a field, used here only to give the reader a frame of reference:

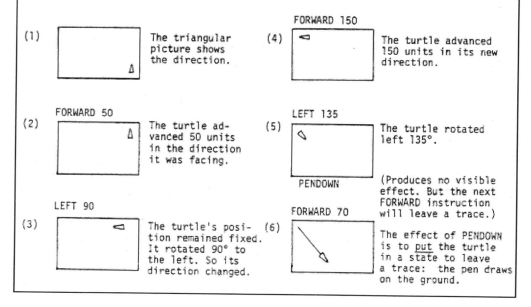

(1) The triangular picture shows the direction.

FORWARD 50
(2) The turtle advanced 50 units in the direction it was facing.

LEFT 90
(3) The turtle's position remained fixed. It rotated 90° to the left. So its direction changed.

FORWARD 150
(4) The turtle advanced 150 units in its new direction.

LEFT 135
(5) The turtle rotated left 135°.

PENDOWN
(Produces no visible effect. But the next FORWARD instruction will leave a trace.)

FORWARD 70
(6) The effect of PENDOWN is to <u>put</u> the turtle in a state to leave a trace: the pen draws on the ground.

-6-

     To make the computer do anything more complicated you have to write a program. For example (using our language, LOGO, in a way that should be self-explanatory) one might type into the computer the following definition:

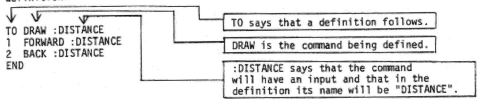

```
TO DRAW :DISTANCE
1  FORWARD :DISTANCE
2  BACK :DISTANCE
END
```

| TO says that a definition follows. |

| DRAW is the command being defined. |

| :DISTANCE says that the command will have an input and that in the definition its name will be "DISTANCE". |

Now if we type the command
DRAW 100
the computer will say to itself: "How do I DRAW? Well, the definition says, "TO DRAW 100, first go forward 100 units then go back 100 units and that's all." So if the turtle is in PENDOWN state it will draw a line and come back to its starting position. Now, using TO DRAW as a sub-procedure, let's give the computer a new command, TO VEE, by typing the following definition:

```
TO VEE :SIZE
1  LEFT 50
2  DRAW :SIZE
3  RIGHT 100
4  DRAW :SIZE
5  LEFT 50
END
```

| A defined command can be used in defining new commands just as if it were a primitive LOGO term like FORWARD or LEFT. |

The command
VEE 100
will now cause the turtle to draw V's as shown in the figures. The starting and finishing positions of the turtle are shown by the usual triangle.

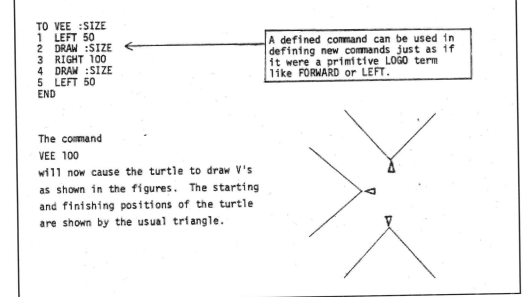

365

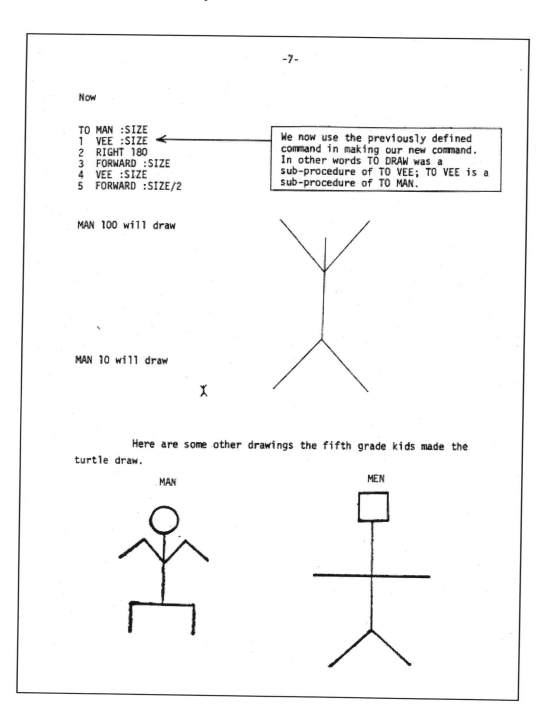

-7-

Now

```
TO MAN :SIZE
1   VEE :SIZE
2   RIGHT 180
3   FORWARD :SIZE
4   VEE :SIZE
5   FORWARD :SIZE/2
```

We now use the previously defined command in making our new command. In other words TO DRAW was a sub-procedure of TO VEE; TO VEE is a sub-procedure of TO MAN.

MAN 100 will draw

MAN 10 will draw

Here are some other drawings the fifth grade kids made the turtle draw.

MAN   MEN

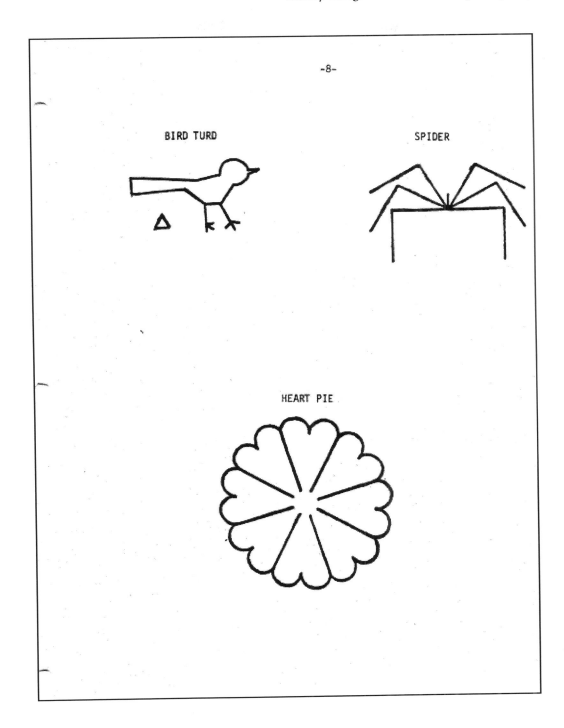

-9-

3. Turtle Biology

To make the turtle more like a living creature we must give it behavior patterns. This involves using sense organs. A well conceived turtle should be very flexible in this respect: instead of fixed sense organs like real animals, it should have a number of sockets (we find that eight is good) into which you can plug any on-off device such as a micro-switch, or light detector or whatever you think up. Such devices are easy and cheap to make.

Let's give the turtle a ridiculously simple piece of behavior based on using 4 touch sensors which we shall call FRONTTOUCH, BACKTOUCH, LEFTTOUCH and RIGHTTOUCH. The behavior consists of going straight ahead until it touches the wall, turning back and so on.

The "and so on" illustrates the need for "loops" or "recursion" in the procedure we are about to write. To prepare yourself for the concept, consider the plight of a person who never fails to keep a promise and who has been tricked into saying, "I promise to repeat what I have just said."

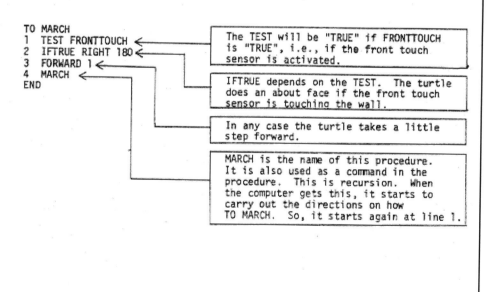

```
TO MARCH
1   TEST FRONTTOUCH
2   IFTRUE RIGHT 180
3   FORWARD 1
4   MARCH
END
```

The TEST will be "TRUE" if FRONTTOUCH is "TRUE", i.e., if the front touch sensor is activated.

IFTRUE depends on the TEST. The turtle does an about face if the front touch sensor is touching the wall.

In any case the turtle takes a little step forward.

MARCH is the name of this procedure. It is also used as a command in the procedure. This is recursion. When the computer gets this, it starts to carry out the directions on how TO MARCH. So, it starts again at line 1.

-10-

The next definition explains this idea in a way that might
be clearer for people who are used to another style of programming.
It also illustrates some flexibility in LOGO by showing other LOGO
idioms to express the same idea:

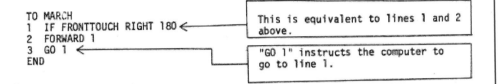

```
TO MARCH
1  IF FRONTTOUCH RIGHT 180  ←        This is equivalent to lines 1 and 2
2  FORWARD 1                          above.
3  GO 1  ←
END                                  "GO 1" instructs the computer to
                                      go to line 1.
```

A more interesting behavior is to go to the wall and circumnavigate the room. Getting the turtle to find the wall is easy: just
as in MARCH. To make it follow the wall we use the important concept
of <u>feedback</u>. The idea is this. Imagine yourself walking next to a
wall on your left <u>with your eyes closed</u>. Every now and then you
put out your left hand. If it
does not touch the wall, you
say to yourself, "I'm wandering
into space, better turn left a
little."

TURN LEFT   TURN RIGHT

If you do feel the wall you say (slightly perversely) "maybe I'm
getting too close, better turn right a little." The result is that
you will follow the wall perhaps in a slightly wavy line

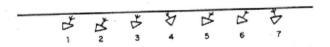

1   2   3   4   5   6   7

<u>Your Progress</u>

369

-11-

Interestingly this procedure would make you circumnavigate a house walking on the outside. Watch what happens at the corner:

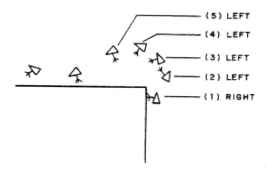

To circumnavigate the room from the inside one could use FRONTTOUCH to know when to turn. A small extension of the procedure could enable the turtle to find a door and escape from the room. Or explore a maze. Or ...

Using light sensors one can imitate a moth's flight to the candle, cause turtles to pursue one another or to engage in dances or fights, and ...

-12-

4. Make a Display Turtle

In our fifth grade class a turtle that walks on the floor is called a "turtle turtle". Another kind is called a "display turtle". This kind exists on a "scope" (i.e. Cathode Ray Tube, i.e. TV-like screen) as a picture just like the triangle we have used to illustrate the same commands, leaving a line of light as a trace when given the command PENDOWN. The disadvantage of the display turtle is that it cannot move physically about the world, touching, pushing and playing. But it has advantages for some purposes. One is that is is very fast and accurate. Another is that one can command it to draw a line which will last only for a stated length of time -- say a tenth of a second. Thus it can make moving pictures.

In LOGO the command

PEN :NUMBER

causes all lines to appear for :NUMBER tenths of a second. Thus

PEN 10

makes all lines last a second before vanishing.

The command

FLY

will cause a bird to move across the screen if the following procedure has been written, as well as a procedure TO BIRD, which draws a bird.

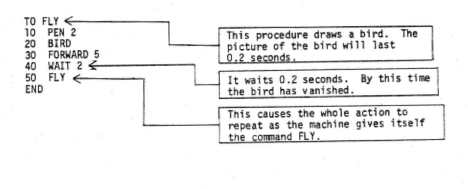

```
TO FLY
10    PEN 2
20    BIRD
30    FORWARD 5
40    WAIT 2
50    FLY
END
```

This procedure draws a bird. The picture of the bird will last 0.2 seconds.

It waits 0.2 seconds. By this time the bird has vanished.

This causes the whole action to repeat as the machine gives itself the command FLY.

-13-

5. Play Spacewar

Spacewar is a famous computer game invented at M.I.T. in the days when display programming was new and unusual. Two people play it. On the "scope" appears two spaceships, together with background frills such as stars, the sun, etc. There are two players; each controls a spaceship and may cause it to turn, go forward, shoot out a stream of rockets. Whoever destroys the other ship, wins. The excitement of the game is increased by such dangers as getting caught by the sun's gravity and vanishing in a brilliant explosion.

When our fifth grade class visited M.I.T., they were caught up by the fun of playing the game. (It really is orders of magnitude better than non-computerized pin-tables.) But unlike most people, our children could go back to school the next day and get caught up by the even greater fun of programming their own versions of spacewar.

6. Differential Geometry

The "turtle language" provides a very remarkable formal system for describing many geometric objects; we think vastly superior to Cartesian coordinates as an introductory path into geometry. To see this let's study a very simple procedure, known in our fifth grade class as POLY. In its simplest form POLY has two inputs called "STEP" and "ANGLE". In LOGO it is written:

```
TO POLY :STEP :ANGLE
1   FORWARD :STEP
2   LEFT :ANGLE
3   POLY :STEP :ANGLE
END
```

The following pictures show the effect of invoking this procedure with different inputs: (the first input is the side size, the second is the angle)

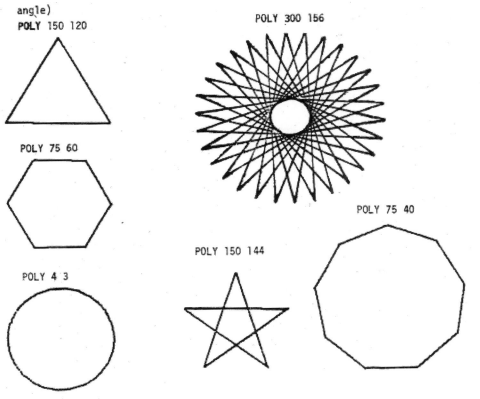

POLY 150 120

POLY 300 156

POLY 75 60

POLY 75 40

POLY 150 144

POLY 4 3

-15-

7. Draw Spirals

To change the procedure called POLY so as to draw spirals we make a very small addition to line 3. We also change the name -- but that is of course unnecessary.

```
TO POLY :STEP :ANGLE          TO POLYSPI :STEP :ANGLE
1   FORWARD :STEP              1   FORWARD :STEP
2   LEFT :ANGLE               2   LEFT :ANGLE
3   POLY :STEP :ANGLE          3   POLYSPI  :STEP+5 :ANGLE
END                           END
```

POLYSPI 5 90

POLYSPI 40 60

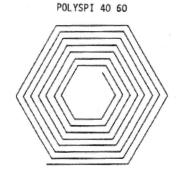

POLYSPI 5 120

POLYSPI 5 121

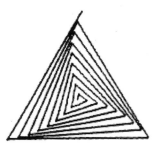

POLYSPI 5 125

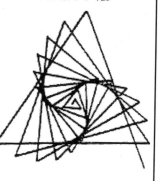

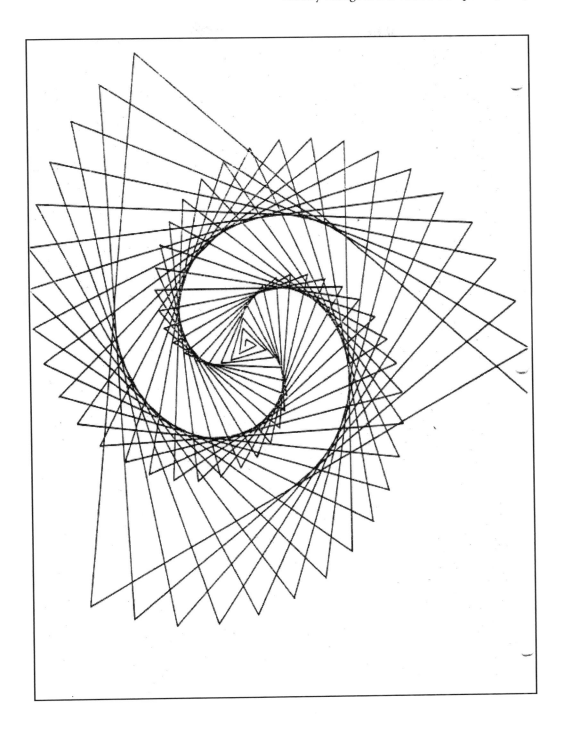

8. Have a Heart (and learn to DEBUG)

Making a procedure to draw a heart went through the following steps.

Step 1: Find something like making a heart that we know how to do.
Idea: a triangle.

```
TO TRI :SIZE
1  FORWARD :SIZE
2  RIGHT 120
3  FORWARD :SIZE
4  RIGHT 120
5  FORWARD :SIZE
END
```

TRI 100

Step 2: Make a plan to modify TRI. Idea: Make a procedure TO TOP.

```
TO TOP :SIZE
1  SEG :SIZE/2
2  RIGHT 180
3  SEG :SIZE/2
END
```

TOP 100

Then replace line 1 in TRI by
1 TOP :SIZE.

This is easy but the result is

HEART WITH BUG

Step 3: Debug. Trying out this idea produced a bug. Why? Because replacing "FORWARD" by "TOP" in line 1 of TRI has side effects we did not anticipate! (And is therefore typical of almost all good ideas in almost all good projects.) To remedy this we must change line 2 as well; and while we are about it let's change the name to "HEART1".

```
TO HEART1 :SIZE
1  TOP :SIZE
2  RIGHT 30
3  FORWARD :SIZE
4  RIGHT 120
5  FORWARD :SIZE
END
```

HEART1 100

-18-

Step 4: Consider: is this a good enough abstract model of a heart.

No. Let's curve its sides. After a little debugging we get:

```
TO HEART2 :SIZE
1  TOP :SIZE
2  SEG 2*SIZE 60
3  RIGHT 30
4  SEG 2*:SIZE 60
END
```

HEART2 100

MINITHEOREM: A heart can be made of four circular segments.

-19-

9. Growflowers

A computer program to draw this flower uses the geometric observation that petals can be decomposed (rather surprisingly!) as two quarter circles. So let's assume we have a procedure called TO QCIRCLE whose effect is shown by the examples. Some of them show initial and final positions of the turtle, some do not.

QCIRCLE 50

QCIRCLE 100

Now let's see how to make a petal.

```
TO PETAL :SIZE
1  QCIRCLE :SIZE
2  RIGHT 90
3  QCIRCLE :SIZE
END
```

PETAL 100

```
TO FLOWER :SIZE
1  PETAL :SIZE
2  PETAL :SIZE
3  PETAL :SIZE
4  PETAL :SIZE
END
```

FLOWER 100

STEM 100

```
TO STEM :SIZE
1  RIGHT 180
2  FORWARD 2*:SIZE
3  RIGHT 90
4  PETAL :SIZE/2
5  FORWARD :SIZE
END
```

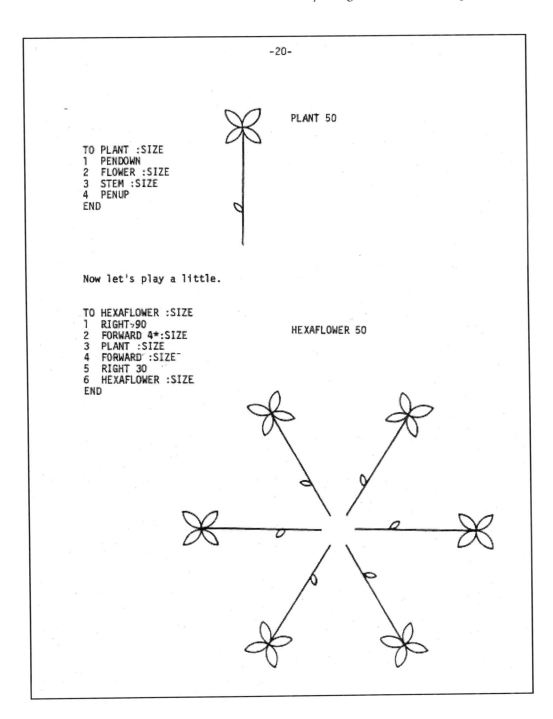

-20-

PLANT 50

```
TO PLANT :SIZE
1   PENDOWN
2   FLOWER :SIZE
3   STEM :SIZE
4   PENUP
END
```

Now let's play a little.

```
TO HEXAFLOWER :SIZE
1   RIGHT 90
2   FORWARD 4*:SIZE
3   PLANT :SIZE
4   FORWARD :SIZE
5   RIGHT 30
6   HEXAFLOWER :SIZE
END
```

HEXAFLOWER 50

10. Make a Movie

        We describe how to make a very simple movie, in which the whole plot consists of a flower growing.

        A flower can be drawn as well by the physical turtle described in Thing No. 1 as by a display turtle. Movies need a display turtle. The following commands in LOGO allow us to take advantage of a special feature of CRT drawings -- their ability to vanish! We recall that the command

```
PENDOWN
```

causes the turtle to leave a trace. The commands

```
PEN 50 (or PEN 10 etc.)
```

cause a trace that will stay for 50 tenths of a second (or 10 tenths of a second etc.) and then vanish. The command

```
WIPE
```

causes everything to vanish instantly.

        Now let's try making successive frames of our little movie. First we do it by direct commands, rather than writing a new procedure.

```
PENDOWN
PLANT 5
WIPE
PLANT 10
WIPE
PLANT 30    etc.
```

This can be automated slightly by

```
PEN 50
PLANT 10
PLANT 20
  :
```
This causes the picture to vanish after 5 seconds. So WIPE is not needed.

We give the commands PLANT 10, PLANT 20, PLANT 30 immediately after the previous picture vanishes.

To automate the process further we build a procedure around the central action command:

```
PLANT :SIZE
WAIT 5
```
A pause of half a second occurs, so that the next round does not rush in before the previous plant is seen. PEN 5 would be chosen to match WAIT 5.

Now make some more exciting movies!

-22-

A superprocedure to issue these commands will be called MOVIE.
It will make successive frames appear at half second intervals

FRAME 1; PLANT 10   FRAME 2; PLANT 20   FRAME 3; PLANT 30

To command itself recursively at any given time it must know the appropriate
input for PLANT. It also needs to know its frame number so as to know
when to stop. We notice that remembering the frame number eliminated
the need to remember separately the input to PLANT -- this is merely the
frame number multiplied by 10. So the little movie program is:

```
TO MOVIE :THISFRAME :ENDFRAME
1   IF :THISFRAME=:ENDFRAME STOP
2   PLANT :THISFRAME*10
3   MOVIE :THISFRAME+1 :ENDFRAME
END
```

The meaning of these inputs is
explained below.

HOW TO THINK ABOUT THE INPUTS

Picture of the Inputs

:THISFRAME is like a moving
clock. It ticks up one after
each frame.

STOP AT
6

:ENDFRAME is like a time posted
up at the beginning of the show
to tell the projectionist when
to stop.

We think of a movie as a process.
As it goes on we need to know two
things: where we are and where
we are going. The two inputs are
set up for this. The first is
:THISFRAME. It starts at 1 and
increases by 1 on each round. It
is the frame number. The second
input remains constant during the
showing of the movie.

-23-

11. Make A Music Box and Program A Tune

A music box is a device for making sound under control of a computer.
Our style of music box "listens in" to the signals sent by a computer to a
teletype.   Just as the teletype "decodes" them as instructions to print
particular characters, and the turtle decodes them as movements, the music
box decodes them as instructions to emit particular sounds.   It is only a
slight technical frill to give the music box several "voices" that will play
simultaneously.

One (very bad) way to make the computer play Frere Jacques
would be to write the following LOGO procedure:

```
TO FJ
1  PRINT "AAA!CCC!EEE!AAA!AAA!CCC!EEE!AAA!EEE!FFF!HHHHHHH!EEE!FFF!HHHHHHH!..."
END
```

A better approach is to program the computer to accept descriptions of
music in a good notation. An example is the following (which is one of
several we are trying experimentally).

> This notation and many of the ideas about
> the musical aspect of our work is due to
> Terry Winograd and Jeanne Bamberger.

Our music box can play a five octave range of notes, with as many as
four at a time. One octave is chosen as the base, and its twelve
chromatic tones are numbered 1 through 12. Notes in the next octave
up can be indicated either by continuing beyond 12 or by using the
sign "!". Thus 13 and 1! represent the same note. The LOGO command
SING takes a sequence of notes as input and plays them in order. Thus
SING "1! 3! 5! 6! 8! 10! 12! 1!" will cause a major scale to be played.

To add rhythm to the tune we use a LOGO operation MUSIC
which takes two inputs: one a sequence of notes, the other a sequence
of durations and combines them in the obvious way.

Now we use LOGO (following Terry Winograd) to write a better
Frere Jacques procedure.

-24-

```
TO FRERE1
1   SING MUSIC OF "1! 3! 5! 1!"  "2 2 2 2"
END


TO FRERE2
1   SING MUSIC "5! 6! 8!"  "2 2 4"
END


TO FRERE3
1   SING MUSIC '8! 10! 8! 6! 5! 1!"  "1 1 1 1 2 2"
END


TO FRERE4
1   SING MUSIC "1! -8! 1!"  AND  "2 2 4"
END


TO FREREJACQUES
1   FRERE1
2   FRERE1
3   FRERE2
4   FRERE2
5   FRERE3
6   FRERE3
7   FRERE4
8   FRERE4
9   FREREJACQUES
END
```

-25-

12. Play with Semi-Random Musical Effects and then Try Serious Composing

Following Winograd again, we write a procedure, called
RANDOMSONG, that will select randomly from a given set of tones.
Trying it with different inputs produces very different musical effects.
Thus
RANDOMSONG "2 4 7 9 11"
is described as "oriental" while
RANDOMSONG "1 3 5 6 9 11"
is described as "spooky".

Then you can try making some effects of your own. And
after a while, you may like to write a piece of music with real structure.

Many people would like to try their hand at musical composition,
but cannot play well enough to hear their ideas. If you are one of
them, this is your chance. The music box is an obedient orchestra
that will play precisely whatever you can describe to it.

-26-

13. Computerize an Erector Set Crane and Build a Tower of Blocks

A turtle is driven by two motors. Detached from the rest
of the turtle the motors can pull strings that can work any mechanisms.
For example a crane built of erector set parts.

To pick up objects make a grab -- or use an electro-magnet.
Make a pile of iron discs, one on top of the other. Program the computer
and crane and magnet to play tower of Hanoi.

-27-

14. Make a Super Light Show

The school computer should have a large number of output ports to allow the computer to switch lights on and off, start tape recorders, actuate slide projectors and start and stop all manner of little machines. There should also be input ports to allow signals to be sent to the computer. We leave to your imagination the possibilities that this opens of making "interactive environments" for the next school festivity or even more solemn purposes.

In a similar spirit, but with a little more work, make an array of light bulbs to display the news of the day like they do it in Times Square. Or generate funny cartoons on the light bulb array. Or put up the scores at ball games and track events.

```
XXXXXXX
      X   X
      X   X          XXXX          XXXX
      X   X          X   X         X   X
      XXXX           X   X         X   X
                     XXXX          XXXX                    X   X XXXXX
XXXXXXXX             XXXX          XXXX  XX                X   X X
X  XX   X            XXXX          XXXXX                   X   X   X
X  XX   X         XX XX XX           XX                    X   X   X
X  XX   X            XX              XX                    XXXXX   X
                     XX              XX                    X   X   X
XXXXXXX              X   X          X  X                   X   X   X
      X   X        X      X       XX     XX               X   X   X
      X   X       XX       XX                             X   X XXXXX
      X   X
XXXXXXXX

XXXXXXXX
X       X                         XXXXXXXXX
X       X                         X   X   X
X       X                         X   X   X
XX     XX                         X   X   X
                                  X  XXX  X
XXXXXXX                           X X X X X
X  XX   X                         XX  X  XX
X  XX   X                         XXXXXXXXX
X  XX   X
```

SUPERPEACE

-28-

15. Write Concrete Poetry

Perhaps we have carried too far our reaction against using computers to write symbols on teletype paper. Here are some examples of teletype output from procedures simple enough for the first weeks of a fifth grade course. We use teletype pictures as an initiation project to learn the very basic principles of using the computer, the terminal, the procedure definition idiom, the ritual for editing procedures and so on. Writing a random sentence generator made a girl exclaim: "So that's why we call words 'nouns' and 'verbs'." What she meant was: for the first time I see a use for classifying words.

```
THE FUNNY PROF TALKED WHILE THAT COOL KID KISSED . . .
SOME FUNNY PROF WALKED BUT A BEAUTIFUL KID CLAPED . . .
A WILD DONKEY KISSED WHILE THE FUNNY PROF CLAPED . . .
SOME GROSS PROF WALKED ALTHOUGH SOME COOL KID HUMMED . . .
```

```
?HAIKU

            ALL GREEN IN THE TWIGS
            I GLIMPSE FAINT BIRDS IN THE COLD
            WHIZZ THE SUN HAS CRACKED

            ALL CURVED IN THE PEAKS
            I SEE CLEAR PEAKS IN THE DUSK
            WHIZZ THE FLOWER HAS CRACKED

            ALL CURVED IN THE PEAKS
            I GLIMPSE DARK TREES IN THE DAWN
            WHIRR THE STORM HAS CRACKED
                                                    X  X
                                    X X X           X X X
                                    X X X X         X X X
  DDD       D                       X               X        X
  DDDD      D                       X       X       X X X X X X
    DDDDDDDD                          X   X         X X X X X X
    D D    D D                        X   X         X X X X X X
    D D    D D                      X X X X X X
    D D    D D                      X       X       X X  X X
    D D    D D                      X       X       X X  X X
  IIIIIIIIIIIIIII                   X X X X X X X X X X  X X X X X

            DOGS BY FIFTH GRADERS AT BRIDGE
```

```
                                    -29-

        .    .
                                              X
           .                                 X X
                                            XXXX                    XXX
           .                                X  X                    X
        .                                  X      X                 X X
      XXX                                  X X X X                 XXX X           XXX
     X   X                                 X     X                 XX   X      X    X
     X   X                                 XX   XX                 XX    X     X    X
     X XXX                                 X     X                 XXXXXXX     X     X
     X  X                                  XXXXXX                  X        X   XXX
    XX    X                                                        X        X   XX
     X     X                                                       X   XX   X   XX
    X       X                                                      X   XX   X   XX
XXXXXXXXXX  X                                                      XXXXXXXXXX XX
    X       X                                                          XX
    X XX  XX X                                                          XX
    X XX  XX X                                                          XX
    X       X                                                           XX
    X XXXX  X                XX        XXX
    X X  X  X              XXXXXX    XXX XXX
    X X  OX  X            XXXXXXX X  XXX XXX
    X    X  X            XXX   X   X  XXX
    X    X  X            XXX  X  X                                      &&&
    X    X  X            XX   X      X                                 &  &
                        XX X         X                                 &  &
                        XXX          X                                 &  &
     XXXX               XX            X                              @@@@@@
    X    X              X              X                               @
    X    X             X               X                               @  @
    X    X            X                 X                              @
    X    X         XXXXXXXXXXXXXXXXXXXXXXX                             @  @
XXXXXXXXXXXX       X                     X                              @
X          X       X   XXXXX     XXXXX   X                            ??????????
X          X       X   X   X     X   X   X                           ?          ?
X  XXX XXX X       X   X   X     X   X   X                           ?   $$$    ?
X  X X X X X       X   X   X     X   X   X                           ?   $  $   ?
X  XXX XXX X       X   XXXXX     XXXXX   X                           ?   $  $   ?
X          X       X                     X                           ?   $$$   ?
X  XXX XXX X       X      XXXXXXX         X                           ?          ?
X  X X X X X       X      X     X         X                           ?          ?
X  XXX XXX X       X      X     X         X                          $$$$$$$$$$$$$$
X  XXXXXX  X       X      X     X         X                          $            $
X X     X  X       X      X     X         X                          $            $
X X XXXX X  X      X      X X X X         X                          $            $
X X X XX X  X      X      X     X         X                          $            $
X X XXXX X  X      X      X     X         X                          $            $
X X  UX  X  X      X      X     X         X                          $            $
X X     X  X       X      X     X         X                          $            $
X X     X  X       X      X     X         X                          $            $
X X     X  X       XXXXXXXXXXXXXXXXXXXXXXXX                           $$$$$$$$$$$$$$

                   HOUSES BY FIFTH GRADERS
```

-30-

16. <u>Try C.A.I. and Psychology</u>

A slight extension of the sentence generator idea leads to generating mathematical sentences that are <u>true</u> (as well as grammatical) though somewhat boring.   For example:

```
TO RANDOMSUM
1  MAKE
       NAME "NUMBER1"
       THING RANDOM
2  MAKE
       NAME "NUMBER2"
       THING RANDOM
3  MAKE
       NAME "SUM"
       THING :NUMBER1+:NUMBER2
4  TYPE (SENTENCE  :NUMBER1 "+" :NUMBER2 "=" :SUM)
5  RANDOMSUM
END
```

The effect is something like

```
7 + 4 = 11
3 + 2 = 5
9 + 6 = 15
```

and so on.

A slight modification will cause the computer to print something like

7 + 4 = ?

and wait for a human victim to type something in order to insult him if he fails to give the appropriate answer.   For example:

```
7 + 4 = ?              (Computer)
ELEVEN                 (Victim)
IDIOT, THE ANSWER IS 11  (Computer)
```

Even when the procedure has been modified to accept "ELEVEN" we can still tease the victim:

```
7 + 4 = ?
ELEVEN
DON'T THINK YOU ARE SMART, YOU TOOK MORE THAN 2 SECONDS.
```

By taking the timing idea more seriously one can do endless experiments to find out such facts as: which multiplications are hardest (for example:

-31-

1 X 1 is very easy but one might disagree about whether 7 X 9 is easier than 8 X 6).   Or if one gets bored with teaching arithmetic one can teach children how to estimate lengths of time, to recognize rhythmic patterns and so on endlessly.

The conclusion from all this is that we have at last discovered the true role of C.A.I. in education.   Writing C.A.I. programs is one of the twenty best projects for the first semester of a fifth grade computer science course!

In a similar spirit it's fun to do "optical illusion" experiments with the display turtle.

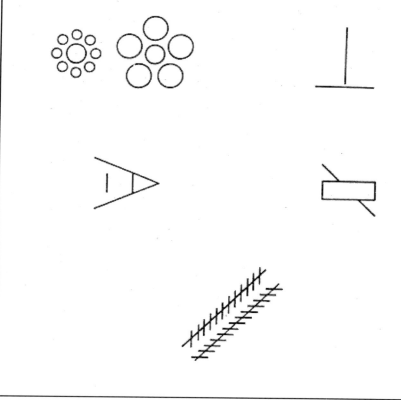

<u>17</u>.   Physics in the Finger-Tips

     We begin by inviting the reader to carry out the illustrated
experiments -- or to recall doing something similar.

     One of the goals of this unit of study will be to understand
how people do this and particularly to understand what properties of a
human being determine what objects he can and what objects he cannot
balance.

     A "formal physical" model of the stick balancing situation is
provided by the apparatus illustrated next:

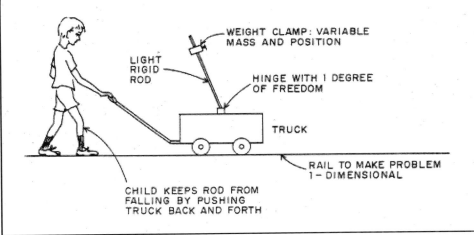

WEIGHT CLAMP: VARIABLE
MASS AND POSITION

LIGHT
RIGID
ROD

HINGE WITH 1 DEGREE
OF FREEDOM

TRUCK

RAIL TO MAKE PROBLEM
1- DIMENSIONAL

CHILD KEEPS ROD FROM
FALLING BY PUSHING
TRUCK BACK AND FORTH

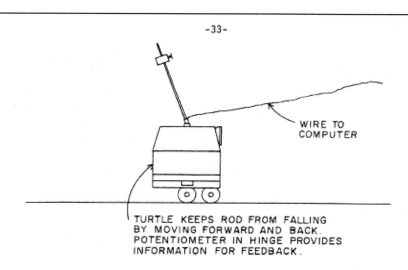

-33-

WIRE TO
COMPUTER

TURTLE KEEPS ROD FROM FALLING
BY MOVING FORWARD AND BACK.
POTENTIOMETER IN HINGE PROVIDES
INFORMATION FOR FEEDBACK.

A computer controlled version replaces the track and the child
by a turtle with the angle sensor plugged into its sensor socket. A
simple minded procedure will do a fair amount of balancing (provided that
the turtle is fast!!):

```
TO BALANCE
1   TEST ANGLE > 10
2   IFTRUE FORWARD 8
3   TEST ANGLE < -10
4   IFTRUE BACK 8
5   WAIT 1
6   BALANCE
END
```

This procedure is written as part of a project plan that begins by saying:
neglect all complications, try something. Complications that have been
neglected include:

(1) The end of the line bug.

(2) The overshoot bug.
(Perhaps in lines 2 and 4 the value 8 is too much or
too little.)

(3) The Wobbly Bug

The TEST in the procedure might catch the rod over to
the left while it is in rapid motion towards the right.
When this happens we should leave well alone!

One by one these bugs, and others can be eliminated. It is not
hard to build a program and choose constants so that with a given setting
of the movable weight, balance will be maintained for long periods of time.

Feeding Energy

Again we begin with some finger-tip physics by considering some
toys:

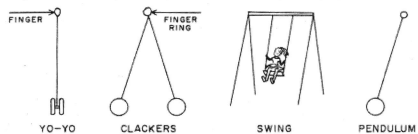

YO-YO   CLACKERS   SWING   PENDULUM

All these systems will run down unless supplied with energy.
How is the energy fed in? A good starting system is the clock pendulum
on a rigid rod.

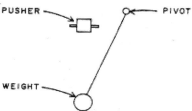

A linear actuator or one of the rotating joints can be used as a "pusher".
A simple experiment will show the need for a good phase relationship.
When this is understood, proceed to the flexible string and finally the
interesting case of the swing in which the source of energy is carried
by the pendulum.

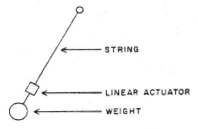

-35-

A mechanical YO-YO player provides a different setting for similar
principles and is an impressive example of a "skill" that can really be
achieved quite easily by machines.   Moreover it opens up a huge vista of
challenging problems.   Causing the YO-YO to SLEEP is a feasible hard project
in our context.   The more elaborate tricks like WALKING-THE-DOG or
ROUND-THE-WORLD would probably succumb, but would need a lot of work and
ingenuity.

-36-

18. Explain Yourself

Building machines to balance sticks did not actually answer the original question about why people can balance broom-sticks but not toothbrushes.   What property of people determines how long (or short) a stick one can balance?   The answer is: reaction time!   Now go back to the balancing machines to give them reaction times rather like those of people (which you will find out by carrying idea number 16 a little further).   How good a model can you make of a person?   Does this explain you -- or at least explain one of your characteristics?   Could similar models explain other human characteristics?

-37-

19. Puppets

The computer controls enough motors to pull enough strings to manipulate the desired number of marionettes. Like many of these projects, this one has this great educational property: some effect can be obtained by extremely simple means; extra effort will produce more exciting effects; and to emulate a skilled human puppeteer will require a very thorough understanding of the geometric and dynamic principles of movement.

-38-

20. Recursion Line

Think up twenty more things to do.

-39-

Epilog: How To Make Those Things Happen

Most of the devices we have mentioned are extremely simple and much cheaper than teletypes. The hardest problem has been getting the computer to communicate with the device. The approach we have developed centers around the concept of a "universal controller". This we define as a black box which looks to the computer like a teletype. So, to use it you would program the computer to print a piece of text which might read

"!!(!!(!!(!!(!!("

knowing that the controller will turn "!" and "(" into turtle signals whose effect will be to cause forward and left steps respectively. Thus any programming language, running on any operating system (including commercial time sharing services) can be used to control a turtle.

In our image of a school computation laboratory, an important role is played by numerous "controller ports" which allow any student to plug any device into the computer. The ports are protected by fuses and suitable interfaces so that little harm will be done if anyone carelessly puts the main voltage into a computer output port. The laboratory will have a supply of motors, solenoids, relays, sense devices of various kinds, etc., etc. Using them the students will be able to invent and build an endless variety of cybernetic systems.

This is not the place to discuss strictly practical problems like where to buy good motors. We do, however, expect that very sooon someone will supply a full range of suitable things. In any case we would be happy to provide advice and information.

On the Cost of Computation in Schools

A final word about the cost of doing all this. Turtles, music boxes, computer controlled motors and the like are less expensive than teletypes. Displays are slightly more expensive but becoming rapidly cheaper. So if computers are being used in a school, there is no good economic argument for accepting the narrowness of the pure teletype terminal.

-40-

Some school administrators and town politicians still consider the cost of using computers at all as too high. If you are engaged in battles on this point, write to LOGO INFORMATION to be briefed on the latest ideas and prices of equipment. At the moment a good estimate of what computation ought to cost is $30 per student per year, for one hour per student per week of terminal time. This is based on the assumption that several hundred students will be involved. The price could be halved within a year if several hundred schools would commit themselves to installing identical systems. Only inertia and prejudice, not economics or the lack of good educational ideas, stand in the way of providing every child in the world with the kind of experience of which we have tried to give you some glimpses. If every child were to be given access to a computer, computers would be cheap enough for every child to be given access to a computer.

Write to:

        LOGO INFORMATION
        Artificial Intelligence Laboratory
        M.I.T.
        Cambridge, Massachusetts 02139, U.S.A.

Also from
Constructing Modern Knowledge Press

Visit CMKPress.com for more information

Invent to Learn: Making, Tinkering, and Engineering in the Classroom

by Sylvia Libow Martinez and Gary S. Stager

An all new and expanded edition of the book called "the bible of the Maker Movement in classrooms," *Invent To Learn* has become the most popular book for educators seeking to understand how modern tools and technology can revolutionize education.

The Art of Digital Fabrication: STEAM Projects for the Makerspace and Art Studio

by Erin E. Riley

Integrate STEAM in your school through arts-based maker projects using digital fabrication tools commonly found in makerspaces like 3D printers, laser cutters, vinyl cutters, and CNC machines. Full color pages showcase the artistic and technical work of students that results from combining art with engineering and design. Written by an educator with experience in art and maker education, this volume contains over twenty-five makerspace tested projects, a material and process inventory for digital fabrication, guides for designing with software, and how-to's for using digital fabrication machines.

Making Science: Reimagining STEM Education in Middle School and Beyond

by Christa Flores

Anthropologist turned science and making teacher Christa Flores shares her classroom tested lessons and resources for learning by making and design in the middle grades and beyond. Richly illustrated with examples of student work, this book offers project ideas, connections to the new Next Generation Science Standards, assessment strategies, and practical tips for educators.

The Invent to Learn Guide to Fun

by Josh Burker

The Invent to Learn Guide to Fun features an assortment of insanely clever classroom-tested maker projects for learners of all ages. Josh Burker kicks classroom learning-by-making up a notch with step-by-step instructions, full-color photos, open-ended challenges, and sample code. Learn to paint with light, make your own Operation Game, sew interactive stuffed creatures, build Rube Goldberg machines, design artbots, produce mathematically generated mosaic tiles, program adventure games, and more!

The Invent to Learn Guide to MORE Fun

by Josh Burker

Josh Burker is back with a second volume of all new projects for learners who just want MORE! Insanely clever classroom-tested "maker" projects for learners of all ages with coding, microcontrollers, 3D printing, LEGO machines, and more! The projects feature step-by-step instructions and full-color photos.

The Invent to Learn Guide to Making in the K-3 Classroom: Why, How, and Wow!

by Alice Baggett

This full color book packed with photos is a practical guide for primary school educators who want to inspire their students to embrace a tinkering mindset so they can invent fantastic contraptions. Veteran teacher Alice Baggett shares her expertise in how to create hands-on learning experiences for young inventors so students experience the thrilling process of making—complete with epic fails and spectacular discoveries.

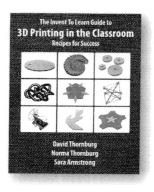

The Invent to Learn Guide to 3D Printing in the Classroom: Recipes for Success

by David Thornburg, Norma Thornburg, and Sara Armstrong

This book is an essential guide for educators interested in bringing the amazing world of 3D printing to their classrooms. Eighteen fun and challenging projects explore science, technology, engineering, and mathematics, along with forays into the visual arts and design.

Meaningful Making: Projects and Inspirations for Fab Labs and Makerspaces (Volumes 1 & 2)

edited by Paulo Blikstein, Sylvia Libow Martinez, Heather Allen Pang

Project ideas, articles, best practices, and assessment strategies from educators at the forefront of making and hands-on, minds-on education.

In these two volumes, FabLearn Fellows share inspirational ideas from their learning spaces, assessment strategies and recommended projects across a broad range of age levels. Illustrated with color photos of real student work, the Fellows take you on a tour of the future of learning, where children make sense of the world by making things that matter to them and their communities. To read this book is to rediscover learning as it could be and should be—a joyous, mindful exploration of the world, where the ultimate discovery is the potential of every child.

Learning to Code – An Invitation to Computer Science Through the Art and Patterns of Nature (Snap! and Lynx Editions)

by David Thornburg

These are books about discovery—the discoveries each of us can make when finding beauty in geometric patterns, beauty in mathematics, and beauty in computer programming. This is also a way to teach children to program computers in uniquely powerful ways.

Underlying the geometric pattern that we experience with our eyes lies a more subtle pattern of mathematical beauty, which is experienced intellectually—a collection of unifying principles that govern the arrangement and shapes of objects, both natural and crafted. Computer programming offers a bridge between the worlds of nature, design, and intellect.

Lynx and Snap! are accessible programming languages in the Logo tradition of constructionism and student-centered learning.

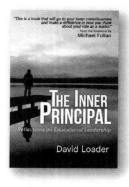

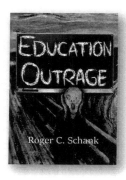

The Inner Principal: Reflections on Educational Leadership

by David Loader

Remarkably candid reflections by one of the most consequential school leaders of the past 50 years.

"This is a book that will go to your inner consciousness and make a difference in how you think about your own role as leader." – from the foreword by Michael Fullan

Education Outrage

by Roger C. Schank

Roger Schank has had it with the stupid, lazy, greedy, cynical, and uninformed forces setting outrageous education policy, wrecking childhood, and preparing students for a world that will never exist. No sacred cow is off limit – even some species you never considered. The short essays in this book will make you mad, sad, argue with your friends, and take action.